THE INTERNET

Effective Online Communication

HARCOURT BRACE *is*

Harcourt College Publishers

A Harcourt Higher Learning Company

Now you will find Harcourt Brace's distinguished innovation, leadership, and support under a different name . . . a new brand that continues our unsurpassed quality, service, and commitment to education.

We are combining the strengths of our college imprints into one worldwide brand: Harcourt

Our mission is to make learning accessible to anyone, anywhere, anytime—reinforcing our commitment to lifelong learning.

We are now Harcourt College Publishers. Ask for us by name.

One Company
"Where Learning Comes to Life."

www.harcourtcollege.com
www.harcourt.com

THE INTERNET
Effective Online Communication

Tyrone Adams
Southern Methodist University

Norman Clark
Appalachian State University

HARCOURT COLLEGE PUBLISHERS

Fort Worth   Philadelphia   San Diego   New York   Orlando   Austin   San Antonio
Toronto   Montreal   London   Sydney   Tokyo

Publisher	**Earl McPeek**
Acquisitions Editor	**Stephen Dalphin**
Market Strategist	**Laura Brennan**
Developmental Editor	**Michelle Vardeman**
Project Manager	**Andrea Archer**

Cover Design: Jane Tenenbaum Design

ISBN: 0–15–507081–9

Address for Domestic Orders
Harcourt College Publishers, 6277 Sea Harbor Drive, Orlando, FL 32887–6777
800–782–4479

Address for International Orders
International Customer Service
Harcourt College Publishers, 6277 Sea Harbor Drive, Orlando, FL 32887–6777
407–345–3800
(fax) 407–345–4060
(e-mail) hbintl@harcourtbrace.com

Address for Editorial Correspondence
Harcourt College Publishers, 301 Commerce Street, Suite 3700, Fort Worth, TX 76102

Web Site Address
http://www.harcourtcollege.com

Harcourt College Publishers will provide complimentary supplements or supplement packages to those adopters qualified under our adoption policy. Please contact your sales representative to learn how you qualify. If as an adopter or potential user you receive supplements you do not need, please return them to your sales representative or send them to:
Attn: Returns Department, Troy Warehouse, 465 South Lincoln Drive, Troy, MO 63379.

Printed in the United States of America

0 1 2 3 4 5 6 7 8 9   039   9 8 7 6 5 4 3 2 1

Harcourt College Publishers

ACKNOWLEDGMENTS

Norm and I have had an interesting year writing this textbook. Throughout the process, we have debated, embraced, and playfully disregarded one another's ideas. I feel fortunate in knowing that we are not only coauthors but friends. If I had to pick someone to be stranded with on a deserted island, Norm would make the shortlist.

First, thanks be to God, who guided me through the year and a half of labor required to cocreate this work with Norm. I would also like to thank my parents, Betty and Fred Adams, for being a supportive foundation in my life. But thanks especially to Professors Marilyn J. Young at Florida State University and Stephen A. Smith and Lynne M. Webb at the University of Arkansas–for being passionate about my ideas when, at times, I had lost the passion for passion itself. And to Professor Wayne Overbeck at California State University, Fullerton, who helped us put the legal chapter into context.

To Paul A. Barefield, A. David Barry, Steve Landry, and President Ray Authement at the University of Louisiana for employing me during the original authorship of this work. To my new colleagues at Southern Methodist University: Gregory Poggi, Nina Flournoy, Kathy LaTour, Ann Mayer-Guell, and Rita Kirk Whillock. Their support during the construction of this textbook's website and other ancillary materials has been remarkable. And to my research assistants Michelle Lemming, Martin Guidry, and Shallie Daire Johnson. Without these good folk, we could not possibly have pulled this work together as quickly as we did.

Tyrone Adams

Make it a tropical island, say Tahiti, and I'll be happy to be stranded there with you Ty. Seriously, it's not every day you find and keep a good friend, and I'm glad this project brought and tied us together.

I couldn't have finished this book without the support of my wife, Heather, and our daughters, Kehvon and Ashlyn. They served as readers, real-world reminders, and morale boosters. Several students helped speed this project: special thanks to Beth Bliss, Lindsay Boyd, Allison Satterthwait, and Dave Barrows. Of course, none of this would have been possible without the training and mentoring I received from numerous teachers. To all those who showed me how to live the life of the mind, my sincere thanks. My colleagues at Appalachian State University also deserve recognition for encouraging me when the sleepless nights grew more numerous and for keeping the coffee flowing. Much credit also goes to my parents, Richard and Colette, for giving me a love of books.

Finally, to God be the glory.

Norman Clark

ABOUT THE AUTHORS

■———————■

TYRONE L. ADAMS, PH.D.

Tyrone L. Adams teaches mass media and society, communication management, and media and technology in the Division of Arts Administration and Corporate Communication at Southern Methodist University in Dallas, Texas. Dr. Adams holds a B.A. in Communication Studies from the University of Florida (1900) and an M.S. (1992) and Ph.D. (1995) in Communication from Florida State University. His research focuses on the individual, organizational, sociopolitical, and economic aspects of new communication technologies. Dr. Adams is the recipient of the 2000 Southern States Communication Association Outreach Award; the University of Louisiana's 1999 Excellence in Communication Education Award; and the 1998 Outstanding Contributions to New Communication Technologies Award presented by the American Communication Association. He is the founding editor of the *American Communication Journal,* the communication discipline's premiere online multimedia journal [http://www.acjournal.org/]. He is also the coauthor of over 15 journal articles, book chapters, book reviews, editorials, and product benchmarking test reviews. Professor Adams and his wife, Brenda, have one very active son named Alexander Frederick Adams.

NORMAN CLARK, PH.D.

Norman Clark's interest in computers started the Christmas he got a Commodore VIC-20 instead of the compound bow he wanted. Since then, Dr. Clark has gone through numerous computers and earned a B.A. (1990) and M.A. (1992) in Speech Communication from the University of North Dakota and a Ph.D. (1998) in Communication Studies from the University of Iowa. He has written several publications on subjects ranging from classical rhetoric to campus portals and done extensive research on computer-mediated communication pedagogy. Currently teaching a wide range of courses at Appalachian State University, including Internet Communication, Dr. Clark is periodically pulled away from the Internet and reminded of the real world by his wife, Dr. Heather Clark, and their two daughters, Kehvon and Ashlyn.

PREFACE

No doubt about it, we're living in the Digital Age. Messages, information, and commerce are all flying around the world at the speed of light, thanks to the Internet. Colleges, businesses, and even families are purchasing domain names faster than you can say "dot-com." But as everyone gets online, one thing is becoming clear: there's a vast difference between simply *being* online and *effectively communicating* online.

The basic goal of this textbook is to provide you with the general information, theories, and practices that will allow you to craft effective messages and get them read, seen, or even heard on the Internet. In the global electronic exchange of information that is the Internet, your message will get buried under an avalanche of competing electrons unless it gets your audience's attention. We're also concerned (and you should be too) that unless you learn to evaluate information, you'll be taken in by the vast amount of misinformation, rumors, and outright lies that exist out there. So another goal of this textbook is to give you the tools you will need to think critically when communicating digitally.

We believe that education should address both theory and practice. That's why this text covers both *what* you should do online, as well as *why*. Much of the text is highly practical: students will learn how to efficiently use e-mail, newsgroups, chat-rooms, MUDs, MOOs, MUSHs, and videoconferencing equipment; how to use Internet search engines to prepare for communication; and how to create or enhance websites. But at the same time, all of this practical information is grounded in various theoretical perspectives. Throughout the book, we draw from interpersonal, small group, mass communication, design, and persuasion theories to give students reasons why they should or shouldn't interact in certain ways when online. We also rely on many theories to both define what the Internet is as well as to discuss what it is doing to us.

This text is divided into five sections. We begin our trip through cyberspace with the *History and Characteristics of the Internet.* If you want to communicate well online, you need to understand where this medium came from and what its key characteristics are. Part 2 focuses on *Personal Communication.* Here you will learn how to effectively communicate with individuals or small groups using e-mail, chat, and video-conferencing. Of course, you don't just use the Internet to communicate with friends, which is why part 3 gets you ready to communicate with larger and more formal audiences. In *Preparing for Communication* we cover online research skills. You will learn how to search and evaluate sites and avoid copyright infringement. All of this preparation will help you move from private to *Public Communication* in part 4. This section will give you the skills you need to reach large audiences through well-designed webpages and sites. Finally, in part 5 we move back out of cyberspace into the "real world" and assess the *Implications of the Internet.* We will consider how other media, society, and your own sense of identity are being influenced and affected by the Internet.

It seems obvious that a textbook about Internet communication would come with online resources, and this one certainly does. Adopting this textbook gives instructors and students access to a website with online quizzes, exercises, discussion boards, chapter-by-chapter links to examples and tools, and much more. We are dedicated to making this textbook fit the needs of instructors and students. They are committed to participating in the discussion boards, answering e-mails, and adapting the book and website. Periodic revisions and updates to the text will be downloadable from the website. But most importantly, we want to develop a community of users of this textbook. The discussion boards will allow instructors to communicate with others using this text, exchange exercise ideas, ask and answer questions, and get assistance from us, as well as contribute their own ideas for improving the textbook and website. Students will be able to interact with other students around the country taking similar courses and using this textbook. In short, what we imagine is an interactive, responsive textbook community—made possible by Internet communication.

The website isn't the only digital resource we provide. In the back of every text students will find a CD-ROM with 30-day trial versions of two of the top editing programs, Macromedia's Dreamweaver 3.0, an HTML editor, and Fireworks 3.0, a Web graphics editor, along with Flash 4.0, a multimedia authoring tool. Students will be able to install these programs on their own computers to complete assignments for the course. Since these are 30-day trial versions, instructors should advise their students to wait until they have started the webpage design section of the course before installing the software. In part 4, where we discuss webpage design and multimedia elements, we use screen shots and examples from these programs. Instructors and students are of course free to use any software that they want, but students may find it easier to use Dreamweaver, Fireworks, and Flash since what they see on the computer screen will then match the examples from the book.

We've worked hard to make this textbook and its accompanying resources fit the needs of instructors and students. Along the way, we had to make some tough decisions about what to include and what not to include. We hope it fits your needs as it is. But a wonderful thing about the Internet is that it makes it easier to get feedback and adapt our book. So we look forward to hearing from and working with you, as we all learn how to effectively communicate online.

Tyrone Adams
Norman Clark

BRIEF CONTENTS

———

CONTENTS

■———————■

PART 3

PREPARING FOR COMMUNICATION: RESEARCHING ON THE INTERNET   135

PART 4
PUBLIC COMMUNICATION: CREATING WEBPAGES   185

Part One

Entering Cyberspace: History and Characteristics of the Internet

Cyberspace: a graphic representation of data abstracted from the banks of every computer in the human system.

WILLIAM GIBSON, NEUROMANCER

In William Gibson's book *Neuromancer,* we were introduced to a new word, in fact a whole new world: cyberspace. In Gibson's vision, people could literally "jack into" the network by plugging a cable into their heads, allowing them to "see" the information. While you can't quite plug yourself in yet, you can access a worldwide network of computers. And while Gibson's cyberspace came from his imagination, the cyberspace that we'll be entering came from a lot of creative human effort. In part 1 of this book, you'll get a sense of where the Internet came from and what it is. You'll learn the history of the Internet and how it evolved from a basic set of programs into the full-fledged communication medium that it is today. And you'll discover the characteristics of this new medium that you'll be diving into more and more everyday. Because knowing where the Internet came from and what it is like today is the key to using it effectively in the future.

CHAPTER 1

How Did We Get Here?

The Development of a New Medium

By Peter Zale ©2000 Peter Zale, www.peterzale.com   Distributed by Tribune Media Services, www.comicspage.com

By the end of this chapter, you should:

I. Grasp the significance of the Internet as it relates to your changing world.
II. Understand how networked computers developed into a communication medium during the latter half of the twentieth century, from Hiroshima to the World Wide Web.
III. Be ready to approach the Internet from a communication perspective, with a focus on:
    A. audience,
    B. purpose,
    C. medium, and
    D. context/culture.

WELCOME TO THE FUTURE OF GLOBAL COMMUNICATION!

Let's face it: if you are a college student today, you spend a lot of time in front of a computer. Writing papers on a word processor, working out accounting problems on a spreadsheet, and putting together presentations are just some of the tasks that force you to stare at a computer monitor for hours on end. Of course, some of that time in front of the computer is entertaining. You probably play an occasional (OK, maybe even more than an occasional) game. And if you're like many students today, you spend hours logged into the **Internet** sending e-mail, browsing for information, and even playing more games.

The idea of a worldwide network of many smaller computer networks has been exciting and troubling people for years. Many visions of this network have been **dystopic** (darkly pessimistic). For example, the artificial intelligence network known as "Skynet" from the *Terminator* series sought to eliminate humanity because it saw us as a threat. In *The Net*, starring Sandra Bullock, corporate criminals erase all of her character's personal records while electronically tracking her to recover incriminating evidence that she comes to possess. And in *The Matrix*, Keanu Reaves's character "Neo" learns that his world is just a vast computer simulation created by machines to keep humans happy as their energy is harvested.

Of course, others have come up with equally fictional **utopic** (idealistically optimistic) stories of what computers might do for us. They promise us that the Information Superhighway will reinvent the way that we interact with our world. Religion, government, education, the individual, the economy—everything will become technologically enhanced to meet the growing needs of our society (Stefik 1996). You can find these visions presented in television advertisements or preached by technology evangelists who tirelessly promote the coming of a new information age. What excites these optimists is not the fact that computers are being connected but the assumption that *people* are getting connected. These advocates envision a planet where access to information, and access to people with information, creates an aware global population (see Borgmann 1999; Negroponte 1995; Leary 1994). As our television sets remind us, in the "university without walls" you will learn to experience a "world without borders" where your most basic question will be Microsoft's "Where do you want to go today?"

Answering that question is more difficult than it may seem at first. If you are a newcomer to the Internet, or haven't even used a computer much before, you might find it challenging to get onto the Internet, much less go anywhere on it. Luckily for you, using the Internet has become a matter of point-and-click common sense. However, this has not always been the case. Just a few years ago, you would have had to master an enormous glossary of confusing terms and abbreviated commands to navigate cyberspace. If you didn't know the commands necessary to access the Information Superhighway, you would be stopped at the symbolic tollbooth—the computer's $ prompt to log in **(Figure 1.1).** As a result, it was very unlikely that the average citizen could even get *on* the Internet, let alone *use it* effectively.

Most of these roadblocks to the Internet were removed in late 1994 with the coming of the **World Wide Web (WWW** or **Web),** a hypertextual, multimedia interface to the Internet. With this invention, you can

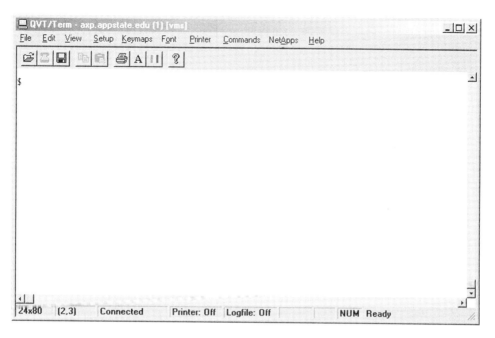

Fig. 1.1. Say what? Unix prompts are not very friendly . . .

easily point and click your way to other sites of information located on the Internet via graphic buttons and underlined phrases **(Figure 1.2).** Computer programs like Netscape's Communicator and Microsoft's Internet Explorer have made the Web easier for everyone to "browse" or "surf." Now, if you would like to search the Web, all you have to do is click the Search button on the interface, and Netscape or Microsoft's search page will instantly appear. Furthermore, the programs you can use to create webpages have become almost as easy to use as a word processor. Anyone with access to an Internet-connected computer and the necessary software can create their own websites for others to view. At present, the range of content being provided on the Internet is astounding. Businesses advertise their wares and offer customer support, university departments provide information about their faculty and courses, job-seeking students post their resumes, medical centers describe their new treatments, and Comedy Central puts up a Pac-Man-like game starring Cartman (Mann 1998). It seems that at least one scene from the utopic vision–any information, from anywhere in the world, available to anyone, at any time–may be close at hand.

But those people who are comfortable browsing around online are painfully aware that this massive amount of information creates another problem: finding the information that you need. Just *knowing* where you want to go doesn't by any means guarantee you'll be able to *get* there.

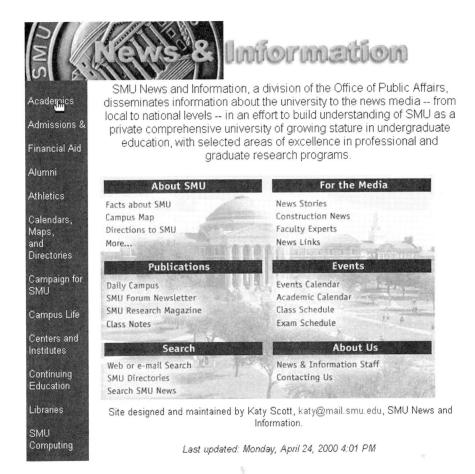

Fig. 1.2. Much better! The graphical interface of the Web is far more user friendly.

With millions of pages of information out there, it's easy to get lost. And just as knowing how to use a word processor doesn't guarantee you'll write a best-selling novel, knowing how to use a webpage editor isn't enough to catch the attention of people browsing the millions of pages online. But if you want to get anywhere, you have to start moving, and it helps to have a map and to be pointed in the right direction. That's the goal of this book: to get you moving in the right direction, into the future of communication.

It is clear that the future of communication is closely tied to the Internet. It is dramatically changing your world and the way that you communicate. And honestly, we find these changes exciting. After all, we wouldn't be writing a book on the subject if we didn't. Just think about it: in an afternoon, you can make a basic website that will reach a world-wide audience. That website could get you in touch with people from New Zealand, Germany, or maybe even your next door neighbor who shares your interests in, say, soccer or designer fashions. In that same afternoon, you could learn everything there is to know about several sport utility vehicles, including what the dealer paid for the model. Maybe you have a problem with your VCR; chances are very good that someone else, somewhere in the world, has had the same problem with the same model. And chances are equally good that they've already asked a group of people how to solve that problem and gotten an answer (possibly from the designing engineer herself). So all you have to do is find that answer stored somewhere on the Internet. You could do *that* in an afternoon, as well.

What's important in all of these exchanges is that the Internet is about **interaction** in many different forms (Johnson 1997). You interact with people, sending **e-mails** (short for electronic mail) to relatives and friends, perhaps even to people in other parts of the world whom you have never met. More and more, you interact with programs. You might go to a travel site such as Travelocity.com to book a plane flight, or to an online retailer such as Amazon.com to order a book, or to a news source such as CNN/SI to check on the latest baseball rankings. But increasingly, you are interacting with a provocative blend of people *and* programs. For instance, you might go to eBay.com, a popular auction site where you can buy anything under the sun. Here you will interact with the program, placing a bid on a set of computer speakers. But you'll also be interacting with people. Because at eBay, and places like it, people feel that they are part of an auctioning *community*. When someone buys something from a seller, they often post a message rating their transaction. So before you buy something from someone, you can review other people's comments about the individual **(Figure 1.3).** Of course, sellers can also post notes about buyers, so you can get blacklisted if you don't pay up.

What should be clear is that if you wish to be an active participant in your changing information-oriented world, you need to be able to effectively communicate on this interactive medium. Effective communicators can both get their messages across to others and evaluate the messages that they receive. And as you no doubt have guessed by the title of this book, the goal of this text is to help you become an effective online communicator so that those hours you spend online are productive ones. To really understand any human invention, you need to know where it came from. That's why your training in effective online communication begins with the history of the Internet from a communication perspective.

Fig. 1.3. Example of eBay Auction Feedback.

DEVELOPMENT OF THE INTERNET: FROM THE 1940S TO THE PRESENT

Before we begin examining the history of this medium, we want to make sure you understand the distinction between two terms you've no doubt heard quite often: the Internet and the World Wide Web. Simply put, the Internet is the worldwide network of computer networks and all of the supporting structure, while the WWW is an immense collection of hyperlinked documents that allows you to easily access vast amounts of information. These words are often used interchangeably. But the Web is only a part of the Internet, although it is a significant and growing part. The Internet also includes numerous other formats for delivering information, including File Transfer Protocol (FTP), e-mail, chat, and a host of others that you will learn about during the course of this textbook. For now, though, it might be most useful to think of the Internet as the physical hardware driving this new medium and the Web as the software interface used to view some of the data stored on it.

HIROSHIMA AND NAGASAKI

To understand the interrelationship between the Internet and the Web, we must revisit the end of World War II in 1945, when the United States dropped atomic bombs on Nagasaki and Hiroshima, Japan (Hogan 1996). While Harry S. Truman's decision to use these weapons may have ultimately produced Japan's unconditional surrender, it also made the threat of having another atomic exchange in the future seem imminent. After all, the world would not sit idly by and allow the United States to become the only nuclear entity. Several nations began developing their own arsenals as a result: USSR (confirmed in 1949), Great Britain (1952), France (1960), China (1964), and India (1974).

SPUTNIK I, ARPA, EXPLORER I, AND EMPS

Still, nothing was as troubling to U.S. scientists and politicians as the launching of **Sputnik I,** Earth's first artificial satellite, by the Soviet Union on October 4, 1957. This event heightened the cold war to an entirely new level (Divine 1993). U.S. scientists concluded that there was now a far more serious threat than standard nuclear war. Given the invention of satellites, nuclear warheads could now be deployed from space. Alarmed, the United States immediately formed the **Advanced Research Projects Agency (ARPA)** to consider the tactical issues made possible by new scientific discoveries. And in 1958, the National Aeronautics and Space Administration (NASA) was also formed to organize U.S. efforts to establish satellites and explore space. Wasting no time, NASA launched its first satellite, **Explorer I,** on January 31, 1958, rivaling the Soviet accomplishment.

Now that the United States had secured the same advantage as the Soviets in space, ARPA began examining new evidence that made the satellite attack scenario even more disturbing. In 1959, physicists investigating the effects of test blasts in Los Alamos, New Mexico, found that the **electromagnetic pulse (EMP)** surging from a nuclear explosion rendered much of their electronic equipment inoperative. As testing continued, pulses were detected hundreds of miles away from the epicenter of the blast (O'Neil 1995). These EMPs neutralized any equipment using electricity–lights, battery-powered radios, gas engines, telephones, and computers. This was made quite apparent when a 1.4-megaton test blast, approximately 250 miles in the atmosphere above Johnston Island in the

Pacific, produced an EMP strong enough to cause unexpected electrical failures throughout Hawaii (over 800 miles away).

RAND ENGINEERS ENVISION A "GALACTIC NETWORK"

While designing contingency plans for nuclear war during the late 1950s, scientists at the Research and Development (RAND) Corporation (a private think tank based in Santa Monica, California) were charged with the additional mission of developing a communication infrastructure that could withstand a nuclear attack. Their assignment was difficult: assume a full-scale nuclear war, where most of the command-and-control operations located in major cities and on military bases had been eliminated. Given this scenario, how could the military coordinate an effective response to defend the nation? How could survivors in one geographical area confirm the fate of others? How could we keep our country, our way of life, together?

Assuming that any nuclear strike would result in some cities being destroyed and others surviving, in 1966 RAND researchers developed a plan to disperse communication systems across the country. At first, RAND's "galactic network" was considered highly unconventional. Then again, we were making contingency plans for some highly unconventional weapons. The RAND plan was revolutionary: where communication had traditionally flowed from a hierarchy downward through formal communication networks, this new supercomputer network had to be organizationally flat and geographically decentralized. In other words, all of the computers connected to this network would possess the same communicative functionality and would be dispersed everywhere (Moschovitz et al. 1999).

RAND designed this network **(Figure 1.4),** based on the assumption that no single computer or communication line would be needed for total system survival. Each computer would routinely look for all of the other computers on the network. If a computer or line went out, the remaining computers would bypass the system malfunction. Likewise, if a computer or communication line came back up, the other computers would immediately recognize it.

Let's look at **Figure 1.4** for a moment to see how this works. If you wanted to transmit a message from, say, computer A to C, the network could either transmit directly, or go from computer A to E to D to C. Depending upon which point or line went down, you could also get a message from computer A to C via several other combinations. Let's pretend for a moment that you want to send an e-mail from Los Angeles (Computer A) to Boston (C). Let's also pretend that Illinois, Iowa, and Missouri no longer exist. In this case, it is safe to assume that your message will not get routed through Chicago (B) or St. Louis (B). Instead,

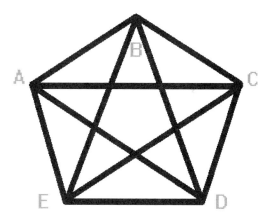

Fig. 1.4. Reliable networks depend on multiple connections between points.

your message may likely find another means through Little Rock (E) or Dallas (D).

THE BIRTH OF COMMUNICATION PROTOCOLS

However hard the RAND scientists may have labored on plans for their network, they had not yet perfected how information would travel through this system. RAND worked in conjunction with the Massachusetts Institute of Technology (MIT) and the University of California at Los Angeles (UCLA) during the 1960s to build a set of communication protocols that would serve to direct information around broken or clogged points on the network. **Protocols** are the generally accepted rules governing the transmission, delivery, and reception of data on the Internet and are normally programmed into a universally installed software suite so that no one computer has a different set of standards than any other machine. The principal theorists who developed these protocols were Americans Paul Baran (RAND) and Lawrence Roberts (MIT). But their ideas were merely notions in articles and had not yet been tested by the realities and rigors of programming.

NPL NET AND PACKETS

Interestingly enough, it would be the British who would first put these American theories into action. At the National Physical Laboratory (NPL) in 1967, Donald W. Davies developed the **NPL Network** using the first "packets" to transfer data. With their theory based upon the American hypotheses, the British team agreed with Baran and Roberts that any data traveling on such a dispersed system would have to emulate the structure of the network (Metcalfe, Walden, and Salus 1996). In other words, if the network were going to function on a distributed model, then so too should the data. As a result, they designed a system that would allocate data streams into **packets,** smaller bundles that made traffic more manageable across the Internet. This way, if a few packets of the whole transmission got lost, at least the general message would probably make it through the network. This system was the first attempt to design a network protocol.

ARPANET

The British NPL Net was a huge success because it demonstrated that the American theories were valid and expanded a larger dialogue on electronic communication between the two allies. After the successful British test, in 1968 the United States launched a full-scale effort to build a national computer-mediated communication infrastructure. Fusing the efforts of several private and public research agencies, RAND began "internetworking" the West Coast. On September 2, 1969, UCLA became the first host connected to ARPA's computer network, known as **ARPANET.** The Stanford Research Institute, the University of California at Santa Barbara (UCSB), and the University of Utah were connected within the following two months, forming the first network.

Because no reliable protocol yet existed to govern network exchanges, the machines at UCLA, Stanford, UCSB, and Utah would periodically crash. Despite this, the system provided some extraordinary benefits for researchers: (1) it could transfer sizable amounts of data from one computer to another; (2) it allowed them to make use of remote computers at other select institutions, which was especially important since access time was scarce; (3) it allowed for the writing or installation of programs on remote computers; and (4) it increased interpersonal exchanges between the people at these institutions. While ARPA wanted to see all four of these benefits materialize, they did not anticipate the growth in interpersonal communication.

A RELIABLE PROTOCOL IN NCP

To keep ARPANET from crashing, ARPA requested that the four test institutions develop a more capable protocol for governing the delivery of data. All that was required, apparently, was a tighter reprogramming of the British protocol. This reworked software was released as the **National Control Protocol (NCP)** in 1970 and stabilized most of the exchanges made among early ARPANET members. The release of NCP as a standard could not have occurred at a better time. After all, the

Date	No. of Hosts	Date	No. of Hosts
12 / 1969	4	10 / 1972	31
06 / 1970	9	01 / 1973	35
10 / 1970	11	06 / 1974	62
12 / 1970	13	03 / 1977	111
04 / 1971	23	12 / 1979	188

Fig. 1.5. Early growth of ARPANET.

network was about to begin its first expansion phase (Metcalfe, Walden, and Salus 1996). **Figure 1.5** shows the increase in the number of **hosts** (computers open to access on a network) connected to ARPANET during the 1970s. Had NCP not been reliable, these hosts would not have come online.

THE COMING OF COMMUNICATION TOOLS

It is important to remember that ARPANET was, at this time, still a network dedicated to military research projects. One could not simply connect to ARPANET if they wanted to do so. Getting onto ARPANET was more a matter of knowledge and privilege than it was choice. Either you were a professor at a major research institution on the cutting edge of science and technology, or you were with a private firm that specialized in a particular niche of research and development. Regardless, all of these newcomers to ARPANET were also human and had the same needs for simplicity, order, and practicality in their online communication. These basic needs, placed in such a chaotic technological context, are what provided the initial demand for some of the most useful and intriguing inventions of our century.

For instance, in 1972 Ray Tomlinson invented the first e-mail program that could deliver messages across ARPANET. In 1973, vocal patterns were coded into transmittable signals, and history recorded the first multiparty conference call using ARPANET. Building upon Tomlinson's invention of e-mail, in 1975 Steve Walker created a way to send one e-mail to many people using one address. But perhaps the most important invention of this era was the 1975 debut of a durable new network protocol called the **Transmission Control Protocol (TCP).** It was initially tested during the first satellite linkup of ARPANET between Hawaii and Great Britain (Zakon 1999). As the satellite link to ARPANET came online, TCP performed flawlessly (to understand how TCP evolved out of

TEXT BOX 1.1

PROTOCOLS AND PACKET SWITCHING

Today, all of our e-mail messages, chat-sessions, and webpages get segmented into thousands of packets whenever we send or receive information. So in a very real sense, whenever you send an e-mail to a friend across the Internet, you are actually sending thousands of smaller e-mail packets. What is important to remember here, though, is how distributed networks function. Not all of the packets will follow the same path to their final destination, and not all of the packets will make their initial transmission. As things change on the Internet–traffic flows, server outages–the network redirects packets, literally switching their flow to the path of least resistance. This process is what we call **packet switching.**

Naturally you are probably wondering how all of these packets ever find their way home. Each packet is tagged with details about its journey in something called a **header.** The header is the part of a packet that identifies (1) who and where the packet is from, (2) when it was issued according to the sending server clock, (3) to whom and where the packet is headed, (4) the subject of the data, or data type, and (5) transmission error information. The entire process of packet switching is governed by the **Transmission Control Protocol/Internet Protocol (TCP/IP)** communication standards. Each protocol set controls certain functions regarding packet transmission:

TRANSMISSION CONTROL PROTOCOL (TCP)	INTERNET PROTOCOL (IP)
Safeguards the reliability of the data sealed in each packet, using a check/recheck confirmation system	Responsible for converting the original communication into transmittable packets
Numbers the packets to ensure that they can be reconstituted at their final destination	Creates and binds the header to each packet
Responsible for the sequenced transmission of all packets	Defines the size of each packet in relation to the overall size of the general communication

The "where from" and "where to" information is technically referred to as the **origination** and **destination protocols** and works much like the basic information you would put on an ordinary postal envelope. This information is important because if packets are lost during the original transmission, the receiving router will often request that those packets be retransmitted before issuing the delivered data to the recipient. To do this, the receiving machine routinely reviews the transmission error information (a numbered inventory log provided by TCP) and determines which packets did or did not successfully make the trip. In short, the sending machine fractions the outgoing data into packets, each of which are individually routed to the recipient machine, then orderly reassembled to produce an e-mail, a webpage, or maybe even a movie clip. Today, the TCP/IP suite is considered the industry standard for governing online communication.

TCP/IP is differentiated from the former NCP standard in that TCP/IP is directly installed on each network host, whereas NCP was installed on the governing **nodes** (computers that serve as major connecting points on the Internet). TCP/IP, therefore, does much of the packet conversion on-site before the data is ever released onto the network. NCP, on the other hand, had to do much of this work at the node machine. TCP/IP greatly accelerated and streamlined the process of packet switching, since the **routers** (the machines dictating where packets will travel on the network) could now focus on delivering the data.

---

the late 1970s as the protocol of choice for ARPANET, read the box on **protocols and packet switching**).

THE PERSONALIZATION OF E-MAIL

As the Department of Defense continued to finance ARPANET, network administrators suddenly found themselves in an unforeseen predicament. As early as 1973, ARPA's internal audits confirmed that e-mail alone was totaling nearly 75% of all network activity. For all intents and purposes, ARPANET had become a prattle parlor. Users were establishing individual ARPANET accounts and were spending a substantial portion of their workday engaged in a series of professional and personal e-mail exchanges with their colleagues. They were not, as had been assumed, spending their time analyzing data. Instead, they were all *communicating through technology*–about their projects, about their friends and families, and about themselves.

TCP/IP AND INTER-NETWORKING

Another surprising event occurred in 1983 when ARPA announced that it would be switching from NCP to **TCP/IP (Transmission Control Protocol/Internet Protocol)** on its network hosts. When they made the move, so did everyone else. During the late 1970s, many corporations and state agencies had invested a considerable amount of money and energy into building their own *private* computer networks. These networks were very helpful because they provided each organization with the means to unify their in-house efforts. The lacking component among these networks was interorganizational communication. A few of the private networks had already adopted TCP/IP well in advance of ARPA's switch. Still, that meant that only a few of the private networks had access to one another. The problems remained: How could accountants for the U.S. Department of State access billing records at Honeywell? How could officials working for the state of Florida interact with Sperry-Rand on an upcoming project? There was a need for continuity in this anarchic network; a means for everyone to connect. That continuity, that means, was TCP/IP.

A large number of previously private and new networks began adopting the universal TCP/IP standard in search of interorganizational communication. By default, this made their computer a host on ARPANET. Each adoption of TCP/IP by a new host augmented the inter-networking reach of TCP/IP as a communication vehicle. In other words, every time a smaller network subscribed to the communal properties of TCP/IP, their hosting made that communication system part of the **inter-network.** This encompassed the lines running to the computer, the host system, the machines (if any existed) networked off of that host, and most certainly the people using those machines. Everything and everybody was now using TCP/IP protocols for inter-networking. Throughout the 1980s, this process continued to grow and incorporate new systems until it took on its own social meaning as a formal place: the **Internet.**

ARPA ABANDONS ARPANET

While ARPA wanted this to happen, they were truly shocked at the speed of the transition to TCP/IP and the rate of network expansion. It seemed that all of the network administrators wanted their communication systems to operate on the same protocol as ARPANET. ARPA rightly feared that when these new users inter-networked into ARPANET, information pertaining to research and development would be overrun by extraneous communication. To protect the research and development community from being overwhelmed by noise, in 1983 ARPA developed a dedicated access-only network called MILNET. They immediately relocated all critical ARPA staff to this network, and abandoned ARPANET to the public.

While this may sound somewhat undiplomatic, ARPA had both knowingly and unknowingly done the public a tremendous favor. Their goal was to make a network that could withstand a nuclear attack. In so doing, they designed it to be counterchaotic from an engineering perspective. Where nuclear weapons were the ultimate centralized statement that humanity could make, this network would become the ultimate decentralized statement. But not knowing that technology would become so powerful so quickly, and so democratically dispersed, ARPANET simply became a victim of its own success. The ultimate decentralized network essentially grew beyond the scope and mission of its designers. While some of ARPANET's original lines are probably still in use today, the network as it once existed is no longer in operation. On its 20th anniversary in 1989, the first supercomputer ever connected to ARPANET was symbolically disconnected at UCLA.

NATIONAL SCIENCE FOUNDATION TO THE RESCUE

One year after ARPA retreated from ARPANET, the National Science Foundation (NSF) emerged in 1984 to continue the crusade for a better Internet. Through their Office of Advanced Scientific Computing, and with the financial backing of both Congress and the White House, plans were made to build a massive new information superstructure named **NSFNET.** With nearly unlimited funds and an army of computer scientists bolstering the design, NSF charged onto the landscape in 1986 by introducing five supercomputing facilities that would provide the nation's major research institutions with high-speed computing access (Zakon 1999). Then, in 1988 NSFNET upgraded the dedicated lines running between these systems to T1 fiber optics, which allowed data transfer rates of nearly 1.5 **Mbps** (millions of bytes [of data] per second). This was quite an upgrade, considering that ARPANET's cross-country network only allowed for flow rates of 56 **Kbps** (thousands of bytes per second). And in 1991, NSFNET once again upgraded the network to T3 fiber optics, allowing for nearly 25 times the flow of data over its T1 predecessor (44.7 Mbps). In less than a decade, NSFNET had constructed an enormous data pipeline stretching across the country. It became known as the **backbone.**

CONVERGENCE OF EFFORTS

However, it wasn't only NSF that was building the information architecture. Almost every government agency with a need for a distributed network was helping fund the effort: the National Institutes of Health, NASA, the Department of Energy, the Department of Education, the Department of Commerce–the list goes on and on. Each agency was dedicated to both their own and their constituents' Internet connectivity, regularly providing grants to geographies and organizations in need of "Internet-working." Every new fiber-optic line branching from the backbone, every dedicated satellite connection, every private Internet service provider bankrolling more development, every university building an infrastructure–each making the Internet a more credible vehicle for the delivery of information, ideas, and knowledge.

1991 was a critical year for another reason besides the upgrade to T3 lines. Before this year, only educational and governmental institutions could use the Internet. But in 1991, that restriction was lifted, opening up the way for commercial institutions to use this global network. Now the number of computers connected, and the amount of information available, began to mushroom rapidly. Eventually, the convergence of efforts built enough of a critical mass in the early 1990s to supernova into a full-fledged mass medium. Naturally, with all of these new organizations providing hosts online, we would need some way to distinguish them from one another.

DOMAIN NAMES

As NSFNET continued to encourage the expansion of the Internet throughout the world, the U.S. Department of Commerce began assigning domain name prefixes and suffixes for the different groups establishing a presence in cyberspace. This was done for two reasons: (1) as a genuine effort to help classify information on the Internet; and (2) to identify which groups were for profit and which groups were not for profit. You may have encountered many of these suffixes already whenever browsing the Internet. They are always tagged on the tail end of any **Uniform Resource Locator (URL),** or the host address which is entered into a Web browser to retrieve online documents. The six staple domain suffixes, one of which will appear on any host address, are shown in **Figure 1.6.**

If you've been online for any length of time, you have probably encountered e-mail addresses bearing multiple suffix components (e.g., user_name@bbicserv.provo.k12.ut.us). These protracted handles are remnants of a chaotic period gone by. At first, the Department of Commerce tried to manage every possible variable pertaining to a host address: the type of network, sponsoring nation, state, organization, and type of organization. But the number of dots (.) in the addresses and the sequence of character sets became difficult to recall, so the Department of Commerce began allowing network administrators to select their own

ABBREVIATION	TYPE
.com	Private "commerce" domains, reserved for business entities who might wish to someday do business online.
.edu	Educational institutions.
.gov	Governmental institutions.
.mil	Armed forces.
.net	Network domains, reserved for those organizations who host gateway services, providing Internet access and network solutions.
.org	Organizations.

F i g . 1.6.   The six primary domain suffixes.

domains as long as the titling was consistent with government policy (Zakon 1999). Unluckily, those first hosts got stuck with their bulky descriptors.

THE WORLD WIDE WEB

Of all of the innovations that have coincided with the development of the Internet, perhaps the most powerful contribution was made in 1991 (that crucial year, again!) by programmer Tim Berners-Lee, who was then working for the European Laboratory for Particle Physics (CERN) in Geneva. Berners-Lee is credited with developing the WWW as a means for users to access information in textual and visual form via computer hosts connected through the Internet. As we noted earlier, the WWW is a network of interactive documents created by millions of users throughout the world and is linked via the **hypertext transfer protocol (HTTP).** HTTP is a special set of protocols used for retrieving webpages that operate in harmony with the Internet-standard TCP/IP suite. You will often see websites listed by their WWW host protocol: for example, http:// www.w3.org/.

Before the Web and HTTP, users utilized a text-based program known as Gopher (named after the Golden Gophers at the University of Minnesota, where the device was invented). Gopher was a simple system of text menus that users had to dig (puns intended) their way through to get to the information they wanted. Berners-Lee made this process more user friendly by designing a simple programming language called **hypertext markup language (HTML)** that would work in conjunction with the new HTTP. HTML allows documents to be interactive because authors can instantaneously refer readers to other documents scattered about the Internet by simply selecting a word or phrase and making that selection dynamic through a hidden set of codes. You will learn more about HTML and how it works in part 4. Still, it is important for you to know that HTML is one of the most easy and useful programming languages ever written. In fact, it is so easy to learn and use that many computer programmers do not deem it an official programming language. Many of these professionals think of HTML as a mere set of codes driving an advanced word processor.

The evidence connecting the Web's contribution to the total growth of online communication is irrefutable. When Berners-Lee engineered the Web, NSFNET traffic was at one trillion bytes per month. Then, in 1993, lightning struck. Students at the University of Illinois wrote a program called Mosaic. This was the first graphical Web browser, which allowed people to point and click at links, view graphic images, and much more. By early 1994, merely six months after Mosaic Communications released Mosaic to the general public, NSFNET was spooling at an astounding 10 trillion bytes per month (Zakon 1999). Of course, much of this data was no longer simple text. It had pictures, audio files, movie clips, and even word processing and spreadsheet documents. By 1995, the Web surpassed all other forms of online data flow to become the primary information being transferred on the Internet.

The Internet is now the fastest-growing medium ever. Much of the explosion in Web use comes from a convergence of five major events preceding and during 1995. The first of these breakthroughs was, of course, the release of Windows 95. This popular product made using the computer easier because it provided a turnkey means of accessing the Internet through a simple telephone line. The second breakthrough came when Netscape released its Web browser designed for Windows 95. With a 32-bit system architecture, Windows 95 could process large streams of data quickly, allowing for multitasking. The third important event was the rise of private Internet service providers like America Online, Prodigy, and CompuServe. To this day, these companies still bombard us with diskettes and CDs, offering free trial periods and relatively affordable Internet connectivity. The fourth event, and perhaps one of the most important, was the beginning of the drop in technology prices as the speed and efficiency of the technology continued to increase. A fifth and final reason for this explosion is that in 1995 ownership of the Internet backbone lines was transferred from the government to private companies like MCI.

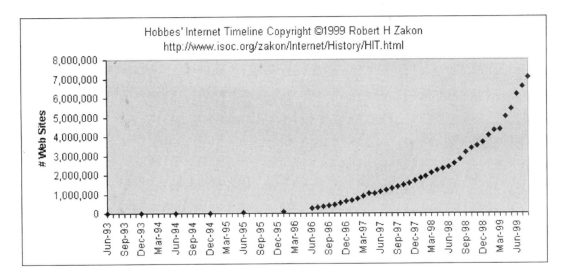

Fig. 1.7. Growth of the WWW.

Figure 1.7 indicates the growth of information on the Web. This chart tells us how many millions of websites (not pages) have been placed on servers since the summer of 1993. What is interesting about this chart is that it demonstrates the explosion of information occurring just after 1995. Clearly, unless an extensive number of webpages are simply deleted someplace, it is doubtful that this number will ever go down. If any conclusion can be drawn, it should probably be that there is an information explosion on the Web. This is an important conclusion, too, since information is what constitutes cyberspace.

THE INTERNET AND THE COMMUNICATION STUDIES APPROACH

You can approach any topic from a number of directions and whichever perspective you choose will affect what and how you learn. You might have heard the story by Rudyard Kipling in which three blind men touch an unknown object. The first man was certain that he had touched a thin piece of rope dangling from the ceiling. The second man believed that he had touched a giant snake. And the third was convinced that he had touched a coarse tree trunk. But they were all wrong, since they all touched an elephant. The first man had touched the elephant's tail, the second the trunk, and the last its leg. This story shows us that what we learn is, fundamentally, a product of our perspective. Before you examine any subject, first ask yourself, What is my angle? What is my approach? These are two crucial questions to keep in mind before examining any important subject. You could approach the Internet from many different perspectives, and actually many people have already done so. We have chosen to focus our attention on how the Internet works as a communication medium. But to get a better understanding for our communication studies angle, let's first see what other parts of the proverbial elephant people have grabbed.

For starters, you could study the Internet from a popular press approach. To do this, you would go down to your local bookstore, or call up BarnesandNoble.com online, and buy any number of popular works on how to use the Internet. Many of these texts are quite good. They take the user step-by-step through some basic software procedures and explain some of the key difficulties and successes that many first-time Internet users experience. We appreciate the way that many of these authors coach their readers into learning applications and tools. And in this book, you'll be learning some of this same basic information. It would be ridiculous, after all, if you finished this book and didn't know how to use many of the basic online applications.

Still, a problem with these popular press books is the focus on the Internet as an information superhighway or web of information. As metaphors for the digital transmission of data through computer networks, these figures of speech have caught the attention of the world. They have also created a breed of literary road hogs: instant book writers and crafty speakers who spin off ad nauseam from this metaphor, creating such sound bites as "Infobahn," "on-ramps," "off-ramps," "road kill," and other horrible mixed metaphors like "surfing the Web." When we look at the Internet through these popular works, we end up focusing solely on information as if it were traveling along actual pathways or roads. This causes us to focus merely on the transmission and reception of information, coldly negating its ability to influence, to change, and what is most important, to communicate. And, what is worse, these books do this without fully acknowledging the fact that *people* are important in this exchange. If you want to reach people in this age of information, you have to be able to craft a message that fits your audience, creating the need for a communication studies approach.

Another way to examine the Internet is from the computer science perspective. Here, you would also study the Internet as an information network, but without the bad metaphors. Instead of learning how to use Internet software, you would learn to design the programs with which you would communicate. In other words, you would learn how to code webpages in HTML, you would write **Java scripts** (simple programs, designed to be sent over the Internet and run on any computer), and you might even work on designing databases. We appreciate the nitty-gritty details found in many of these books, and you'll even get exposed to some of them when we discuss HTML design in part 4. Yet we also believe that the Internet is far more than a collection of complex computer programs. When we strictly focus on learning the ins and outs of computer code, as these books do intentionally, we lose sight of the communicative and cultural implications of this powerful new medium. For as we interact more and more through the Web we literally change our understanding of the world, our society, ourselves, and even knowledge. Because our focus is on communication, we'll approach webpages as a way to connect with people, and not as a collection of codes.

You could also approach the Internet as a resource for doing research. For example, people in the information sciences (also known as library sciences) do an excellent job of outlining the proper methods for classifying and categorizing online data. You'll find many of these methods in the chapters about online research. One of the biggest challenges is to find *useful* information on the Web, and the field of information science is doing much to make our searches more fruitful. However, unless you simply wish to know where information can be found, this perspective is limiting. To actually do something with the data that you find, you will at some point have to communicate.

In short, the way that we approach the Internet greatly affects what we learn about it. Rather than learn how to follow the flow of information, or program a computer, or discipline data, in this text you will learn how to connect with people. From a communication studies perspective, the emphasis in this text will be on using the Internet to effectively connect with the endless range of audiences that you will meet on this new medium. After all, anyone can build a website with some basic instruction. Think about it for a moment: if *everyone* is building a website, that's an awful lot of websites. How can you make your information stand out? If everyone is sending e-mail, how can you make sure that yours gets read? If you have to find some specific information quickly to make your communication more powerful, how do you go about doing it? That's the perspective that this book takes: it is about effective online communication.

Throughout this text, we'll look at the Internet through a communication lens, consisting of the following key components: (1) audience, (2) purpose, (3) medium, and (4) context/culture.

AUDIENCE

Central to communication, whether face-to-face or mediated, is understanding and adapting to your audience. You understand this at a basic level: if you built a webpage about how televisions work, you would use different language and images if you were targeting children than if you were targeting adults. Effective communication on the Internet starts with thinking about for whom your message is intended and how best you can reach them.

PURPOSE

Deeply connected to considerations of audience are considerations of purpose. Communicators must constantly ask themselves, Why am I trying to reach this audience? From this basic question of purpose, you then need to consider how you can best achieve your goal. Which interface will work best? What form should your message take? Throughout this text we will consider how to effectively achieve your purpose when communicating.

MEDIUM

One thing we have learned in studying communication is that the medium, or channel by which we communicate, is extremely important. We can communicate in ways now that were impossible before the Internet. The medium with which we communicate not only affects how we say things but also has social consequences. For example, the printing press made it much easier and cheaper to duplicate the written word, leading to an increase in literacy, the invention of the newspaper, and the spreading of ideals like freedom of thought and expression. Effective communication means you need to be aware of the effects of this new medium on your message, on your society, and even on your own identity.

CONTEXT/CULTURE

Communication doesn't take place in a vacuum—at least, not very often. Instead, it takes place in a context. Thus effective communication means being aware of the context in which your communication occurs and of the most appropriate and efficient means of getting your message across in that setting. But again, at a deeper level, communication also *creates* a context or culture. To effectively use the Internet, you'll need to be aware of how the style of communication creates a particular community, how rules of interaction develop, and how to fit your message into this evolving electronic world.

Throughout the pages of this book, you will be learning concepts and tactics that have been gathered from a growing body of research. Just as the Internet is still growing and changing, so too theories about electronic communication are developing even as you read this text. Searching through research journals, you can find a wide range of approaches to studying computer-mediated communication (CMC), including the following:

- Fundamentals and how-tos of CMC and online databases
- Educational dimensions of CMC
- Legal implications of CMC (copyright law, First Amendment law, etc.)
- Uses and gratifications of CMC users
- Small groups and their interaction on CMC systems
- Diffusion of CMC technology in organizations
- Characteristics of online communities
- Impact of CMC on personal identity
- Political communication on the Internet

What ties all of these studies together, and this textbook as well, is the emphasis on communication. And after all, since that is one of the main reasons you will be using the Internet, why not start from that perspective?

BACK UP AND RELOAD

There's a saying (which is sometimes used as a curse) that goes, "May you live in interesting times." These certainly are interesting times, as a new medium rooted in a worldwide network of computers starts to shape all areas of your life. In this chapter, you have been introduced to this interactive communication medium. You've learned how the Internet began as a military research project in the years of the cold war and evolved into a global communication system. This evolution took place in several stages as the various components of the World Wide Web were developed and put into place. Finally, you have seen why we chose to approach the Internet from a communication studies perspective. This focus on audience, purpose, medium, and context/culture has guided a wide range of research, the results of which will help you become an effective communicator in cyberspace.

> # BROWSE *and* BUILD
>
> For sites to visit, exercises, quizzes to test your learning, and more, go to
> *www.harcourtcollege.com/communication/inetcomm*

References and Readings

Borgmann, A. 1999. *Holding on to reality: The nature of information at the turn of the millennium.* Chicago: University of Chicago Press.

Divine, R. 1993. *The sputnik challenge.* Oxford: Oxford University Press.

Hogan, M. 1996. *Hiroshima in history and memory.* Cambridge: Cambridge University Press.

Johnson, S. 1997. *Interface culture: How new technology transforms the way we create and communicate.* San Francisco: Harper San Francisco.

Leary, T. 1994. *Chaos and cyberculture.* Berkeley: Ronin Publishing.

Mann, J. 1998. *Tomorrow's global community: How the information deluge is transforming business and government.* Philadelphia: Trans-Atlantic Publications.

Metcalfe, R. M., D. Walden, and P. Salus. 1996. *Packet communication.* New York: International Thomson Computer Publishing.

Moschovitz, C., H. Poole, T. Shuyler, and T. Senft. 1999. *History of the Internet: A chronology, 1843 to the present.* Santa Barbara: ABO-CLIO.

Negroponte, N. 1995. *Being digital.* New York: Knopf.

O'Niel, D. 1995. *The firecracker boys.* New York: St. Martin's Press.

Pinch, T. J., and H. Collins. 1998. *The golem at large: What you should know about technology.* Cambridge: Cambridge University Press.

Porter, D. 1997. *Internet culture.* New York: Routledge Press.

Stefik, M. 1996. *Internet dreams: Archetypes, myths, and metaphors.* Boston: MIT Press.

Zakon, R. 1999. *Hobbes Internet timeline v4.2.* Accessed 21 December 1999 <http://www.isoc.org/zakon/Internet/History/HIT.html>.

CHAPTER 2

What Is It?
Characteristics of the Medium

By Peter Zale ©2000 Peter Zale, www.peterzale.com   Distributed by Tribune Media Services, www.comicspage.com

By the end of this chapter, you should:

I.   Know how the Internet compares and contrasts to other communication media.

II. Appreciate three of the problems of distant communication that the Internet is trying to solve:
     A. reliability,
     B. speed, and
     C. distribution.

III. Be familiar with the six key qualities of the medium:
     A. multimediated,
     B. hypertextual,
     C. interactive,
     D. (a)synchronous,
     E. packet based, and
     F. digital.

IV. Understand how visuals persuade us, and the implications of this for Internet literacy.

In chapter 1, we established the importance of studying the Internet from a communication perspective. In this chapter, we'll essentially give you a pair of "communication goggles" through which you can view the Internet. First, we'll compare and contrast the Internet in relation to other communication media. Regardless of what type of medium it is, problems will ordinarily occur whenever communicating across long distances. We'll talk about how the Internet is resolving the issues of reliability, speed, and distribution in the second part of this chapter. Next, we'll cover the six key qualities of this new medium, showing how it has evolved from existing media and pointing out how these characteristics affect communication on the Internet. And finally, because the Internet is at present a primarily visual medium, we will discuss how visual images persuade us, and what this means for us as consumers of information.

THE INTERNET AS A COMMUNICATION MEDIUM

Exactly what kind of medium is the Internet? This is a question without an easy answer. The study of communication has traditionally been divided into categories based on the number of people involved in the transmission of the message. Thus we have interpersonal (one-to-one), small group (limited numbers of interactants), public speaking (one person addressing a group of varying size), and mass media (one group broadcasting messages to the general public) categories. However, the Internet does not fit neatly into any of these categories, since the medium allows so many different forms of interaction.

E-mail, chat-rooms, MUDs (multiuser dungeons), telephony, and videoconferencing are typically used for more personal forms of communication. While some people do resort to **spamming** (distributing e-mail messages indiscriminately to multiple audiences), such tactics violate the norms of the Internet community. Instead, we typically use these tools to send mail to our friends, to interact with people who share our interests in a hobby or sport, to hear and see a coworker, or to announce news to specific and appropriate audiences. Thus interaction on these submedia typically resembles interpersonal communication, small group communication, and on some occasions public speaking.

But the Internet is not just used for personal communication. Quite often it is used for public communication and resembles a mass medium more than an interpersonal one. Webpages and sites are typically produced for mass audiences (although here again we find exceptions; for example, most people in the world probably won't want to browse your personal homepage). Companies use websites to get product information to consumers or to sell their products. Universities use them to provide information and courses. Traditional media outlets, such as CNN, use websites to enhance their broadcast programs. In these and many other ways, the Internet builds upon and extends the application of our more traditional media. At different times it can resemble an interactive newspaper, an augmented television program, or, quite often, a highly targeted advertising campaign.

If you are reading carefully, you will have noticed that we still have not answered the question of exactly what sort of medium the Internet is. Is it an interpersonal medium? A mass medium? Or is it something else entirely? Part of the challenge presented by the Internet is that it is dramatically altering our understanding of communication media since it does not fit easily into any one particular category. In fact, as you will see later in this text, it is causing significant changes in the way our preexisting media operate. The Internet itself is still changing, evolving, adapting as new technologies and applications come and go. Even though we cannot yet get a good picture of what exactly the Internet is, or will someday become, it should be helpful in the meantime to consider the following two terms: macromedium and metamedium.

We would like to suggest that the Internet is a **macromedium.** The prefix "macro" is useful here in two senses. First, macro denotes large scale or size. Macroeconomics, for example, is the study of system-wide economic processes. The Internet is a macromedium because it is immense in size and can be used to reach audiences on a global scale. But we also use the word macro in connection with photography to talk about taking nearly life-size pictures of small objects at a very close range. The Internet is also a macromedium in the sense that it can be used to access or publish the smallest bits of personal trivia, or webpages tailored to an audience of one. As a macromedium, the Internet is a synthesis of interpersonal and mass media, a unique new blend of communication genres.

This global system, which can be accessed and used at an extremely personal level, provides us with a unique platform for interaction—a platform that is altering how we communicate. If it started out as a network of networks, the Internet has become a medium of media, or **metamedium.** It is a communication system that serves as a platform for older media, including telephony, print, and broadcasting. But more than that, it now enables us to operate on both ends of traditional mass media. We can now both send and receive live audio or video feeds, enabling us to both have a television or radio *set* and a television or radio *station* on our desktop. Once you have the requisite software components installed, you can quickly and easily switch between sending e-mail, listening to streaming audio, and broadcasting a video feed—all without moving from your computer.

RESOLVING PROBLEMS IN DISTANT COMMUNICATION

Obviously it's difficult to pinpoint just what type of medium the Internet is going to become since it is still undergoing significant development. Still, regardless of their specific form, throughout history communication media have been used to increase humanity's ability to share information across larger distances. Whenever people try to communicate between spatially distant points, they have to resolve a number of problems. The three we discuss here are *reliability*, *speed*, and *distribution.*

RELIABILITY

The Internet represents another stage in our age-old quest to make communication reliable between people in distant places. Throughout history, communicators have been worried about the frailty of communication. For the ancient Greeks, the weakest link in communication was the memories of the people involved. The technology of **formulaic invention** was vital to communication in ancient Greece (Havelock 1963). If a citizen needed to send a message during the ages before writing, the message had to be memorized. To aid memorization, they developed set patterns for the order of information in the message, set phrases that were repeated periodically, and a rhythmic and melodic language that was much closer to singing than our language today. This formulaic expression of content made the message easier for the messenger to memorize and ensured that the message would not be distorted (or at least minimized the risk).

In the middle ages, when memory was replaced by fixed type, communicators became more worried about the frailty of language. Even though you could put your message down on paper and duplicate it a thousand times, ensuring it would not be forgotten, there was no guarantee that the other person would understand exactly what was meant. The words in any language do not mean the same thing to everyone: if I were to say the word "house," everyone hearing it would picture something else in their head. Some would see a split-level two-story home, others might see a ranch-style hacienda, while still others might picture an A-frame cottage. People began to recognize that language was hopelessly imprecise and incapable of directly transferring meaning. This concern was most evident in the rise of the field of science (Ong 1971). While the ancient Greeks used formulaic expressions to aid in the storage and retrieval of information, scientists tried to develop formulas that could not be misunderstood by anyone. For example, formulas for chemical compounds, while complicated to learn, are universally understood.

Once knowledge could be formulaic in this new sense, the inventor of that knowledge could be erased. The author of the formula was irrelevant; all that mattered was that the formula was accurate.

While the ancient Greeks were concerned about the frailty of memory, and scientists of the middle ages about the frailty of language, the inventors of the Internet were concerned about the frailty of the medium. The problem with any network is that the larger it is, the more distributed through space it is. As a result, the network gets more fragile. If something goes wrong, repair technicians first have to find the break in the network and then travel to that point and repair it. Under even the best conditions such a task would take time, and the planners of the Internet were trying to build a system that would work under the *worst* possible conditions (travel during a nuclear attack might be hazardous, they rightly assumed). The formulaic expressions of the past, whether the mnemonic structures of the Greeks or the abstract symbols of the scientists, would not resolve this problem. Thus, as we discussed in chapter 1, the Internet's inventors designed formulaic packets, which would allow any computer anywhere to pass the message along. The formulaic address was not a way to augment the storage or precision of information, but its transmission. Communication between distant points had been possible for decades. Now it was approaching levels of reliability necessary for the transfer of digital data.

SPEED

Of course, reliability was not the only problem that engineers trying to eliminate the impact of space or place had to solve. As researchers began to transfer larger and larger files, speed began to emerge as an issue. The top speed of data transmission during the 1970s was 56,000 bits per second. At the time, this was considerably faster than any available modems for home or personal use, which ran at 300 bits per second. At top speed, researchers could transmit an article-length paper in a second. As you learned in the last chapter, the National Science Foundation (NSF) began hooking up campuses across the nation in the 1980s, and use of the net began to increase exponentially. As use increased, so did the variety of uses and the types of content. Now researchers wanted to send graphic images or vast amounts of statistical data. The speed kept increasing until it reached 45 Mbps in 1991.

At such speeds, researchers could send over 5,000 pages every second. Yet it is important to remember that this top rate is only on backbone lines, and messages often have to travel the last stages of their journey over much slower lines. In addition, graphic images are much larger than text files. At 45 Mbps, you can only send 100 large graphic images per second. Video is even worse, since 30 seconds of compressed, choppy video the size of a postage stamp is an enormous amount of digital data (although new compression schemes are constantly improving video transfer rates). Even so, at these speeds it is possible to access entire books over the Internet, and many libraries and other institutes are working to make this dream come to life. No longer do you have to physically travel to Washington, D.C., to check out a book from the Library of Congress. You don't even have to wait for the physical book to be mailed to you through interlibrary loan. Instead, you can ignore the spatial distance, or, more accurately, transform the distance into an insignificant amount of time, and read the book within seconds of pressing a button on your mouse.

The interrelatedness of space and speed/time became even more clear as people began to use the Internet for interpersonal communication. Since communication among humans began, interpersonal communication has had the richest sensory impact in face-to-face settings. As the distance between the communicators increased, the richness decreased. Communicators could not give or interpret nonverbal cues, provide or receive feedback, use multiple senses, or engage in extensive synchronous dialogue. But as the speed with which data could be transmitted on computer networks increased, so did the richness of the communication. Faster modems permitted audio conversations over the Internet, adding the older communication technology of the telephone (but without long distance charges) to this metamedium. When Internet phones were combined with cheap videoconferencing systems and fast data transmission speeds, video and audio conversations became possible. The day when two people wearing virtual reality suits will be able to conduct conversations with full sensory input while standing in cities thousands of miles apart is arguably not far away. In short, as the speed of transmission on the Internet increased, the number of senses that you could use to interpret communication also increased.

DISTRIBUTION

A fast, reliable network–whether a computer network, a telephone network, or a postal network–still requires a third quality: distribution. A postal system that cannot reach all of the people in its domain is inefficient and unreliable. Telephone penetration is at 93.9% in the United States, while cable television is in more than 65% of television households in the country (Federal Communications Commission 1997, 9; *Industry statistics* 1997). These figures far outstrip present Internet penetration. In 2000, the Stanford Institute for the Quantitative Study of Society (SIQSS) suggested that approximately 43% of U.S. households are connected to the Internet. Measuring the full distribution of the Internet is a difficult task. Since the Internet has no central location, no one place knows everything about the rest of the network. Since some sites choose to limit access, it is impossible to precisely determine the extent and size of the network. Even best guesses are complicated by the multiple means available to define and measure the network's distribution and by its ever-changing size. However, it is possible to estimate the extent of the Internet through space by using a few different measures.

The size of the Internet could be judged by the number of sites connected to it, the number of different *places* people can visit. As of July 1999, 56,218,000 different hosts were connected to the Internet (*Internet Domain Survey* 1999). However, this figure does not give any indication of *where* the Internet is being used or *who* is using it. The problem is that it is almost impossible to even estimate how many people might be using the Internet because people can access it from public libraries, colleges, their homes, etc. Estimates on the number of users vary. The *1997 American Internet Survey* conducted by Find/SVP, "one of the most conservative and rigorous market research companies around," put the number of Internet users in the United States at 27 million (Electric word 1997, 41). One of the most respected historians of the Internet, Robert Hobbes Zakon (author of the famed *Hobbes' Internet Timeline*), was asked why he does not chart the number of Internet users. His answer was, "This is too controversial, and relatively inaccurate, an issue which the author does not want to get flamed or spammed for. His guess would be between 1 (himself) and 6 billion (but then again, one never knows if you're a dog on the Net)" (Zakon 1999).

Most statistics about the Internet are more accurately labeled estimates, and by the time anyone reads this paragraph they will be hopelessly out of date. The only conclusion that can be drawn from the data we have is that the global computer network is growing at a phenomenal rate (for now). The number of hosts connected to the Internet **(Figure 2.1)** and the speed with which new ones come online continue to rise. Much of this growth is occurring at the international level, for although many computer networks in the United States are connected, the level and density of connectivity varies around the globe.

By looking at the distribution of Internet nodes around the globe, an observant researcher would come to an important conclusion: the problem of distribution is solved by money. Countries with more wealth, or those willing to invest what wealth they have in new technology, are more connected than those unwilling or unable to connect themselves. This is true in the United States as well. People living in urban areas have more Internet service providers (ISPs) to choose from and lower rates than people living in rural areas. Access to this new medium is still highly dependent on income, since the $700 or more necessary just to purchase a computer is too high of a start-up fee for many. This disparity has not gone unnoticed, and some activists have been working hard to rectify it in their local communities by providing free or very inexpensive local Internet access.

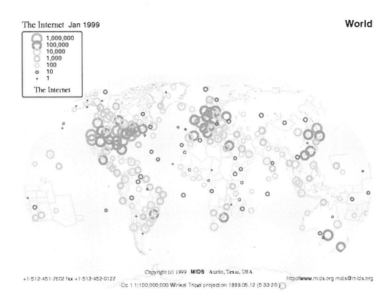

Fig. 2.1. Distribution and density of host computers connected to the Internet.

As the reliability, speed, and distribution of the Internet increase, so too does the variety of uses people create for it. Now might be a good time to check out the *Trends* section of the text website. Here you'll find links to a wide range of cutting-edge websites that are making innovative use of this new communication medium.

SIX KEY QUALITIES

It is an understatement to say that the Internet is changing. Trends come and go faster than we can count. But one thing we can pin down is the important qualities of this medium, or the characteristics that influence our changing communication patterns. Rafaeli and Newhagen (1996) suggested six defining qualities for the Internet, which we will discuss here (with some adaptations and additions): the Internet is *multimediated, hypertextual, interactive, (a)synchronous, packet based,* and *digital.* These qualities affect how we communicate over the medium, so you should expect to see them resurface throughout this text as we discuss effective communication skills for each interface.

You should remember one important fact (and we'll do our best to remind you): new media do not come from Neverland. The characteristics of the Internet have their foundations in the media that preceded it. So as we go through these six qualities, we will talk both about how they are evolving from past media and their importance for our future communication.

MULTIMEDIATED

When you visit a webpage, you most likely encounter a wide range of media: graphics, words, sound, and video. Some sites will even add the dimension of virtual reality to your sensory experience. The most popular browsers (Microsoft's Internet Explorer and Netscape Navigator) both support many different file formats, or different ways of storing and transferring the multimedia content. Not only that, these browsers also allow you to add in small programs called plug-ins that run inside the browser and allow you to view still more types of content. You can watch videos, listen to audio clips, and even play games online if you have the necessary plug-ins.

The concept of combining different media in one message is not really new, as you no doubt realize. Books have both text and pictures; television combines audio and visual forms. But the Internet, and more importantly the personal computer, have popularized the term multimedia because they have taken the combination of forms to a new level. Anyone who has ever done any video production will tell you that the computer has made it far easier to combine text and video, sound and still images. This ease is due to digitization, which we'll discuss in more depth.

Depending on which website you are visiting, the Internet might resemble a radio, a book, a television, or something out of a science fiction movie. And it is exactly this shifting, fluid quality that makes the Internet different. A significant change that the Internet brings to mediated communication is its capacity for mixing together a wide range of media. Designers of webpages can blend together text, audio, video, and still or animated graphics with relative ease (and unfortunately sometimes do so with little concern for the electronic eyesores they create). This is leading to significant changes in our expectations for messages, as well as significant industry changes. What we're seeing more and more in our news today is **convergence:** "the integration of the once separate technologies and industries of print, broadcasting and telecommunications" (Dutton 1995, 82). Our televisions, radios, and computers are becoming one and the same. Our Internet data is traveling over our cable lines. Networks have websites, and radio stations broadcast over the Web. We're expecting more and more for messages to come to us in multiple forms, for them to be as visually and aurally stimulating as possible.

To be an effective communicator on this metamedium, it's going to take the development of some discernment. You will need to learn what types of messages work best in what form. This judgement will not be easy to develop since, to a large extent, it will be based on your audience

BOX 2.1

POPULAR PLUG-INS

Plug-ins are supplemental programs that work with Web browsers or other applications to expand their communicative capacity. You may also hear the term used for non-Internet-related software such as Adobe Photoshop photo filters or audio-editing effect programs. However, for our focus, we will deal strictly with Web-based plug-ins. If these plug-ins aren't currently on your computer, you can easily install them. You can find links to download the plug-ins on the textbook website.

Documentation

Adobe Acrobat Reader–Allows users to create documents however they would like and convert the page into a .pdf file, which can then be read in the plug-in accessory. This is one of the most widely used tools on the Internet, allowing organizations to seamlessly transfer their paper documentation into an online version that will retain the original format. Most forms and intricate documents are transmitted through this universally accepted application.

Multimedia

Flash and Shockwave Players–These plug-ins add an impressive array of sophisticated multimedia capabilities to webpages, including animation, games, interactive displays, sound, and much more. To see what can be done with these players (often automatically installed with newer browsers), check out the links to multimedia sites provided on the textbook website.

Audio and Video Streams

RealPlayer–By far the most widely used means of transferring rich digital media content through the Internet. With this plug-in, you will be able to watch live television or streaming video clips saved on a server. You will also be able to listen to live audio events, Internet radio broadcasts, and prerecorded audio files. Microsoft's Media Player is a competing player that is installed with Windows 98 (and newer versions).

QuickTime–Made by Apple Computer, QuickTime is another popular player valued for its versatility. As the Apple.com site reads, "QuickTime is the latest version of Apple's complete technology for handling video, sound, animation, graphics, text, music, and even 360-degree virtual reality (VR) scenes. A gateway for rich media including images, music, MIDI, MP3 and more, QuickTime lets you experience more than 200 kinds of digital media with your Mac or PC."

> **Virtual Reality Worlds**
>
> **Viscape**–Superscape's Viscape plug-in allows you to view and interact in graphical, three-dimensional, virtual worlds. Viscape, and other 3-D plug-ins use a language called VRML (virtual reality modeling language) to create virtual realities. With Viscape you can walk through artificially created environments, interact with objects, communicate in real time with other "visitors," and even race cars against other people online.

and on still-evolving technologies and standards. But we'll try to point out along the way which forms work well for what types of messages.

HYPERTEXTUAL

If the Internet was simply a new mix of media, it would not be much more than a glorified, easier-to-produce television show. But with the addition of **hypertextuality,** the Internet becomes much more. Hypertextuality is essentially the ability to link any type of content to any other type of content. So when you visit a multimedia site, clicking on an underlined word may bring up a new document, clicking on a picture may start a video, and clicking on a graphic may play a sound. For example, the CNN website **(Figure 2.2)** allows you to read related stories, hear sound bites, and view video clips all by simply clicking on the appropriate word or picture.

Hypertext has been around for a few decades–at least in theory. The term was "coined by Theodor Nelson in the 1960s" and was first used to talk about "text composed of blocks of text . . . and the electronic links that join them" (Landow 1992, 4). As media have converged, the links have connected more than just blocks of text, so that now people sometimes talk about hypermedia: electronically interconnected information in a variety of forms. Today, the World Wide Web is based on the concept of hypertextuality. In fact, as you've already learned, the language used to format the pages on the WWW is called HTML: *hypertext* markup language.

Hypertextuality means that all of the mixed content on the Web is easily navigated. You can get from one thing to the next with a simple click. But the impact on communication goes deeper than this. Landow (1992) talks about three key implications of hypertextuality: **intertextuality, multivocality,** and **de-centering.** Intertextuality is a word used to denote the connections between texts. For example, when you read a book (even this one) you'll find references to other books, cultural phenomenon, and so forth. On the WWW, thanks to hypertext, you can

Fig. 2.2. With a simple click on words or pictures, you can access more words, pictures, sounds, or videos.

actually see these other texts, so it is possible to provide greater depth and context for those viewers who want to learn more (for example, see the CNN webpage in **Figure 2.2**). When done well, linking multiple texts and materials to a document can provide the user with a much richer experience and, hopefully, a fuller understanding of an issue.

With linked content, you, the reader/viewer/audience/consumer of a webpage, can pick and choose to whom you want to pay attention. This is the essence of multivocality, or many voices. Unlike a book, which is designed to be read by itself from beginning to end (unless you cheat), hypertexts allow you to read text by one author, jump to text by another author, and then view a graphic put on the Web by a third person. Because of this multivocality, it is relatively easy on the Web to quickly lose a sense of what belongs to whom, which means that copyright issues get very complicated (an issue we'll discuss in depth in chapter 12).

On the Web, it's also easy to lose a sense of just exactly who the producer of the text is and who the consumer is. In a very real sense, you write your own text or script each time you get online. As you move from page to page *selecting* your links, you literally build the text that your mind, in turn, encounters. You choose what you want to focus your attention on instead of the author choosing it for you. This de-centering, or loss of a single organizing principle, means that texts on the Web have to be organized differently. If you want people to interact with your material on the Web, you need to provide them with multiple ways to access your information and multiple ways to organize or make sense of it. We'll talk about this in more detail when we talk about effective navigation systems in chapter 10.

INTERACTIVE

The ability to choose your own path as you "surf the Web" (a painful but popular mixed metaphor) means that the Internet is far more interactive than older media. With television and radio, you choose a station or program. With books, you choose which text to read. But with the Web you have much greater control over the medium, and the medium itself has a much greater ability to respond to you. Your choices are much greater: you can choose to interact with other people via e-mail or chat; you can choose the content you want to view and the format in which it comes; and you can order products. But the Web can also interact with you: you can submit personal information and get news tailored to your interests, sophisticated websites alter the content of pages based on your personal preferences, and much more. For example, Amazon.com (an online bookseller) will give you recommendations based on prior purchases and your self-entered preferences **(Figure 2.3)**.

In essence, with the Internet you can choose to interact with either people or programs—people who will respond to you in the endless variety inherent to human interaction, or programs that will respond to you in predictable obedience and ever-increasing specificity and sophistication. Over the past years, and no doubt in the coming ones, the richness of interactivity on the Internet has increased. At first, communication on the Internet consisted of exchanging text messages via e-mail. Now you can interact with full motion video and sound. In this environment, you need to learn how to choose the level of interaction appropriate to your message, audience, and goals. We'll return to this issue throughout the text. People also expect more from websites, so you'll want to make your webpages as interactive as possible. Fully interactive pages are beyond the scope of this book and (we imagine) the course that you're in, so you'll need to learn CGI (Common Gateway Interface, a programming language) scripting elsewhere. But one of the benefits of a communication-

Fig. 2.3. Your computer knows you better than you know yourself, and it wants to interact with you—or at least sell you something.

centered approach is the focus on adapting to your audience. We'll talk about ways that you can make your website fit your audience, increasing their desire to interact with your message.

(A)SYNCHRONOUS

When we interact on the Internet, time gets stretched in both directions. At times, we want to communicate **synchronously** (at the same time), where your response follows my comment instantly. At other times, we want some time to think in between our exchanges—our communication is then **asynchronous** (not at the same time). Other media have had the possibility of becoming synchronous or asynchronous. Telephones, for example, are augmented by answering machines. Televisions can create the illusion of displaced time through the use of VCRs. But the Internet is different in the extremes to which it stretches time. We can have faster-than-synchronous communication: you can download information faster than you can read or view it. We can have extremely asynchronous communication by storing messages in archives and then retrieving and replying to them at any date in the future. We can have a bizarre blend of both, as in chat-rooms where your comment and another person's synchronous reply might be separated in the flow of text by several others' comments. Or worse yet, you might type up a long thoughtful response only to look at your screen and realize someone else already answered the question. Time on the Internet does not adhere to the normal linear constraints presented by either conversation or traditional media.

As if you didn't have enough to worry about in communicating over the Internet—now you have to worry about time, too! Each interface that we discuss in this text, whether e-mail, chat, video conferencing, or webpages, has its own sense of time. So to use them effectively, you'll need to be aware of each one's relative speed and interactivity and then match your goals and time constraints to the appropriate interface. On a medium that is growing and evolving at an unprecedented rate, where information is flowing at a rate too fast for human comprehension, it is vital that you have a very strong grasp on time.

PACKET BASED

Getting the message through has always been a key component of communication, as we will see later in this chapter. The Internet's solution to making sure that communication traffic gets correctly routed is the technology called packet switching. You learned about this technology in the last chapter. To refresh your memory, all data transmitted over the Internet is sent in segments (packets), and attached to each segment is information about where it came from and where it needs to go. This technology revolutionized communication, leaping far past our prior addressing system used by the postal service. As we noted earlier in the chapter, the formulaic address attached to each chunk of the message is responsible for the reliability of the medium.

This is a crucial technological advance that has significant implications for communication. For the most part, you don't need to be aware of this to use the Internet effectively. But the effect of what goes on behind the scenes shouldn't be overlooked. This design makes it almost impossible to control the flow of information since each chunk of information, in a sense, controls its own transmission through the network. It knows where it is going, and it can find any route among hundreds of possibilities to get there. You can't really block it since the system is designed to work around blocks automatically. This makes any attempt to censor the Internet extremely difficult, if not impossible. For you personally, it means you do not have to worry about the route the message must take. If the delivery information is correct, it will find the recipient. If not, it will return to you.

DIGITAL

What makes packet switching, and really all of the Internet, possible is the digitization of information. Negroponte (1995) has written a great deal about the impact of digitization, and here we will present just a brief summary of his studies.

Data can be stored in one of two ways: with an analog or a digital device. An analog device creates a physical analog, or analogy, of the information to be stored. Thus the bumps on a phonograph are analogous to the shape of the sound wave that they represent. Digital devices use numbers to store information instead, usually using a binary system where 0 = off and 1 = on. Digital encoding of information has many advantages over analog. For one thing, digital information isn't as easily distorted as analog recordings, in which a small imperfection (a scratch, for example) can cause large changes. Digital devices typically are less vulnerable to wear and tear since the device does not have to come into physical contact with the medium (e.g., the laser mechanism does not touch the CD) as it does with an analog device (e.g., the needle rubs along a record groove). Finally, almost any information can be digitally encoded and stored in very compact form. Of course, no format is perfect. Digital information has some limitations: an early error can corrupt an entire file, digital encoding of analog information such as audio waves requires a massive amount of data, and digital formats come and go at a frustrating rate—the format in which you saved a bunch of video clips may disappear next month, forcing you to resample the videos. But for most people, these limitations are outweighed by the advantages.

Data can also be transmitted in one of two ways: physically (as atoms) or electronically (as bits). Communication used to depend on physical transportation, a potentially difficult, time-consuming, and expensive task (think of the history of exploration, or the postal service, for example). But once information is digitally encoded, the bits can be moved across copper wires, fiber-optic cables, or even the airwaves easily, instantly, and very cheaply. Now, instead of having to purchase a CD from a record store, which means that a physical object has to be shipped and stored, you can download the music off the Web and store it on your computer still in bit form. The most searched-for term on the Web used to be *sex;* now, it's *MP3.* **MP3** is a format for digitally encoding music. Right now, you can visit sites like MP3.com **(Figure 2.4)** and download CD-quality songs, and if you're lucky enough to own a CD-R, you can **burn** (record) those songs onto a CD of your own. If you are unscrupulous enough, you can download pirated popular songs by nearly any artist—a fact that has music corporations understandably concerned and taking legal action.

The ability to transform information into bits has had an enormous impact on communication. We can have **bits about bits:** information can be encoded into the message itself, allowing it to be somewhat self-reflexive and communicative. A website can tell screening software what its rating is, its content, who can view it, and much more. Bits are highly **compressible,** and sophisticated **algorithms** (formulas used for

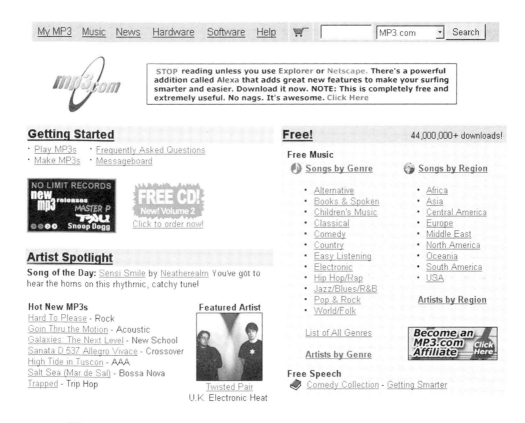

Fig. 2.4. Why wait to buy atoms (in the form of a CD) when you can instantly download bits?

manipulating data) make it possible to reduce the size, and thus the downloading time, of large graphic files or video clips. CD-quality MP3 songs now run about five megabytes in size, a previously unimaginable feat. Bits are extremely **malleable.** Once you have information encoded digitally, it is extremely easy to alter it almost undetectably. The Internet is full of faked pictures called *pasties* where fans put the heads of stars, such as Gillian Anderson, on the nude body of a model. And once information is in digital form, it can be **commingled:** bits can mix with other bits. A website can have video, audio, text, graphics, and any other digital content all connected and blended together. Finally, digitization of information raises a dilemma that has yet to be resolved: how do you put a **price on bits**? Pricing schemes that charge by the bit have been proposed, but have yet to be implemented largely because putting them into practice is extremely complicated. Should grade school students accessing information from the Library of Congress pay as much as college students downloading pictures of the latest Playboy Playmate?

VISUAL RHETORIC AND INTERNET LITERACY

As a student, you have firsthand knowledge of the fact that you do not pop into this world fully literate. You have spent many years learning to read and write with increasing effectiveness and sophistication—and no doubt you're still taking writing classes. You hopefully had some training at public speaking, and if you were lucky, you were taught how to listen more effectively. But being a literate user of the Internet means you need to acquire even more skills. Obviously, you need to learn how to use the software programs that help you interact on this new medium. A portion of this textbook is dedicated to teaching you the basics of some of these programs. One of the first skills required is the ability to browse the Web. In this chapter, we've included a box on how to use Netscape Navigator that will help those of you new to the Web get started, and should give those of you for whom browsing is old news some tips on how to browse more effectively.

But clearly, there is more to the Web than words, sounds, and programs. Much of the communication that occurs online happens through images. After all, Netscape Navigator and Internet Explorer are not called graphical Web browsers for nothing. At this point, you might be thinking that everyone knows how to look at pictures—even toddlers look at picture books! But obviously if you wish to be an effective online communicator, you need to be more visually literate than a toddler. You need to understand that images do more than just decorate a webpage; they communicate, persuade, and even deceive. More importantly, to be a skilled producer and consumer of messages you need to know *how* images persuade, otherwise known as **visual rhetoric.**

Obviously, entire books have been written about how images and visuals persuade us. One of the most famous writers is Edward Tufte, who has written several books that should be required reading for anyone interested in the visual display of information. We cannot cover everything about visual rhetoric here, but we do want you to understand the fundamental differences between how words and images persuade us. In his book *Visual Persuasion,* Paul Messaris uses a classification system developed by the American philosopher Charles Pierce to differentiate between words and images. Pierce identified three different types of signs: **icons, indexes,** and **symbols.** Iconic signs are similar or analogous to the object that they represent. For example, the little image of a house on your Web browser's button bar stands for your homepage. Indexical signs point to an object's existence. A footprint is a sign that a person walked there, and a photograph of your friends is a sign that they were alive. Finally, a symbol is an arbitrarily chosen sign; words are the most obvious examples. The word "cat" doesn't look like a cat, nor does it prove a cat was there.

B O X 2 . 2

BROWSING THE WEB

Graphical browsers such as Netscape Navigator have made browsing the Web a fairly intuitive process. And no doubt many of you are already familiar with how to use a browser. But we want to provide you with a quick introduction to browsing for two reasons: (1) to give you some advanced tips so you can use the browser more efficiently, and (2) to introduce those of you who have never used a browser to this new communication interface. We'll be using Netscape's Navigator for our examples; Microsoft's Internet Explorer, the other popular browser, is essentially the same. At the top of the screen, you see the name of the page you are visiting and the name of the program (in this case, Netscape).

Most of what you're likely to do in Navigator can be accomplished with the click of a button on one of the toolbars. When Navigator first opens up, it normally shows three toolbars at the top of screen: the navigation, location, and personal toolbars. If any of them are not visible, you can make them appear (or disappear) by going to View > Show on the menu and checking (or unchecking) the desired toolbar. You can also shrink up any of the toolbars by clicking on the "bumpy" buttons on far left edge.

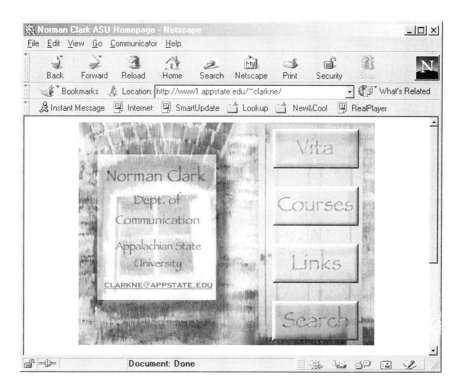

The first toolbar is used for navigating around the Web. The metaphor used for navigation on the Web is turning the pages of a book. The Back button takes you to the previous page. If you go back, the Forward button becomes active, allowing you to return to the page from which you went backward. If you press and hold down either button, a list pops up that allows you to jump backward or forward to a specific page. The next button will Reload the page, forcing the browser to retrieve the page from the Internet again, instead of just from the cache (temporary storage on your local computer). This will make sure that the page you're viewing is the most recent version. Many times pages will be altered by a program on the fly (in real time, even as the page is being displayed) and you will need to reload it to see those alterations.

The Home button takes you to homepage. You can designate any page to be the homepage by going to Edit > Preferences and filling in the homepage location in the Navigator settings. Clicking on the flashlight allows you to Search the Internet using Netscape's Net Search. This page offers one-stop access to several popular search engines. My Netscape allows you to set up a personalized start page that provides you with easy access to a wide range of online content. The Print button should be self-explanatory. Pressing the Security button will give you security information about the page you're visiting. If you get tired of waiting for a page to download, you can always hit Stop. Finally, the big animated "N" at the end of the toolbar will take you to Netscape's homepage.

Directly below the navigation toolbar is the location toolbar. One of the most useful features of browsers is their ability to set **bookmarks.** Just like real bookmarks, virtual ones allow you to go straight to the desired page. When you visit a page that you want to revisit sometime, you can add a bookmark by clicking the Bookmarks button and selecting Add Bookmark. If you start to collect a lot of bookmarks, you should sort them into groups and store them in folders. Folders are created with the bookmarks editor, which you can get to by clicking on the Edit Bookmarks option. Selecting File > New Folder brings up a dialog box to name and create a new folder. Then you can use the File option on the Bookmarks button to store a link to a webpage in a particular folder. When you want to return to any page that you have bookmarked, simply select the correct site from the drop-down list. The bookmark editor also allows you to move bookmarks to different folders, sort them, delete them, change their names, and much more. The icon next to Bookmarks, which looks like a page with a green bookmark on it, allows you to create a link to the page that you are on. Do this by simply clicking and dragging the icon to the desktop, to an e-mail message, or to any other location.

One of the most important parts of the location toolbar is the location box. The location box shows the URL of the page that you are currently viewing. But more importantly, this is the box into which you type the URL of a website that you want to visit. In Netscape, you do not need to type in the "http://" and in the case of a site whose address is www. name.com, all you need to enter is the name. Thus typing in "toyota" will take you to http://www. toyota.com. But the location box can do even more. In newer versions of Netscape, you can also type in a word (or words), and

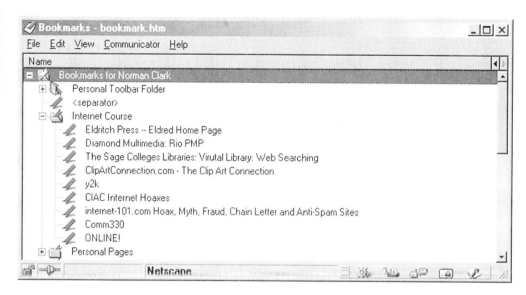

Netscape will search for that word using its NetCenter search tool. Finally, the What's Related drop-down button pulls up a list of sites that Netscape's NetCenter has registered as similar to the site you are visiting. Sometimes the sites that show up here seem rather unrelated, but this feature can come in handy. If, for example, you are on a travel site such as Travelocity.com, hitting the What's Related button will pull up a list of several other travel sites.

The personal toolbar, just below this, is one that you (and other programs) can modify. Here you can add bookmarks to sites that you visit often. To add to the personal toolbar, simply go to the Bookmarks drop-down (or editor) and file the bookmark in the personal toolbar folder. You will find that as you add some plug-ins to your copy of Netscape, some will add buttons to this toolbar. Here you can see that RealPlayer added a link to its homepage when the plug-in was installed.

At the bottom of the Netscape window, you see the status bar. The first icon tells you if you are visiting a secure site. It will have a yellow background, and the lock will be shut if the site is secure. The next icon shows the status of your network connection: if the wires are connected, you are online; if they are separated, you are offline. The next box shows a moving shaded bar that gives you an indication of how much time is left to finish downloading a page. If you are waiting for a page to load, and you notice that the shaded bar keeps moving back and forth for a long time without any progress (or stops), you may want to hit the Stop button and then hit Reload. Next to this is a section that shows messages from Netscape or scrolling text that webpages can insert. Finally, you'll see a series of small icons that allow you to switch between Netscape Navigator, Messenger, Newsgroups, Address Book, and Composer. Sometimes these buttons will show up in a floating box that you can move around the screen. If you want to dock (lock it in place in the status bar) this box, simply click the X to close it.

So what are the implications for Internet literacy? First, icons work best when the analogy is obvious. They move audiences by simulating the appearance of something else. In doing this, icons often connect unrelated emotions to objects: the homepage icon may evoke feelings of comfort and security, for example. Second, because indexical signs "prove" that something exists, people often believe photographs must be true, since pictures supposedly cannot lie. Even though we know that photographs can be manipulated, we rarely assume that they are (unless the alteration is obvious). Part of being an effective consumer of online communication means that you are aware of the emotional connections that iconic signs might be drawing on and of the implied but not necessarily actual reality of indexical signs. Producers of online communication need to know how to design visual elements that are persuasive, effective, and ethical. We'll discuss design in more detail in chapter 9.

But what about symbols? The important implication here is that there are some things images cannot do. We can use symbols to explicitly point out causal connections: for example, you can use words to say "buying this beer will cause you to be sexually appealing to incredibly attractive members of the opposite sex." But if advertisers were to say that, you would not believe them (I hope). Images cannot explicitly make causal connections, but they can *imply* them: beer commercials often connect beer with sex appeal. This is a great strength of images, but also a great danger for the visually illiterate. Advertisers can use images to imply a link between beer and sex that they could not make with words because they would violate truth in advertising laws and because the link is ridiculous when stated so explicitly. A key component of Internet literacy is being aware of how images imply connections that do not exist and resisting those connections when they are illogical. The power of visual rhetoric is that it is often unthinkingly accepted. That is why a vital aspect of Internet literacy is the awareness and critical analysis of visual persuasion.

BACK UP AND RELOAD

Now that you've read this chapter, you should have a solid understanding of the Internet as a communication medium. Traditionally, the study of communication has been divided up according to the number of interactants involved. But with the Internet, you might interact with one person or one million. For this reason, we have suggested that you think of this new communication medium as either a macromedium or a metamedium.

When you communicate over long distances, problems inevitably crop up. The Internet is trying to resolve three key problems: reliability, speed, and distribution. Reliable online communication is made possible through the technology of packets, which ensure that a message will get through. Faster and faster data transmission rates are making it possible to communicate with audio and video, not just text. And even though the distribution of the Internet is nowhere near 100%, more people are getting connected daily, increasing the size of your potential audience even as you read this.

In this chapter you also learned about six defining characteristics of the Internet. It is clearly multimediated, presenting users with combinations of audio, video, graphics, and text. All of this content is linked together through hypertextual connections. The various interfaces allow you to interact with people and programs in a wide variety of ways–programs even interact with each other. Online communication can either be synchronous, as in chat-rooms, or asynchronous, as is the case with e-mail. All messages carried over this medium are sent in packets, making communication extremely robust and difficult to block. Finally, every message is encoded digitally, which impacts communication in several ways.

As you go further in this book, you will learn the skills necessary to communicate effectively online. But along with those skills, you need to develop an awareness of visual rhetoric, or how images persuade us. Icons, indexes, and symbols all work in different ways to persuade audiences, and competent communicators need to be aware of how they work and what the implications are. Don't just file this information away somewhere. As you continue through this book, keep these fundamentals in mind. As we deal with the various interfaces of the Internet and the impacts of the medium, these themes will constantly resurface.

BROWSE *and* **BUILD**	For sites to visit, exercises, quizzes to test your learning, and more, go to *www.harcourtcollege.com/ communication/inetcomm*

References and Readings

Dutton, W. 1995. Driving into the future of communications? Check the rear view mirror. In *Information superhighways: Multimedia users and futures,* edited by S. Emmott, 79–102. London: Academic Press.

Electric word. 1997. *Wired* 5(8):35–42.

Federal Communications Commission. 1997. *Statistics of communication common carriers.* Accessed 20 August 1999 <http://www.fcc.gov/Bureaus/ Common_Carrier/Reports/FCC-State_Link/SOCC/961-all.pdf>.

Havelock, E. 1963. *Preface to Plato.* Cambridge: Harvard University Press.

Industry statistics. 1997. Accessed 15 August 1999 <http://www.catv.org/GIP/industrystats/>.

Internet domain survey. 1999. Accessed 21 December 1999 <http://www.isc.org/ds/WWW-9907/report.html>.

Landow, G. 1992. *Hypertext: The convergence of contemporary critical theory and technology.* Baltimore: Johns Hopkins University Press.

Messaris, P. 1997. *Visual persuasion.* Thousand Oaks, Calif.: Sage.

Negroponte, N. 1995. *Being digital.* New York: Knopf.

Ong, W. 1971. *Rhetoric, romance, and technology.* Ithaca: Cornell University Press.

Rafaeli, S., and J. Newhagen. 1996. Why communication researchers should study the Internet: A dialogue. *Journal of Communication* 46:4–13.

Tufte, E. 1983. *The visual display of quantitative information.* Cheshire, Conn.: Graphics Press.

———. 1997. *Visual explanations: Images and quantities, evidence and narrative.* Cheshire, Conn.: Graphics Press.

Zakon, R. H. 1999. *Hobbes' Internet timeline.* Accessed 10 December 1999 <http://www.isoc.org/guest/zakon/Internet/History/HIT.html>.

Personal Communication: Interpersonal Interfaces of the Internet

■———————■

This is a free country. Folks have a right to send me letters, and I have a right not to read them.

WILLIAM FAULKNER

Now that you understand what the Internet is, it's time to begin learning how to use it effectively. If you're like most people, your first form of online communication was e-mail. As you got more familiar with using this interface, you may have moved on to more synchronous forms of textual interaction, including chat-rooms and instant messaging. Today, with a fast connection and some inexpensive equipment, you can even conduct video conferences over the Web. In this next part of the text, we're going to cover what each of these interfaces is and how they were developed, their cultural significance for our changing communication environment, and how to use them effectively. Hopefully, you'll learn how to send letters that even Faulkner would have wanted to read.

Chapter 3

Don't Just Hit Reply!

Effectively Using E-mail, Listservs, and Newsgroups

By Peter Zale ©2000 Peter Zale, www.peterzale.com   Distributed by Tribune Media Services, www.comicspage.com

By the end of this chapter, you should:

I.   Know the difference between e-mail, listservs, and newsgroups.

II. Understand how e-mail is shaping our culture, including:

    A. the types of power that can be used online,

    B. the persona effective communicators assume,

    C. the roles that are required, and

    D. the shifting of some types of messages from face-to-face to e-mail.

III. Be familiar with the basic e-mail commands.

IV. Be able to effectively use e-mail by following the rules of netiquette and usage guidelines.

Chances are very good you have sent or received some e-mail. And you're not alone. The popularity and growth of e-mail is staggering. In 1998, one estimate put the number of e-mail boxes in the world at 263 million. And in that same year, according to eMarketer, 3.4 *trillion* e-mail messages were sent in the United States. That's 9.4 billion messages per day! For comparison, only 107 billion pieces of first-class mail were delivered during the whole year in the United States (*eMarketer tallies the number* 1999). In the past few years, free e-mail accounts offered by sites such as Yahoo! and HotMail have become increasingly popular. Many people have acquired at least two e-mail addresses, one for work and one for personal use. Who knows, perhaps the day isn't far off when you'll even have one for the family dog.

As you learned in the opening chapter, e-mail is the oldest form of computer-mediated communication used on the Internet today. Since it has been around the longest, it has had a chance to grow and mature. Researchers have had a chance to study how people use e-mail and how it influences communication. As a result, many reports, books, and guides have been written. But researchers aren't the only ones who have learned about the Internet. The general public, through day-to-day use of e-mail, has developed a general sense of what works and what doesn't work on e-mail. In this chapter, we're going to strive for something more than a general sense. We will start by differentiating between three terms most often used to designate this communication interface: e-mail, listservs, and newsgroups.

DEFINING THE INTERFACE

E-MAIL

When people talk about messages they receive on their computer, they typically use the word **e-mail.** E-mail is a shortened version of the phrase electronic mail and refers to messages exchanged through networked computers. These messages are primarily text, although recent mail programs have made it easier to include graphics and more. Under the umbrella term of e-mail, however, we can talk about several subcategories of messages. Sometimes you get personal e-mail: messages from relatives, friends, or coworkers that are addressed to you. These messages are usually interpersonal in nature. Think of these messages as similar to personal letters.

LISTSERVS

This isn't the only e-mail you can receive. One advantage (and disadvantage, as we'll discuss in a bit) of e-mail is that it is easy to send one message to many people. At some point, you will probably subscribe to a **listserv.** A listserv (named after one of the popular programs used to manage lists) is a server-maintained database of subscribers' addresses, allowing messages to easily be sent to a group. Think of mailing lists as an electronic version of a small group. You send a message to one address, and it goes to a whole group of people who joined that list because they share something in common–a hobby, profession, or even a class. A second address is used to send mail to the program (the most popular ones are Listserv, ListProc, and Majordomo) running on a mainframe computer, which keeps track of who is on the list and sends out mail to everyone who is subscribed. This program also allows you to control some options, which we'll cover later. The list is usually given a title related to the topic that is supposed to be discussed. For example, if your instructor set up a list for your class, it might be called INETCOMM. Hundreds of lists are out there. If you're interested, check out the textbook website, where we provide links to several tools that help you search for and join lists on almost any topic.

NEWSGROUPS

This isn't the only form of group communication on the Internet, however. Another popular service, called **Usenet,** is an extensive collection of electronic bulletin boards. Each topical bulletin board, or **newsgroup,** is a place where interested parties may visit to post and view one another's data on an ongoing basis. This data may be in the form of textual messages, photographs, graphics, audio clips, and even video segments. Since Usenet is so versatile, allowing users to create new discussion topics on a whim, hundreds of thousands of these newsgroups exist.

The primary technical difference between a listserv and a newsgroup is that postings to a newsgroup are not actually delivered to your personal mailbox. Instead, they are posted to and stored on a mainframe computer. But newer mail programs (including Netscape Messenger) make accessing newsgroup messages as simple as getting your regular e-mail. Each Usenet service provider maintains a set of newsgroups to which they ordinarily subscribe. Most major universities maintain a Usenet server to provide their students, faculty, and staff with newsgroup access. Even so, because of the provocative nature of some of the material available via newsgroups, some institutions have decided not to host specific newsgroups (and in some cases, some schools have abandoned the support of Usenet altogether) due to the liability presented by hosting such data on state equipment. In turn, campus activists are quick to point out that the state has no authority to legislate between "good" and "bad" information, especially on a university campus where the free exchange of ideas should be allowed to occur.

Newsgroups differ from listservs in other ways as well. For one thing, listservs are typically smaller than newsgroups in terms of the number of subscribers/readers. You have to subscribe to a listserv, which means you have to send a command to the program that runs the list so it will add you to its database. Since newsgroups do not require this, they are easier to join and consequently more people do so. Listservs are typically, although not always, more professional in nature. The programs that run listservs allow for more control so that, quite often, they are **moderated.** On a moderated list, one person or a group of people serve as gatekeepers. They read through messages and sort out ones that aren't on topic or are too inflammatory, and they only pass on to the subscribers those

Table 3.1

CHARACTERISTICS OF DIFFERENT FORMS OF E-MAIL

FORM	DELIVERED TO	ADDRESSED TO	PRIMARY COMMUNICATION FORM
Personal E-mail	your mail box	you	interpersonal
Mailing Lists (Listservs)	your mail box	group	small group
Usenet (Newsgroups)	mainframe	group	group (varying size)

messages that fit the topic and environment of the list. If you're interested in interacting with other mature adults about a specific topic and want to get good information, you probably ought to start with a listserv. If you're interested in joining a sometimes raucous group of people discussing a particular rock band, for example, you should check out newsgroups. Since newsgroups are very public in nature, and you are not required to subscribe to them, they often have a much lower **signal-to-noise** ratio. In other words, most of the messages are garbage (noise), and you end up deleting them, and only a few are actually worth your time to read (good signals). **Table 3.1** summarizes the differences between these three mailing interfaces.

Postings to a listserv or newsgroup may take any shape or form of communication. Commonly, someone interested in a newsgroup topic will post a question or make a statement to get things rolling. Then another respondent will attempt to answer the question, provide some additional insight, or express an opinion. Eventually, as more and more participants contribute postings to the newsgroup, an online dialogue will unfold. This dialogue is called a **thread.** Most mail programs allow you to sort your mail by these threads, indenting replies to a message and placing them below it in a list that can be expanded by clicking on the + **(Figure 3.1)**. Threads are often exciting to watch because the exchanges can, at times, be piercingly critical. Some people are not used to communicating in this fashion and are put off by e-mail as a result. Others seem to thrive on the heated exchanges and actually bait responses by sending taunting posts to newsgroups.

Almost any topic that can be reasonably imagined probably has a newsgroup. After all, there are over 34,000 unique newsgroup classifications. Usenet employs a naming hierarchy that works both to give the newsgroup a recognizable title and to arrange high-volume newsgroups into subcategories. For instance, the newsgroup "rec.travel.caribbean" is obviously reserved for discussions involving recreational travel in the Caribbean, whereas "rec.travel.cruises," a neighboring newsgroup, is clearly established for discussing recreational travel on cruises. **Table 3.2** shows some of the primary headings used to abbreviate newsgroups:

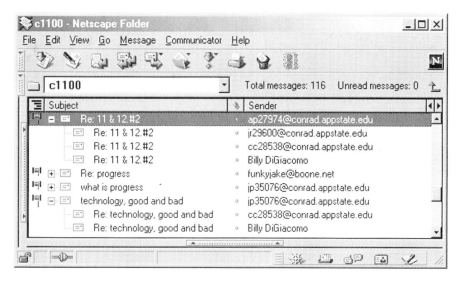

F i g . 3 . 1 . Threading messages makes it easy to see the flow of conversation. Clicking the "+" expands a thread and the "–" shrinks it up again.

Table 3.2

USENET PRIMARY HEADINGS

alt.	alternative topics	almost anything goes!
biz.	business topics	commercial, retail, and trade issues
comp.	computer topics	computer hardware, software, and cyber-culture
humanities.	academic topics	the arts, crafts, humanities, and languages
misc.	miscellaneous topics	topics that do not meet any of the predetermined newsgroup categories
news.	news | usenet	news on or about Usenet
rec.	recreational topics	recreational activities, sports, travel, and hobbies
sci.	science topics	science, agriculture, biology, engineering, physics, and technology
soc.	social topics	clubs, cultures, families, lifestyles, organizations, religions, and social activism
talk.	discussions	conversational topics

We mentioned earlier that sometimes the ability to send one message to many people can have a down side. The down side is **spam,** or unwanted mass e-mail, usually of a commercial nature. Spam is the electronic version of junk mail and includes such messages as get-rich-quick scams, advertisements for pornography sites, diet programs, and other messages you (and hundreds of other poor souls) didn't ask to receive. Many Internet service providers (ISPs) are working hard to reduce the amount of spam that their users get, and some programs (see, for example, MailShield at http://www.mailshield.com) can automatically filter out (and delete) spam that is sent to you.

BRIEF HISTORY OF E-MAIL

To understand how e-mail has evolved into the prolific means of communication that it is today, we must recall the context surrounding its early development. While e-mail had its beginnings in the 1960s, it was only available to users working on the same mainframe computer. Relaying messages from machine to machine had not yet been made possible because computer networking was still in development itself. In the late 1960s, Ray Tomlinson, a computer-networking specialist at BBN Consulting, set out to convert this single-computer utility into a multicomputer messaging system. He combined the intracomputer e-mail system used on mainframes with an ARPANET file transfer system (known as CPYNET) and designated remote computers with locator addresses. To do so, he used the "at" symbol, @, to segment the user from the whereabouts of their system. As simple as it may sound today, in the 1970s this was considered maverick engineering. Tomlinson's first e-mail message to a remote computer read: "QWERTYUIOP" (the top row of characters on a typewriter/computer keyboard). While not quite as historically poetic as "Watson, come here, I need you . . . ", it does illuminate the alphanumeric symbolism inherent to e-mail (Baron 2000).

Tomlinson released two programs in 1972 that worked together on ARPANET: READMAIL and SNDMSG. The applications were quickly adopted by early ARPANET adherents, even though they were rather primitive (Johnson 1999). READMAIL had one major design flaw in that the program would download all e-mail messages into a single lengthy text file. So, later that year, Lawrence Roberts and Steve Crocker improved upon Tomlinson's concept by installing an e-mail management device named RD. RD allowed ARPANET users to view an e-mail menu by sender, subject line, and date stamp, and to retrieve a specific e-mail file from the menu rather than having to go through the list item by item (Stewart 2000). All the same, users had to use two different programs, at two different times, to communicate online.

Throughout the early 1970s, ARPANET developers expanded the functionality of e-mail. For instance, in 1973 Barry Wessler augmented the RD e-mail reading program by adding the ability to delete messages from the mainframe, calling this version NRD. Then Marty Yonke revamped the NRD e-mail reader in 1974 to include a simplistic help file system that would tell the user exactly how to use the interface, renaming this software BANANARD (Stewart 2000). While improvements were constantly being made to *how* e-mail messages were being read, SNDMSG remained the traditional means of sending e-mail. What was needed, clearly, was an all-in-one e-mail utility. In 1975, John Vittal bettered BANANARD with his all-in-one release, which he named MSG, by adding features such as automatic addressing for e-mail replies and e-mail forwarding (Stewart 2000). Many consider MSG to be the first fully developed e-mail utility. In part, this is because there have not been many changes to e-mail functionality since the release of MSG. Most of the changes that have been made in e-mail since 1975 have been more matters of style than engineering substance.

These matters of style, however, may be of some importance. In the late 1980s, private companies began providing Internet and e-mail access to the public. For instance, CompuServe and MCI Mail emerged in 1989, providing e-mail service to the public for the first time. The early technological successes of CompuServe and MCI Mail made Internet pioneer Steve Case, founder and CEO of AOL, design a business plan and secure venture capital during the early 1990s. His idea was to provide phone-based Internet and e-mail access to every home in the United States (Swisher 1999). While total market saturation is unlikely in any business endeavor (except for monopolies . . .), AOL is definitely responsible for driving the popularization of e-mail since their services went online in 1993. This is due, in part, to the company's commitment to interface simplicity.

If you have been an e-mail user for any length of time, you realize that e-mail comes in many different formats. Today some ISPs such as AOL, CompuServe, and Prodigy have their own messaging interface. Others provide you with a Web-based e-mail account, which is good if you travel a lot and wish to check your e-mail via the Web. Still others want you to use an e-mail program such as Netscape Messenger to retrieve your messages. On occasion, the ISP will combine all of these approaches, allowing you, the consumer, to use whichever e-mail option may be the best for you in the given circumstances (Baron 2000).

CULTURAL SIGNIFICANCE OF E-MAIL

Clearly e-mail is becoming a popular form of interpersonal and group communication. But the e-mail interface is not the same as **face-to-face (FTF)** communication, or even the telephone, although in some ways they are similar. Because of this, e-mail forces us to reexamine the basic concepts of interpersonal and small group communication and adjust some of them. We are going to talk about three in particular: power, expert persona, and group versus individual roles. Finally, we'll also draw on communication research to show that because of the way the e-mail interface has evolved, some of the messages we used to send by meeting face-to-face are now being sent via e-mail–but some messages should not be.

POWER

Whenever two or more people get together to communicate, power comes into play. One of the basic aspects of communication is that it is about influence, persuasion, and change: in other words, the exertion of power. No doubt you want to be able to influence people, particularly in the business world. So how do you go about gaining power online?

The first thing we need to figure out is what type of power is available when interacting through e-mail. In interpersonal communication research, six different bases of power are identified (French and Raven 1968; Raven, Centers, and Rodrigues 1975). They are listed in **Table 3.3.** It's important to realize that all power in interpersonal communication depends on a relationship. **Table 3.3** describes each type of power in terms of how it works between people.

It's also important to realize that you typically rely on more than one power base at a time. You can certainly remember times in your own life when your parents used a combination of legitimate, reward, and coercive power to get you to come home at 11:00 P.M. But think for a moment about which of these power bases work online. You probably won't know much about the people you interact with on a listserv, so they probably won't have much referent power over you (with some exceptions, of course). The Internet is by nature anticentralized power, so there is very little legitimate power. Sometimes on a moderated list, the moderator will have some legitimate power, but other than that the Internet prides itself on being very egalitarian (at least in theory). Reward and coercive power is fairly minimal on the Internet as well. After all, if the other person is far away from you there isn't much they can do to reward or punish you (although, obviously, it is possible).

This leaves expert and information power, the two sources of power you'll need to rely on in e-mail interaction. When you're writing in to a listserv about your hobby, people will pay attention to your messages and be influenced by them when you demonstrate some sort of expertise or when you construct a logical, understandable, convincing message. When you have the information that others need, you will have greater power. And since we're living in an information age, in an information society, this is one of the key bases of power today.

One word of caution about power online: it's **insulated.** Think about this analogy for a moment. Power cords are wrapped with insulating materials so you don't get a shock. Online power is somewhat similar in that you don't feel much of a shock from your messages. If you yell a profanity at someone right in front of you, you might get hit. If you do it online, chances are nothing will happen to you immediately. So you're more likely to say extreme things online since you don't fear any negative consequences. In the long run, people will get a negative impression of you, but in the short run they'll probably just delete your message. In effect, you don't really feel the impact of your own power use and neither does anyone else. It's just as easy (in fact, easier) for them to hit the delete key as it is for you to hit the four keys necessary to type that nasty word. This insulation factor means that online messages are not as likely to be persuasive as face-to-face encounters—an issue we'll return to later in the chapter. In fact, we'll talk more throughout this chapter (and throughout this book) about how to use expert and information power, starting with constructing an expert persona.

Table 3.3

POWER BASES

POWER BASE	RELATIONAL EXPLANATION
Referent	You have referent power over another when they want to be like you ("I wanna be like Mike"). Power is based on that person's desire to conform.
Legitimate	You have legitimate power over another when you are in a position that gives you authority over them (police officer, teacher, parent). Power is based on society agreeing that you should have control.
Reward	You have reward power over another when you control something they want (money, sex). Power is only present when that person (a) values what you have and (b) believes you will give it to them.
Coercive	You have coercive power over another when you can punish them in some way. Power is only present when that person (a) is afraid of your threatened action and (b) believes you will do it.
Expert	You have expert power over another when you have some special expertise that they need (doctor). Power is present when that person requires that knowledge (a plumber wouldn't have power when you need surgery).
Information or Persuasive	You have information power over another when you construct an argument that they find persuasive. Power is present when that person finds the content of your message logical or convincing.

EXPERT PERSONA

An "old" saying goes, "On the Internet, no one knows if you're a dog." Since you are not physically present with the other person when you communicate via e-mail, you can be whomever you choose, or at least you can be whomever you can write like. When people first meet you, whether **in real life (IRL)** or online, they form an opinion of you. When they meet you face to face, their opinion is based on a wide variety of sensory data: your clothes, your appearance, the sound of your voice, your smell, etc. They can quickly discern your race, sex, and even social class.

But this is not the case with online interaction, where the amount of information that people get about you is very limited. Your identity when you use e-mail is based, to a large extent, on what you write. In essence, you are what you write. So you can create any sort of **persona,** or constructed identity, for yourself. You can be either sex or even no sex at all. Ever wanted to be a genderless alien? Now's your chance! The possibilities are limited only to your imagination and writing abilities.

So, what sort of person do you want to be online? If you want people to think positively of you and to respect what you have to say, you should try to construct an *expert* persona for yourself. Gaining this respect is a process of continually posting in a manner that lets people know that you are knowledgeable and that your messages are worth reading. So, how do you construct an expert persona? Here are some guidelines:

- Stick to facts. Don't spread rumor or inferences. If you don't know it for sure, be sure to preface your remarks with a disclaimer or, better yet, don't send the message at all.

- Stick to what you know. If you have a certain degree of expertise, share your knowledge with others. If you don't know much about the topic, don't say anything. Someone else who is an expert on that topic will be sure to chime in when necessary.

- Don't just ask questions, *answer* them. Offer thoughtful responses. Take the time to craft your answers. One of the major benefits of e-mail is that you have a chance to make your message as artistic and polished as possible. Nothing will gain you more respect (and power) more quickly online than a correct, timely answer.

- Be a resource for others. Stretch ideas that others have posed. Make connections to others' concepts. Offer summaries when lots of ideas have been thrown out and the discussion starts to lose coherence. Push others to think harder. Give something back to the community that you joined when you subscribed to the mailing list. This will increase your limited referent power immeasurably. People will start to want to emulate you.

- Avoid language that diminishes your power. This includes being self-critical and hesitant. And avoid slang and vulgar words unless it's appropriate for your audience and the cultural context of the mailing list. Swear words are associated with a lower social class, and thus less power in some peoples' minds. So if you don't know your audience well, and they don't know you, don't swear.

If you consistently stick to facts that you know, answer questions well, act as a resource for others, and follow the rules of expected behavior (explained later in this chapter), you'll soon be considered an expert by the people who read your mail. Who knows, someday you may even become a cyber-celebrity!

GROUP VERSUS INDIVIDUAL ROLES

Usually, when people get together in a group, they have some sort of goal in mind. That goal might range from simply discussing a hot topic to planning a shuttle launch. Most of your interaction online will fall somewhere in between, and probably a lot closer to the general chatting end of the scale. What you need to remember is that an effective group member tries to keep in mind the goal of the group and pays less attention to his or her own needs.

If the group is to be successful, certain roles have to get filled. Group roles fit into two large categories: **task** and **maintenance roles.** Task roles are related to getting the group's job completed: some people in the group have to contribute information, some have to clarify issues, some have to keep track of what's going on, some have to propose new ideas, and so forth. Maintenance roles are about making sure that people are happy with the group. Groups need people to encourage others, to mediate disputes, and to keep social harmony. No one person fills just one role. You might find yourself fulfilling many different roles the longer you interact with a particular group.

What's important is that if you want to be a valued member of an electronic group, you need to fulfil *group* roles, not individual roles. You want to focus on the needs of the group, not on your own needs. Small group research has identified several individual roles that you generally want to avoid when interacting with your online groups (Benne and Sheats 1948):

- Aggressor: attacks others to feel stronger.
- Blocker: generally disagreeable for no apparent reason.
- Recognition Seeker: spends all their time boasting.
- Self-Confessor: uses group for therapy. Granted, some listservs will welcome your discussion of your bad day or the problems you are having with your spouse. On most professional lists, however, this would be inappropriate.
- Playboy/girl: disrupts groups with inappropriate messages.
- Dominator: attempts to take over all decisions for own gain.

Pay close attention to your messages when you are interacting with an online group. Are you furthering the goals of the group, whatever they might be? Or are you compromising the integrity of the group with your personal agenda? If you want to be influential online and continue communicating with the group, work on fulfilling task and maintenance roles, not individual ones.

TO E-MAIL, OR NOT TO E-MAIL?

Just as people in groups take on different roles, so too do media. Different media have different strengths and weaknesses and are appropriate for different purposes. For example, if you were sitting across the table from another person, you probably wouldn't call them on your cell phone (although there might be times when that's the only way you can get their attention). So in wrapping up this section, we want to consider for a moment when you should or shouldn't use e-mail.

Four key factors determine whether someone will even think about using e-mail: knowledge, comfort, access, and perceived benefit. Hopefully this book is solving the first problem: knowing how to use the basic interface. If people perceive the effort involved in learning to use e-mail as too high, they won't bother with it. Second, many people are still uncomfortable around computers in general. We can't do much about that in this book except to argue that your comfort level will typically increase as you learn more about the medium. To use e-mail, you have to have access to technology–specifically, a computer and an Internet connection. This access is usually fairly good on campuses; however, access is still not universal. Finally, people are unlikely to use e-mail if they don't see it serving a purpose. When people discover they can use e-mail to keep in touch with friends very cheaply or get notices of discounted airfares, they start to increase their use of this medium. If you are trying to get some of your friends or relatives to start using e-mail, keep these four factors in mind when planning your persuasive strategies.

E-mail has some definite advantages over other media (Palme 1995). Since it is asynchronous, it is easier to use at your convenience. You can send and read messages when you have the time. It is also especially helpful if you have to share information in written form since it can be reused and stored. E-mail also makes it easier to share information that is in electronic form. For example, you can attach a word processing file to an e-mail message, and the person who receives the message can then open up that file in their own program to add to it or make changes.

When should you use e-mail instead of other forms of communication? Most people who use e-mail extensively develop a sense of when e-mail is effective. But rather than just having a vague sense, we want you to have some researched knowledge on when to use what media. Dr.

Jacob Palme (1995) has done extensive research on using e-mail efficiently and offers the following suggestions:

- Use e-mail instead of the telephone when you have to reach more than one person. Otherwise, you end up having to say the same thing over and over. If you only have to reach one person, only use e-mail if you can wrap things up in four or fewer messages. If it's going to take more messages than that, use the phone.

- Use e-mail instead of postal mail when the message will be short. If you have to send a very long message, either use an attachment or the post. If you have to send a critical or formal document, you're better off using the postal system (legal documents that require signatures, for example).

- Use e-mail instead of face-to-face meetings for large groups if people have to travel, or if the meeting would be short.

E-mail does have disadvantages, however. As we noted earlier, power is insulated when online, so persuasion is more difficult. Without all of the nonverbal elements of communication, it is far easier for misunderstandings to occur. Because of these things, it is difficult to make formal decisions or reach a consensus using only online communication. In sensitive situations, or when you need all of your persuasive powers, you are better off using e-mail to arrange a time and place to meet face to face. Don't fire someone over e-mail, for example, unless you want them to have a negative impression of you and your company.

In the business world, you will undoubtedly use e-mail for completing projects. But e- mail is not best for all stages of a project. Palme (1995) divides projects into three phases: preparation, where you gather ideas and propose solutions; the actual decision making stage; and the execution of the plan. E-mail is not well suited to the decision-making phase, but it can be used very effectively for the first and last phases. Ideas and solutions can be tossed out to the group quite easily via e-mail, and the details of how exactly things will be done can also be worked out online. Thus, for groups who need to work together, e-mail can reduce the time spent meeting face to face. Each person can spend a few minutes a day (whenever it is convenient for them) getting and sharing background information through e-mail before the meeting takes place. Once the decision has been made, simple issues and questions can quickly be resolved online instead of having to call another meeting.

BASICS OF E-MAIL

When it comes time to start using e-mail, you can choose among a wide range of programs for reading and composing. Two programs that are widely available and free, so you're likely to have access to them, are Netscape Messenger and Pine. Pine is a text-based program that runs on a mainframe server, and unless you are using a network terminal, you would normally use it from inside another program called **Telnet.** Telnet basically connects your computer directly to a server, turning your system into a dumb terminal. When your computer operates as a dumb terminal, it simply shows on your screen the results of a program that actually runs on the server. **Figure 3.2** shows the opening screen for Pine. Netscape Messenger is a graphical program that runs on the computer you're sitting in front of (it can run on Windows, Unix, or Macintosh machines). **Figure 3.3** shows the main window for Netscape Messenger.

Messenger has a number of advantages over Pine: it uses a familiar graphical interface, you can see individual messages and a list of all your mail at the same time, it is easier to edit your message since you can cut and paste text, and it can handle **attachments** (files sent with an e-mail message, which we'll discuss more in a minute) much more easily. So for the rest of this chapter, we'll be showing example screens from Netscape Messenger (version 4.5 and up) and explaining how to use the program. Just realize that most of the same commands also apply to Pine. You just use keystrokes instead of moving the mouse around.

READING A MESSAGE

The opening window of Netscape Messenger **(Figure 3.3)** is divided by default into three frames. The frame on the left side lists your mail server

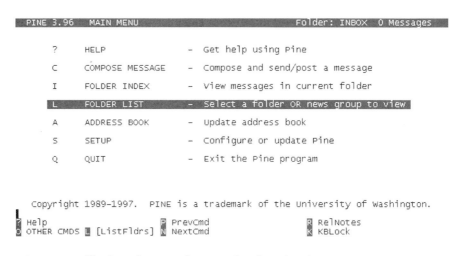

Fig. 3.2. Pine's main menu is sparse but functional.

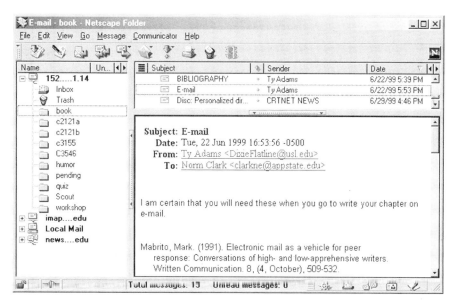

Fig. 3.3. Netscape Messenger's interface.

and any folders that are created on it. The right top frame shows the basic information for the messages in the folder that you currently have open. The lower right frame shows the actual e-mail message itself. Reading an e-mail message is quite easy. All you have to do is click on the message you want to read in the upper right frame, and it will appear in the lower right frame.

HEADERS

All e-mail messages that you receive share a basic structure, starting with the **header.** The header is a block of information at the start of an e-mail message that tells you who sent it, what it's about, and other technical information. If you look back at **Figure 3.3,** you can see the header at the top of the sample message in the lower right frame. The **Subject:, Date:, From:,** and **To:** lines are self-explanatory. Sometimes you'll see a **Cc:** line, which tells you if any other people received carbon copies of the message. If a message comes to you from a listserv, you'll usually also see a **Reply-To:** line. This lists the address that will be used if you reply to this message. Note that in the case of messages sent out to a listserv, the from line and reply-to line will be different. The from line shows the individual who sent the message, and the reply-to line has the address of the list. Finally, you might also see an **Organization:** line, which tells you who employs the sender of the message.

TEXT BOX 3.1

POP OR IMAP?

POP3 mail (short for Post Office Protocol 3) is usually just called **POP mail.** This software acts as a bridge between your PC and the server where your e-mail is collected. Your e-mail software will periodically (based on the time interval you set in the preferences) retrieve all of your messages from the server, alerting you when new messages arrive. You can also force the POP mail client to retrieve your new mail now with a mouse click, just in case you are anticipating incoming messages and do not want to wait for them. The software will then download your e-mail into your POP mail client and either leave or delete a copy from the server (depending on how you set up the preferences). Generally speaking, POP mail is a way to *transfer* e-mail files from the server to your PC.

   On the other hand, the **IMAP** (Internet Message Access Protocol) allows you to view your e-mail messages as if they were stored on your computer, while, in fact, they stay stored on a remote mail server. You can create folders on the server and automatically sort mail before you ever open it. Depending on how you set the preferences, deleting a message will either mark it as deleted, transfer it to a trash can

Table 3.4

COMPARING POP AND IMAP MAIL SERVERS

POP	IMAP
Widespread availability, supported by most ISPs and most e-mail programs	Less available and supported, although growing
Relatively simple setup	Can be more involved
Mail is stored on your local computer, using up space on your hard drive	Mail is stored on the mainframe, using little space on the local computer
Mail can be accessed even if you aren't online	Must be connected to access mail
Multiple POP accounts are not supported by many programs	Most programs allow you to setup and check multiple IMAP accounts
Accessing mail from different places can create problems if mail is downloaded from mainframe and then deleted; also, cannot access stored mail except from the computer it is stored on	IMAP's biggest strength is its ability to access all of your mail from anywhere; can access old mail since folders are on server; less concerns about mail being moved off server and made inaccessible

(which can be emptied as you see fit), or immediately erase the message. Generally speaking, IMAP mail is used to *access* your e-mail from the server.

So how do you choose which one to use? Well, that question may be easy to answer: not all ISPs or schools provide both types of servers. POP is almost universally available, while IMAP is less common. So you might only have access to POP. But if you can choose, pick the one that best fits your needs.

SENDING E-MAIL

Suppose you want to send an e-mail to one of the authors of this book. The first thing you'll need to know is his e-mail address. E-mail addresses have two parts: the user ID and the mail server address, separated by an @. So, for example, one author's e-mail address is *clarkne@ appstate.edu.* The *clarkne* portion is his user ID, and the computer that receives the mail is named *appstate.edu.* To send an e-mail in Messenger, you need to press the New Msg button in the toolbar **(Figure 3.4).** This will pull up a composition window **(Figure 3.5).** In the to line, you'll need to enter in the person's address. Then you will want to enter in a pertinent subject line and start writing the message. When you're ready to send the message, hit the Send button.

REPLYING AND FORWARDING

Replying is even easier than sending e-mail. When you receive a message from someone and want to write back, just hit the Reply button (yes, we told you not to do that in the title of the chapter, and we'll explain why in a minute). You can also use Reply to All, which will send your message to anyone who got the original message (an easy way to communicate with a group). Sometimes you'll want to send a message you received to someone else. The best way to do this is to forward the message. With Messenger, all you need to do is press the Forward key and then enter in the address of the person to whom you want to send the mail. You might want to include a brief note at the beginning of the message you are forwarding. Later in this chapter we'll talk about some dos and don'ts for forwarding.

F i g . 3 . 4 . Messenger's main button bar.

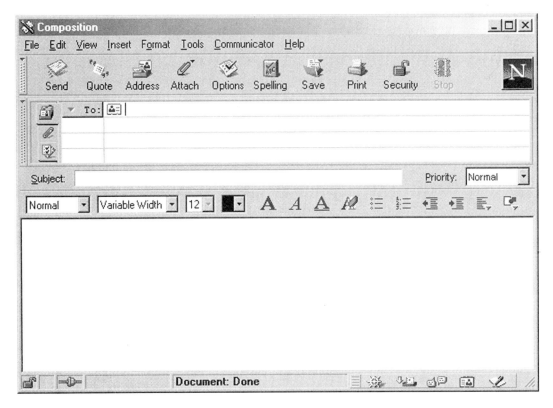

Fig. 3.5. Want to write a letter? Messenger's composition window.

ADDRESS BOOK

Once you learn someone's e-mail address, the best thing to do is store it in your mail program's address book. Suppose you get an e-mail from an old friend. If you click on their address listed in the header, it will pull up a New Card dialog box **(Figure 3.6).** It will already have the person's e-mail address filled in. You might have to make some changes to the name, and you might want to add some other info (like a nickname). Now all you have to do to mail that person is enter in their name, or the nickname, and the program will fill in the correct e-mail address. You can also create new entries even if you don't have a message from them. Simply go up to the menu and click on Communicator > Address Book and then press the New Card button. Finally, you can use the Address Book to create your own distribution lists, which will send mail to multiple people. By clicking on File > New List, or on the icon of a card with three heads, you can name the distribution list and add in the addresses of the people that you want included in the list. This is a simple way to repeatedly mail groups of people without having to create a listserv.

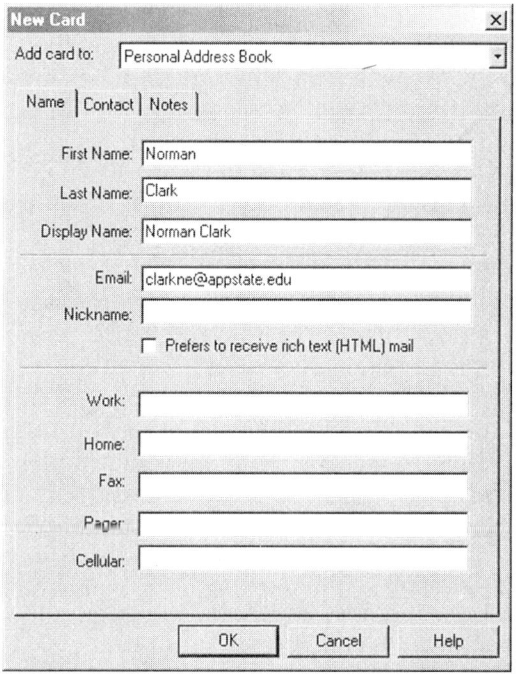

Fig. 3.5. Want to write a letter? Messenger's composition window.

ATTACHMENTS

An attachment is a file that someone sends to you in an e-mail message. The file might be a graphic image, a word processing file, or a program. With Messenger, it is quite easy to send and receive attachments. If you want to send an attachment, click on the Attach button. Then select File and enter in the location and name of the file you want to send (you can browse around your computer until you find the file if necessary). When you get an attachment that Messenger knows how to handle, like most graphic images, it will simply show up in the message window. If it is a type of file that Messenger can't deal with, like a word processing file,

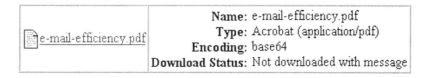

Fig. 3.7. You've got more than mail—you've got an attachment!

then it will show up as an icon inside a box that also describes the content **(Figure 3.7).** When you click on it, Netscape will ask you if you want to open it or save it. We would recommend saving it, for reasons we'll go into later. Once it is saved, you can open up that file in the appropriate program or run the file if it is a program.

FOLDERS

Once you have used e-mail for a while, it's very easy to start to feel swamped. It is not unheard of to get a hundred messages in a day. Now suppose you keep some of those messages. After a while, your **inbox** (the initial mail folder, into which all new mail is put) could get very full. And unless you want to have a thousand messages in it, eventually you'll want to create some other folders in which you can save messages. On the left side of the Messenger window (assuming your window is set up in the default configuration), you'll see a list of folders. In the example in **Figure 3.3,** one of your authors has several folders set up: some for classes, a folder for jokes, etc. Creating a new folder is very easy with Messenger. You can either right-click on the name of the server, which is listed in the left-hand frame, or click on File > New Folder on the menu. Either way will pull up a dialog box **(Figure 3.8)** into which you can enter the name of the new folder that you want. Once this is done, you can simply drag the message into the desired folder. This way, you can keep track of important messages (and not-so-important ones) much more easily.

FILTERS

Of course, now that you have folders set up, why not have Messenger automatically move mail into the appropriate folders for you? You can do this with filters, which you set up by clicking on Edit > Message Filters on

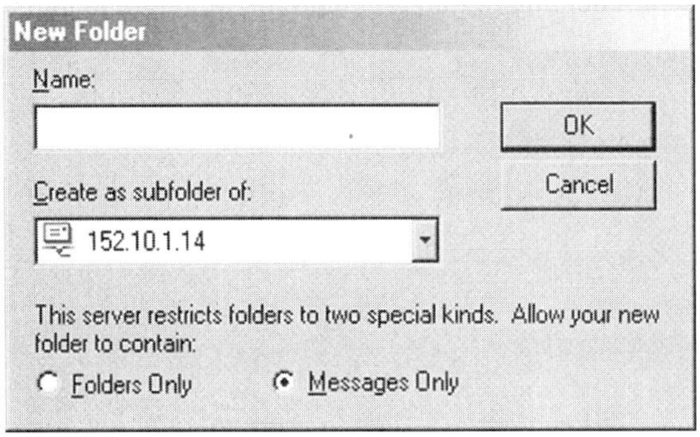

Fig. 3.8. Folders help you store mail.

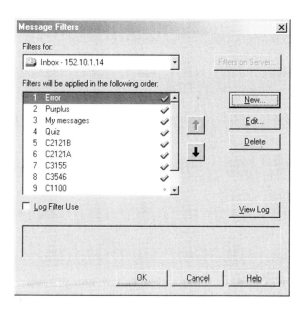

Fig. 3.9. Filters will sort your mail automatically.

the main menu. This pulls up a list of the current working filters **(Figure 3.9),** which in your case is probably empty or has one "error" filter. If you click on the New button, it will pull up a dialog box **(Figure 3.10),** which allows you to create a new filter. Give it a name that will help you remember what it does, then set the options for what you want the filter to do. You can have it check your mail based on text in any of the headers.

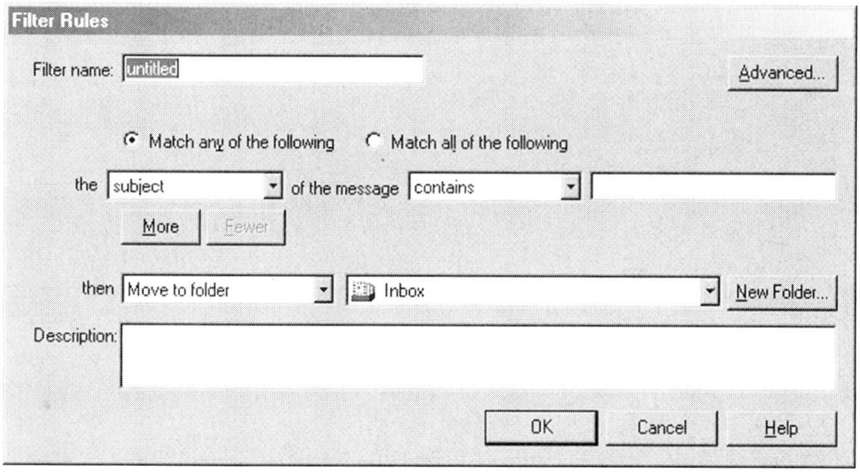

Fig. 3.10. Creating a filter is a "powerful" experience.

Perhaps you want mail with the word "quiz" in the subject heading to get sorted into one folder and mail that comes from a person who annoys you to get automatically deleted (a filter known as a "kill filter"). You can easily set up two filters to do this. Look over the options available in the New Filter dialog box, and you'll see that filters can be quite powerful and useful.

EFFECTIVE USE OF E-MAIL

NETIQUETTE

Etiquette, in its broadest sense, is proper social behavior as prescribed by some authority. Each culture that you encounter has its own rules of etiquette. This holds true for different countries, but it also holds true for different cultures, such as the upper versus lower class, young versus old, even different sides of the train tracks in some towns. Since the Internet is a conglomeration of cultures, the rules of net etiquette (or **netiquette,** for short) vary from listserv to listserv, or newsgroup to newsgroup. But some general guidelines do exist.

First and foremost, be sensitive to other people's feelings and be cautious with the words that you use about them. Remember that at the other end of every message is another human being–a fact that is all too easy to forget when all you see in front of you is a computer screen. Ask yourself, Would I say this to their face? If not, reconsider your message. If you are not nice, you may log in to your e-mail account one day to find over a thousand flaming messages from some extremely upset people. Or, you may be tracked over an extended period and coaxed into revealing some delicate information about yourself, only to find this information posted throughout the Internet. On the Internet, what goes around definitely comes around.

An important thing to remember is that whenever you enter a new culture, you will make mistakes. So expect that you will make some mistakes on the Internet. Hopefully when you do, you will be helped by someone who shows patience and compassion. When you become more accomplished, try to be one of those people who show patience and compassion to newcomers to the Internet, also known as **newbies.** Remember that you were once a newbie, too, and a little kindness shown to a person now can reap great rewards later.

You should also keep in mind that intercultural communication research tells us that people often have one of three responses to unusual behavior: confusion, pity/disdain, or anger/hate. When you first start e-mailing, you might do some things that others will consider unusual, since you aren't accustomed to the culture you've entered. Some people will wonder what you're doing, others will assume you're an idiot, and still others will send you nasty replies that will startle you with the quantity of expletives included. Expect to see all three of these types of responses. But hopefully, you'll also get some helpful replies that explain to you the mistake you made and what you ought to do instead. After you get more experience with e-mail and some newcomer makes a mistake, think carefully about how you want to respond: with confusion, pity, anger, or helpfulness.

What should be getting gradually clearer is that net cultures can often be unforgiving. Newbies are treated especially harshly since they often ask questions that have been answered a hundred times. Most of this harsh treatment can be avoided by taking the time to learn the culture first. The culture of the Internet varies a great deal. On some newsgroups, it might be appropriate for you to discuss your personal hygiene problems. On many listservs this would be a terrible faux pas. You need to take the time to learn what is appropriate for every new culture (list, newsgroup, whatever) that you join. So when you start interacting with a new group, take a few days (or long enough to observe several message exchanges) to read the messages that members of the group send without posting one of your own–a procedure called **lurking.** You'll quickly learn what comments are tolerated, which ones annoy people, who to avoid, and who to seek out for help. To avoid making simple mistakes, take to heart this simple advice: *lurk before you leap.* Also check the **FAQs (frequently asked questions).** Many newsgroups and listservs have files stored in their archives that answer these questions. Locating and reading these files will give you a good sense of the culture and procedures of the group, and keep you from making too many mistakes.

Another aspect of the unforgiving side of the Internet are **flames,** or strong opinions expressed bluntly. Flames are, for the most part, an accepted part of the Internet culture. Don't get too offended when someone slams you with a sarcastic e-mail. Sometimes flames are almost an art form, and particularly funny or biting ones are often repeated. If you're really bothered by the message, just delete it. Don't complain about it, unless the person continually sends you nasty messages. Most e-mail providers won't do anything about an occasional biting letter. The one thing you should definitely NOT do is engage in a **flamewar.** If one person flames another, don't join in and flame them back, since then 5 people will flame you, 10 others will flame them, and soon the whole list will be consumed by flames. This will get you into hot water with your ISP very quickly.

Finally, one last thing that is especially difficult for Americans to remember is that the Internet is international. Granted, right now most of the people you encounter online come from the United States, but more and more countries are coming online. You will increasingly need to explain references to your culture that might not be obvious to others.

And watch out for ethnocentrism–don't assume that your way of doing things is right and all other ways are wrong.

The key to netiquette is respect. All of the above reminders are rooted in the concept that you need to respect others that you encounter online. Aretha Franklin said it best: "R-E-S-P-E-C-T, find out what it means to me." Take the time to learn the culture of the Internet. When online, you can demonstrate respect for others by following some basic guidelines related to using mainframes, composing messages, replying, and mailing to groups.

USING MAINFRAMES

Your e-mail doesn't just come to your local computer. It first goes to a mainframe computer, either on your campus or in the office of your ISP, and you pull it down from there. Because of this, you need to keep the following in mind:

- Check e-mail daily.
- Delete unwanted messages.
- Store messages in folders and clean them out periodically.
- (These three tips are important to follow. Otherwise, your mailbox may get too full. When this happens, your e-mail might get deleted or returned, you might not be able to send messages, and in general, it will create a hassle for you.)
- Realize others can read your e-mail. Even if you are deleting your messages, they might be backed up on the mainframe somewhere. Just ask Oliver North, who carefully wiped out his e-mail files that had incriminating evidence about the Iran-Contra affair. Imagine his chagrin (and fear) when those messages resurfaced in the hearings, since the White House staff had been faithfully backing up the computers. Don't say something that might come back and haunt you later.

COMPOSING

When you're typing up the message, remember that more is involved here than just keyboarding.

- DON'T TYPE IN ALL CAPS. It's annoying and the typographical equivalent of shouting. This will get you flamed for sure.
- Use asterisks to make a *strong point*.
- Use underline marks for *Book Titles* (in text editors like Pine, you can simulate this like so: _Book Titles_) and other citations.

- Use special formatting features (boldface, colors, underlining, etc.) with caution. Many people will not be able to see them. If they aren't using an HTML-enabled e-mail program, your message will be messed up with a bunch of special codes. If you're not sure if the person you're mailing is able to see your special features, just ask them. Or, to be safe, just send plain text.

- Use acronyms with caution. Some popular ones on e-mail include IMHO (in my humble opinion), YMMV (your mileage may vary), FTF (face-to-face), BTW (by the way), LOL (laugh out loud), and RTFM (read the friendly, or sometimes a nastier word starting with "f," manual). Use them when you're sure your audience understands them. Otherwise, explain them.

- Include a signature line with your credentials and e-mail address when communicating to unknown people. However, don't include personal information like your home address and phone number unless you enjoy being stalked.

- Remember that since people can't see you, your communication lacks the emotional cues that people normally get from your non-verbal messages. So use **emoticons** (typographical emotional symbols) when necessary. Let people know when you're being friendly :-), funny :-D, sarcastic, :->, mad >:-(, or joking ;-).

- Write out the month for dates, since 5/6/97 means May 6 in America, but June 5 in the rest of the world.

- Be simple and to the point. E-mail is best used for short exchanges, not for ranting epistles or book-length expositions on your position.

- Include pertinent and useful subject lines. This allows people who check their mail off-line to search and skip unwanted messages. Warn your receiver about long messages. Some people will get very annoyed if you don't tell them your message is actually a sermon (see the previous tip).

REPLYING AND FORWARDING

We titled this chapter "Don't Just Hit Reply!" There are several good reasons for hesitating over that Reply button.

- Only send the message to people who need it. Reply to individuals when necessary, rather than to an entire list. If you get an e-mail from a private person and want to e-mail them back, go ahead and reply. But if the message came from a listserv, and you hit Reply, it's going to go to *everyone* who is subscribed to the list. Everyone who has used e-mail for a while has their own horror story of the time they sent a very personal message that was

TEXT BOX 3.2

EMOTICONS

On the Internet, no one can hear you scream—or see you smile, or hear laughter in your voice. To get around this, use these emoticons, often called "smileys." Smileys are invented daily, so check out the links provided on the textbook website to some smiley collections.

Basic Smileys

:-) Your basic smiley. Use this to designate that you're joking or being sarcastic.

;-) Winky smiley, used to note a flirtatious and/or sarcastic remark. More of a "don't hit me for what I just said" smiley.

:-(Frowning smiley. Sad, upset, or depressed about something.

:-I Indifferent smiley.

:-> Really biting sarcastic remark.

>:-> Devilish remark.

>;-> Winky and devil combined: a lewd remark.

Less Widely Used Smileys

(-: Left-handed smiley.

:*) Drunk smiley.

[:] Robot smiley.

8-) Smiley wearing sunglasses.

::-) Four-eyes smiley.

B-) Horn-rimmed glasses smiley.

:-{) Smiley with mustache.

:-{} Smiley with lipstick.

{:-) Toupee smiley.

} :-(Toupee in an updraft.

:-[Vampire smiley.

:-E	Bucktoothed vampire.
:-7	Wry smiley.
:-*	Sour face.
:-)~	Drooling smiley.
:-~)	Smiley has a cold.
:'-(	Crying.
:'-)	So happy, you're crying.
:-@	Screaming.
:-#	Braces.
:-&	Tongue tied.
-:-)	Punk rocker.
|-I	Asleep.
| O	Yawning/snoring
:-Q	Smoker.
:-?	Pipe smoker.
:-`	Spitting out chewing tobacco.
:-D	Laughing (at you!).
:-X	Lips are sealed.
:-C	Really bummed.
:-/	Skeptical.
:-o	Uh oh!
3:]	Pet smiley.
:-9	Licking lips.
[:-)	Wearing a Walkman.
<:-I	Dunce.
X-(	Dead.
[]	Hugs and . . .
:*	Kisses.

Some Celebrity Smileys

~(_8^(|)	Homer Simpson.
(@@):^)	Marge Simpson.
((-_-))	Cartman.

supposed to go to just one person to an entire list by mistake. You'll probably do it sometime, too. Just try not to do it often.

- Don't quote the entire message when you reply—just include the section(s) you're responding to. Some mail programs are set up to automatically stick in the old message (the one you're replying to) in your new message as a big, long quote. If you don't need to refer back to that old message, delete the quoted material. If you need to refer back to some part of that message, delete everything else.

- Be careful with the subject line. When you reply, the program automatically uses the subject line from the original message and puts "RE:" in front of the subject. If you're still talking about the same subject, go ahead and leave the subject line the same. This makes it easy for people to follow the conversation, since most mail programs out now will allow you to sort the messages by threads (replies are indented below initial messages). But if you're changing the subject, change the subject line too!

- Don't be a dittohead. Don't reply to a message by sending it back and saying "I agree," or "Me too!" If you do, get ready for flames.

- Don't post netiquette reminders to the whole listserv. If an individual makes a mistake, and you think you need to correct it (think carefully about this!), send a note to the individual, not to everyone.

- Don't forward chain letters. This is *never* (that might be too strong of a word for some people, but we don't think so) appropriate and may even get you kicked off some listservs and ISPs.

- Don't forward virus warnings without verifying their validity with a site such as Symantec Antivirus Research (http://www.symantec.com/avcenter/index.html). Almost all warnings that you get are bogus, especially ones that warn of a virus from an e-mail message. About the only way you can get a virus from e-mail is from an attachment—that's why we said to save attachments instead of opening them. Before you open them, scan them for a virus.

- Don't forward urban myth e-mails that tell you that Disney will donate money to some child with cancer for every e-mail they get or that Congress is going to tax every e-mail message. Check if such messages are myths at an online myth site, many of which can be found at Internet101.com (http://internet-101.com/hoax/).

- If you do forward a message, make sure you delete all of the unnecessary header information that gets tacked on to the message and all of the old headers and ">" marks that others haven't deleted. Otherwise, people have to scroll down 20 screens to get to the message, and they just might get annoyed.

GROUP MAILING

If you decide to join a listserv or newsgroup, you'll need to keep some additional tips in mind.

- Choose your groups wisely and modestly. If you sign up for too many, your mailbox will rapidly overflow, and you won't be able to keep track of the conversation. It would be rather like trying to listen to 20 conversations at once at a party. You can't really listen to any of them.

- One way to handle your listserv mail more efficiently is to use the **digest** mode. When you set the list to digest mode, you get one message that groups together a set number of messages, or all of the messages received in a certain time period, say a day. This way you get 1 message per day instead of possibly 50 on a very active list. To find out the command to do this, you will need to check the help file for the listserv program being used.

- Remember the different orientations of listservs and newsgroups. Listservs are generally more professional, and newsgroups are more chatty.

- Remember that listservs have two addresses: the address to which you send commands and the address to which you send messages. For example, the list address might be INETCOMM@ APPSTATE.EDU, and the corresponding command address would probably be LISTSERV@APPSTATE.EDU. If you accidentally send a command to everyone on the list, instead of to the computer controlling it, someone will probably yell at you.

- When you first sign up to a listserv, you'll get a notice that welcomes you to the list, tells you a little about the list, and most importantly, tells you how to unsubscribe. Hold onto that message because at some point you might want to leave the group. If you don't know how, you'll have to post a message asking people how to unsubscribe. You'll get flamed by someone, we guarantee it.

- Check the validity of what you post. Ensure that your e-mail address is properly listed. Check to see that the details of your message are correct. No one likes a rumormonger, especially online.

- Make sure that you avoid repetition, both in message content and in the number of your posts. Generally, you should only post one message to one newsgroup once. And you should not bombard every newsgroup that you come across with your message. Contrary to popular belief and practice, Usenet is not an advertising service. Avoid repetitious replies on a particular thread. If you really must repeat something, send it to the individual instead of the whole list. It may begin a new friendship, and it will certainly reduce the clutter of interpersonal messages on what should be a mostly public forum.

- Consider your purpose: are you trying to get an answer to a question? If so, make sure you phrase the question as specifically as possible. Vague questions reap no answers. Also, most people won't answer a question that has an easily available answer. Do some digging in likely places first (the library is a good place to start!) before asking others on e-mail. If you are looking for advice or feedback, again be as specific as possible. If you are responding to another posting, be as direct as possible. Coyness and vagueness have their place in face-to-face interactions, but they rely too heavily on nonverbals to be very effective when online. Convoluted, complex, and obscure statements might make you feel really smart, but you're going to feel really dumb when no one responds to your statement or someone misinterprets what you said.

- Consider your audience: judging from your experiences with the group (hopefully you've taken the time to lurk, as we suggested earlier), what kinds of messages are appropriate? Are there some topics or people you should avoid? What kind of tone (argumentative, conciliatory, questioning, etc.) will work best with this group? What sort of support and opposition can you expect? Answering these questions before you post will ensure that your audience won't just hit Delete (instead of Reply) when they read the first line of your message.

This is just an introduction to proper online behavior. Just as you can't write down all the rules of a face-to-face culture, you can't really write down all of the rules of the Internet. And just as you don't learn the rules of your culture by reading them, so, too, you'll learn most of the rules of online interaction by living it–making mistakes, but also making friends. If you still want to read more, check out the textbook website for links to online netiquette guides.

BACK UP AND RELOAD

E-mail is the most mature of the Internet communication interfaces. Personal e-mail resembles interpersonal communication, while listservs and newsgroups resemble group communication. From communication research we learned that power is limited online to expert and information power, which necessitates the development of an expert persona in order to gain online influence. Since e-mail interaction often resembles small-group communication, it is important to take on group maintenance and task roles and not individual roles. And like all media, e-mail has its strengths and weaknesses and should be used appropriately.

Even though several programs are out there for checking your e-mail, the basic interface is fairly consistent. In this chapter we covered the basic commands for receiving, composing, sending, and managing e-mail. But it's not enough to just know how to use a program. To communicate effectively with e-mail, keep in mind the netiquette rules and guidelines for using mainframes, composing messages, replying and forwarding, and mailing to groups.

BROWSE *and* **BUILD**	For sites to visit, exercises, quizzes to test your learning, and more, go to *www.harcourtcollege.com/ communication/inetcomm*

References and Readings

Anderson, D., B. Benjamin, and B. Paredes-Holt. 1998. *Connections: A guide to online writing.* Boston: Allyn and Bacon.

Baron, N. 2000. *Alphabet to email: How written language evolved and where it's heading.* New York: Routledge Press.

Benne, K., and P. Sheats. 1948. Functional roles of group members. *Journal of Social Issues* 4:41–49.

eMarketer tallies the number of e-mail messages sent in 1998. 1999. Accessed 21 July 1999 <http://www.emarketer.com/estats/020199_e-mail.html>.

French, J. R. P., Jr., and B. Raven. 1968. The bases of social power. In *Group dynamics: Research and theory.* 3d ed. Edited by D. Cartwright and A. Zander, 256–69. New York: Harper & Row.

Holmes, M. E. 1995. Don't blink or you'll miss it: Issues in electronic mail research. *Communication Yearbook* 18:454–63.

Johnson, K. 1999. *Internet e-mail protocols: A developer's guide.* Reading, Mass.: Addison-Wesley.

McLaughlin, M., K. Osborne, and C. Smith. 1995. Standards of conduct on Usenet. In *Cybersociety: Computer-mediated communication,* edited by S. Jones, 90–111. London: Sage.

Palme, J. 1995. *Electronic mail.* Norwood, Mass.: Artech House.

Parks, M. 1996. Making friends in cyberspace. *Journal of Communication* 46(1):80–97.

Raven, B., C. Centers, and A. Rodrigues. 1975. The bases of conjugal power. In *Power in families,* edited by R. E. Cromwell and D. H. Olson, 217–34. New York: Halsted Press.

Rice, R. P. 1997. An analysis of stylistic variables in electronic mail. *Journal of Business and Technical Communication* 11(1):5–23.

Stewart, W. 2000. *The living Internet: How email was invented.* Accessed 6 May 2000 <http://www.livinginternet.com/>.

Swisher, K. 1999. *aol.com: How Steve Case beat Bill Gates, nailed the netheads, and made millions in the war for the Web.* New York: Times Books.

CHAPTER 4

Shall We Chat in the Dungeon?

Effectively Using Text-Based Multiuser Synchronous Interfaces

By Peter Zale ©2000 Peter Zale, www.peterzale.com Distributed by Tribune Media Services, www.comicspage.com

By the end of this chapter, you should:

I. Be familiar with the primary forms of online text-based interaction and their histories:
    A. chat-rooms and
    B. MUDs.
II. Understand how these interfaces can affect our culture by:
    A. stimulating critical thinking,
    B. constructing a shared cultural context,
    C. allowing identity play,
    D. encouraging creative means of emotive communication,
    E. relying on an architecture of belief,
    F. bringing us back to the written word and
    G. leading to addiction.
III. Know the basics of connecting to and using chat-rooms and MOOs.
IV. Be able to effectively communicate in chat-rooms and MOOs.

When people discuss the Internet, they are usually referring to sending e-mail and browsing the Web. While e-mail and the Web have been widely employed since 1995, many users are still unfamiliar with **text-based**

multiuser synchronous interfaces (TMSIs). TMSIs use only letters or numbers (making them **alphanumeric** interfaces). People type messages to others using computers anywhere in the world in close-to-real time, similar to a group conversation. These interfaces often use text to create a context, describing the "scene" in which the conversation is occurring. These contexts range from virtual dungeons to textual universities. In this chapter, we will provide an insider's view of these interfaces, with (as always) the goal of effective communication in mind.

DEFINING THE INTERFACE: CHAT-ROOMS AND MUDS

CHAT-ROOMS DEFINED

A **chat-room** is a synchronous portal where communicators can engage in an abrupt text-based conversation. Imagine a chat-room as a public space, like a local coffee shop or a hairdresser's salon, where patrons come to mix and mingle. Chat-rooms simulate these public spaces, and each "room" has a different name that normally designates the topic of conversation (although not always). A limited number of people can send and receive text messages in each room. Since people rarely take the time to type in complete sentences, the conversation is often abrupt, and acronyms and abbreviations abound. Also, each message is relatively short (and potentially confusing). This is because while you are typing in your message, the other people in the room are typing theirs. So by the time you finish writing a response to one person, four other people have sent messages in reply to previous messages. The flow of conversation in a chat-room might looks something like this:

ONLINEHOST: *** You are in "Movie Hall Reviews". ***
ASTROT: what about Wild Wild West?
FUDGIE: I love Star Wars Ep 1!!!!!
JOECOOL: WWW had way too much action, not enough humor
    IMHO >:-(
SAM12: too much action, should have let Kline have more fun
GARION: Jar-Jar Binks must DIE!!!! >:-[
YOU: Fudgie, SWE1 was way overrated.

While initially confusing to the novice, chat-rooms can be both functional and entertaining. Today, chat-rooms are used by organizations, cultures, and game groups to create virtual spaces where collective thought can unfold (Dieberger 1994). Or, at the very least, they are used to create a space where people can meet anonymously and have some fun. Often they serve as breeding grounds for online and real-life relationships. This is especially true when one is considered a regular. To become a regular in a chat-room you will need to dedicate some time getting to know other regulars. Of course, you must grasp the language, syntax, and particular communication patterns of chatting itself before you join. Figuring out the emoticons, abbreviations, and style of chatting is much like learning a new language.

An alternate type of chat interface has developed recently: the **instant messenger chat-box.** Instant messenger programs run on your local computer. When you have them running, they alert you whenever people on your "friend" or "buddy" list open their chat-box, providing the opportunity for interpersonal exchange. These programs make it easy for people to stay in contact with a select group.

A BRIEF HISTORY OF CHAT-ROOMS

No one is certain who invented **Talk,** but it was heavily used between the lines connecting MIT, BBN Consulting in Massachusetts, RAND in Santa Monica, and UCLA in the late 1960s. Talk was a simple program that allowed users on networked computers to type messages to one another in real time. As more computers were connected to ARPANET during the 1970s, Talk became a means of communicating with anyone linked to ARPANET. This valuable tool, however, began to affect the productivity of government and corporate employees. Mandates were issued not to use Talk unless it was truly important. But throughout the 1970s and 1980s, users continued to hold chat-sessions. Not only was the exchange of information useful but communicating with others in this fashion was enjoyable and personable.

In 1988, a Finnish programmer named Jarkko Oikarinen wrote a program called **Internet Relay Chat daemon (IRC-d)** to allow for multiuser real-time communication. Oikarinen and his friends were **bulletin board service (BBS)** participants. BBSs allowed participants to post text messages to a virtual bulletin board for public reading. After his BBS became uselessly cluttered with brief personal messages, Oikarinen announced on the BBS that everyone should download his new software application, IRC, and connect to his server. From that moment on, his server was flooded with a flow of participants. IRC was truly revolutionary because it allowed up to 100 participants to engage in synchronous chat-sessions.

Hundreds of variations upon the original IRC model are still being made today, but the basic model remains the same. Some chat software may allow you to select your own participants if they are online, while others will require you to join a common server. Some chats may allow users to define themselves by an alias so as not to be tracked by unwanted individuals. Some chats may allow the user's text to be emboldened, colored, or stylized. Some chats may allow for graphics and audio files to be tossed into the discussion, providing a lively multimedia quality. And some chats (like the popular ICQ) provide all of these services and much, much more. If you are interested in reviewing a certain type of chat program, then use our list of the top chat programs, found on the textbook website, to locate the company's latest downloadable version.

MUDS AND THEIR DESCENDANTS
(MOOS, MUSHS, AND MUCKS) DEFINED

MUDs (multiuser dungeons) and their descendants are text-based, real-time fantasy role-playing games where communicators have the ability to navigate their way through an imaginary environment. They can also interact with the environment, objects, and other players through a variety of simple verb commands. Like chat-rooms, all of the interactions inside MUDs are expressed with text. However, instead of everyone being inside a fixed chat-room, in a MUD users can "move" through a series of chat-rooms connected together to form a building, perhaps even a landscape. These connected rooms are described with words and are built around a theme: a space station, a medieval country, a nightmarish underground world, or any other setting that the human imagination can create. These rooms can be examined more closely by their visitors. The best way to see what MUDs are all about is to visit one. **Figure 4.1**

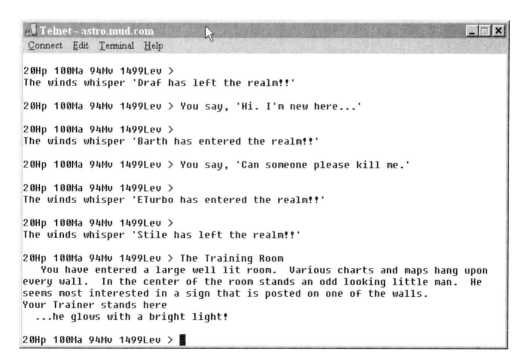

```
20Hp 100Ma 94Mv 1499Lev >
The winds whisper 'Draf has left the realm!!'

20Hp 100Ma 94Mv 1499Lev > You say, 'Hi. I'm new here...'

20Hp 100Ma 94Mv 1499Lev >
The winds whisper 'Barth has entered the realm!!'

20Hp 100Ma 94Mv 1499Lev > You say, 'Can someone please kill me.'

20Hp 100Ma 94Mv 1499Lev >
The winds whisper 'ETurbo has entered the realm!!'

20Hp 100Ma 94Mv 1499Lev >
The winds whisper 'Stile has left the realm!!'

20Hp 100Ma 94Mv 1499Lev > The Training Room
   You have entered a large well lit room.  Various charts and maps hang upon
every wall.  In the center of the room stands an odd looking little man.  He
seems most interested in a sign that is posted on one of the walls.
Your Trainer stands here
   ...he glows with a bright light!

20Hp 100Ma 94Mv 1499Lev > █
```

Fig. 4.1. A common scene in AstroMud.

is an example of the type of online communication that players at the AstroMud enjoy. We have provided a list of MUDs, MOOs, MUSHs, and MUCKs (each defined in this section) for you to visit on our website.

MUDs have administrators, strangers, doors, staircases, open fields, springs–anything that the designer can imagine. In this virtual reality, users have the ability to move from one room to the next, holding conversations with people in each area. Or, if the user chooses, he or she may "shout" throughout the complex, alerting a friend who may have taken a wrong turn at a tricky corridor. On everyone's monitors, a message appears: "GreySword, where are you?!!!" The communication patterns in a MUD are extremely complex, since participants may either: (1) say something in view of all participants, (2) say something only within the room in which they occupy, or (3) whisper comments discretely to specific players. Thus, communication can be within the public, small-group, or interpersonal spheres. Or, of course, all three at the same time.

There are several varieties of MUDs, each with its own acronym to distinguish its unique properties. MOOs (multiuser, object-oriented interfaces) are essentially the same thing as a MUD. So, you are probably asking yourself, Why the different name? The best rule of thumb is that if interaction revolves around Medieval fantasy play, these environments are called MUDs to retain the word "dungeon" in their description. But since many corporations, universities, and government agencies are spending respectable sums of money to deploy these interfaces as business tools, the MOO acronym is used to distinguish serious virtual communication from "play." MOOs are essentially the professional version of MUDs, where much less gaming transpires (Daft and Lengel 1986, 1984).

Two other less common variants of MUDs also exist: MUSHs and MUCKs. Multiuser simulated hallucinations simulate a hallucinatory experience. Users log in to a MUSH to eat a virtual "mushroom" before they depart on a free-falling adventure paralleling Alice in Wonderland. Conversations with Mickey Mouse and the Lion King need not be part of a hallucinatory experience, however. All that you will need is a little imagination and a nice, clean multiuser character/chat kingdom. MUCKs are generally reserved for the Disney crowd, since almost all of the company's major releases in the past decade have been converted into popular navigable environments by their fans. Players can assume roles similar to the cast of characters in famous fables or films and play out their favorite scenes–this time without knowing the outcome.

A BRIEF HISTORY OF MUDS/MOOS

As you know, the last letter in MUD stands for "dungeon." Throughout the late 1970s and 1980s, a role-playing game (RPG) named *Dungeons & Dragons* became popular among adolescents and young adults. In fact, the game became so popular in the United States that many parents worried about "D & D addiction." Its popularity among computer programmers guaranteed that a computer version would be developed. And in 1971, William Crowther, a senior programmer at Xerox's Palo Alto Research Laboratory, invented a non-networked program called Cavern whereby the gamer would encounter a series of textual lines describing a cavern. Donald Woods teamed up with Crowther in 1972 to enhance the original Cavern program by adding verb commands, renaming it ADVENT (short for adventure). A player could now "look," "get," or "eat" objects if they desired. But ADVENT was still a one-user game because networked computers were still being developed.

It would take six years of computer networking advances before the first network-ready MUD would be designed in 1978 by Richard Bartle and Roy Trubshaw at the University of Essex in England. The original MUD was not popular by any account. In fact, only 10 to 15 users ever encountered the environment. Importantly, though, most of these 10 to 15 players became MUD programmers themselves, transforming their imaginary worlds into independent MUDs. In 1986, at the request of CompuServe, Bartle designed a MUD titled British Legends, which is still played on that Internet service today. In the early 1990s, computer networking ignited and MUDs took off, as people left their dice and game boards for monitors and keyboards.

Eventually, MUDs were used for more than just games. One of the first serious attempts to make a simulated academic environment occurred in 1992. At the Massachusetts Institute of Technology, Amy Bruckman and her associate M. Resnick's hypothesis was that MUDs were versatile enough to satisfy serious organizational needs and not just gaming desires (1995). Bruckman created mediaMOO, a virtual space for academicians and students in media and communication, which served as an archetype for other academic MOOs. Designers of MOOs are primarily interested in how these spaces can be better designed (whether in their textual forms or their more contemporary Web models) to enhance education, community, and business. It seems that the need to establish contexts for business and academic interaction is as universal as our human need to play.

CULTURAL SIGNIFICANCE OF TMSIS

Since these interfaces are now used throughout the world for a wide variety of purposes, it stands to reason that they are the focus of a respectable amount of research. TMSIs possess the ability to affect us, and our communication, in seven distinct ways. These seven themes, which regularly emerge in the scholarship regarding TMSIs, are discussed in the following sections of this chapter. Understanding these effects is the basis for more effective communication in chat-rooms and MUDs.

STIMULATE CRITICAL THINKING

Studies reassure us that TMSIs can stimulate critical thinking among new users (Cherny 1995). While the behavior of those involved in a chat-session or MUD may appear mindless, communication research tells us that the users are actually engaged in an intense process of logical conditioning. Learning and using unfamiliar verb commands, maintaining a sense of position when running from one room to another, or simply holding conversations in a nearly foreign language can be a rather taxing experience. This is especially the case when you must perform all of these feats in concert.

When entering a chat-room or a MUD, new users generally encounter a mild version of the fight-or-flight syndrome: either they seek to adopt the new mode of interaction immediately or they disapprove of the means altogether. It is this unfortunate dynamic that keeps many from ever really experiencing the playfulness of a MUD or the genuine community residing within a MOO (Cutler 1995). Accordingly, we should not feel taken aback because we do not know exactly what is being said or everything that is going on in these textual frontiers. New users almost always feel a little misplaced at first. Not to worry, however. This knowledge will come with time, experience, and a little help from your online friends.

CONSTRUCT A SHARED CULTURAL CONTEXT

Another widespread conclusion is that these tools build virtual communities, united around specific interests (Moshell and Hughes 1996). The titles of rooms and MUDs serve both to draw and deflect potential participants. So, unless you are prepared to engage in gory rampages, it would be advisable not to log in to BloodMUD. Likewise, The Crochet-Club might not be the most exciting chat-room unless you happen to be working on a new set of mittens. However, the claim that these interest groups constitute a community might be too strong. We will return to this very philosophical question in chapter 13. For now, let's just talk about these tools as the creators of a cultural context.

When you hear the word culture, you might imagine picturesque scenes of people in native costumes, eating an ethnic dish, spinning around in a traditional dance, and listening to music played on folk instruments. And actually, your understanding of culture wouldn't be completely incorrect. **Culture,** according to Williams, is "one of the two or three most complicated words in the English language" (1983, 87). The definition of culture used here is the shared activities, values, ways of life, and problem solutions of a group of people. Users of TMSIs all share a context in which they interact and solve problems; sometimes these problems revolve around slaying dragons and at other times debating a topic. In this textual world, one must learn how to communicate and read between the lines, without the normal nonverbal cues available in face-to-face communication (Reid 1995). The specific strategies, tactics, and language usage that develop in any one MUD or chat-room constitute its culture. But just as you wouldn't know all of the cultural norms when you first arrive in a foreign country, so too you won't know how the culture of a given MUD works when you first log on. Your best course of action is to see what people are talking about and how they are interacting first. Then, when you feel comfortable, by all means participate.

ALLOW IDENTITY PLAY

While communication research tells us that the virtual communities develop among people with shared interests, remember that what your online sidekick tells you might not be true (Rintel and Pittam 1997). When people first meet online, they often feel obliged to ask each other their location, whether they are male or female, their age, and even their ethnicity. These are markers that we use to understand who people are, where they are coming from, and what they mean (Curtis 1992). Thus one of the most common blurbs posted in a chat-room is the "age/sex check" (often simply expressed as a/s). This type of primitive discussion serves as something of an icebreaker to get more specific data moving between parties. Yet remember that this data cannot be verified and should under no circumstances be trusted. To borrow a phrase from general semantics, "The symbol is not the thing."

Normally, when you first meet someone they disclose a great deal of information about themselves without saying a word. You can tell from their appearance (most of the time!) their sex, age, and maybe even socio-economic class. But when communicating these attributes online, the other person has much more control over their self-disclosure. They can try out new identities by describing themselves as of a different sex or even a different species. Some people go so far as to use pictures of other people on their websites, creating totally new personas for themselves. Your ability to wear different masks is only limited by your imagination and your ability to convincingly create an alter ego through words. This identity play is a powerful way for people to explore new, or previously hidden, sides of themselves. And some researchers believe that this phenomena is increasing people's awareness that much of our identity is socially constructed and is thereby expanding our understanding of gender (Danet 1998).

ENCOURAGE CREATIVE MEANS OF EMOTIVE COMMUNICATION

Studies continue to show that the use of emoticons, abbreviations for repetitive phrases, and ALL CAPS to demonstrate language intensity truly helps people understand the emotive meaning of online messages (Murray 1989; Hiltz and Turoff 1981). Drawing upon interpersonal communication theory, we know that there are two levels of meaning that are constantly being shared in our daily communication activities: these are the **content** and **relational** levels of meaning. The content level refers to the pure data that you are communicating. The relational level refers to how you interact with this information and how this affects the relationship between you and the other. These interpersonal dynamics carry over into the technological context (Walther 1992). If they did not, there would be no need for our friend the emoticon.

Imagine getting an e-mail or a message in a chat-room or a MUD that simply said, "NO." A message like that is wide open to interpretation for the relational meaning, even though it is quite direct in content meaning. How did the person mean to say "NO"? Did they mean to use all caps? Was it a friendly "NO"? Or was it an ugly, insulting "NO"? Without being able to hear the tone of their voice, you have no way of knowing what relational message was being sent. You could go mad thinking about all of the possible insinuations. We have provided a list of commonly used abbreviations in the box on this page to help you communicate relational meaning. Use them in conjunction with the list of emoticons found in chapter 3. These abbreviations and emoticons help people know how you *feel* about issues, as much as what you *think* about them.

DEPEND ON AN ARCHITECTURE OF BELIEF

No doubt in the course of your education, you've heard the phrase "the social construction of reality." Peter Berger and Thomas Luckmann wrote an influential book with that title in 1966, in which they argued that human societies create ways of behaving and knowing and then forget that they were created. We start to see our creations–our institutions, our education systems, our religious orders–as natural, as the way things just are, as "real." When these ways of knowing and acting get repeated over time, they reinforce themselves until we no longer see that they are not the only ways of thinking and doing. They become "habits" that are "normal."

MUDs in particular are excellent places to see the social construction of reality taking place. When you enter a MUD, you create a character that fits the setting. So if you enter a fantasy-based MUD, you might decide to become a dwarf. Thus the constructed reality of the fantasy realm determines what type of role you can play. But this constructed reality is in turn reinforced by the roles that people take inside the MUD.

TEXT BOX 4.1

COMMON ABBREVIATIONS

AAMOF	as a matter of fact
ADN	any day now
AFAIK	as far as I know
AFK	away from keyboard
ASAP	as soon as possible
A/S/C	age/sex check
A/S/S/C	age/sex/state check
ATK	at the keyboard
B4N	bye for now
BAK	back at keyboard
BBL	be back later
BBS	be back soon
BF	boyfriend
BFD	big friggin' deal
BFN	bye for now
BRB	be right back
BTDT	been there, done that
BTW	by the way
CYA	see ya
CYO	see ya online
EMFBI	excuse me for butting in
EOD	end of discussion
EOM	end of message
EOTWAWKI	end of the world as we know it
FAAK	falling asleep at the keyboard
F2F	face to face
FAQ	frequently asked question
FUBAR	frigged up beyond all repair
FWIW	for what it's worth
FUD	fear, uncertainty, and doubt
FWD	forward

FYI	for your information
GAL	get a life
GC	good cover
GF	girlfriend
GL	good luck
GMTA	great minds think alike
GR8	great
HTH	hope this helps
IE	Internet Explorer by Microsoft
IAE	in any event
IDK	I don't know/I didn't know
IMHO	in my humble opinion
IMNSHO	in my not so humble opinion
IOW	in other words
IRL	in real life
ISRN	I'll stop rambling now
ITA	I totally agree
JAM	just a minute
JK	just kidding
JJ	just joking
JOOTT	just one of those things
K	ok
LMAO	laughing my ass off
LOL	laughing out loud
LSHMSH	laughing so hard my side hurts
LTNS	long time no see
LTR	letter or long-term relationship
MOTD	message of the day
MYOB	mind your own business
NFI	no friggin' idea
NP	no problem
OIC	oh, I see
OOTB	out of the box
OTOH	on the other hand
OTW	on the whole

PC	politically correct or personal computer
PDA	public displays of affection
POTS	plain old telephone service
PPL	people
POV	point of view
ROTF	rolling on the floor
ROTFL	rolling on the floor laughing
ROTFLMAO	rolling on the floor laughing my ass off
RSN	real soon now
RTFM	read the friggin' manual
RYO	roll your own
SOP	standard operating procedure
SS	so sorry
TANJ	there ain't no justice
TCB	taking care of business
TPTB	the powers that be
TTFN	tah-tah for now
TTYL	talk to you later
UNK	you never know
UTT	under the table
VBG	very big grin
VEG	very evil grin
WB	welcome back
WTG	way to go
XXXX	kisses
XOXO	kisses and hugs
YWSYLS	you win some, you lose some
YAOTM	yet another off-topic message

As you "walk" around the MUD and encounter knights, elves, gnomes, and dragons, the "reality" of the fantasy realm is socially reinforced by all of the characters you meet. This is what Rheingold called an "architecture of belief" (1993, 148), where you and everyone else in the MUD build a mutual reality that is held up by the sheer force of imagination. Consequently, when you describe your character to others as "Jerico, a short muscular dwarf with reddish hair and a graying beard, bearing a double-bladed long-handled axe over his shoulder," you are doing far more than just constructing a new identity for yourself. You are helping to birth a new social reality. The reality creates the roles, and the roles reinforce the reality.

Since MUDs rely entirely on text, you and the others inside the virtual reality are essentially coauthoring a narrative. To write a believable narrative and to interact effectively in a virtual realm, you need to understand one of the basic principles of "narrative probability" (Fisher 1987). Stories (and your MUD interactions) are believable when they have something called **characterological coherence,** which means that we expect characters to act reliably. As you read a book or interact in a MUD, you get a sense of what the character is like, and soon you are able to predict their behaviors. If characters in a book suddenly do something out of character, you can either get puzzled, expect some explanation, or get angry with the author for messing up the book. The same thing is true in a MUD: as you interact with various characters, you will begin to expect them to do certain things. When they act out of character, you will feel one of three emotions: confusion, expectation, or anger. Unfortunately, anger is often the option chosen, because when people "act up," they are destroying the architecture of belief that everyone has created, and at a deeper level, betraying a communal trust.

BRING US BACK TO THE WRITTEN WORD

Due to the steady diffusion of cable television and the proliferation of simple-minded and sometimes violent video content, U.S. teachers have been concerned about a media-exploited "Generation X" over the past decade. Prior to the popular diffusion of the Internet, one of the main accusations leveled against Gen X'ers was that they were aliterate. Not that they could not read, mind you, but that they possessed the skills *to* read, yet elected not to exercise the craft. In the face of declining standardized test scores in English, the argument that these young adults did not engage print seems convincing.

However, this trend of declining English skills might be slowing. The Internet's focus on text as a primary method of interaction has contributed to the societal return to the written word. Of course, this includes the younger segments of our population that are becoming increasingly Internet savvy. By flocking to e-mail, chat-rooms, MUDs, computer screens, and the like, we begin to emphasize text as a primary form of communication (Ackerman 1994). Of course, Internet enthusiasts await the day when we can reliably and easily e-mail video clips of ourselves or do multiuser video-chat-sessions with one another. When this day comes, text may once again be sidelined for yet another round of media transformation. But at present, TMSIs are a popular means of expression through text.

CAN BE ADDICTIVE TO SOME

Of course, all things *should* be done in moderation. That said, we all realize that some minds are not satisfied with anything other than total completion. When encountering chat-rooms and MUDs that never end but simply acquire new participants, those obsessed with completion may find it difficult to enter the command "quit." Some of the most rational minds log in to their first MUD, never to log out. You might see these addicts connected to machines all night long because participants in seven time zones create a never-ending cycle of activity. They might be huddled together in computer labs, usually logged onto the same MUD, campaigning against other parties. Here they sit day after day, over long durations of time, mastering the repetitive keystrokes of their craft.

As a consequence, you will also likely see these people experience personal disarray. It is true that these users may have connected with other kindred spirits about the planet. And, as advocates for the Internet ourselves, we well know that this is a very exciting benefit of the interface. But when the user replaces real-life considerations with the events presented by artificial contexts, dependency arises as something of an issue (Turkle 1997). If you suspect you might get assimilated into the matrix, then establish a predetermined time to quit chatting or playing–and stick to it.

We do want to caution you against too quickly calling the frequent use of the Internet "addiction." While there might be similarities between Internet use and other forms of addiction, those similarities do not mean they are the same. Your cat might be similar to your dog, but that doesn't make them compatible. Walther and Reid (2000) have argued that we have applied the label of addiction to Internet activities too quickly, without carefully defining the terms. Almost anything can be called an addiction, including perhaps a love of chocolate. But the label of addiction brings with it an implication of a high degree of dysfunctionality that may not apply in this situation. Then again, it just might.

BASICS OF CHAT-ROOMS

Keeping this framework in mind, it is now time for us to learn the basic commands for these interfaces. First, we will cover the how-tos of chat-rooms. Then we will outline the fundamental mechanics operating behind MOOs. Our reasons for profiling the MOO interface rather than the MUD are twofold: (1) MOO commands function as a good foundation for using most TMSIs, and (2) it is more likely that your professor will want you to encounter an academic MOO environment for class purposes. It would be best to explore MUDs on your own time. The commands between a MOO and a MUD may be a little bit different, even though the general principles are universal. So, if the commands listed here fail to work, type "help" at the cursor line whenever in doubt. Almost every interface recognizes *that* simple command.

CONNECTING TO A CHAT-ROOM

The first thing that you will need to do is connect to a chat-room. This can be done through most university-networked computers and private ISPs. Many of the popular online services–like AOL, CompuServe, and Prodigy–already make in-house chat-rooms available by preinstalling their chat software within their proprietary interface. For example, when logging on to AOL, you could click on the People Connection button on the menu interface and select from the following basic options: (1) chat now, (2) find a chat, (3) start your own chat. Generally speaking, all of the other popular online services also make connecting to a chat-room this easy and intuitive.

The only drawback with using a service's chat is that you are restricted to holding conversations only with other users of that particular service. Say, for instance, that you are on CompuServe and wish to have a conversation with someone on AT&T Worldnet. Unless you both download a specific piece of chat software to use outside of the two proprietary interfaces (see our chat list on the textbook website), it will be nearly impossible to do. In fact, this became such an issue with AOL customers that in 1998, the company released its own free AOL Instant Messenger (IM), which circumvented this problem. Anyone may download IM from AOL's website and use the simple interface to connect with other IM users. Other Internet services (like CompuServe and Yahoo!) are beginning to release their own cross-ISP chat programs.

So what do you do if you are not using AOL, CompuServe, Prodigy, or any of the other ISPs offering in-house chats? How do you go about talking with your friends throughout the world? If you do not have an ISP-made interface, you will have to download and install an independent program. This is not a major issue since most experienced users primarily use these stand-alone programs anyway. By using a stand-alone chat program, you gain several benefits: (1) the ability to know when your friends are online, no matter their means of connectivity, (2) the freedom to use whatever form of expression you and your friends decide without an ISP community policeman, and (3) the security of maintaining uninterrupted chat-sessions without unwanted drop-ins.

There is, obviously, a third way to chat. Many websites host chat-rooms embedded within a webpage, using a specialized type of programming called Java. Many of these chat-rooms are popular because they provide organizations and interest groups with a place to hold online discussions. Major sports websites, like NFL.com, NBA.com, and NASCAR.com, make use of these tools to interact directly with their fans. Also, these chat-rooms are popular among users who lack a private ISP connection or use a networked computer that does not allow the installation of software on the hard drive. There are many means by which users can hold chat-sessions with others. It is simply a matter of connectivity and personal preference.

SELECTING THE CHAT-ROOM

As the saying goes, "You can't always judge a book by its cover." This also holds true for the names selected for chat-rooms. Realize that any given chat-room may be a month-old creation that has attracted a completely different set of participants over this extended time period. For instance, the participants discussing matters in FishChat today will be very different from those chatting there tomorrow. One minute, a local fishing troop might be holding an online strategy session. Then, suddenly, the room might be taken over by everyone in the world interested in fishing, or tropical fish, or maybe even good sushi. The composition, participants, and discussions in chat-rooms will change drastically from one minute to the next.

This is why it is important for you to know how to properly select a chat-room. First, you need to make sure that you have considered a decent range of chat-room titles before you impulsively select one to investigate. Once you enter the chat-room, make sure that you monitor the conversation a bit before contributing. This way, you will have some idea as to whether you plan to remain or not. If you wish to stay, then it is customary for you to introduce yourself by greeting the others in the room. Something as simple as "Hi room!" will suffice. Depending upon the friendliness of the participants, you may or may not get immediate feedback. Usually, someone will respond by acknowledging your presence in a similar fashion. If not, be patient. There are a great number of communication processes going on about you—some of which you cannot even see. It will take a little persistence and contribution on your part if you are to join in the conversation flow. That said, you may elect to leave the chat-room at any time. Or, you may prefer to lurk. Since chat-rooms are considered public forums, lurking is regarded as an acceptable form of participation.

GOING PRIVATE

If you repeat this process enough, moving from one discussion to the next, you may discover that the language flow in these chat-rooms is rather, well, chatty. You will also find that other participants are moving about from one chat-room to the next, just like you. This fragmented means of communication can be very confusing and frequently dissatisfying to those seeking more substance. That is why some users will target specific participants for a private chat-session by monitoring the public conversation. Going private need not be considered a sneaky activity. In fact, some of the most meaningful discussions that you may ever experience might occur in these private rooms, where the conversation is unaffected by the disjointed nature of heavy communication traffic. Most chat software and ISP-driven chats have clearly marked buttons that will allow you to privately invite participants to your discussions.

Ultimately, how you communicate and what you say in these chat-rooms is your business. If you seek a wide anonymous audience with which to commingle, then 11–35 participants in a room probably fits your public communication needs. If you desire a more thorough discussion, then a small-group setting with 3–10 companions might be better. And, when you really need to relate with someone online, the chat tool can be configured for one-to-one interpersonal communication. We believe that the chat program's best uses remain at the interpersonal and small-group communication levels. Possessing a wide range of applications, the chat program is one of the more popular features used on the Internet following e-mail and the Web.

BASICS OF MOOS

CONNECTING TO A MOO

No matter whether you connect to the Internet through a private ISP or a networked system, MOOs can be accessed via two common types of software: (1) Web browsers, or (2) the program called Telnet. If you have version 2.0 or better of Netscape's Navigator or Microsoft's Internet Explorer, you will probably be able to access most any MOO through a Web connection. *We wish to make this point very strongly: It is easier for you to access a MOO through a Web browser than it is to connect directly via Telnet.* We urge you to acquire the recommended software for these exercises (V. 2.0 or better of Netscape's Navigator or Microsoft's Internet Explorer) before connecting to a MOO. Learning the environs and arcane commands can be confusing enough without having to wrestle an outdated interface at the same time. Of course, if you are connecting to the Internet by way of a networked machine that does not provide Web access, you may be forced to use Telnet.

In either case, you'll need the address of the MOO in order to connect to it. You can find lists of MOOs (and MUDs) on the Web, and if it uses a Web interface, all you have to do is click on the link to enter it. Many

MOOs require you to fill out information about yourself before you are given a user ID and password. You also might have to initialize your character: what it looks like, its defining characteristics, etc. If the MOO uses Telnet, you will need to open up a Telnet program and connect to the server address that you are given.

BASIC MOO COMMANDS

Where chat-rooms seem to be best equipped to handle interpersonal and small-group communication, MOOs seem lifeless without a large number of participants. It also seems like a waste of "space" for only two or three people to be inside a MOO. After all, since the number of rooms in a MOO is almost infinite, the number of participants can be very large. Because you'll be interacting with a large group in a large space, it is important that you know the basics of communication, emoting, movement, and object manipulation. Again, we only explain the most frequently used commands for these categories. More advanced MOO features can be acquired through the program's **help** command. Whenever you feel unsure about something, simply type "help" and a topic list will appear. Then, type "help [name of topic]" for more specific information on the issue. Please remember, we only plan to provide you with a functional knowledge of MOO commands. You must master the more obscure commands on your own. At this time, we strongly suggest that you log in to a MOO to learn these basic commands through practice. You can find several different MOOs on the textbook's website.

Basic Communication Commands

The following are basic MOO communication commands.

say   "say" allows you to say something in full view of the participants in the same room. No one else outside of that room, unless they are system administrators or the message is reposted elsewhere, would see these comments.

You type:
say Hello everyone! My name is CaliDude!
Everyone in the room sees:
CaliDude says, "Hello everyone! My name is CaliDude!"
"   The quotation mark (") is shorthand for the say command.

to   "to" allows you to speak directly to a particular person within a room, while allowing everyone else to hear you. If you wish to speak in private with a person, it is best to relocate to a private conversation room or to whisper (see the following command).

You type:
to FLAGrrl Would you like a glass of Chardonnay, FLAGrrl?

> **Everyone in the room sees:**
> CaliDude [to FLAGrrl]: Would you like a glass of Chardonnay, FLAGrrl?

whisper   "whisper" allows you to speak quietly to people within the same room. This command implies that what you are saying is meant to be kept confidential. No one else inside that room would see these comments, unless they were system administrators or the recipient decided to post the message elsewhere.

> **You type (quotation marks included):**
> whisper "Hey, have you seen Frenchy lately?" to FLAGrrl
> **Only FLAGrrl sees:**
> CaliDude whispers, "Hey, have you seen Frenchy lately?"

page   MOOs are arranged to make communication function much like it does in real space. So, whenever you "say" or "whisper" something, it only works within that room. To communicate with people throughout the MOO complex, you will need to use the "page" command.

> **You type:**
> page FLAGrrl with "I miss you, FLAGrrl. @join me . . ."
> **FLAGrrl sees:**
> You sense that CaliDude is looking for you in the SUB HUB. He pages, "I miss you FLAGrrl. @join me . . ."
> **You see:**
> Your message has been received.

gagging   Sooner or later, you will encounter noisy players. Or you may encounter a player that really likes to talk to you, in particular, a lot. The gagging command will allow you to mute communication from a specified player. Use this feature judiciously, since the other party will inevitably question whether or not you are ignoring them or have them gagged.

> **You type:**
> @gag FLAGrrl—to add FLAGrrl to your gaglist
> **You type:**
> @ungag FLAGrrl—to remove FLAGrrl from your gaglist
> **You type:**
> @listgag—to list all of the participants you have gagged

Emoting Command

As you can probably tell, communicating in a MOO is easy. But you have to know how to tell the machine exactly *how* you want to convey your message. MOOs are sophisticated communication interfaces that allow the programmer to mimic reality while stretching how this reality functions in the mind's eye of the virtual. Capitalizing upon this sophistication, early MOO programmers installed an interesting feature called "emote."

emote   This feature allows you to announce whatever follows the command to those in the same room. Your name will come before the actual text, which is typically action-oriented communication. This tool is most often used to express nonverbal communication, emotion, or action.

You type:
emote cries and rubs his eyes.
Everyone sees:
CaliDude cries and rubs his eyes.
: The colon (:) is shorthand for the command "emote."

Emote allows you to be specific about your feelings and actions. Even though the utility is *called* emote, do not let that dissuade you from experimenting with its possible uses. When you type "emote [fill in the blank]," whatever follows the word emote will appear on screen for others to see, with your character's name as the subject. As far as the MOO is concerned, emote is a way to "do" things in an environment, even though you are not really "doing" them. When you enter "emote gets glass of water," you are not really getting a glass of water. Your character is just acting out the behavior for others to see. Everyone will simply see "CaliDude gets glass of water." In the world of communication make-believe, everyone thinks you just got a glass of water.

For this reason, the "emote" command is both useful and annoying. Often you will see people do things like smile and wave, take off their shoes, order pizzas, pull semi trucks out of their pockets, or put a CD in a jukebox (that does not even exist!). Confusing? Sure. The only way that we can really explain how this works is to have you try out some emotes for yourself.

Basic MOOvement Commands

Once you have this feature mastered, you'll probably want to start exploring your new world. Movement in MOOs is fairly intuitive. Most rooms will specify the possible ways in which you can move. To move to the area that you wish, tell the program which way you want to navigate with the "go" command.

go (direction)   Use this command with a direction to move your character. Common directions are: **north, south, east, west, northeast, southeast, northwest, southwest, up, down,** and **out.** You can usually use a number of different common variations on the command, including the following: (1) **go down,** (2) **go d,** (3) **down,** or (4) **d.**

You type:
go down
You see:
[a description of what awaits you in that place]

When your character departs, others will see:
CaliDude goes down.

When you visit MOOs or MUDs, it is a good idea to map out where things are on graph paper. Once you know where things are located, you can use the sequence move command. When you wish to get from point A to point P in a given area, but do not wish to read all of the details and enter all of the commands repeatedly, the "go" command can be used to navigate a series of tricky turns. Check your map and write down the sequence on a piece of paper to consult later. You type something that looks like this: "go s, e, u, e, n, d, s" and then hit Return. If your sequence is correct, the machine will automatically take you from point A to point P, without any time delay.

@who, @join   If you know of someone inside the MOO that you would like to visit, "@join" is an easy command that allows you to teleport to their side. Experienced users travel within a MOO by using the "@who" command to list not only who is in the MOO, but where they are located. Then, to move to that area, they simply type "@join [participant]."

You type:
@who–to get a list of all participants and their locations
You type:
@join FLAGrrl– to teleport to wherever she is

home   Remember, if you ever get lost within a MOO, all you have to do is type "home" to return to the main log-in station.

Basic Object Manipulation Commands

Now that we have covered the basic concepts of communication, emoting, and movement, we will lastly address the object-oriented principles that have made MOOs legendary. Environments can not only be given rich descriptions to provide a picturesque setting but objects can also be placed within this environment to augment the virtual experience. When you encounter these objects–ranging from handbags to toothbrushes to motorcycles–ask yourself a question. Is this a virtual object that actually "exists" in the room, which you can manipulate, or is it simply an *emoted* virtual object? If you see "FLAGrrl gets on her new motorcycle and peels out around the room," you can be fairly sure that the motorcycle does not actually exist in the room. Of course, some players have been known to gain Wizard-like privileges and create items like these for themselves, so the best way to tell is to use the following two commands:

look   This command will tell you everything that your eyes see in the room. This way, if you look at the room and something does not appear in the description, it is probably not an object you can manipulate.

examine (object)   This command can be used to look specifically at the object in question. It will provide all of the pertinent details necessary for you to use the object.

You type:
examine sign
You see:
The sign says "Hello, you are reading the sign!"

Many objects that you encounter can be picked up. Here are some of the universal commands that apply to picking up objects:

get or **take**   This command adds an object to your inventory. By default, when you "get" an object, it is placed in your personal inventory.

drop or **throw**   This command subtracts an object from your inventory, placing it in the room.

put   This command takes an object from your inventory and places it somewhere. Usually, you put something in your "containers."

give or **hand**   This command gives an object to another participant.

inventory   This command lists the items in your inventory available for use.

Many of the verbs that we use in everyday conversation are viable MOO commands. In fact, to control the possible combinations between the number of verbs that could be used, MOO programmers have attached specific verbs to specific objects. So, when you see an object that begs for a certain type of action, be instinctive. What would you ordinarily do to make the object work for you? Do not be afraid to try some verbs out on the object. Sooner or later you will hit the right command.

EFFECTIVE USE OF CHAT-ROOMS

Now that we understand the basic commands of these communication tools, let's examine their effective use. One of the first issues is whether you ought to use a chat-room or an instant messaging program. Which of these devices you will use depends upon whom you intend to be chatting with and the context for your communication. For instance, if you wish to interact with strangers interested in similar topics or have a large number of known discussion participants (4 to 25 or more, depending upon your chat-room's capacity), a formal chat-room is probably the best place to go. On the other hand, if you have one to four online communicants who need to chat, and do so in a sporadic manner over the course of an afternoon or evening, it is better to use an instant messenger chatbox. Consider some of the following suggestions when planning for the most strategic use of your chat interface:

- If using a chat-room for a planned discussion, make sure that you tell all of your partners where the chat-room is located well in advance. If you don't, your last minute efforts to plan a meeting may only have you, alone, in your chat-room. Include the time (translated and marked by time zones), date, subject, participants, agenda, and materials required. Detailed directions on how to find the online meeting are always best.

- When using a chat-room for a planned conversation, make sure that you use a "private room." Private rooms are not listed in the chat-room topic directories. If you do not use a private room but instead use a public room, your conversation may be frequently interrupted by drop-in visitors. And nothing might be more embarrassing or disconcerting than having several middle-school students drop in on your business meeting.

- Someone should serve as an online moderator in these planned meetings, regardless of the chat device used. The worst possible outcome here would be that everyone logged on and discussion ground to a halt. The preparation and predistribution of an agenda can help prevent this.

- Make sure that everyone in the room is allowed to have a chance to contribute. A good way to ensure this is to ask silent participants on the chat-list if they have any questions or anything that they'd like to add to the discussion. Do this throughout the meeting rather than at the end of the session, to foster collaboration and collegiality.

- Use emoticons and abbreviations to express emotions when communicating to friends. But when using these interfaces for business communication, it is best to avoid the use of emoticons. Depending upon the situation, context, and possible recipients of your message (remember that your text can be copied and re-delivered), emoticons could be perceived as being sophomoric even though they may have the best of intentions. Smiley faces and frowny faces definitely mean one thing between friends and another thing between employees and employers. Remember to always use your best grammar, spelling, and writing style whenever engaged in online business communication. If the other person decides to loosen up, then you may decide to follow suit. But do so only with great caution and forethought.

- Instant message chatting often decreases the use of e-mail between parties, but increases chatting exchanges significantly. This can be both a blessing and a curse, since your computer becomes more of a chat-station than a workstation. It is best to store only the names of those with whom you truly wish to interact. Also, be stingy about whom you give your instant message screen name to, and ask these people not to give it out to anyone else as a general rule. Otherwise, you might be chatting on your computer all day long instead of getting that big project into shape.

- Only open your chat-box when you are open for conversation. Some of the instant messengers install the device so that it opens upon system start-up. This can be reconfigured so that you can turn it on and off as you like.

EFFECTIVE USE OF MOOS

MOOs are unique interfaces because they can easily adapt to multiple communication contexts. For starters, when two participants run into each other, interpersonal communication can occur. When three or more are within range of one another, the MOO becomes a context for small-group communication. And when the house is really rocking, with 25 or more visitors all in the same room, this constitutes the public communication situation. Again, the interesting thing about a MOO is that all of this can occur simultaneously. When you have 25 or more people in a MOO, the question is not, Does this constitute public communication? The answer is yes. The question should be, How much of each communication element is going on at the same time? Given that lines of communication frequently overlap and sometimes blur, here are some suggestions for effectively communicating when in a MOO.

- Whenever logging in to a MOO, remember that the object of this exercise is directed more at communication than slaying dragons. Use the "@who" command to locate those who may be present in the environment. Once you do this, it is common MOO netiquette to locate the parties and introduce yourself.

- If you happen to get involved in a heated discussion and notice that your contributions seem to be outweighing the posts of others to the communication stream, adjust your means of interaction as quickly as possible. You can whisper to specific individuals, which muffles what you say only to those whom you specify. Or you can ask those interested to walk with you to another room where the discussion can begin again–this time without prevailing over the entire room.

- Always excuse yourself if breaking from parties, just as you would give oral or nonverbal indicators that you were detaching from a conventional discussion. Perhaps because the communication environment is synthetic and not natural, we often shoot from one discussion to another without adhering to traditional conversational protocol. Make sure that you tell the four to five people with whom you are discussing a topic that you need to be excused for whatever reason.

- Use the "emote" command and emoticons frequently to ensure that the other participants understand your intended relational meaning. Part of the problem with text-based online communication is that it allows us to bring our habits of ordinary conversation into the MOO environment. We instinctively scan all text for the emotional message, just as we would for all of our incoming communication. The problem is, we primarily use nonverbal communication to understand this relational meaning. In a MOO, the only nonverbal communication that exists is that which we emote or create by way of text :-).

- Remember that when online, people can create their own identity. They may not be who they say they are. Since user attributes can be easily invented without verification, it is best to assume that they do not exist. Unless you physically know the person with whom you are communicating, try to connect with others as fellow humans, rather than as man or woman, senior or child.

- Some users purposefully hide their characteristics and motives, pulling juvenile pranks on unsuspecting newcomers (Chayko 1993). Because of this, many online communities have responded by establishing standards for behavior. Be very aware of these standards, and do not break them under any circumstances (Dibbell 1993).

BACK UP AND RELOAD

It didn't take long for the developers of the Internet to realize that this network could be used for playing games and chatting. Chat-rooms and MUDs/MOOs allow users to exchange text-based messages in almost real time and even to create a whole fictitious environment with words. The creation of user-friendly interfaces such as AOL Instant Messenger and ICQ have made online chatting a popular phenomenon.

A considerable amount of communication research has taught us a great deal about the changes that come with these interfaces. They stimulate critical thinking, as users work to solve problems in a new environment. In this new environment, users work together to construct a shared cultural context with its own rules for interaction. Here, people can play with their identity, becoming (at least for a while) any character they can imagine. The text-based environment encourages creative means of expressing emotions. The imaginary worlds created in MUDs rely on an architecture of belief, where all members help create the illusion of inhabiting a fictitious realm. All of this text-based interaction brings users back to alphanumeric textuality, to a valuing of text that many thought lost with television. Finally, the immersive experience of TMSIs can lead to addiction in some people.

Using TMSIs can be an overwhelming experience at first, as you can be bombarded by rapid-fire messages, or sliced in half by a virtual sword. But in the end, using a chat-room involves getting connected, finding an appropriate room, and perhaps going to a private room. MUDs and MOOs add movement, emoting, and objects to text-based communication. Learning the basic commands and applying communication effectiveness tips will help you become a respected resident of these virtual environments.

BROWSE *and* BUILD	For sites to visit, exercises, quizzes to test your learning, and more, go to *www.harcourtcollege.com/ communication/inetcomm*

References and Readings

Ackermann, E. 1994. Direct and mediated experience: Their role in learning. In *Lessons from Learning,* edited by R. Lewis and P. Mendelson. Amsterdam: North-Holland.

Bruckman, A., and M. Resnick. 1995. The MediaMOO project: Constructionism and professional community. *Convergence* 1(1):95–109.

Chayko, M. 1993. What is real in the age of virtual reality? "Reframing" frame analysis for a technological world. *Symbolic Interaction* 16(2):171–81.

Cherny, L. 1995. The modal complexity of speech events in a social MUD. *Electronic Journal of Communication* 5(4). Accessed 14 September 1999 <http://www.cios.org/getfile/CHERNY_V5N495>.

Curtis, P. 1992. Mudding: Social phenomena in text-based virtual realities. *Intertek* 3(3):26–34.

Cutler, R. 1995. Distributed presence and community in cyberspace. *Interpersonal Computing and Technology Journal* 3(2):12–32.

Daft, R. L., and R. H. Lengel. 1984. Information richness: A new approach to managerial behavior and organization design. In *Research in Organizational Behavior.* Vol. 6, edited by B. M. Staw and L. L. Cummings, 191–233. Greenwich, Conn.: JAI Press.

———. 1986. Organizational information requirements, media richness, structural determinants. *Management Science* 32:554–71.

Danet, B. 1998. Text as mask: Gender, play, and performance on the Internet. In *Cybersociety 2.0: Revisiting computer-mediated communication and community,* edited by S. Jones, 129–58. Thousand Oaks, Calif.: Sage.

Dibbell, J. 1993. Rape in cyberspace or how an evil clown, a Haitian trickster spirit, two wizards, and a cast of dozens turned a database into a society. *Village Voice,* 21 December, 36–43.

Dieberger, A. 1994. *On Navigation in textual virtual environments and hypertext.* Ph.D. diss., Vienna University of Technology.

Fisher, W. 1987. *Human communication as narration: Toward a philosophy of reason, value, and action.* Columbia, S.C.: University of South Carolina Press.

Hiltz, S. R., and M. Turoff. 1981. The evolution of user-behavior in a computerized conferencing system. *Communications of the ACM* 24:739–62.

Moshell, J. M., and C. E. Hughes. 1996. The virtual academy: A simulated environment for constructionist learning. *International Journal of Human-Computer Interaction* 8(1):95–110.

Murray, D. 1989. When the medium determines turns: Turn-taking in computer conversation. In *Working with language,* edited by H. Coleman, 319–38. New York: Mouton de Gruyter.

Reid, E. 1995. Virtual worlds: Culture and imagination. In *Cybersociety: Computer-mediated communication and community,* edited by S. Jones, 164–83. Thousand Oaks, Calif.: Sage.

Rheingold, H. 1993. *The virtual community: Homesteading on the electronic frontier.* Reading, Mass.: Addison-Wesley.

Rintel, E. S., and J. Pittam. 1997. Strangers in a strange land: Interaction management in Internet Relay Chat. *Human Communication Research* 23(4):507–34.

Turkle, S. 1997. *Life on the screen: Identity in the age of the Internet.* New York: Touchstone.

Walther, J. 1992. Interpersonal effects in computer-mediated interaction. *Communication Research* 19(1):52–90.

Walther, J., and L. D. Reid. 2000. Understanding the allure of the Internet. *The Chronicle of Higher Education* 46(February 4):B4.

Williams, R. 1983. *Keywords.* Rev. ed. New York: Oxford University Press.

CHAPTER 5

Will That Be with or without Video?

Effective Net Conferencing

By Peter Zale ©2000 Peter Zale, www.peterzale.com   Distributed by Tribune Media Services, www.comicspage.com

By the end of this chapter, you should:

I.   Know the difference between videoconferencing and Internet telephony.
II. Understand the cultural significance of net conferencing:
    A. immediate feedback,
    B. emotional/relational content,
    C. nonverbal content,
    D. proxemics,
    E. out of synch,
    F. microexpressions, and
    G. no real physical presence.
III. Know how to initiate a net conference.
IV. Be familiar with the collaboration tools built into net conferencing programs:
    A. chat,
    B. whiteboarding,
    C. program sharing, and
    D. file transferring.
V.   Improve your net conferencing effectiveness by optimizing the:
    A. setup,
    B. conversation, and
    C. collaboration.

"**P**ut them on-screen, Uhura." For years we've dreamed of being able to do just that: both hear and see the person that we're speaking to, even if they're in another state (or galaxy). In recent years, you've probably even seen commercials for video phones. One place where this is now possible is on the Internet. With a fairly simple program and some additional hardware, you can turn your PC monitor into the bridge of the Starship Enterprise. If you have some high-tech friends and relatives, you can use the Internet to stay in closer touch, maintaining your relationships through sight and sound. But chances are probably better that you'll encounter this technology in the workplace. Businesses are putting cameras on every employee's computer, allowing them to meet with other people without leaving their desk. But conferencing is about more than just being able to hear and see the person to whom you're speaking. As you'll learn in this chapter, net conferencing programs allow people to share a program, work together on whiteboards, chat, and more.

Two key factors are making this communication revolution possible: faster Internet connections and cheaper hardware. Transmitting a video signal requires sending a lot of data. The larger the picture size and the smoother the video, the more data it takes. Just a few years ago, video transmitted over the Internet could only be about the size of a postage stamp and was very choppy due to a low **frames per second (FPS)** rate. Now that people have faster connections to the Internet and programmers have developed better compression algorithms, net conferencing is becoming a reality. But speed wasn't the only issue; the cost had to come down, too. Now, with free programs like Microsoft NetMeeting and video cameras that are as inexpensive as $100, full video and audio conferencing is well within the reach of the average computer owner.

This technology, however, is far from perfect. In fact, if you have a slow network connection, it can be fairly frustrating. Since net conferencing is still evolving, it is vital that you learn how to use it effectively because errors get magnified. In this chapter, you'll learn about the different components of net conferencing, what communication research can tell us about conferencing, the basics of using these programs, and how to communicate effectively with this medium.

DEFINING THE INTERFACE

NET CONFERENCING

A **conference** is essentially a task-oriented meeting between two or more people. We use the term **net conference** as an umbrella term to refer to any conference mediated by networked computers. Net conferencing can take place either with or without video. **Internet telephony** is audio-only network-mediated communication; essentially, it's using your computer as a telephone. In fact, at this point Internet telephony is inferior to the standard telephone. Both you and the person to whom you wish to speak have to have a significant amount of additional equipment. Besides computers, you both need a sound card, a microphone and speakers or a headset, and a fast Internet connection. Sound cards can be either **full** or **half duplex;** if you have a half-duplex card, you'll have to wait until the other person is done speaking before you can begin, much like an old CB radio. If you have a full-duplex card, you can both speak at the same time, but the sound quality is not as good as a normal telephone. Because of the additional equipment requirements and reduced quality, few people use the Internet for their telephone calls. But it does have one

---

TEXT BOX 5.1

What's So Big about Video?: FPS, Bandwidth, and Compression

Sending video over the Internet is a rather daunting task when you think about it for a second (all puns intended). That's because video signals are essentially created by sending several pictures (called frames) every second. The rapid succession of changing images is what creates the illusion of movement on the screen. The more frames you send per second, the smoother the video looks. 30 frames per second is considered full-motion video. When you send fewer frames each second (which often happens if you have a slow connection or the network gets congested), the motion gets jerky. You've probably been in a dance club when they turn the strobe lights on. That's what it looks like on your screen when the frame rate drops down to 10 or even fewer frames per second. People's arms jerk across the window as they wave, and you may not even catch their smiles.

It takes so much bandwidth to send video because what you're asking the computer to do is send at least 15 pictures every second. Early video images were very small, since tiny postage-stamp sized pictures use much less data than full screen images. But video image size is increasing, thanks in part to faster Internet connections, but more importantly because of ingenious compression schemes. One of the most basic—and yet at the same time very creative—ways to reduce the amount of data required is to *only send the information that changes.* Say, for example, you are sitting in front of a plain white wall. Nothing on the wall changes, except perhaps for shadows. So why resend all of the bits that make up the image of the wall? Instead, the program can just send the bits that change in that frame; for example, the bits that make up your image as you talk. The program combines the changed bits with the unchanged bits from the previous frame to create the next frame.

key advantage over the regular telephone: no long distance charges. The only charges you incur are for accessing your ISP; from that point on, the data is flowing over the Internet, not over the phone network.

Videoconferencing refers to audio and video network-mediated communication. Like almost all other technologies, it exists on a scale. At the high end are very costly group videoconferencing systems, typically found in the boardrooms of large corporations. In this chapter we will focus on the other end of the scale: personal videoconferencing, where one person sits in front of their computer and speaks with one or perhaps two other people sitting in front of their computers. Like telephony, videoconferencing requires additional equipment. You need a full-duplex sound card, speakers, a microphone or a headset, a video camera, a video input card (unless you have a **USB** [universal serial bus] video camera), and a fast Internet connection. Despite these additional requirements, personal videoconferencing is becoming increasingly popular because of its one major advantage: you can see the other person.

But net conferencing, as we noted at the beginning of this chapter, is about more than just being able to see the other person. It involves a range of communication and collaboration tools. Rosen (1996) coined the term **collabication** as a combination of collaboration and communication to denote the dual nature of conferencing tools. The communication tools include the audio and video signals. Three key collaborative tools include application sharing, whiteboarding, and file transfer. Application sharing allows you and the other person to work on the same program at the same time. Say you were coauthoring a paper with a person on the other side of the country or world. You could open up the paper in your word processing program, and you and the other person could simultaneously edit the document. **Whiteboarding** involves using a virtual version of the whiteboard that you might find in a classroom. You and the other person can draw on the whiteboard, underline or highlight things, or write text on it, and both people will see it at the same time. Finally, most net conferencing programs allow people to easily transfer files to each other. Of course, much of this can also be done asynchronously, but the advantage of conferencing is that you can work together at the same time.

BRIEF HISTORY OF NET CONFERENCING

Even though videoconferencing seems relatively new, it actually has been around since the 1960s. AT&T introduced its Picturephone at the 1964 World's Fair. For a number of reasons, including a lack of bandwidth, a lack of desire by executives to use the technology to communicate, and high cost, the product did not catch on (Rosen 1996). For this reason, most of the effort during the 1970s and 1980s went into developing high-end, expensive conferencing systems that were sold to corporations for use in boardrooms.

It wasn't until the 1990s that personal videoconferencing became possible for the average user. In the early 1990s, AT&T introduced five product lines, including the VideoPhone 2500 for home use. But according to most experts, it was Intel's involvement that caused net conferencing to come to life (Rosen 1996). In late 1990, Intel's CEO Andy Grove pushed the company to add richer multimedia capabilities to PCs, which would require greater processing power and thus drive sales of their more expensive high-end microprocessors. Video in particular requires a great deal of microprocessor power, which is why Intel decided to focus its efforts on video instead of shared applications. By 1993, Intel had created a conferencing program called ProShare to take advantage of (and help sell) its more powerful chips.

In the next few years, several companies jumped into this breakthrough market. PictureTel worked with Microsoft, eventually creating in 1995 a conferencing program called NetMeeting (which we'll use as our example in this chapter). Apple released QuickTime Conferencing in 1995, and Intel introduced their Video Phone in 1996. All of these programs could run on a home PC over **plain old telephone service (POTS).** CU-SeeMe, another company that sprang to life in the 1990s, introduced the first net conferencing system that let multiple people participate simultaneously in a conference over POTS. All of the other desktop programs could only be used by two people at a time.

In order for net conferencing to be practical and affordable, many technological developments had to occur. We don't want to drown you in jargon, but we do want you to be aware of three key advances, in addition to the increased processing power of PCs, that made net conferencing possible.

- Compression standards: in order for various computers connected up to the Internet to exchange video signals, they have to speak the same language. Since video signals have to be compressed, both computers have to know how to compress and then decompress the signal. The development and widespread use of the H.32* compression standard has made this possible. Even though many conferencing software manufacturers have their own compression standards, nearly all also include H.32* so that both people do not have to be using the same program.

- Inexpensive video cameras: obviously, to get a video signal you need a video camera. The development of cheaper **CCD** (charged coupled device) chips, which are used to capture images, brought the cost of a PC video camera down to under $100.

- Onboard digital signal processors **(DSPs):** to convert the video and audio signals into digital information for transmission over the Internet, you need a digital signal processor. This used to require purchasing a separate card that had to be installed into your computer. But now, DSPs often are already part of the motherboard of your computer (hence the term "onboard"), making the installation of video cameras much easier. If you have a USB port, all you have to do is plug the camera in and install the conferencing software, and you are ready to roll (Szuprowicz 1997).

CULTURAL SIGNIFICANCE OF NET CONFERENCING

Much like e-mail, net conferencing resembles interpersonal or small-group communication. Thus, much of our discussion about power and persona in chapter 3 applies here as well. However, with video, you can once again see the other person. Because of this, we need to discuss how net conferencing is different from textual interfaces like e-mail and chat, and yet not quite the same as face-to-face communication. Here we'll rely on principles and theories from both interpersonal and mediated communication.

IT'S NOT E-MAIL

Clearly, net conferencing is a much different communication interface than e-mail, or MUDs and chat for that matter. The most obvious difference is the richer interaction possible because you're able to see the other person. The addition of a visual signal is not the only difference, however. A synthesis of interpersonal communication research reveals four significant factors to consider.

Immediate Feedback

E-mail is an asynchronous interface. When you get an e-mail message, you don't have to reply right away. You can think about the message for a while, and reply when you're ready. Net conferencing, however, is a synchronous interface. This means that you and the person are talking and listening *at the same time*. So you can give and receive feedback immediately. This may help speed up the decision-making process. But at the same time, you may feel more pressure to act quickly.

Emotional/Relational Content

When you interact with other people, very little of the emotional content is communicated through words. For example, when you say "hello," that one word can have many different meanings depending on how you say it. Mehrabian (1972) concluded that only about 7% of the emotional content of a message is in the words. Research since then has indicated that this figure is probably too low, and that more emotional content is present in words. However, most of the emotion in a message comes through in facial expressions, gestures, tone of voice, volume, and other nonverbals. Since all of this data is transmitted in net conferencing, you can express emotions much more easily. Most of the time, these emotions communicate something about your relationship to the other person. The richer sensory data provided by net conferencing makes it easier to establish whether you view the other person as your friend, superior, enemy, or inferior.

Nonverbal over Verbal

Suppose you begin telling your friends about a problem. You notice that they don't seem to be paying attention, so you ask them if they care about your problem. They say, "Of course," without looking up from the television. Chances are, you don't believe them. Most of the time, when we get contradictory nonverbal and verbal messages, we believe the nonverbal one. This is because we assume that nonverbal messages are more difficult to fake. Since nonverbal messages are part of the net conferencing interface, we can once again send contradictory messages. And when we do, the nonverbal message is the one that will be believed. We'll discuss the problems that this can cause later.

Interpreting Nonverbal Content

When you make sense of nonverbal cues, you interpret them primarily in three dimensions: **immediacy, arousal,** and **dominance** (Mehrabian 1972). When you like someone, you usually move closer to them, either physically or symbolically. Liking is communicated through such immediacy cues as leaning forward, reaching toward them, smiling, and others. We also use nonverbals to determine how interested the other person is in us. They communicate their interest to us through cues such as an animated voice, face, or body posture. Finally, status is communicated through dominance cues. If you're the person with higher status, you tend to communicate this through a relaxed posture: leaning back in your chair, for example. If you stay fairly formal in your stance, it's pretty clear that you're the one in an inferior position. Since the nonverbal dimension returns with video, your message when net conferencing is shaded by these dimensions of immediacy, arousal, and dominance far more than it is when using textual interfaces.

IT'S NOT FACE-TO-FACE, EITHER

If you were to ask most people if net conferencing was more similar to e-mail, chat, or face-to-face communication, most would answer "face-to-face." And they would be right. When you first start using net conferencing programs, you might be tempted to think that this interface is basically the same as talking to someone in the same room. However, research has revealed some significant differences between net conferencing and face-to-face communication.

Proximity

Normally, when you interact with another person, you negotiate the amount of distance between each other. You move closer to people to demonstrate intimacy, and they might move away from you if they don't know you well or are angry with you. But with net conferencing, the distance between you and the other person is only a function of how close you are to your camera. You can't really communicate intimacy through social distance anymore. The other person may be leaning back in their chair, and to you they are going to look far away. But they may not be trying to communicate that they're angry with you; they may just be tired of being so close to their computer screen. Media researchers use the term **para-proxemics** (Meyrowitz 1986) to talk about the illusion of physical distance that can be created by how close the camera is to the person being recorded. Close-ups can be seen as intimate, but extreme close-ups are usually perceived as threatening. Thus, proxemics can be simulated with net conferencing, but not duplicated. One other spatial problem is that when you are net conferencing, you are tied down to your computer. You can't gesture as expansively as you might want to, since the camera might not pick it up. It's difficult to move around much at all, and this feeling of restrictedness might start to shape your communication.

Out of Synch

It's relatively easy, when you're talking to someone face to face, to take turns. When the other person pauses, you can start talking immediately. If you want to make sure you get your turn, you might hold up your hand to stop the other person from talking. This turn taking becomes problematic when net conferencing. This is because there's a delay of about a half of a second between when you speak and the other person hears you. So when you start talking after the other person pauses, there's a good chance that the other person has already started speaking. Being slightly out of synch alters the conversation considerably. Your feedback is slightly delayed, and it is difficult to respond to the other person's feedback. Studies have shown that net conferences are less interactive, contain less humor (since humor requires precise timing) or other complex interactions, and typically consist of long monologues instead of active conversations (Tang and Isaacs 1995). Another danger is that this out-of-synch communication unfortunately creates two cues that we normally associate with lying: a delay in responding to a question and unfilled pauses (Zuckerman, DePaulo, and Rosenthal 1981).

Microexpressions

Your face moves very quickly; some expressions only last as little as 200 milliseconds. Others, like the blink of an eye, are much faster. Net conferencing video cameras on a very good Internet connection might manage to capture and transmit 24 frames per second. If the Internet gets congested, the frame rate might drop down to 1 frame per second, or even worse. When this happens, many of those microexpressions are lost (Bruce 1995). As we noted earlier, most of the emotional content of the message comes from the nonverbal elements. When you are net conferencing, you might miss out on a lot of the emotional content that you would normally get in a face-to-face interaction. Quite often, nonverbal messages are part of a package: the meaning comes from the smile, the raised eyebrows, and the shrugged shoulders. If part of the package is lost, the meaning can very easily be changed.

No Real Physical Presence

One obvious difference is that you aren't physically present with the other person when net conferencing. You can't touch the other person, which we know to be an important way to show emotion. Depending on what kind of equipment we have and our connection, you might be able to see me but I might not be able to see you. Since I'm not in the room with you, I can't tell how my voice has been altered by the connection. And since the camera might not show the entire room, others could be in the room without my knowledge.

Mechanical Difficulties

It almost goes without saying that putting a machine (actually, several machines) between you and the other person will create some problems. An inability to get the equipment working often leads to frustration. If people have negative initial experiences, they are more likely to avoid using videoconferencing in the future. This can cause serious problems if you're working with a group of people and one person refuses to use videoconferencing to communicate (Johansen et al. 1991). Of course, problems can occur in the opposite direction as well. Some people get so enamored with the technology that they will set up a videoconference when e-mail would work just as well. These enthusiastic adopters of the technology often find that they are less productive when they first begin videoconferencing. This is because they spend so much time working (more like playing) with the interface that they don't accomplish their objectives.

It should be clear that there are some significant differences between net conferencing and face-to-face interaction. Being able to see the other person can make it easier to understand what they mean, but a poor Internet connection may lead to some serious misunderstandings. Sometimes, getting no nonverbal data is better than getting just a little. As we noted earlier, this is a relatively new interface. If both you and the other person are inexperienced, you'll almost certainly make some mistakes. When you combine a new medium with new users, those mistakes can quickly lead to frustrating and problematic exchanges. But if you're aware of the potential problems, you'll be able to avoid them. We'll talk later in this chapter about how to apply this information so you can use net conferencing effectively.

BASICS OF NET CONFERENCING

Using net conferencing is a bit more complicated than using e-mail. Some of this complication is due to the newness of the medium. Most of us are used to composing at a keyboard, but not many are used to speaking into a microphone in front of a camera. With net conferencing, this is complicated by the need to add hardware: a video camera and sound card, and perhaps a video capture card. Chances are good that if you're using net conferencing at work or school, the hardware is already set up. But if you're going to be using it at home, you'll have to install the hardware yourself. Since there are so many different cameras and software packages available, we can't really cover setup. But our universal advice is this: follow the directions that come with the equipment.

Once the video camera, sound card, speakers and microphone or headset, and software are installed, you can start using your net conferencing program. Given the number of conferencing programs available, we can't explain all of them. We're going to use Microsoft NetMeeting for our examples because it is widely used and available, it can be downloaded for free (no doubt a major reason for the former), and it is similar to many other programs. **Figure 5.1** shows the opening screen for NetMeeting. The first time you use the program, you will need to fine-tune the audio settings. Simply follow the directions that the tuning wizard provides.

GETTING CONNECTED

Obviously if you want to communicate with someone over the Internet, you first need to get your computers talking to each other. The first decision you need to make is who is going to host the meeting. As you can see from **Figure 5.2,** the host of the meeting is in control of the security and many other options. Once one person has set their computer to host the meeting, the other person needs to place the call.

You can place a new call in one of two ways. If you know the other person's **IP address** (the address that has been assigned to a computer

Fig. 5.1. Microsoft's NetMeeting interface.

Fig. 5.2. Hosting meetings gives you more control.

by an Internet service provider) or e-mail address, you can click on the telephone icon and enter that address in the To box **(Figure 5.3).** If not, you'll need to use a directory service to locate the other person. You won't be able to find someone, however, unless s/he has entered identifying information into the directory. NetMeeting uses the Microsoft Internet Directory by default, and you can add your personal information to it by clicking on Tools > Options **(Figure 5.4).** However, Microsoft requires you to install the MSN Messenger service and sign up for a Hotmail account to use their Internet Directory. Other directory services that do not require you to install other software or sign up for e-mail are listed on the textbook website.

Since one of the primary reasons for using NetMeeting is to be able to see the other person, you normally want to automatically send and receive video. To make sure that this is enabled, click on Tools > Options and then select the Video tab **(Figure 5.5).** Check the boxes to automatically send and receive video. Otherwise, to start sending video you need to click on the play button (the small triangle below the video window).

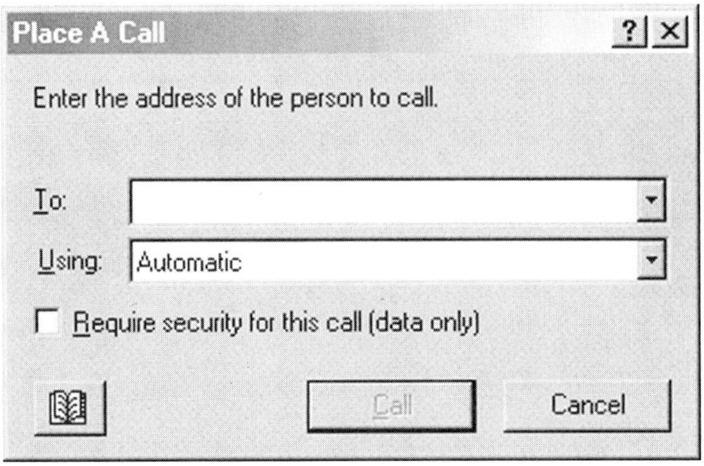

Fig. 5.3. Contacting another person is just a matter of knowing where they are.

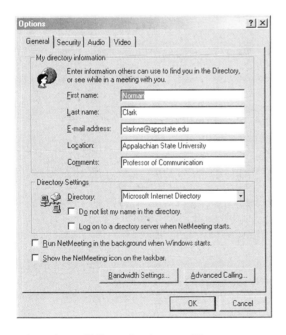

Fig. 5.4. Tell us about yourself!

Fig. 5.5. Use the Video tab to optimize the image you receive.

NEGOTIATING THE CONNECTION

Typically, you'll need to spend the first few minutes of your conference adjusting various settings. One of the first things you'll probably need to adjust is the position of your microphone. Here you will need to rely on feedback from the other person, who can tell you when you have your microphone positioned best. If you are wearing a headset, you want the microphone about a thumb's width away your mouth, off to one side. Clicking on the speaker/microphone icon will allow you to adjust the volume of your speakers and the sensitivity of your microphone. Rely on your own ears to set the speaker level, and either allow the program to automatically set the microphone sensitivity or get feedback from the other person.

The Options dialog box allows you to fine-tune your video **(Figure 5.5)** and audio **(Figure 5.6)** settings. For audio, you are typically better off allowing the program to automatically adjust the microphone volume and silence detection, and enabling full-duplex audio and auto-gain control (if your sound card has these capabilities). With video, you may need to do more adjusting. If your connection is running at a slow speed, a smaller image could be necessary. You also might want to adjust the

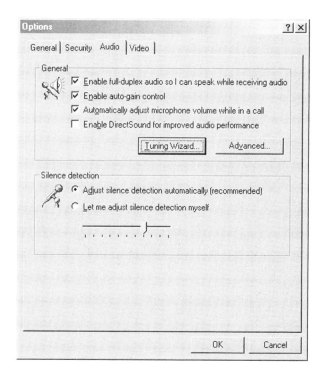

Fig. 5.6. Can you hear me calling? If not, adjust the audio here.

video quality and perhaps the lighting in your room, which we'll talk about in more detail when we discuss how to use this medium effectively.

YOU MAKE THE CALL

Once you are connected and everything is working, you can begin to converse. One of the first things you will notice is that it is somewhat difficult to carry on a smooth conversation. This is because of the audio time lag. There can be as much as a second of delay between the time the other person speaks and you hear it. In face-to-face conversations, we use pauses to signal when we are done speaking. With net conferencing, however, by the time you hear the pause, the other person might have already begun speaking again. This can lead to some frustration, since you and the other person might simultaneously say, "you go ahead," be unsure of who said it last, and so both start speaking again. It can take a little time to work out turn-taking. Don't forget that you can use the video signal: gesturing for the other person to speak is usually effective.

DROPPING IN TO CHAT

If you become frustrated with the audio time lag, or if your network connection gets congested, you might find it useful to use the chat feature. Chat can be especially effective when you are first trying to set up the conference. If your audio connection is not working well, you and the other person can use chat to work out problems. Clicking on the icon that looks like a speaking balloon opens up the chat window **(Figure 5.7).** The messages that the other person sends appear in the upper part of the window, while you type in the Message box.

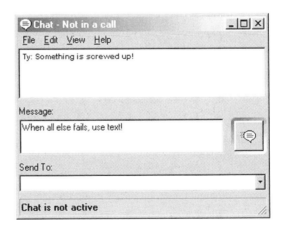

Fig. 5.7. Sometimes, text is best.

WHITEBOARDING

As we noted at the beginning of the chapter, net conferencing programs allow you to do more than just see and hear the other person. These programs also provide collaboration tools, including whiteboards **(Figure 5.8).** Think of whiteboards as a virtual version of the dry erase boards that you might find in classrooms and boardrooms. To bring up the whiteboard, click on the icon that looks like a pen on a white surface **(Figure 5.1).** You and the other person can draw lines, shapes, and text on the whiteboard surface, and you will both be able to see what's been drawn. Clicking on the icon of a hand brings up a pointer that you can move around the whiteboard and the other person can see what you're pointing at. Of course, while you are working on the whiteboard you can continue to talk with the other person. This is where net conferencing programs really begin to shine. Imagine being able to sketch out the solution to a problem, while being able to hear and see the other person, even though they are a thousand miles away!

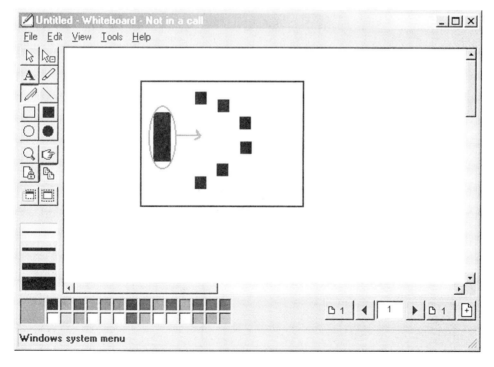

Fig. 5.8. Whiteboards allow you to get creative together; for example, you can plan the table layout for a face-to-face conference.

SHARING PROGRAMS

While the whiteboard is useful for sketching out ideas, it is a fairly limited program. However, most net conferencing programs allow you to
share any program that you are running on your computer with the other
person. Clicking on the icon of a hand holding up a program window
brings up the Sharing Program dialog box **(Figure 5.9).** Listed in this
box are any programs that are currently running on your computer. You
can select the programs that you want to share with the other person in
the conference. You can also allow the other person to take control of the
program. For example, when we were writing this textbook, one of us
could open up the chapter in our word processor and both of us could
work on that file at the same time. We could both edit the document
simultaneously, talk about the changes we were making, and see the gri-
maces on the other's face when we didn't like what the other was doing.
Being able to share programs like this makes it much easier for people to
collaborate on projects even though they are miles apart.

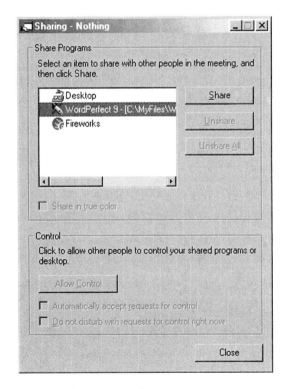

Fig. 5.9. NetMeeting allows you to share computer programs from across the
globe.

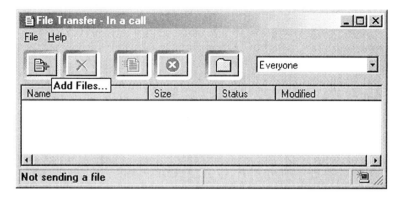

Fig. 5.10. Need to send a file? NetMeeting's File Transfer makes it easy.

TRANSFERRING FILES

Finally, net conferencing programs often allow you to transfer files. Clicking on the icon that looks like a flying piece of paper **(Figure 5.1)** brings up a file transfer window **(Figure 5.10).** Chances are you won't use this feature very often. Transferring a file while in a videoconference will degrade the audio and video quality. If you do need to share a file with another person, it makes more sense to send it to them as an e-mail attachment. However, if you are in the middle of a conference and want the other person to look at a file but don't want to share the program, the file transfer option might fit your needs.

EFFECTIVE CONFERENCING

At the beginning of this chapter, we noted that net conferencing is a relatively new phenomenon. You are more likely to make mistakes on a medium with which you are unfamiliar. And unfortunately, if the other person is also unfamiliar with the medium it is difficult for them to work through your mistakes and figure out what you really meant. For these reasons, it is important for you to learn how to communicate effectively with net conferencing programs. It is also important for you to share what you have learned with the other person. In this section, we'll talk about how to optimize the setup, the conversation, and the collaboration.

OPTIMIZING THE SETUP

Before you even begin the conference, you need to consider a number of factors. Your level of satisfaction with the overall conference will depend a great deal on how well you prepare for it.

- Appearance: remember, people can see you in a videoconference. Since conferencing is typically used for peer collaboration, casual attire is usually appropriate. However, if you're using net conferencing to conduct an important meeting, you'll probably need to dress more formally. Regardless, avoid white or light colored shirts; because they are so bright they will wash out the picture. You also want to avoid shirts with narrow stripes, since the stripes often appear to wiggle on video. Red outfits tend to bleed, busy prints are distracting, and shiny jewelry reflects a lot of light. Your best bet is to wear a solid blue shirt, or a dark shirt with a subtle pattern (Rosen 1996).

- Lighting: as any camera operator will tell you, lighting can make or break a video image. Don't rely on just the overhead fluorescent light that you find in most offices: the top of your head will be bright, while the lower half will be in shadow. Don't shine a light directly on your face either, since this will wash out your face. Too much light behind you will cause your face to be very dark. Your best bet is to use a variety of indirect light sources **(Figure 5.11).** To make sure that you are looking your best, click on the Play button of your net conferencing program to preview your image. This will give you a good idea of what you look like to the other person on their screen.

- Background: any photographer will tell you that you need to pay attention to what is behind the subject of the picture. Otherwise, you can have trees growing out of people's heads. Pay attention to what is behind you; you might need to do some rearranging. A neutral-to-dark, plain background is best. Movement in the background will detract from the overall video quality and should definitely be avoided.

- Arrangements: before you use this medium, you need to make use of a more common, reliable medium to set up the conference:

Fig. 5.11. Light in front, light behind, or (your best bet) a variety of indirect lighting sources.

typically, either the telephone or e-mail. Select the time and date for the conference. Decide who will be the host and make sure that the caller knows the host's TCP/IP or e-mail address. Identify which net conferencing program you'll both use. Finally, state the objectives of the net conference and make sure that a net conference is really required. If all you're going to do is exchange e-mail addresses, a full videoconference is probably not necessary.

OPTIMIZING THE CONVERSATION

The lights are on, you're looking good–now what? As with any new medium, it will be difficult at first to have a smooth-flowing conversation. But with practice, and with the help of these suggestions, you should be able to participate in a productive conference.

- Eye contact: we all know how important eye contact is in face-to-face conversations. The same is true with videoconferencing: good eye contact communicates interest in the other person and that you are paying attention. With videoconferencing, unfortunately, when you look at the other person's image on your screen you are not making eye contact. To make good eye contact, you have to look directly at the camera. Of course, then you can't see the other person. The best compromise is to mount your camera to your computer monitor, and then move the NetMeeting window so that it is as close as possible to the camera. So, for example, if you have your camera mounted to the top of your monitor, move the program window to the top of the screen directly below the camera. To be able to see your own image while still maintaining good eye contact, set NetMeeting to display your image in picture-in-picture mode. Do this by clicking the center icon below the video box, which looks like a small box inside a larger one **(Figure 5.1).**

- Para-proxemics: the distance that you stand from another person communicates a great deal as well. The closer you stand, the more intimate the conversation is; the further away that you stand, the more formal. While you can't move closer to the other person in a net conference, you can simulate social distance by how close you get to the camera. Don't get extremely close to the camera, since extreme close-ups are perceived as threatening (and nobody really wants to count your nose hairs). On the other hand, avoid sitting far back from the camera, since this may communicate a lack of interest in the other person. Adjust your position so that your head and shoulders fill most of the video frame. You should have no more than three people crammed into the video window at one location.

- Audio over video: most of the research that has been done on videoconferencing suggests that even though video is pretty cool, audio is more important for effective communication (Tang and Isaacs 1995). If you have to choose between a videoconference with delayed and broken audio or an audio-only conference, choose the audio. By shutting off the video, you can reduce or even eliminate the delay between when you speak and the other person hears you. This can make the conversation flow much more smoothly. In fact, in some instances you might decide to use the telephone for the audio side of the conference and use your computers for just the video signal. However, you need to be aware if you do this that the video signal on your computer will be slightly delayed and out of sync with the audio signal from the telephone.

- Audio quality: you will end up with the best audio quality, and the least frustrating experience, if both people use headsets. If you use standard speakers and a microphone, the other person will hear an echo of their own voice, since your microphone will pick up the sound of their voice coming out of your speakers. This can be very disconcerting and annoying, much like the childhood game of copying everything the other person says. With a headset, the microphone will rarely pick up the sounds coming out of the headphone speaker, unless you have the volume turned up to eardrum-shattering levels. The headset also keeps the microphone positioned at a constant distance from your mouth, resulting in greatly improved audio quality.

- Turn-taking: for most people, the most frustrating aspect of net conferencing is the delay between when you speak and the other person hears your voice. The reason this is so frustrating is because in face-to-face conversations, you jump in to speak within a fraction of a second after the other person finishes. However, with the time delay in conferencing, you often will find yourself speaking over the top of the other person. To overcome this difficulty, use the video channel. You can gesture for the other person to speak or hold up your hand if you wish to continue speaking.

- Video over audio: even though we stated that responsive audio is more important than video, there are some times when video is extremely valuable. We know from interpersonal and nonverbal research that most of the emotional and relational dimensions of messages are communicated nonverbally. Use the video signal to determine the other person's attitudes and feelings when you can't infer them from the sound of their voice. Obviously, the video signal is also crucial when you need to demonstrate actions—

show them, don't tell them (Tang and Isaacs 1995). Microsoft NetMeeting allows you to adjust the video that you receive to have either a higher quality picture or a faster image **(Figure 5.5).** You should adjust this setting until you are satisfied with the image that you are receiving. You may find that a faster video allows you to catch more expressions on the person's face. Or, you may prefer a clearer picture with jerkier motion, especially if the other person is not very animated.

- Etiquette: when you meet face to face, you typically shake hands. The equivalent greeting in a net conference is to smile and wave. We are still working out many of the etiquette issues for video-conferencing. For example, if the phone rings while you are in a net conference, do you answer the phone? When you are on the telephone, you can work on other tasks at the same time; can you write a memo while the other person is watching you? The best answer we can give you at this time is that it depends on your relationship to the other person. If it is someone you know fairly well, you can get away with not devoting your full attention to the net conference. However, if it is a superior or someone you need to impress, you ought to devote your full attention to the conference. It is probably best if your first contact with a person whom you never met before is over the telephone instead of a net conference, since the addition of the video signal makes it far more intrusive (Rosen 1996). Finally, if there are other people in the room but out of the camera's eye, you ought to introduce them to the other person. Otherwise, some uncomfortable foot-in-mouth situations might occur.

OPTIMIZING THE COLLABORATION

As you get more adept at using net conferencing programs, you'll likely begin to make use of many of the collaboration tools. Keeping in mind what the tools are appropriate for and remembering some basic interpersonal skills can help make your work more productive.

- Choose wisely: with Microsoft NetMeeting, you have several collaboration tools available. Choose chat when you're having problems with the audio. Choose the whiteboard when you need to sketch out some rough ideas or anytime you need to draw out a concept. Share programs when you need to mutually work on a specific file, such as a word processing document or a spreadsheet. When you are using these collaboration tools, you may find that the video window is unnecessary. It is difficult to look at the word processing file and the video window at the same time. Much of the time, you'll find that it works best to shut off the video so that you can have smoother control over the program and better audio quality.

- Negotiate sharing: suppose you are working on a document with another person. With NetMeeting, you can decide whether or not you want to allow the other person control over the program **(Figure 5.9).** Your first instinct might be to say, Sure, why not let them have control? But think about this for minute. Are you going to take turns controlling the document? And if so, is your conference going to turn into a competition? And how might you react when you see another person changing a document you worked on for many hours, right there on your own computer screen? Obviously, these are issues that you need to take seriously and negotiate with the other person before you begin the collaboration. However you decide to work out these issues, strive to maintain a positive, supportive communication climate in which you can continue to collaborate. One basic interpersonal skill to remember is to describe what's going on, instead of evaluating the other person's behavior. Talk about yourself (using "I" statements) instead of the other person (using "you" statements).

BACK UP AND RELOAD

In this chapter, you learned about the basic components of net conferencing. Hopefully, one thing that has stuck in your mind is that net conferencing is more than just being able to see the other person. You also learned that conferencing is different from both e-mail and face-to-face interaction. The possibility of immediate feedback, the richer emotional content, and the return of nonverbal communication separates conferencing from e-mail. The lack of real proximity and physical presence, the problems of being slightly out of synch, and the loss of microexpressions mean conferences lack some of the richness afforded by face-to-face interaction.

Even though net conferencing hardware and software vary in some details, what you learned about using Microsoft NetMeeting is applicable to most other programs. You should now be able to get connected, converse and use the collaboration tools that NetMeeting provides. But most importantly, the application of communication theory to this new medium provided you with some vital advice on how to net conference most effectively. Keep the advice on optimizing the setup, conversation, and collaboration in mind as you conference over the Internet.

References and Readings

Bruce, V. 1995. The role of the face in face-to-face communication: Implications for videotelephony. In *Information superhighways: Multimedia users and futures,* edited by S. Emmott, 227–38. San Diego: Academic Press.

Duran, J., and C. Sauer. 1997. *Mainstream videoconferencing: A developers guide to distance multimedia.* Reading, Mass.: Addison-Wesley.

Johansen, R., D. Sibbet, S. Benson, A. Martin, R. Mittman, and P. Saffo. 1991. *Leading business teams: How teams can use technology and group process tools to enhance performance.* Reading, Mass.: Addison-Wesley.

Mehrabian, A. 1972. *Nonverbal communication.* Chicago: Aldine-Atherton.

Meyrowitz, J. 1986. Television and interpersonal behavior: Codes of perception and response. In *Inter/media: Interpersonal communication in a media world.* 3d ed. Edited by G. Gumpert and R. Cathcart, 253–72. New York: Oxford University Press.

Rosen, E. 1996. *Personal videoconferencing.* Greenwich, Conn.: Manning.

Szuprowicz, B. 1997. *Multimedia tools for managers.* New York: American Management Association.

Tang, J., and E. Isaacs. 1995. Studies of multimedia-supported collaboration. In *Information superhighways: Multimedia users and futures,* edited by S. Emmott, 123–60. San Diego: Academic Press.

Zuckerman, M., D. DePaulo, and R. Rosenthal. 1981. Verbal and nonverbal communication of deception. *Advances in Experimental Social Psychology* 2:1–59.

Part Three

Preparing for Communication: Researching on the Internet

If you have an anecdote from one source, you file it away. If you hear it again, it may be true. Then the more times you hear it the less likely it is to be true.

ANTHONY HOLDEN

E-mail, chat, and videoconferencing are often used for relatively informal communication. But eventually, you are going to need to communicate with people on a more formal level. In the life of the student, this need comes up every time you sit down to write a paper or prepare a speech. When you make a formal argument, it is not enough to simply state your opinions. You have to back up your claims with evidence. In these next two chapters, you'll learn how to search the Internet for information to support your communication efforts. You'll also learn how to evaluate that information, since much of what you'll find on the Internet is not much better than rumor.

Where Do I Find It?

Searching the Web

By Peter Zale ©2000 Peter Zale, www.peterzale.com   Distributed by Tribune Media Services, www.comicspage.com

By the end of this chapter, you should:

I.   Understand the basics, advantages, and disadvantages of nine tools for finding data online:
   A. search engines,
   B. directories,
   C. bibliographic databases,
   D. site-specific search engines,
   E. subject-specific search engines,
   F. metasearch engines,
   G. topic rings,
   H. FAQs, and
   I. expert inquiries.
II. Improve your use of these tools as you:
   A. initiate a search,
   B. refine a search, and
   C. complete a search.

Locating on the Internet the exact data you need is one of the most difficult skills to master. The confusing number of search engines and lists of lists creates the impression that the Internet is nothing more than loosely organized chaos. To be honest, this impression is generally correct. For the most part, everyone is still trying to define some standard methods for retrieving online data (Falk 1998). Setting these standards is so difficult because the information is constantly being altered, replicated, moved, or deleted.

An additional challenge is the rapid growth in the amount and types of information available. Recent estimates report some 1.25 billion documents available on the Web. What type of data—exactly—is it that you require? Are you looking for text-based data? Court cases? Specific types of photographs? Video? CD-quality digital audio? Software? And do you need this data in English? Spanish? French? Sorting through a network where data is growing in size and scope at an astronomical rate has become rather complicated. But thanks to the various research tools available, it is not impossible.

UNDERSTANDING ONLINE RESEARCH TOOLS

The goal of research is to provide you with the data you need to effectively communicate to others. But first, you need to know how to effectively find the materials you need, using the wide variety of tools available. Acquainting yourself with the various online search methods allows you to search more accurately, saving yourself valuable time and energy. Plus, it can certainly help you shorten your library visits, provided you rely upon credible data. We'll cover nine different research tools; for each, we'll talk about what it is, how to use it, and what its advantages and disadvantages are.

SEARCH ENGINES

What Are They?

A **search engine** is a device that allows the user to submit key-term search requests to an online database that stores most of the Internet in a compressed format. You have probably heard of some of these search engines: Altavista.com, Excite.com, HotBot.com, Infoseek.com, Look Smart.com, Lycos.com, Microsoft Search or MSN.com, Netscape Search at Netscape.com, and Yahoo.com. These engines normally appear as rectangular input boxes with a button marked Search or Submit off to the side. Into these input boxes you enter the most important word or words that you are looking for information about and then hit Enter (or the button next to the input box). The search engine takes the exact words of your entry and scans for them in its database to locate matches containing the key terms you entered. The search engine then gives you a results page that lists all of the documents in its database that contained the words you told it to look for. The results are listed in order of decreasing relevance (the ones at the top are most likely to be related to your search terms) and will usually include an abstract about the page (or the first few lines of text from it). If you happen to have misspelled your search, as we did purposely for our example in **Figure 6.1** (*Atlana* rather than *Atlanta*), the search engine will still retrieve documents stored on the Web containing that misspelling. This is because the search engine, as is the case with all software, does only what you tell it to do.

You need to know that the input box is just an entry point for your particular request. The real search engine is stored on a powerful set of computers housed in the sponsoring company's physical location. Search engine input boxes can show up in the most peculiar places, since Web programmers can easily borrow the computer code used to create input boxes and place them into websites removed from their original location (Ackermann and Hartman 1998). In other words, do not be surprised if you come across an Altavista, Infoseek, or Yahoo! input box on a friend's webpage. Boxes can even be set up to allow you to easily search several different search engines, as is the case at Netscape Netcenter **(Figure 6.2).**

Search engines first appeared in 1994 as an effort to bring order to the wealth of data being placed online (Berry and Browne 1999). They are indispensable tools that have become so popular that many have evolved into **portals,** or customizable entry points to the Internet. Billed as something of a one-stop shop for online needs, portals usually offer a bundled array of services (Calishain and Nystrom 1998). Often the user can secure a free e-mail account, get free webpages, use free chat-rooms, and, depending upon the host, download free software. These services are provided at no cost to the user in an effort to keep the company's webpage bookmarked as your primary starting point. The company can then sell

Fig. 6.1. Even misspelled searches generate documents with similar keystroke errors.

Fig. 6.2. Netscape's Netcenter is an easy interface to use to quickly search several engines.

advertising space on their website and simultaneously promote their product in publicly traded stock markets.

It is important to realize that when you use a search engine, you are not actually searching the entire Web. You are only searching the database used by that engine. It is true that these databases are very large, but they do not contain information about everything on the Web. Information about webpages gets into the database in one of two ways: knowbots or site notification. Whatever the search engine sponsor chooses to call them, the majority of data provided by search sites is gathered through "knowbots," "robots," "'bots," "spiders," or "crawlers" (Berry and Browne 1999). **Knowbots** are programs designed to retrieve all of the publicly available data posted on the Internet and store it in a compact version on the main search engine server. If you have placed something online (say, in the form of a webpage or discussion-group posting), eventually one of the knowbots will record that data. Twenty-four hours a day, seven days a week, knowbots crawl around the Web, finding and then storing data in a mammoth index (Sonnenreich and MacInta 1998). The second method, site notification, is really just a way to speed up having your site indexed. When people or organizations build new websites or place important documents online, they usually like to have interested parties know about it. To list their data on any particular search engine, they submit their URLs directly to the service. Then the engine's knowbot is sent to abstract the site, which is then added to the database (Snyder and Rosenbaum 1998). A fast way to get your site into the search engines' databases is to use one of the online website registration services that send out notifications to multiple search engines for a fairly reasonable fee (anywhere from $20–100 depending upon how many search engines are to be contacted) (Deulloa 1999).

Pros and Cons

The obvious advantage of using a search engine is that it searches the entire Web—or at least that portion of it that is stored in the engine's database. Out of all of the tools we're discussing in this chapter, search engines search the largest portion of the materials online. You'll get the most results for your key term when you use a search engine. However, this can also be a disadvantage: using a search engine can give you more hits—or search results—than you know what to do with. If you were to type in the word "toy," for example, you would get back thousands of pages, since that word shows up on countless websites.

Another problem with using search engines is that you are relying on the people who put up the pages to correctly identify their pages. To understand why this leads to problems, you need to know a little bit about how knowbots work. When these programs find a page on the Web, they don't just store information about that page in the database at random. They use complicated algorithms to rank the importance of that data. For example, most databases will pay the most attention to the words in the title of the page, and those that show up in the first few lines of text or frequently on the page. Some pages also use a **keywords meta-tag,** which is a line in the HTML code of a page that programmers can use to identify what the page is about. How can this cause problems? Well, many webpage designers who are aware of this will use it to their advantage, putting a word such as *sex*, which they know will be searched for a great deal, into the title or keyword section of the code, even if the page has nothing to do with the subject. And many other beginning Web designers fail to properly identify their pages in the title through simple ignorance, or even fail to title the page at all. Or they might start off the page with a paragraph that is irrelevant to the rest of it.

For these reasons, when you use search engines that index the entire Web you are likely to get a very long list of results, including many pages that have little or nothing to do with the subject for which you were searching. You're also not likely to get the pages put up most recently, since the knowbots haven't had a chance to index those pages yet. But despite these drawbacks, many people continue to use these pages as their initial research tools because they are the easiest to find and use. But ease should not be equated with quality.

DIRECTORY OUTLINES

What Are They?

The second most familiar research tool is the interactive **directory outline,** an extensive series of general to specific lists of subtopics and websites that can either be browsed through or searched. Directory outlines evolved from the early days of the Web (circa 1995), when ambitious

TEXT BOX 6.1

SEARCH ENGINE ADD-ONS

Natural Language Inquiries

Some of the more advanced search engines, such as AskJeeves.com, understand questions entered into the search engine that are worded naturally. For example, you could ask, How do I use search engines? The machine grammatically filters out all unnecessary words, focusing in on the key terms, and directs the question to the appropriate source. In this case, the word "how" and the question mark would probably lead Jeeves to send you to a frequently asked questions page (FAQ). Many of these software developments come from the work of noted linguists and semanticists (Lappin 1997). They make searching a little easier for the average person who is unfamiliar with advanced searching techniques.

Language Translation

If you speak another language or are currently learning another language, pay attention. Many search engines now house documents compartmentalized by their given language. If you speak Russian, German, Chinese, or even Latvian, you can select your language and enter key terms just as you would in your other tongue. Some search engines even have Web-based translation devices that convert foreign documents to your selected language of choice. These tools have done wonders for international and intercultural communication. Imagine having the ability to read a website written in German through a translation program, or have Germans view your site in their native language!

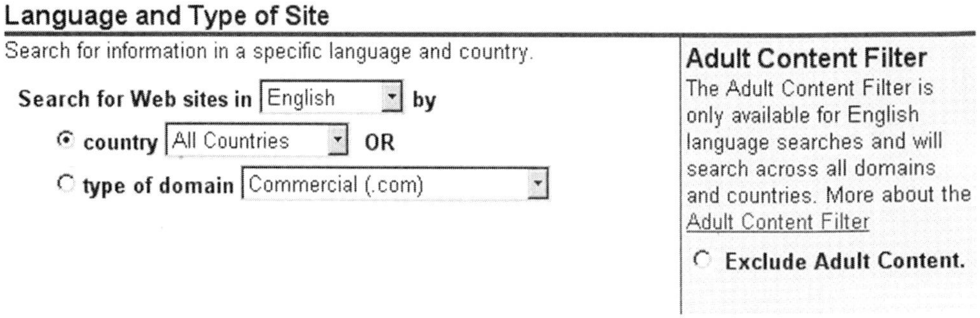

Language and Type of Site

Search for information in a specific language and country.

Search for Web sites in [English ▾] **by**

  ⊙ **country** [All Countries ▾] **OR**

  ○ **type of domain** [Commercial (.com) ▾]

Adult Content Filter

The Adult Content Filter is only available for English language searches and will search across all domains and countries. More about the Adult Content Filter

  ○ **Exclude Adult Content.**

Fig. 6.3. Controlling the content of your search.

Content Control Settings

Several sites have now installed content control features that allow the owner of a given computer to define what that machine's browser can and cannot access when visiting that company's search engine. This is a mutually beneficial relationship for both the company and the user because this not only ensures that the users may be more inclined to engage in repeat visits but it also protects the user from undesired data. Content control settings can be set for multimedia products (such as audio and video) as well as textual references to whatever is defined as "offensive" by the user. Altavista, for example, farms out this responsibility to a group known as SurfWatch, which monitors data on the Web and classifies it into several borderline categories. Among the more popular items blocked from viewing by these content control settings are drugs, alcohol, tobacco, gambling, hate speech, sexual explicitness, and violence. The ability for users to easily control the data-gathering components of their favorite search engines is becoming a necessity in the ever-expanding wealth of online content.

individuals began trying to categorize everything online. Moving from general to more specific sets of categorization, directory outlines provide structured option sets. In other words, you can actually see and select the categories of data containing links to other suggested topic areas or web-sites **(Figure 6.4).** If you wanted to search for a fan page for your favorite musical group, you would work your way down through categories such as entertainment, music, classic rock, Aerosmith, and fan groups. Finally, you would find links to several fan groups, perhaps grouped by location.

Over the last few years, search engines and directory outlines have begun to merge. As the number of Internet users began to substantially increase in the latter half of the 1990s, the two formats became an integrated platform (Miller 2000). Today, search engines that used to be exclusively key-term driven now offer directory outlines, and search engines that used to be just directory outline-oriented now allow for key-term input. Not to be outdone by the other model, each adopted the properties of the other.

Pros and Cons

The biggest advantage, which once again can turn into a disadvantage, is that directories are organized by humans. Directories such as Netscape and Yahoo! do not subscribe to the practice of knowbot data retrieval. The argument against knowbots is that they gather far too much insignificant data. Their method is to employ actual people to categorize new data. From its inception, Yahoo! has always adhered to this model, hiring

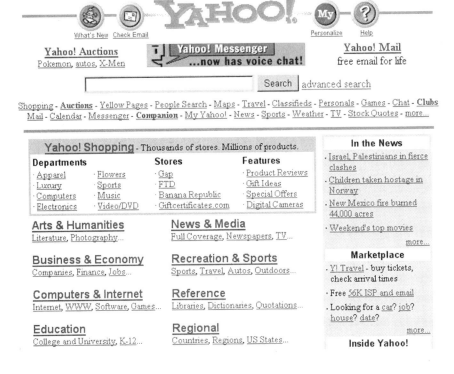

Fig. 6.4. When people think of searchable topic directories, they often think first of Yahoo.com.

employee topic managers to classify and categorize links. Netscape, a relative newcomer to this practice, is still recruiting user-editors to volunteer their net knowledge and services.

Two benefits come from using humans to categorize websites. First, unlike many of the knowbot-generated databases, Netscape and Yahoo!'s community-based attention provides for the consistent monitoring of dead or abandoned sites. As a result, their users generally encounter far less **link rot,** a term used to describe the deletion or relocating of a particular website without its location being erased or fixed in search engine databases. Second, some people find Internet searching confusing (Robbins 1997; Teicher 1999). For them, the directory outlines are of great help, because another human being has already done some of their research for them by classifying the sites. This classification system also makes people feel more confident that the site will actually have what they're looking for.

But classifying websites is not without its problems. Imagine you're trying to find a "custom ping pong paddle manufacturer." To find it, you have to figure out the correct sequence of subcategories. Looking under "recreation," then "sports," then "table tennis," then "equipment," may seem intuitive enough when presented in this sentence. But figuring out the correct category to go to next when you're using the directory can be difficult, not to mention time consuming if you have a slow connection. Thankfully, most directories also provide a search tool to quickly jump to the correct category.

A final disadvantage of directories is that they are more limited than search engines. You will only find the sites that have been categorized. This may be to your advantage if you are just browsing, since you won't be overwhelmed by unrelated sites. Directory outlines make it easy to quickly check out a number of related sites, a task that is much more difficult with a search engine. But it is a disadvantage if you are looking for something very specific and fairly unusual. For instance, if you were looking for the now-infamous sound clip of President Clinton stating that he "had no sexual relations with that woman, Ms. Lewinsky," we suggest sticking with a search engine. While you may quickly find hundreds of Clinton websites via a directory outline, it is unlikely that the person managing that section of the outline has reduced the world of Bill Clinton to such a microscopic level. Then again, you might just get lucky and happen upon the file while reading someone's webpage.

BIBLIOGRAPHIC DATABASES

What Are They?

Bibliographic databases are focused collections of reference and research materials such as journals, books, etc. These databases are put together by professionals, indexed according to keywords, and often have abstracts of the article/book or even the complete text. Because of the massive amounts of work that go into creating and maintaining these databases, there is often a fee to access them. However, most college libraries subscribe to several databases, which you can access from computers in the library and sometimes from any computer on your campus. For example, EBSCO*host* **(Figure 6.5)** allows you to search through popular periodicals, research journals, ERIC documents, and much more, and includes the full text of many of the articles. And of course, most libraries today provide a Web interface to the database of books held in the library's collection **(Figure 6.6).**

Pros and Cons

It is important for you to understand that if you're doing academic research, your best bet is a bibliographic database. Most of the "stuff" that

Tip: To search within a single database, click on the database name listed below. To select more than one database to search, check the boxes next to the databases and click on the ENTER Button.

`Enter`

☑ **MasterFILE Premier**
Provides full text for 1,820 periodicals covering nearly all subjects including general reference, business, health, and much more. Click here for a complete title list. Click here for more info

☑ **Academic Search Elite**
Provides full text for over 1,250 journals covering the social sciences, humanities, general science, multi-cultural studies, education, and much more. Click here for a complete title list. Click here for more info

☐ **Business Source Elite**
Provides full text for over 960 journals covering business, management, economics, finance, banking, accounting, and much more. Click here for a complete title list. Click here for more info

☑ **ERIC**
Provides citation and abstract information from over 750 educational journals and related documents from the Educational Resource Information Center and educational symposium report literature dating back to 1967. Click here for more info

☐ **Health Source Plus**
Provides full text for nearly 270 health periodicals, over 1,000 health pamphlets, and 23 health reference books. Click here for a complete title list. Click here for more info

☐ **USP DI Volume II, Advice for the Patient**
Provides patient-oriented drug information in lay language. Monographs are organized into the following sections: Brand Names commonly used in both the United States and Canada, Description, Before Using This Medicine, Proper Use of This Medicine, Precautions, and Side Effects. Click here for more info

☐ **Clinical Reference Systems**
Provides over 7,000 reports, in every-day language, describing symptoms, treatments, risks and after-effects of a vast array of medical topics and conditions. Click here for more info

☐ **Newspaper Source**
Provides selected full text articles from 143 U.S. and international newspapers. Click here for a complete title list. Click here for more info

Fig. 6.5. EBSCO*host* allows you to search indexes of research journals, newspapers, and much more–for a fee.

Western North Carolina Library Network
Appalachian State University   Western Carolina University
University of North Carolina at Asheville

Search the Library Catalog

- AUTHOR
- TITLE
- KEYWORD
- SUBJECT
- PERIODICAL TITLE
- AUTHOR/TITLE
- CALL NUMBERS

- Search Reserves by Instructor | Course
- View your library record or renew books
- Suggestions for your library | new books

- About ABC Express
  Request materials from another WNCLN library
  ABC Express Calendar

- Frequently Asked Questions
- Telnet to WNCLN
  Text version of catalog

About WNCLN | ASU Library | WCU Library | UNCA Library | Other Library Catalogs
Comments? Problems? Send e-mail to the Webmaster.
Copyright 1995, 1996 (C) by Innovative Interfaces Inc. (INNOPAC) All rights reserved

Fig. 6.6. Most libraries let you search their collections from the Web.

general search engines and directories find or catalog is just that: stuff that anyone could have published. The "stuff" in a bibliographic database is academic research, which has been carefully and scientifically conducted and has been reviewed and edited by experts. We'll talk more about standards for evaluating what you find online in the next chapter; for now, it's enough to know that the materials you find here have already passed many of these rigorous standards.

Most of the time, what you find in a bibliographic database is a reference to the actual printed material. For example, the library database will tell you the call number of a book, and you will have to go through the book stacks to find it. Some databases do provide the full text of some of the more recent periodical articles, but often you'll have to go to your library's collection of journals to find the research article that you need. This may seem like a disadvantage, but online bibliographic databases are much easier to use than printed catalogs. And if you're trying to find rigorous, scientific research that will be acceptable to your instructor, you won't find a better tool for your search than a bibliographic database. Of all the searching tools we discuss in this chapter, bibliographic databases provide you with the most reliable information.

One acknowledged drawback of these databases is that they rely heavily on human effort. Because of this, they are likely to be slightly out of date. It is difficult for a periodical index, for example, to stay on top of thousands of publications that come out monthly, biweekly, or even weekly. However, with advances in automation these databases are doing an increasingly better job of staying current.

SITE-SPECIFIC SEARCH ENGINES AND SITE MAPS

What Are They?

Site-specific search engines are search engines that only search the data on a given website **(Figure 6.7)**. **Site maps** are dedicated outlines of a site's layout, which can be used as a navigational guide. Site maps are very much like directory outlines, except that they are dedicated to the site at hand and show how its pages are connected. Both of these tools, often used in conjunction with one another, are very effective at helping users find the data they seek when visiting an unknown site. You have probably seen a site-specific search engine or directory outline without ever realizing it. Often, when you visit the site of a company that sells products online, you will notice that they have a key-term input box built into their interface for customer searching. Computer equipment companies, news sites, financial and trading institutions–just about any online entity that keeps track of products or data now uses these tools.

The main order of business for site-specific search engines and directory outlines is to provide quick access to the data contained on that

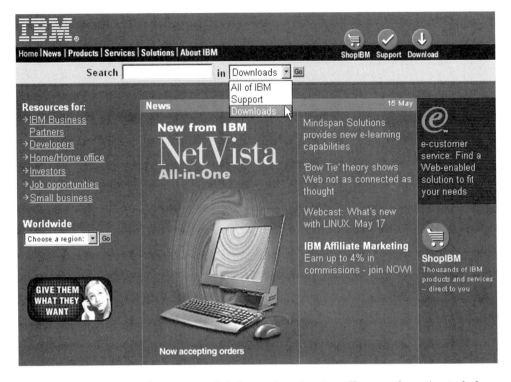

Fig. 6.7. Some sites have so much information, they install a search engine to help you find what you need.

site. Most site-specific search engines do this rather well. When using these tools, treat them just as you would a major search engine or directory outline. Since most of the software driving these search engines has either been purchased from, installed by, or is actually being run on the computers of the very companies who authored the major search engines, it really is a case of "learn one, you've learned them all."

Pros and Cons

Since site-specific engines only search the site to which they are attached, obviously they are far more limited than general search engines. But this is not necessarily a disadvantage. If you can find the right site, a site-specific search will give you very specific, specialized, highly targeted information without a lot of unrelated results. If, for example, you're looking for information about the types of engines in the latest line of Toyota pickups, you could use a general search engine to try to find this information. But it would be a lot faster and less painful to first go to www.toyota.com and use the site-specific search tool.

You've probably picked up on an obvious disadvantage, however. If you are doing research into Toyota trucks because you are planning to buy one, only using the Toyota site search engine is going to result in highly biased data from only one source. A second disadvantage is that you have to either know the location of the site that you wish to search or else find it with a general Web search. And that is quite often the approach that researchers take: find a good site with a general search engine, then search that site with its own site-specific tool.

SUBJECT-SPECIFIC SEARCH ENGINES AND DIRECTORY OUTLINES

What Are They?

Once programmers figured out how to direct knowbots to read specific files and directories across the Internet, the introduction of a new type of search interface emerged around 1996: the subject-specific search engine. These tools are unique because they do not attempt to organize the entire Web, nor do they focus upon the data contained on any one site. Instead, subject-specific search engines and directory outlines seek out the data stored on many different websites about a particular topic or theme. Basically, if you want to know anything about Captain James T. Kirk, pregnancy and parenting, or water sports **(Figure 6.8),** it is possible that a search engine dedicated strictly to that data already exists.

Pros and Cons

Obviously, subject-specific search engines have many of the same limitations as do site-specific ones. Granted, subject-specific tools have limited

Fig. 6.8. Aqueous.com, and sites like it, attempt to pull topic areas together on the Web through one searchable interface.

applications because they only search through a very specific type of data. But if you happen to want that type of data, they can be invaluable. Of course, you have to find them first, which is an additional challenge. The website Search.com **(Figure 6.9)** can help you with this, since it is a clearinghouse of subject-specific search engines.

These tools raise an ethical issue as well. Many of the subject-specific search engines and directory outlines are being created by topic enthusiasts. Occasionally, they will advertise these subject-specific engines as comprehensive, when, in fact, they are not. For example, if you were interested in purchasing some new golf equipment, you might consult one of these search engines and feel confident that it was covering all related sites. However, the engine might be programmed to omit a certain brand or distributor of equipment that might present competition at some level. These subject-specific engines are excellent tools to use when the data is not critical. If you are making large purchases, health decisions, or other critical issues, be forewarned that they are only as good (and biased) as the person who programmed the knowbots.

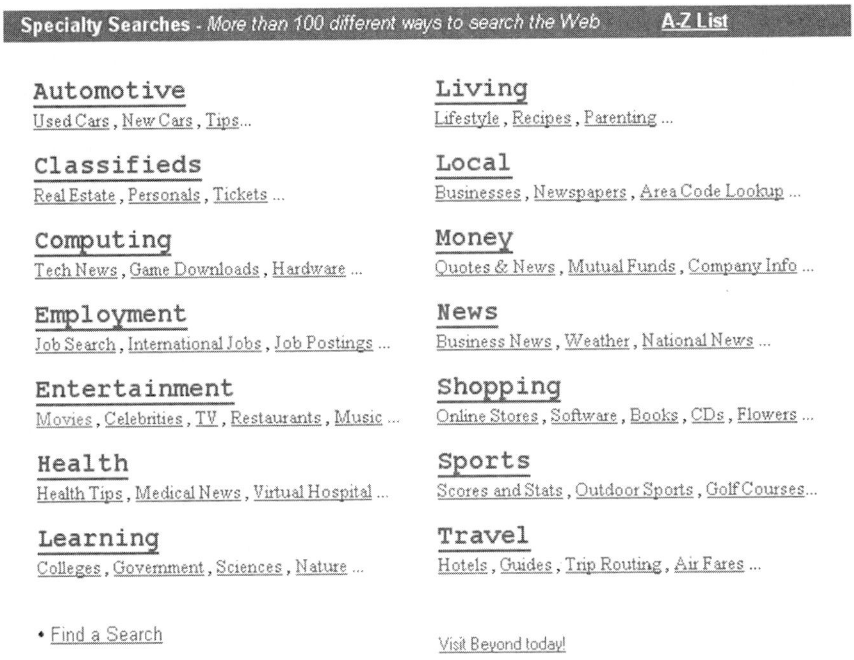

Specialty Searches - *More than 100 different ways to search the Web*   **A-Z List**

Automotive
Used Cars , New Cars , Tips...

Classifieds
Real Estate , Personals , Tickets ...

Computing
Tech News , Game Downloads , Hardware ...

Employment
Job Search , International Jobs , Job Postings ...

Entertainment
Movies , Celebrities , TV , Restaurants , Music ...

Health
Health Tips , Medical News , Virtual Hospital ...

Learning
Colleges , Government , Sciences , Nature ...

Living
Lifestyle , Recipes , Parenting ...

Local
Businesses , Newspapers , Area Code Lookup ...

Money
Quotes & News , Mutual Funds , Company Info ...

News
Business News , Weather , National News ...

Shopping
Online Stores , Software , Books , CDs , Flowers ...

Sports
Scores and Stats , Outdoor Sports , Golf Courses...

Travel
Hotels , Guides , Trip Routing , Air Fares ...

• Find a Search

Visit Beyond today!

Fig. 6.9. Some of the categories of specialty search engines available at Search.com.

METASEARCH ENGINES

What Are They?

Metasearch engines (or **metaengines**) are search engines that submit a key term to several independent search engines, comparing and contrasting the results **(Figure 6.10).** In other words, type your search terms into one spot, and the metaengine will send it to several different engines for you. Many people use metasearch engines because the assumption is that they will do the most complete search of the Web. They believe that the metasearch engine is the answer to most, if not all, of their searching problems. In theory, metasearch engines make a lot of sense. This is, of course, why they are so widely used. Unfortunately, in practice they are not as efficient or commanding as we would like them to be (McGonagle and Vella 1999).

Metasearch engines do not put together their own data; each is merely a portal, or interface, to many other search engines. Unlike general search engines, metasearch engines do not use knowbots to gather their own data. The metasearch engine's only contribution to the actual search comes in the content-comparison formula that each site creates as a means for sorting through the various results. These comparison formulas vary from one metaengine to the next. In general, the metaengine gives higher importance to sites that show up toward the top of the results on several of the engines that it searched. Metasearch engines

Fig. 6.10. Metasearch engines like AskJeeves.com are very popular.

also often include other capabilities; for example, the ability to remove duplicate hits and rank or sort materials in multiple ways.

Pros and Cons

It is true that metaengines can make it easier for you to search several engines at once. But while the metasearch engine may sound like a clever way to search for content, it is important to realize that these engines have several critical shortcomings. Some metasearch engines do not adapt the search request to fit the required syntax of each of the various search engines. As a result of its inability to, say, capitalize the word "and" for a search engine that requires it, the metaengine simply misuses a particular engine's data. As is the case with any "universal" tool, metasearch engines sometimes lack refinement and sophistication.

Two other problems: first, metasearch engines cannot possibly go deep enough into each database to get accurate results. Because it queries several search engines, only about 5% to 15% of the data on every responding search engine is successfully queried before the metaengine moves on to the next search tool. If the metasearch engine did not do so, a query might take several minutes instead of several seconds. Finally, metaengines are often a bit behind the times. Major developments in search technology occur on the general search engines far before they do the metasearch engines (Kahaner 1998; Burwell, Ernst, and Sankey 1999).

Beyond these deficiencies, there are a couple of benefits to using the metasearch engine. The leading benefit is that you get a snapshot sample of the online data available about a specific topic. The results of a metasearch tell you what most people who query these search terms in search engines believe to be representative of the topic. For a preliminary search, metasearches are one of the best tools. The other benefit of the metasearch engine is that it can search through more documentation than webpages alone. Depending upon which metasearch engine you use, most of these services scan Usenet newsgroup postings, FTP sites, and intercompany subscription databases. For instance, Dogpile.com, one of the Web's better metasearch engines, has the ability to scan Headhunter.net's employment database for the positions it lists throughout the Internet.

TOPIC RINGS

What Are They?

Topic rings (a.k.a. **webrings**) are a method of interconnecting topically related material on the Web into an easily navigated collection. Topic rings are a way for Web designers to link their page to similar efforts. These rings are like a community of data, a virtual neighborhood of similar sites. Most of the time, topic rings appear as small tables at the bottom of a site's homepage. Ordinarily, inside these small boxes you will also find hypertext selections like: First, Last, Next, Back, Random, Next 5, Last 5, and Ring Center. By selecting First in the option box found on every page admitted into the ring, your browser will go to the very first site on that particular topic ring.

Let's say that you have been browsing the Web, looking for some new basketball shoes. Using a search engine, you find someone's personal website dedicated to everything Michael Jordan–including, yes, his favorite brand of basketball shoes. At the bottom of this Michael Jordan page, you see a small box marked The MJ Fan's Michael Jordan Webring. What you probably did not know is that you are viewing Air Jordan topic ring document number 352 out of 917 possible. As far as you could tell, you were simply on someone's website reading about Mike. And you would be right too, because the topic ring navigation system is merely a means to reach related sites. Topic rings do not interfere with the data, operation, or behavior of the individual website. What makes this Jordan website different from a traditional standalone site is that it is part of a confederation of sites related to that topic.

From this topic ring site, you may now browse the Web as if it contained *only* Michael Jordan documents. You can either go page by page, clicking the hypertext terms Next and Back, which will walk you forward and backward through the sites flanking your current site, or you can randomly retrieve a new site in the ring by clicking Random. Or, you could even advance forward in the ring by five documents, or backward by five documents.

Typically, topic rings are managed from a remote site that has a special program installed to govern the operations of the topic ring. The "ring leader" often recruits sites about the topic into the ring via e-mail and enters their location onto an enumerated list. This enumerated list is then used by the ring program to govern which site is next or back, which link will be the random site, et cetera.

Pros and Cons

Topic rings are a different sort of research tool, since generally they are not searchable. The advantage to a topic ring is that it allows you to quickly reach related sites that have been organized by a group of living and breathing people. These groups often serve an editorial function, ensuring that the sites on the ring are active and to some extent reliable sources. However, just as you can encounter built-in biases in subject-specific search engines, so too you can encounter topic rings that only present one side of the story. Since you can't search through topic rings, you have to browse through them. We should forewarn you that some topic rings have as many as 2,000 participant sites, while some are merely 10 to 15 sites small. Browsing through a small ring can be an enjoyable way to see what many different people have to say about a subject; browsing through 2,000 sites in an attempt to see everything is probably not a good idea.

FREQUENTLY ASKED QUESTION PAGES

What Are They?

Frequently asked questions (or **FAQ**) **pages** are compilations of the most frequently asked questions pertaining to a given topic, usually assembled on a single webpage that is updated by the proprietor. FAQ pages are typically a series of questions with corresponding essay responses **(Figure 6.11).** Traditionally, the questions appear in a logical sequence, moving from general to more specific items of inquiry. FAQ documents are usually very thorough, well-organized products–usually. These are documents created by authors at the request of or for the benefit of a particular group. In most cases, these communities create FAQ pages that have been cross-checked and are fairly reliable. FAQ pages often evolve over time as a result of much online dialogue. If the same question is asked and answered over and over, someone will eventually post the answer to a page where people can read the answer at any time.

FAQ pages can be extremely powerful resources for answering some of life's little (and big) questions. There seems to be a FAQ page available

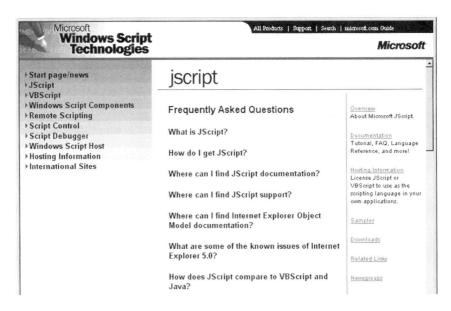

Fig. 6.11. Frequently asked question pages can be found on almost any topic where there is a community in need of data.

for almost every topic imaginable: lawnmower engine repair, bass fishing, personal finance, chemotherapy, etc. The makers of these documents do not charge for their topic-oriented research. Even though some of the authors of these documents are professionals in their respective fields, the creation of a FAQ page is regarded as something of an online public service. FAQ pages also relieve online experts of the burden of having to answer 400 e-mails asking the same question.

When setting out on a quest to find a FAQ page specific to your data requirements, you should always begin with a legitimate **FAQ library.** FAQ libraries are websites dedicated to storing and updating FAQ pages. Many of these FAQ libraries ask the authors of outstanding FAQ pages to submit updated versions of their document whenever they are renewed. Since this is a public service effort, many authors comply, understanding that their data will be made available to new audiences who come to entrust the FAQ library's claim to recency, immediacy, and quality. We have listed several of the better FAQ libraries on the textbook's website, and encourage you to visit them.

Pros and Cons

As we noted earlier, online data is always changing. FAQ libraries attempt to authenticate FAQ documents. But the decentralization of the Internet breeds a certain type of **data chaos.** Data chaos occurs when authors lose track or control of their webpages, resulting in time-based stagnation, multiple counterfeit versions, or false authorship. You may find that some FAQs are hopelessly out of date, or have been so distorted that you end up making plastic explosives in your oven instead of a double-fudge birthday cake.

But most importantly, the advantages and disadvantages of any FAQ depend on the authorship. Most FAQ pages are excellent sources of well-researched, cross-checked, and verified answers. But some groups that put together a FAQ page may share a unique view of the world. The Heaven's Gate cult members who committed group suicide were known to disseminate FAQ pages explaining the particulars of their belief system that, while considered unorthodox (even insane) by outsiders, were considered factually accurate by the cult members. So pay careful attention to the source of a FAQ page. We'll discuss the importance of checking the authority of a page more in chapter 7.

EXPERT INQUIRIES

What Are They?

Expert inquiries are direct requests for data from a recognized expert or body of experts. Once you have thoroughly exhausted the online searching process and still cannot find the data that you need, it is probably time to contact an expert or two. Several websites can help you find an expert in a given area. However, many of these sites function as something of a clearinghouse for speakers and consultants who are more than willing to help—for a fee. If money is no object, then many of these services are quite good. In fact, you are more likely to get a well-grounded and solidly researched series of answers from a paid professional than not. We provide a list of the better expert-referral agencies on our website for you to consider. On the other hand, if you cannot afford the services of your own personal online expert, knowing where to look for friendly experts and how to ask for data may be extremely beneficial (Lane and Burwell 1996). By the way, there's nothing wrong with contacting an unpaid expert. It simply depends upon the degree of advice that you require and the level of interaction you wish to maintain over time.

Finding an expert depends on the topic of interest. If the topic is, say, medical science, you could consult your local hospital's website and try to locate your medical practitioner's phone number or e-mail address. Your best bet is to search for the e-mail addresses of experts at sites dedicated to public research and service, including hospitals, colleges and universities, research think tanks, and professional or academic organizations. Colleges and universities are an excellent choice, for several reasons. First, it is the mission of every college and university to help distribute knowledge. Second, they commonly house a wide range of experts. The likelihood that you will find an expert in biology, business administration, chemistry, or even communication is almost certain. A final reason, which must not be overlooked, relates to simple geography and the collection of resources available on any given campus (Jones 1997). If you contact an expert source at a local institution, chances are you could set up a face-to-face meeting to get even more detailed information. And when you have such a powerful collection of intellectual resources at your disposal, it only makes sense to use them whenever necessary. If this, too, fails, then try consulting the organizational site of your local government agency (Andriot 1999; Notess 1998; Berinstein and Bjorner 1998).

If you can't get in touch with an expert, you might want to try reaching a whole group of them instead. You can reach these groups by using either a listserv or a newsgroup. Chances are good that if you can find a listserv or newsgroup related to your topic, one of those people knows the answer to the question you have. For example, one of the authors of this text once had a quotation from Bertrand Russell, and he needed to find the source. He could have searched through everything Russell wrote, but that would have taken forever. Instead, he went to a site that indexes listservs (www.tile.net), searched for "Bertrand Russell," and found a listserv dedicated to studying Russell's work. He subscribed to the listserv, sent a message with the quoted text, and asked the group for the source of the quotation. Within 15 minutes, he got a reply back telling him the book and page number of the quotation.

Many newsgroups are archived, which means that old messages are stored. If they're stored someplace, that means they can be searched. Chances are good that if you have a question, someone else has already asked that same question and gotten an answer. Many search engines can be told to search through newsgroup archives. One of the best sites to use for such a search is http://www.deja.com **(Figure 6.12).** At this site, you can search through thousands of messages, and perhaps find just the advice that you need.

Pros and Cons

The advantages and disadvantages of using expert inquiries can be summed up in two words: human nature. Some people are by nature extremely giving of their time and helpful; others, frankly, are not. If you

F i g . 6 . 1 2 . In the vast online discussions, you can find almost any information.

contact an expert that is unhelpful, do not give up. Instead, seek out another one. Eventually (hopefully quickly) you will find someone who is willing to take a minute or two to send you a quick answer to your question. If all of your inquiries are ignored, take a minute to read the next section of the book, which talks about how to improve your searches. There might be something about your message that is causing people to ignore it. One other thing to remember about expert inquiries and human nature: the quality of the answer you get back depends on the qualifications of the expert who answers. We'll talk more in the next chapter about evaluating the authority of data.

IMPROVING ONLINE RESEARCH

As we noted at the beginning of this chapter, the massive amount of shifting data on the Internet can be a bit overwhelming. Thankfully, several different tools have been developed to help you sort through that data and find what you are looking for. But as is the case with any tool, if you don't know how to effectively use research tools, you can end up wasting a lot of time and energy. In this next section, we'll talk about ways to improve your online research at three stages in the process: initiating, refining, and completing a search.

INITIATING A SEARCH

An old saying goes, "Well begun is half done." Even though this saying was coined long before the World Wide Web came into existence, you might think it was thought up by someone using the Web for research. Starting your search well is probably the best way to save yourself the most time.

- Pick the right tool for the job: with nine different choices, you need to think about which one is the most appropriate for your task. Think back on the various pros and cons that we discussed. If you have specific content that you're looking for, a site- or subject-specific search engine is probably your best bet. For example, if you are looking for a news story, don't waste your time searching the entire Web. Instead, go to a news source such as CNN.com and use their search engine. If you are looking for a friend's e-mail address and you know what school they attend, go to that school's website and use their directory search engine. In short, don't use a jackhammer to drive in a nail. If you know that the information you're looking for has a tool devoted to it, use it.

- Pick good keywords: when querying a search engine, you are better off using very specific search terms. The more specific you can be, the more likely you'll get relevant results. Try to use multiple keywords: think of synonyms and related people, events, or places. For example, if you are looking for information comparing the Intel and AMD chips, simply entering in the word "Intel" will pull up thousands of pages. Instead, enter in a series of terms: "Intel AMD chip compare speed processor." Also think about alternate spellings of words, and even misspellings. Some search engines will automatically search for variants of a word: for example, if you enter the word "house," they will also look for "housing, houses, housed," and others.

- Don't be lazy: chances are good that no matter how unique you think your question is, someone else has probably already asked it. Rather than asking the question again, search through archived materials such as FAQs and newsgroups first. While experts, generally, are more than willing to help people find their way, they typically don't tolerate laziness. Many people simply do not realize that these experts are bombarded with questions on a daily basis. That is *why* the FAQ page was invented in the first place. So before you waste the group's time, and more than likely invoke their wrath, make every possible effort to obtain the data on your own. It is a simple, but important, courtesy. If this genuinely fails, it is then logical to consult an expert.

- Phrase your questions to experts precisely: whether you are asking a search engine or a group of experts, the more specific your question is, the better response you will get. If you sent an e-mail message to a newsgroup of Web designers asking them how to design a webpage, you'd probably only get a very sarcastic or even vulgar reply. If, however, you ask them how to remove the border from a table using Macromedia Dreamweaver, you are more likely to get the answer you need. Many times you'll get better replies if you tell the group what you already know. That way, they will better understand what you are looking for, and you will be less likely to get data that you already have.

REFINING A SEARCH

Since these tools search through vast databases, they are more likely to give you too many results than not enough. Many of the sites that they recommend will probably be completely irrelevant. Luckily, most search engines have a whole series of commands that you can use to narrow your search, called **Boolean operators.** Boolean operators are terms used to manage the logical operations of the search engine. These operators are entered into the search input box along with your key terms and will give you much greater control over the search, with much better results.

- **And:** This operator forces the search engine to only pull up pages that contain all of the words that you enter. Say that you wanted to locate data about horse ranches in Mexico. You could simply type: "horse ranch Mexico." The search engine would then retrieve all of its known documents containing "horse," all of its documents containing "ranch," and all of its documents containing "Mexico." When the results came up you might find several documents containing the terms "horse" and "Mexico," without the word "ranch" appearing. To ensure that only documents containing all three of these words would appear in your results pages, you would enter: "horse **and** ranch **and** Mexico." On most engines, **and** can also be expressed by using the (&) or (+) characters.

- **Or:** This operator expands the search to include pages that contain any of the words that you enter. For instance, if you were doing research on the classic debate between Demosthenes and Aeschines titled On the Crown, you could try to locate the full text of the work by entering: "Demosthenes **or** Aeschines **or** 'On the Crown'." The search engine would find all of its known documents containing any of the three search terms. Using "or" will naturally expand your search, so if you are trying to get fewer results, use it in conjunction with "and." But if you continually run into walls with your searches, using this operator will definitely increase the number of results. On some search engines, you can substitute the symbolic character (|) for "or."

- **Not:** This operator excludes pages that have a particular term in them. Let's say that in this instance you wanted to find out more about an upcoming trip to Northern Africa that you have been planning, but did not want to waste time reading any solicitous data from a travel agency. A proper use of the Boolean operator "not" would appear as follows: "travel **and** 'Northern Africa' **not** agency." The search engine, recognizing the argument for "not," would disallow any documents containing the term "agency." As a result, only those documents containing "travel" and "Northern Africa" without the word "agency" in them would be issued to your results pages. Substitute characters for "not" include (!) and (-).

- **Near:** This operator pulls up pages that have specific words located close to each other. For example, you might be looking for data on making a good seafood gumbo. To do so on a search engine, you would enter: "gumbo **near** shrimp." This would inform the search engine that it needed to look for the word "shrimp" within 10 other words from "gumbo." Most search engines are automatically programmed to use a 10-word separator count, though some will use more or less. On some search engines, a tilde (~) can substitute for the word "near."

- **Asterisk:** The final Boolean operator we discuss is the wildcard asterisk, **(*)**. When you are unsure about the full or correct spelling of a particular word, or are interested in seeing what combinations a root word may have, the computer will search for the rootword either preceding or following the asterisk. For example, if you are looking for documents about litigation, or litigant, or litigator, or litigatious, you could do this easily by entering in "litigat*". The search engine will look for pages that have any word that starts with the letters "litigat."

- **"":** Although not technically Boolean operators, quotation marks are vital to maximizing the effectiveness of your search. They are used by many search engines to tell the program to look for a specific phrase. You may have noticed them in some of the examples above. If you are looking for an exact phrase and do not put it in quotation marks, the search engine will simply pull up pages that have any of those words anywhere in the page. So for example, if you are looking for a specific article on "recent trends in distance education" be sure to put it in quotation marks; otherwise, you are going to get hundreds of irrelevant results.

- **Advanced searching:** Many of the standard search engines have released a new service called the "advanced search." This service automates the Boolean techniques into a user-friendly, click-button environment **(Figure 6.13).** If you are familiar with Boolean operators, you will generally have no problem using the advanced search page.

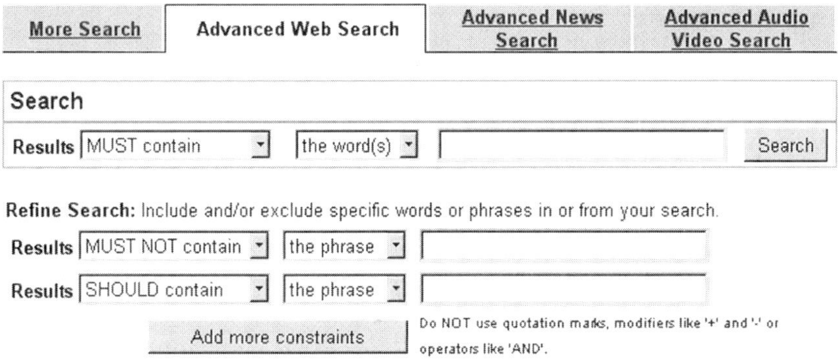

Fig. 6.13. Boolean searches made easy.

- **Read the directions:** Real researchers read the directions. Even though the Boolean operators we discussed here are fairly standardized, you will find some variation from one search tool to the next. So take a minute or two to read the help page that almost all of these tools provide. You just might find out, for example, that when using one particular tool you have to put Boolean operators in all capital letters.

COMPLETING A SEARCH

Once you get a research tool to generate some useful results, you might be tempted to think that your search is over. But before you start to celebrate your successful quest, you need to do three basic things.

- Verify the pages: if you're using a tool that provides you with a page of results, your obvious next step is to visit some of those pages. Some pages may not be what they claim to be. Remember that some unscrupulous Web designers will insert popular keywords into their page, so your search for data about MP3 files might turn up some pornography sites. And since, as we noted earlier, the Internet is undergoing constant change, some of the links may no longer work.

- Verify the results: every tool has its pros and cons. That is why thorough researchers will try multiple searches on a variety of different tools. Remember that many tools may have built-in biases that can taint your results. Using more than one tool can help you avoid this problem.

- Evaluate the results: once you find the information you are looking for, you need to assess how valuable it is. This is such an important issue that the next chapter is devoted entirely to discussing how to evaluate online resources.

BACK UP AND RELOAD

In this chapter, you've learned about the many tools for online research. Search engines can search the entire Web, which makes them an excellent tool for general searches. Directories provide users with a well-organized catalog of sites, which makes browsing far easier and more productive. Bibliographic databases search the most reliable sources of information, because they index research and reference materials that have met rigorous standards. Site- and subject-specific search engines only search through limited parts of the Web, but since they search through smaller and more specific databases, they can often generate highly relevant results. Although they are somewhat flawed, metasearch engines make it possible for you to submit your query to several search tools at once. Browsing the Web for information can be more productive if you find a topic ring, which connects related sites with a simple navigation tool. Finally, you can use FAQs and expert inquiries to get accurate, highly targeted answers to very specific questions.

But without a skilled user, any tool is useless. To increase your skill, remember the tips we discussed. Initiate your search by selecting the right tool and asking your question well. Use Boolean operators and advanced searching techniques to refine your search. Finally, be sure to verify what you find. Because it's not enough to simply find a needle in a haystack; you need to make sure that the needle is sharp.

BROWSE *and* BUILD

For sites to visit, exercises, quizzes to test your learning, and more, go to *www.harcourtcollege.com/ communication/inetcomm*

References and Readings

Ackermann, E., and K. Hartman. 1998. *The information specialists guide to searching and researching on the Internet.* Wilsonville, Oreg.: Franklin, Beedle, & Associates.

Andriot, L. 1999. *Internet blue pages.* Medford, N.J.: CyberAge Books.

Basch, R. 1998. *Cybersearch: Research techniques in the electronic age.* New York: Penguin Reference.

Berinstein, P., and S. Bjorner. 1998. *Finding statistics online.* Medford, N.J.: Information Today.

Berners-Lee, T., and M. Fischetti. 1999. *Weaving the Web.* San Francisco: HarperSanFrancisco.

Berry, M., and M. Browne. 1999. *Understanding search engines: Mathematical modeling and text retrieval.* Philadelphia: Society for Industrial and Applied Mathematics.

Burwell, H., C. Ernst, and M. Sankey. 1999. *Online competitive intelligence.* Tempe, Ariz.: Facts on Demand Press.

Calishain, T., and J. A. Nystrom. 1998. *Official Netscape guide to Internet research.* Albany: Coriolis Group Books.

Denning, D. 1998. *Information warfare and security.* New York: Addison-Wesley.

Deulloa, J. 1999. *The step-by-step guide to successfully promoting a website.* Escondido, Calif.: PromoteOne.

Doyle, A. 1999. A practitioner's guide to snaring the Net. *Educational Leadership* 56:12–16.

Engholm, C., and S. Grimes. 1997. *The Prentice Hall directory of online business information.* Paramus, N.J.: Prentice Hall.

Falk, J. 1998. The meaning of the Web. *Information Society* 14:285.

Forno, R., and R. Baklarz. 1999. *The art of information warfare: Insight into the knowledge warrior philosophy.* Upublish.com.

Glossbrenner, G., and E. Glossbrenner. 1998. *Search engines: For the World Wide Web.* Berkeley, Calif.: Peachpit Press.

Glymore, C., and G. F. Cooper. 1999. *Computation, causation, and discovery.* Boston: Massachusetts Institute of Technology Press.

Jones, G. 1997. *Cyberschools: An education renaissance.* Englewood, Colo.: Jones Digital Century.

Kahaner, L. 1998. *Competitive intelligence.* New York: Simon & Schuster.

Kennedy, S. 1997. *Best bet Internet.* Chicago: American Library Association.

Kushilevitz, K., and N. Nisan. 1997. *Communication complexity.* Cambridge: Cambridge University Press.

Lane, C., and H. Burwell. 1996. *Naked in cyberspace: How to find personal information online.* Wilton, Conn.: Pemberton Press.

Lappin, S. 1997. *The handbook of contemporary semantic theory.* Oxford: Blackwell Publishing.

McGonagle, J., and C. Vella. 1999. *The Internet age of competitive intelligence.* Westport, Conn.: Quorum Books.

Mead, H., and A. Clark. 1997. *The online research handbook.* New York: Berkeley Books.

Miller, H. S. 1997. The little locksmith: A cautionary tale for the electronic age. *Journal of Academic Librarianship* 23:100–108.

Miller, M. 2000. *The complete idiot's guide to Yahoo!* Indianapolis: Que Publishing.

Newhagen, J. E., and S. Rafaeli. 1996. Why communication researchers should study the Internet: A dialogue. *Journal of Communication* 46:4–13.

Notess, G. 1998. *Government information on the Internet.* Lanham, Md.: Bernan Press.

Reed, B. S. 1997. What kind of lever? How scholars use the Internet in their work. *American Journalism* 14: 217–18.

Renfro, C. G. 1997. Economic database systems: Further reflections. *Journal of Economic & Social Measurement* 23:43–86.

Robbins, C. 1997. *Exploring the Web: Using Internet hypermedia.* Berkeley: NetQuest Publishing.

Rowland, L. M. 1994. Libraries and librarians on the Internet. *Communication Education* 43:143–50.

Schlein, A, and S. Kisaichi. 1999. *Find it online: The complete guide to online research.* Tempe, Ariz.: Facts on Demand Press.

Snyder, H., and H. Rosenbaum. 1998. How public is the Web? Robots, access, and scholarly communication. *Proceedings of the ASIS annual meeting* 35: 453–62.

Sonnenreich, W., and T. MacInta. 1998. *WebDeveloper.com's guide to search engines.* New York: John Wiley & Sons.

Teicher, J. 1999. An action plan for smart Internet use. *Educational Leadership* 56: 70–75.

Want, R. 1999. *How to search the Web: A quick reference guide to finding things on the World Wide Web.* New York: Want Publishing.

Whitesitt, J. E. 1995. *Boolean algebra and its applications.* Dover: Dover Publications.

CHAPTER 7

What Do I Do with It?

Evaluating and Citing What You Find

By Peter Zale ©2000 Peter Zale, www.peterzale.com   Distributed by Tribune Media Services, www.comicspage.com

By the end of this chapter, you should:

I.   Understand how to evaluate webpages, based on the following criteria:
   A. accuracy,
   B. authority,
   C. audience,
   D. purpose,
   E. recency, and
   F. coverage.
II. Understand how to cite webpages.
III. Improve your use of Internet sources for research.

Imagine that you are taking a course in interpersonal communication, and you have a paper due. In this paper, you are supposed to make use of some expert sources to come up with a plan to improve some aspect of your interpersonal communication. You decide to visit your residence hall computer lab and hop onto the Internet for some expert information. The area that you think you need to work on is trusting other people, so you go to your favorite search engine and type in a few keywords: "trust," "self," "others," and "love" (for good measure). One of the pages the search engine retrieves looks promising: Putting Faith in Trust, at http://www.healinggateways.com/FaithInTrust.shtml. On this page, you find some quotations that you put into your paper–correctly citing the web-page, of course.

Now imagine your surprise when your paper comes back with a mediocre grade and the following comment: "This is not an expert source." How did your instructor come to this conclusion? Well, he or she probably visited the webpage that you cited, and then backtracked to the homepage of the website: http://www.healinggateways.com. If you had more thoroughly investigated the site where your document was located, you would have discovered a lack of any formal research studies supporting the site's suggestions–not to mention a link to "aura-soma consultations." The absence of credible research should have been an indication to you that this was not an expert source on trust and interpersonal communication.

The goal of this chapter is to help you avoid making this hypothetical situation into a reality. You are living in the information age, which means that you are being bombarded by advertisements, e-mail, television and radio broadcasts, and countless other sources of information. What that means is that one of the most necessary skills you need to develop is the ability to critically evaluate information. We want to help you become a careful consumer of information. You also no doubt will want to use some of the information that you find in papers or speeches. Thus in this chapter we will also discuss how to use what you find ethically and accountably. As in the last chapter, we will focus on understanding and improving: that is, understanding how to evaluate and cite Web resources, and improving your use of those resources in your research.

UNDERSTANDING EVALUATION CRITERIA

For as long as people have been producing information, other people have been trying to answer the question, How valuable or reliable is this information? Over the past few hundred years, researchers, librarians, editors, and other careful consumers of information have developed criteria for evaluating that information. There are numerous criteria out there; we have selected six that are the most relevant to evaluating information on the Internet: accuracy, authority, audience, purpose, recency, and coverage. This list of criteria is based primarily on the criteria proposed by Alexander and Tate (1998), with some of our own modifications and additions. These criteria were originally applied in one form or another to physical texts: books, newspapers, and other such ancient forms of information transmission. However, putting information on the Internet creates many unique challenges for the careful consumer of information. For each of these criteria, we will talk about the additional concerns that you need to be aware of when applying the criteria to web-pages.

ACCURACY

One of the first and most crucial questions you typically ask people about the things they tell you is, Is that true? What you are really asking here is how accurate and reliable the information is. One of the most common criticisms of the Internet is that it is full of unchecked, unverified rumors. If you already have an e-mail account, you've no doubt received messages urging you to send an e-mail to Disney so they will donate money to a child with cancer, or a message warning you about the "It Takes Guts to Say Jesus" virus. These are only two of the countless **urban legends** (stories that circulate throughout society, that might at one time have been based in fact but now have a life of their own) and virus hoaxes floating around the Web **(Figure 7.1).** Some standard tests of accuracy for information have evolved over time, and each of these must evolve

Fig. 7.1. The alt.folklore.urban newsgroup has a website devoted to urban legends of all kinds.

even further with the advent of the Internet. The three means of verification we discuss here are editorial checks, multiple sources, and personal experience.

Editorial Checks

In the case of traditional book and newspaper publication, information has to flow through several filters before it is deemed publishable. One primary filter is the editor, or more often editors, who are charged with the task of checking that the information was detailed as accurately as humanly possible. Before a textbook like this one is published, for example, the copy must be scrutinized by editors and reviewers to check for mistakes and omissions. However, the Internet has radically changed the dynamics of publication. Now, anyone with a basic computer, a connection to the Internet, and storage space on a server can publish their information to the world. Generally speaking, no team of editors and reviewers exists to verify the information for accuracy before publication on personal websites.

This lack of an editorial check is often celebrated as evidence that freedom of speech is advanced by this new medium. Unfortunately, freedom is sometimes advanced without a concurrent advance in argumentative accuracy or responsibility. When browsing the Web, pay close attention to whether or not the author has tried to ensure that the information on their webpages is accurate. Larger news sites will often have an editorial staff that checks the reliability of the information—partly because they are concerned about being sued for publishing inaccurate information. If the site has no obvious system of editorial checks (and even if it does), you ought to proceed with further verification steps.

Multiple Sources

A fundamental procedure that journalists use to verify information is to search for more than one source. If they cannot find another source to corroborate what they have learned from one source, they will not publish that data. This slows down the publication of news, but improves its accuracy. As traditional news outlets (such as the *New York Times* and CNN) develop their own websites, they have fallen prey to the momentum of the medium, emphasizing speed over accuracy. Traditional media are often scooped by Internet sources, since it is so simple to publish information on the Web. Without question, this has led to some embarrassing situations for traditional media outlets. Concerned that they might get beaten to the news market by a competitor, some established agencies have rushed stories to their websites without sufficient corroboration, only to later learn that the story was a rumor.

An advantage of the World Wide Web is that you can quickly seek out multiple sources, either by conducting a search and then looking at several of the results, or by following related links to new pages. However, you need to beware of **linked ethos,** which is the tendency to transfer your trust of the source of the original page to the source of a nonrelated linked page. If, for example, you are on a site that requires editorial checks and uses multiple sources such as CNN.com, and you follow one of their links to a different site, be aware that your impulse may be to assume that the information you find on the new site has gone through the same checks on accuracy. Many times, reliable sources will warn you when you are leaving their site so that you can reset your trust levels **(Figure 7.2).** Also, be wary of **linking loops,** where two or more websites link to the same information. Just because you can find a fact by following links on two different pages doesn't mean you've found a corroborated fact: it could just be the exact same fact, on the exact same page.

Personal Experience

If the information has gone through some sort of formalized review process and/or is confirmed by multiple sources you can probably trust it. But don't sell your own abilities short: one of the most basic tests of reliability is your own experience. And this one hasn't changed much with the coming of the Internet, except that you might not trust your other experiences if you are not familiar with the medium. But don't hesitate to apply your other knowledge bases to this situation. For example, how many times in your experience have companies donated money to any cause based on the number of letters they receive? None, in our experience. Now, do you think this would change simply because the letters arrive electronically? Doubtful, to say the least, wouldn't you think?

AUTHORITY

If you decide that the information is accurate, the next question you would likely ask is, Where did you hear that? Determining the source of

RELATED SITES:

NASA
NASA Human Spaceflight
Shuttle Countdown Online
The Hubble Space Telescope

Note: Pages will open in a new browser window
External sites are not endorsed by CNN Interactive.

F i g . 7 . 2 . Warning labels for when you are about to surf off the home turf.

information is another one of the most basic steps that we take in evaluation. Some sources are more credible than others: for example, we usually grant articles published in the *New York Times* more authority than those published in the *National Enquirer.* Additionally, we look at the source to determine if the information might have a known bias. If a classmate is trying to persuade you that gun control laws are unnecessary and cites statistics from the National Rifle Association to prove her claim, you might not question the accuracy of her information. But you certainly ought to suspect that the data could be slanted.

Authority can be either individual or collective. If you're looking for quality information about a new nasal spray for treating mold spore allergies, you might ask a friend who has had allergic rhinitis for years and thus has a great deal of practical experience. Or you might ask a doctor, since he or she has had years of formal education. In either case, you assign some authority to what they tell you based on what you know of them as an individual. On the other hand, you might decide to read up on the subject, looking for articles in medical publications that you respect, such as the *Journal of the American Medical Association* or *Prevention.* In this case, you may be more inclined to accept the information not because you know the author of the article but because you believe in the collective authority of the publication.

Assigning collective authority to websites works in much the same way. A site such as CNN.com is considered a credible authority on the news because of their adherence to journalistic values and information verification procedures. On the other hand, appraising individual authority is a far more difficult task. Many webpages do not include authorship information, making it difficult to figure out who posted the webpage in question. Many times you will encounter information out of context. A link that you get from a search engine, for example, might drop you onto a page that has no identifying marks and is somewhere in the middle of a website. Luckily, you can take some basic, straightforward steps to remedy this problem.

- Check the page for a **mailto** link: most pages will have some means of providing feedback to either the author or administrator of the page. Normally, you will see either an e-mail graphic or a hyperlinked e-mail address that you can select to send an e-mail to the person in charge. In the e-mail message you send, simply ask who the author of the page is and what their credentials are. Always copy the link of the webpage in question into your e-mail so that the network administrator can track your information down.

- Go home: if a search engine sends you to a page in the middle of a site, and there is no information about the author on the page, try finding a link to the homepage of the site. Often you will find the information you need there.

- Backtrack the URL: if you can't find a link to the main page for the site on the page you are viewing, then try deleting from the end of the URL by slash mark segments. For example, let's suppose you were searching for information on netiquette and one of the result links led you to http://www1.appstate.edu/~clarkne/ emailnet.htm. If you didn't notice the author identifying information listed at the bottom the page, you could still find out more information by cutting off everything after the last slash in the URL. Going to http://www1.appstate.edu/~clarkne/ would take you to the homepage of the author. This technique would have saved our example student at the beginning of this chapter from receiving a poor grade.

- Use the source, Luke!: sometimes, the program that the person used to make the page inserts his or her name automatically into the hidden HTML code. In Netscape Navigator you can click on View > Page Source (or hit "Control-U") to see the source code for the page you are viewing. If you look at the top of the source code, you might see something like this: <META NAME="Author" CONTENT="Norman Clark">. This still won't tell you anything about the author, other than his or her name. But it will give you a good place to start.

If these methods fail to provide you with information about the author, that doesn't mean you should entirely disregard the information found on the webpage. If it passes all of the other evaluation criteria that we list in this segment, it is probably worthy of your consideration. That said, you should treat this (or any) information that you encounter with a solid dose of skepticism.

AUDIENCE

As we noted in the opening chapter, communication has a lot to do with audience adaptation. When an author writes a book, or an agency creates an advertisement, or a production company develops a television series, they do so with a target audience in mind. It is obvious why the producers of communication are endlessly concerned about audience; after all, if they want to reach people who are constantly bombarded by information, they have to construct a message that speaks directly to those people, meets their needs, and attracts their interest. They must frame a message that *identifies* with their audience and find an audience that *identifies* with their message.

When considering a message, you ought to ask the question, For whom did they make this information? Careful consumers of communication know that the intended audience of a message ultimately shapes the motive behind and the content of a message. For example, a book about cancer would be quite different if it were written for doctors than if it were written for children, or parents of children with cancer, or adults with cancer. Figuring out the intended audience can help you determine whether or not the information is appropriate for your needs.

Even though webpages can reach an audience of millions, as technology enthusiasts are quick to point out, they are still usually produced for a limited audience. You can determine for whom the page was intended by looking at the following information:

- Identity statements that say who "we" are: for example, the intended audience for the Sting fan club page Sting etc. (http://stingetc.com/) should be blatantly obvious.
- Language level: pages intended for children obviously would use a more limited vocabulary and simpler syntax.
- Jargon level: pages intended for professionals in a particular field will include more specialized terms.

Once you've determined the audience for the page, you have to evaluate whether or not you, as a consumer of information, fit into that audience. Sometimes you will find that highly accurate information, from well-respected authorities, may be too esoteric and advanced to be useful for your purposes. Because, as you evaluate this information, you have to consider if it is appropriate not just for yourself but also for *your* intended audience. If the page is too simplistic or too difficult, keep searching until you find something that speaks to an audience at the same level as the audience you plan to address. Otherwise, you will have to "translate" the information into language that your audience will understand. This is a bit risky, since unless you understand the subject very well errors will probably crop up in your translation.

PURPOSE

Communication, according to noted critic Kenneth Burke, is human action and not just animal motion. What he meant is that when we communicate, we do so with a motive, a purpose. Whether we are writing a letter, talking on the phone, or sending e-mail, we have a goal in mind. For example, when *Consumer Reports* prints an article comparing the safety features of that year's new pickup trucks, their primary purpose is to *inform* you. When Toyota airs an advertisement for a new truck, their primary purpose is to *persuade* you to buy one. When Greenpeace sends you a brochure detailing the negative impacts of oil spills, their primary purpose is to *advocate* social change and possibly even get you to contribute to their campaign. And when film directors shoot a pickup truck jumping across a canyon, their primary purpose is to *entertain* you.

Sometimes, the purpose of the communicator is clear cut and easy to distinguish. This isn't always the case, of course. If you have watched late-night television, you have likely seen programs discussing the wonders of food dehydrators, spray-on hair, and the infamous buns of steel. The infomercial has become a blend of information, persuasion, advocacy, and (if you have a particularly bizarre sense of humor) entertainment. Much of our communication is blurred to the point where it becomes difficult to identify a message as being purely informative, persuasive, advocative, or entertaining. It is safe to say that very little of our communication has solely one purpose.

On the World Wide Web, multipurpose communication is definitely the norm. Many people still refer to the internet as the Information Superhighway, implying that its role is informative in nature. However, the emphasis would probably be better placed on the word "superhighway," since, like our interstate highways, the Web is cluttered with the virtual equivalent of advertisement billboards: banners trying to persuade us to buy the latest and greatest products. As you browse the Web, keep the following tips in mind to help you evaluate the varying purpose(s) behind the blast of communication you will encounter.

- Post-dot analysis: pay attention to what comes after the last dot (".") in the URL address for a website. If the address ends in .com, it is a commercial site and its primary purpose is probably to persuade you to buy a product. If it ends in .gov, its primary purpose as a government site is probably to inform. A .org site, the home for an organization, probably intends to advocate for their cause.

- Balance: pay attention to the presentation of information. Are both sides of an issue given equal treatment, or is only one side discussed? Is one side consistently presented in a positive light, and the opposite side presented negatively? If you sense an imbalance, the purpose of the site is probably either to persuade or advocate and not to inform. To be an effective communicator, you need to be familiar with both sides of an issue. So either seek sites that present balanced information, or go to more than one site to strike a balance in your reasoning.

- Is that a fact?: pay attention to the presentation of facts and opinions. If you see many statements beginning with phrases such as "I think," or "in my opinion," be aware of the intended persuasion behind such statements. Warning lights should go off in your head when opinions are presented as facts. Go back and look for the author of this information. Is their opinion a valuable one? If you're searching for valuable information, you ought to be looking for facts and not opinions. After all, everyone has an opinion, including you.

RECENCY

If you had to write a report about current trends in interactive television, you would (hopefully) know better than to use a source dated 1997. Many fields, especially within the area of new communication technologies, are changing so rapidly that it is difficult to stay current. The recency of information has always been a concern for effective communicators. The assumption is that newer information is likely to be more accurate. Of course, some fields of study, such as the classics, are less affected by this concern. Generally speaking, though, every field of formal study is striving to develop a more recent, more applicable body of knowledge. Thus, any time you are doing research, you need to pay attention to the date on the source you are using.

A major advantage of using the Internet for research is that you can get extremely current information. While books can take years to be published, websites can be posted in an afternoon. So if you are doing research in a rapidly changing field, such as new technologies, you will often find the most recent developments posted online.

Just because you find something online, however, does not necessarily mean it is current. And unfortunately, quite often webpages do not tell you the date that the information was published. Many webpages will simply have no date on them. Most pages on a professional news website will probably have a date at the top of the page; some private individuals put dates at the bottom. But even when you can find a date (on a webpage), that information can be ambiguous. Is this the date the webpage was first written? Or is this the date that the document was first placed online? Or is this the date the page was last revised? Or does the date stand for something else entirely? If it was last updated on that date, was the content updated or did the author simply change the color scheme? There are an infinite number of dimensions to this issue.

If you cannot find a date on the page, or you are not sure exactly what the date means, look for another source of information: the e-mail address for the developer of the page. Most pages on the Internet do have an e-mail link on them so that you can send feedback to the Web administrator. This person may not actually be the author of the page, but they may be able to help you determine the recency of the information, perhaps by helping you get in contact with the actual author. Following these simple suggestions will help you ensure that the information you use from the Internet remains current.

COVERAGE

Once you've found a site that has a credible author, is recent and up-to-date, objective, and accurate, the final question you will probably ask is, Is the topic covered in sufficient depth? With traditional media outlets, the depth of coverage is directly related to the time it takes to produce the message. Nightly news broadcasts and newspaper staffs, for example, have a little less than 24 hours to develop their content. Weekly news programs such as *60 Minutes* and *20/20* are allotted more time, and therefore usually provide better in-depth coverage of their stories. Magazines and academic journals are often released in either monthly or quarterly periods, depending upon their circulation. And books can take months, or in some cases years, to write. Thus we have come to expect that a book about the history of the Internet will go into more depth and offer more complete coverage than, say, a newspaper article or a news broadcast on the same topic. It is a matter of time and expectations.

That's why even though the Internet speeds up the publication of information and your access to that information, you won't necessarily find the most complete coverage online. In fact, speed of publication and access almost always result in lower quality information, with more superficial coverage. This is not to say that there aren't some high-quality websites out there with a great deal of in-depth content; it's just that those sites are few and far between. What you are far more likely to find online right now, however, are pages with links to other pages, with little original content. Most of the news sites offer the same type of limited-depth coverage that they put out in their newspapers and television shows.

Regardless, the advantage of the Internet is that if you can't find the depth you need at one site, chances are pretty good that you can find several additional sites with more information. In fact, most news sites take advantage of their ability to archive old stories and will include at the bottom of a current page a list of links to older, related stories. By making use of a variety of sources, and by going back into archived materials, you should be able to increase the quantity and quality of information that you gather about your topic. However, if you need highly detailed information about the migratory patterns of African swallows, your best bet may be to find a good old-fashioned book.

UNDERSTANDING HOW TO CITE

Once you've found information that you believe will help you in your communication efforts, you need to correctly use it. In the context of college writing and speaking, this means you have to cite any information that you get from other sources. Citing sources is necessary for two very important reasons. First, if you do not cite the sources you use, it is called plagiarism. Plagiarism is defined as presenting someone else's ideas as your own. At the college level, plagiarism is an extremely serious offense and often results in penalties as severe as expulsion from school. It is treated so seriously because academia is built upon the exchange of ideas. If you take someone else's money and use it as your own, this is stealing. If you take someone else's ideas and use them as your own, it is the exact same concept. Thus, in academic writing you must identify any information that you get from other sources to acknowledge your debt to the person who did the original research or had the original thought.

Second, citing your sources is necessary so that your reader can find the same information you found, where you found it. If you find a particularly intriguing quotation, or some startling new statistics, chances are good that your listener or reader will want to look up your source. They might not trust your account of the details and need to double-check to see if you quoted your data accurately. Or you might have succeeded in sparking their interest, and they might simply want to learn more about your find. Either way, you need to give them enough information to find the source that you used. This is standard academic and professional protocol, which you will be required to follow no matter the career you select.

This is where the Internet brings almost insurmountable challenges to research. As you might have already discovered, pages on the Internet do not last very long. Entire websites come and go faster than you can download a *Star Wars* movie trailer. Sometimes the information is still available somewhere online, but it has been moved to a new directory or location. The file structure instability of the Internet means that you need to be even more careful when citing the information you find. It's not enough to simply list the URL for the page, since chances are good that within a matter of days or weeks, typing in that URL will bring up a totally different page. Or, even worse, you might find no data except the dreaded "404: Not Found" error message.

The main thing to remember when citing information on the Internet is that your reader (or your instructor) needs enough identifying information to find that page. One of the advantages of the Internet is that it has several different search engines and ways of finding information, as you learned in the last chapter. Your goal should be to give your reader enough data so that even if the page does get moved, it can still be found. Obviously, the title of the page is crucial, since that is what most search engines pay attention to. And nearly every webpage will probably have a title. Traditionally, you also cite the author and date of publication, but as you learned in this chapter, quite often webpages do not list either. However, academicians skilled at style guide precision have developed some excellent solutions to these challenges.

TEXT BOX 7.1

CITING AND REFERENCING WEB MATERIALS

Citation

**American Psychological Association
(*Electronic Reference Formats* 1999)**

Citing Entire Websites

Format:

APA states that if you are citing an entire website, it is not necessary to list it in your references. Instead, you can simply give the address in the text.

Example:

Online retailers such as Amazon.com (http://www.amazon.com) are rapidly increasing their sales.

Personal Webpages

Format:

Author/editor. (Year published). *Title of page* (edition). Retrieved [date] from the World Wide Web: address.

Example:

Adams, T. (1999). *C.V. of Tyrone L. Adams.* Retrieved December 19, 1999 from the World Wide Web: http://www.cajuncomm.com/faculty/adams/vita2000.htm.

Online Journal Articles

Format:

Author. (Year). Title. *Journal Title, volume* (issue), paging or indicator of length. Retrieved [date] from the World Wide Web: address.

Example:

Gronbeck, B. (1998). Underestimating generic expectations: Clinton's apologies of August 17, 1998. *American Communication Journal, 2*(2). Retrieved December 19, 1999 from the World Wide Web: http://www.americancomm.org/~aca/acj/acj.html.

Online Magazine and Newspaper Articles

Format:

Author. (Year, month day). Title. *Magazine Title, volume* (if given), paging or indicator of length. Retrieved [date] from the World Wide Web: address.

Example:

Makovsky, D. (1999, December 17). Preparing for the end times. *U.S. News-Online.* Retrieved December 19, 1999 from the World Wide Web: http://www.usnews.com/usnews/issue/991227/jitters.htm.

Discussion List and Listserv Messages, Personal Communication (E-mail)

Format:

APA treats all such messages as personal communication. Thus, they are not cited in the reference list, but only in text. You should provide the initials and surname of the person who sent the message, as well as the exact date.

Example:

Community network pages at times lack a sense of connection to their physical communities (N. Clark, personal communication, November 17, 1999).

Modern Language Association (*MLA Style* 1999)

Personal Webpages

Format:

Author/editor. Page Title. Access date <address>.

Example:

Adams, Tyrone L. Homepage. Accessed 20 Dec.1999 <http://www.cajuncomm.com/faculty/adams/vita2000.htm>.

Online Journal Articles

Format:

Author. "Title." *Journal Title* volume.issue (Year of publication): Access date <address>.

Example:

Gronbeck, B. "Underestimating Generic Expectations: Clinton's Apologies of August 17, 1998." *American Communication Journal* 2.2 (1998): Accessed 20 Dec. 1999 <http://www.americancomm.org/~aca/acj/acj.html>.

Online Magazine and Newspaper Articles

Format:

> Author. "Title." *Newspaper or Magazine Title* Date of publication. Access date <address>.

Example:

> Flanigan, James. "IBM's Shift to Information Services a Model for New Era." *Los Angeles Times* 20 Dec. 1999. Accessed 20 Dec. 1999 <http://www.latimes.com/business/19991219/t000115526.html>.

Discussion List and Listserv Messages

Format:

> Author. "Subject of Message." Posting method. Date. Contextual information. Accessed date. <Archive link or discussion/listserv address>.

Example:

> Baym, N. "Call for Papers: Association of Internet Researchers." Discussion list posting. 30 Nov. 1999. Posted on the Computer-mediated Communication Listserv of the Communication Institute for Online Scholarship. Accessed 30 Nov. 1999. <CMC@cios.org or Support@cios.org for support>.

Personal Communication (E-mail)

Format:

> Sender <sender's e-mail>. "Subject of Message." E-mail to recipient (Recipient's E-mail address). Date. Contextual information. Access date.

Example:

> Whillock, R. K. <rkwhillock@mail.smu.edu>. "Revisions to Our Manuscript." E-mail to Tyrone L. Adams. 10 Dec. 1999. Pertaining to publication release in ACJ. Accessed 10 Dec. 1999.

In-Text References

American Psychological Association

- It has been suggested that the U.S. is in the midst of a great postmodern renaissance (McGee, 1999, paragraph 3).
- McGee suggested that the U.S. is in the midst of a great postmodern renaissance (1999, paragraph 3).
- In 1999, McGee suggested that the U.S. in the midst of a great postmodern renaissance (paragraph 3).

Modern Language Association

- It has been suggested that the U.S. is in the midst of a great postmodern renaissance (McGee 1999, paragraph 3).

- McGee suggested that the U.S. is in the midst of a great postmodern renaissance (1999, paragraph 3).

- In 1999, McGee suggested that the U.S. is in the midst of a great postmodern renaissance (paragraph 3).

All of the major style guides have developed forms for referencing webpages. The most commonly used style guides for academic writing are the **American Psychological Association (APA)** and the **Modern Language Association (MLA).** In the accompanying text box you will find guidelines for citing basic electronic resources. If you have an unusual resource, check the style guide texts for specific guidelines. Note that we made one minor change to the MLA style guide. In front of the accessed date, we added the word "Accessed." This makes it more clear why two dates are listed.

Of course, it's not enough to simply list webpages at the end of your paper. You also need to reference where you use these sources in the body of your work. Here again, the Internet brings several new challenges. Traditionally, when you use a direct quote from a source, you are required to list the page of the quote. However, webpages do not have page numbers. You could list paragraph numbers, or you could count the number of screens that you have to go down to get to the quoted words. But if you think about the logic behind listing a page number, you will understand that neither of these are necessary. You are supposed to list the page number of a direct quote so your reader can quickly find those words in a long document. With a webpage, however, it is quite simple to find where those words are located even in a long document, since Web browsers allow you to search in the page to find a specific word ("Control-F" to find). Thus page numbers are not only impossible to identify with Web references but also unnecessary. The correct format for in-text references for the APA and MLA styles is also in the text box.

You should always consult your instructor as to how, exactly, in-text references are to be formatted. Every scholar has their own preference. But in general, three methods based on the (author, date, location) system are used. Where pagination or paragraph numeration cannot be supplied, simply use the (author, date) system. If there is no author, you should use the first three words in the title to identify the reference. The only major difference between the two styles is the lack of a comma between the author and the date in the MLA style.

IMPROVING ONLINE RESOURCE USE

What we have been talking about in this chapter and the previous one is preparing for effective communication. And as we noted in the first chapter, a key component of communication is considering the nature of your audience. In the case of writing college research papers, your audience will be your instructor. So to improve your use of online resources, this section will discuss how instructors evaluate papers that use Internet resources. This "insiders" look through your instructor's eyes should make your paper writing more effective.

First, you ought to begin with the understanding that most of your instructors will probably have a bias against Internet resources. As you have learned in this chapter, this bias is not without good reasons. A large part of being a professor has to do with research, and the goal of research is to produce verifiable and credible knowledge. This means that professors tend to privilege (or value most highly) information that goes through a process of careful critique and review before it is published. This is the exact opposite of most information on the Internet, which is often placed online without any editorial checks. We're not saying that all information on the Internet is garbage; after all, we wouldn't be dedicating so much time to the topic if we didn't think it was important and valuable. But you should realize that even the authors of this textbook are more likely to trust information found in a scholarly journal than information found on the Internet. This means that of the tools we discussed in the last chapter, your safest and most reliable tools are the bibliographic databases.

Some of your professors have been online for at least as long as you have, if not longer. And even those who haven't been online as long are aware of the Internet's reputation as a source of ill repute. You will probably even find some who believe that the Internet is simply too easy; that "real" research requires great effort and rigor. And to some extent, they're right: information quickly obtained is often less valuable than knowledge acquired through careful and painstaking work. If you are aware of this bias, you can take steps to ensure that it does not interfere with your message:

- Use websites that your instructor will recognize and that have built-in credibility. The URL www.nationalgeographic.com will be less likely to raise your instructor's suspicions than, say, www.geocities.com/~bubba/.

- Confirm the information that you find online with another source. Using multiple sources will reduce suspicions that the information is inaccurate.

- Try to find information online that has gone through a peer-reviewed process. Many academic journals and magazines are now launching content online and maintain the peer-review process, which makes this data more valued.

Besides a general bias against the Internet, many instructors also know that the Internet has become a repository for plagiarized works. Many students find it difficult to resist the temptation to cut and paste entire paragraphs from their Web browser directly into their word processor without properly citing them. Graphic images are also grabbed and stuck into papers without proper documentation, often in violation of copyright laws. Worse yet, several sites on the Web make papers available to students, allegedly "for research purposes only," that can be downloaded for free or a fee. These prefabricated papers are then turned in for credit. Besides being against every academic integrity code in existence, this practice is extremely dangerous because scholars are now aware of this maneuver. Antiplagiarism sites are already springing up; these sites will analyze a suspect paper to see if it has come from a paper mill. Search engines make it relatively easy for your instructor to find exact phrases in any page online, as you now know. So if you could find the information with relative ease, chances are certain that your instructor will be able to do so. After all, remember that we do research for a living. To avoid being suspected of or charged with plagiarism, take the following precautionary steps:

- Cite your sources carefully. Make sure you use the style guide recommended by your instructor, make sure you put the complete citation information in the reference list, and make sure you correctly note any place where you use the sources in the body of your work. Ignorance of the correct citation format is, unfortunately, no excuse (especially since so many online versions of style guides now exist).

- Use few direct quotes. Instead, paraphrase or summarize information, putting it into your own words to show that you understand what you are talking about. Make sure to cite the source that you used to develop the paraphrase or summary, of course. Identify the source of the paraphrase or summary as soon as you begin: for example, "According to the CIA World Factbook, terrorism has been increasing in the following countries . . ." Make sure that your paraphrases really are paraphrases; don't use the same phrases or sentence structure that the original source used.

Finally, a common problem with papers that rely heavily on Internet sources is that they develop a structure much like the Internet itself: an almost random collection of statements and facts, without a central organizing theme or sustained argument. As beginning researchers browse the Web, they encounter a useful page, then another, and then another. The connections between the pages seem obvious while browsing; after all, the pages were linked, so the information must be related! Unfortunately, their reader didn't share that same browsing experience, so the connections may not be obvious to him or her. But when these students write their papers, they often simply insert ideas from these sources one after another, without spelling out the connections for the reader. Sometimes the connections are there and just need to be explained with a transition sentence that links the two ideas together. But sometimes two linked webpages actually have no logical connection. You can avoid the patchwork quilt paper effect by doing the following:

- Develop an outline of your argument first, then find evidence to support your position. This will help keep you from inserting "cool stuff" from a webpage that you found while browsing, but that really has nothing to do with the argument you are trying to make.

- Between ideas, use strong transition sentences that review the previous idea, preview the upcoming idea, and show the connection between the two. This is good advice for any writing or speaking, but particularly so when using Internet sources. Remember that your reader wasn't with you when you browsed around the Web and thus didn't experience the connections as you did.

BACK UP AND RELOAD

Even though the Internet is called the Information Superhighway, that doesn't mean you should blindly race down it at 100 mph, ignoring the rules of the road. In this chapter, you learned six key criteria for evaluating the information that you find online. The test of accuracy asks whether or not the information is correct. The test of authority asks whether the source is a credible one or not. The test of audience asks whether or not the information is appropriate for your intended audience. The test of purpose asks about the objectivity of the page. The test of currency asks how old or new the data is. Finally, the test of coverage asks if the material goes into enough detail for your purpose.

Once the online content passes these tests, you need to cite it correctly in your own work. Citing is necessary so that you are not charged with plagiarism, and so that your readers can find the same information if they desire. You learned how to use the two most common citation styles, APA and MLA, to cite Web documents.

To help you make more effective use of online material, we put you inside your instructor's head for a while to see how they view Internet resources. Be aware of your instructor's probable biases against the Internet. Understand that plagiarism is a serious concern of your instructor that has been taken to a new level by online paper mills. Lastly, show the connections between ideas so your instructor is not left with the impression that all you presented was a string of random thoughts.

BROWSE *and* **BUILD**   For sites to visit, exercises, quizzes to test your learning, and more, go to *www.harcourtcollege.com/ communication/inetcomm*

References and Readings

Alexander, J., and M. Tate. 1998. *Web resource evaluation techniques.* Accessed 10 November 1999 <http://www2.widener.edu/Wolfgram-Memorial-Library/webeval/eval1198/index.htm>.

Electronic reference formats recommended by the American Psychological Association. Washington, D.C.: American Psychological Association. Accessed 12 November 1999 <http://www.apa.org/journals/webref.html>.

MLA style. 1999. New York: Modern Language Association. Accessed 15 December 1999 <http://www.mla.org/set_stl.htm>.

Part Four

Public Communication: Creating Webpages

Architecture starts when you carefully put two bricks together. There it begins.

LUDWIG MIES VAN DER ROHE

God is in the details.

LUDWIG MIES VAN DER ROHE

Now that you know how to find information on the Internet, you're ready to begin communicating what you know to the global audience of Web surfers and to add your knowledge to the database of cyberspace. Since the World Wide Web is a relatively new interface, the theories to explain it are still in development. But graphic design principles have been around for ages, and many of them can be applied to this new context. There are also more technical things to learn, because you need to know how to work with Web editors and graphics programs. In the next few chapters you'll learn the basics of creating effective webpages using these programs. Through it all, remember the words of the architect Mies van der Rohe. For your webpages to be effective, you have to pay attention to the details. And it all begins at the most basic level.

CHAPTER 8
What a Tangled Web
We Weave!

The Basics of Hypertext Markup Language (HTML)

By Peter Zale ©2000 Peter Zale, www.peterzale.com   Distributed by Tribune Media Services, www.comicspage.com

By the end of this chapter, you should:

I.   Be familiar with the development of HTML.

II. Understand how HTML:
   A. resolves system incompatibility issues,
   B. formats text,
   C. creates interactive documents,
   D. inserts multimedia content, and
   E. places data into a global communication context.

III. Know what a WYSIWYG HTML editor is, including its:
   A. definition,
   B. general layout,
   C. benefits, and
   D. drawbacks.

IV. Recognize the importance of learning HTML, since this knowledge helps you:
   A. teach others how to communicate online,
   B. be prepared for innovations in online communication, and
   C. borrow design techniques to use on your webpages.

If you are fortunate enough to speak more than one language, you are well aware of the benefits of being multilingual. Multilingual communicators possess the skills necessary to relate to new people, cultures, and ways of life. This is why most schools require some level of foreign language proficiency to ensure that their students mature and prosper in our increasingly multicultural world. On the other hand, if you are still a monolingual communicator, you probably know how difficult it can be to learn a new language. The reorientation in thinking and communicating can be challenging, to say the least.

The purpose of this chapter is to introduce you to a new language and in a sense a new way of thinking and communicating. But instead of studying a formal language like Arabic or Spanish, you will be learning a fairly simplistic computer programming language. We say "fairly simplistic" because, as programming languages go, hypertext markup language (HTML) is about as easy as they come. In fact, most professional computer programmers do not even consider HTML to be a bona fide programming language. They think of it as more of an advanced word-processing code with some added multimedia sizzle for effect. Still, if you have never before formatted documents in HTML, you will probably *feel* as if you are learning a new language. This anxiety will decrease, however, as you immerse yourself within the culture, customs, and techniques of coding. Our goal is to familiarize you with HTML–in concept and in practice–so that you can begin the process of self-education that is Web authorship.

In this chapter, we first introduce you to a definition and brief history of HTML. Next, we examine the significant characteristics of HTML, taking you behind the scenes of the code so that you can understand how it works. Third, we show you how to use a **What You See Is What You Get** (**WYSIWYG,** pronounced whiz-ee-wig) HTML editor, explaining both the benefits and drawbacks. And finally, we discuss the need to become as proficient as possible with HTML, to enhance your online communication.

DEFINITION AND BRIEF HISTORY OF HTML

DEFINITION OF HTML

HTML is a set of computer codes written in standard text that tells Web browsers how to assemble webpages, including the general layout, color schemes, text formatting, and graphical design. The collection of HTML commands that make up a webpage is known as its **source code.** Source code is what your Web browser reads from left to right, top to bottom, assembles, and then displays as the document you see onscreen when browsing the Web. Following are two screen shots. **Figure 8.1** is a portion of the webpage's source code, and **Figure 8.2** is the actual webpage that you would ordinarily view in your Web browser when visiting the *New York Times* online.

While the source code may look like gibberish to you right now, you should understand how webpages are assembled in browsers by the time you finish this chapter. Try going to one of your favorite websites and selecting View > Page Source in the Netscape Navigator menu bar. This will reveal the source code compiling that document. From this source code, try to get a feel for how HTML is being used in that document. When you start to feel overwhelmed, come back to the textbook to learn the theories behind this gibberish.

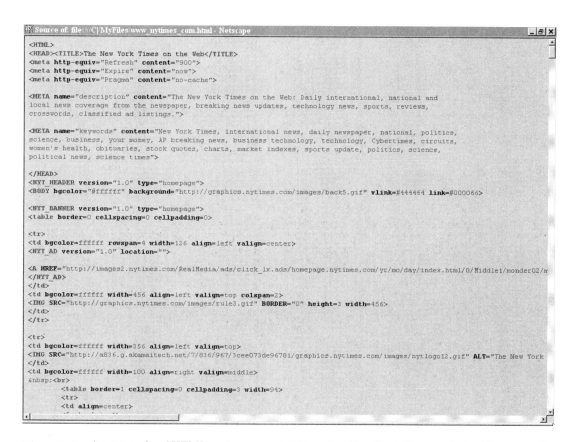

F i g . 8 . 1 . An example of HTML code, excerpted from the *New York Times* website. You can only see a small segment of the code.

The New York Times

ON THE WEB

NYC Weather
36° F

THURSDAY, DECEMBER 30, 1999 | Site Updated 12:20 AM

QUICK NEWS
PAGE ONE PLUS
International
National/N.Y.
Politics
Business
Technology
Science/Health
Sports
Weather
Opinion
Arts
Automobiles
Books
CareerPath
Diversions
Living
Magazine
Photos
Real Estate
Travel
MARKETPLACE
SITE INDEX

Nasdaq Index Ends Day Above 4,000 Points for the First Time

The milestone came less than two months after the index first topped 3,000, and was based largely on the strength of the technology stocks. Go to Article

A Bold Welfare Effort Leaves Much Unchanged for the Poor

After three years of tracking the nation's boldest antiwelfare campaign, what seems most noteworthy about the lives of the poor is not the change at all. Go to Article

Fund-Raising by Insurgents Outpaces Vice President Gore

Bill Bradley and John McCain made significant

(NYT)

Nearly six years after Baruch Goldstein killed 29 Muslims at a West Bank mosque, Israeli soldiers demolished a shrine at his grave. Go to Article

INTERNATIONAL
Hijackers Lessen Demands

POLITICS
Anti-Politician McCain Shows Political Skills

Fig. 8.2. This is the final product that you actually see in your browser.

BRIEF HISTORY OF HTML

You already know that the Web was developed by researchers in computer science and information technologies. Interestingly, however, the original proposal for a device that would operate in a fashion similar to the Web was made in 1945 by cognitive scientist Vannevar Bush (Moschovitis et al. 1999). In his landmark *Atlantic Monthly* essay, Bush proposed that ordinary microfiche films could be interconnected through a mechanical device called a Memex. As designed, the Memex would be able to interlink the data embedded within the microfiche, remembering points of interest. This would expedite research in the library, leaving a more permanent data impression on the human memory. Using the mind's natural inclination toward associative thinking rather than deductive thinking would accelerate human memory and thus knowledge, according to Bush. While the Memex never materialized, Bush had a profound impact on the author of hypertext.

At a trade show 15 years later, Douglas Englebart debuted an electronic communication package featuring e-mail and a text-based filing system called hypertext. Hypertext allows users to select predefined, highlighted words on a document by using the keyboard (or mouse) to control a floating point of reference (these days, an arrow-shaped cursor). If the highlighted word were selected by the user, the computer would retrieve a new document on-screen. Englebart's hypertext behaved exactly as the Memex device was theorized to, by associating keywords and statements with new documents. As the keyboard got more difficult to use with hypertext, Englebart invented the mouse in 1964 to provide for a more free form of textual interactivity (Abbate 1999). The two inventions, now inseparable, are the very tools that have made the Internet so accessible.

Englebart's innovations were quickly adopted by Xerox, IBM, Apple Computer, and Microsoft throughout the 1970s and 1980s, becoming accessories for the emerging personal computer. During the late 1980s when inter-networking began to diffuse throughout state agencies, universities, and major corporations, many administrators turned to the Internet's ability to unite work efforts (Cailliau and Gillies 2000). And, while upgrading computer equipment and software was easy, upgrading the humans that would accomplish these tasks was always a challenge. People simply did not want to learn the complex jargon necessary in those days to make the Internet work. So a more intuitive means of collaborating electronically became an early necessity for those who wanted to use the Internet for research and collaboration.

This problem was shared by Tim Berners-Lee, a programmer at the European Laboratory for Particle Physics in Geneva. By 1988, Berners-Lee had grown tired of having to reformat the latest version of a research document into each of the differing computer formats supported at the laboratory. Further, Berners-Lee and his staff were quickly becoming linguists because many of the researchers using these reports spoke one of Europe's many languages (Berners-Lee, Fischetti, and Derotouzos 1999). As fate would have it, they also shouldered the responsibility of machine translating these documents and reformatting each translation into each format supported at the laboratory. Five computer formats and three European languages quickly became 15 documents, all of which needed to be released simultaneously. The task became a tedious, energy-consumptive chore from which Berners-Lee and his staff wanted to free themselves. So they set out on a mission to create a means of making highly formatted data available to their researchers through the laboratory network. The unspoken mission here was to also create a means simple enough to allow the original authors of the documents to format their own work. The team's innovation became known as the hypertext transfer protocol (http), or the World Wide Web–powered by HTML. **Figure 8.3** is a copy of Berner-Lee's ingenious draft of the Web.

However well the browser worked with text, it lacked the graphical user interface (GUI) environment becoming popular in the early 1990s.

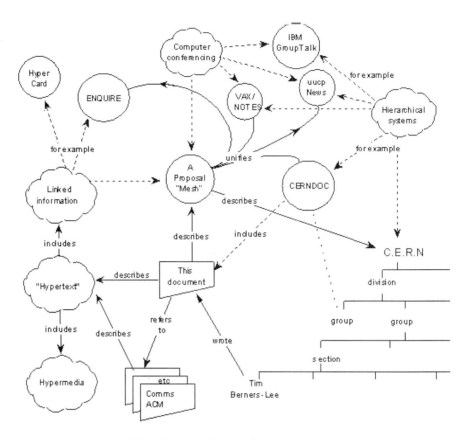

Fig. 8.3. A copy of Tim Berners-Lee's original rough draft plan for the hypertext markup system.

It had no icons to click, no pictures, and was in a drab version of black and gray. The browser's focus on functionality lacked the multimedia flair that was becoming an expectation of many users. All of this changed when Marc Andreessen was introduced to Berners-Lee's browser and protocol set in 1992. Andreessen, a multimedia specialist from the University of Illinois at Urbana-Champaign (UIUC), was involved with the institution's NSF supercomputing project. There he had unlimited computing resources and a group of kindred minds focused upon making the supersystems at UIUC more accessible to the nation's networked institutions. Up until that time, Andreessen and others were trying to find a way to synthesize several data formats into one "experience." They correctly bargained that they could add the media components that the Berners-Lee hypertext browser lacked. Their mission was twofold: to make the new browser (1) user friendly and (2) able to handle as many media properties as possible. Within several months, they released the National Supercomputing Agency's multimedia-capable browser, named **NSCA Mosaic** (Reid 1997). By 1993, it had been installed on over one million machines.

The paths taken by each of these two researchers-developers after 1993 are important in the evolution of the Web and HTML as public resources. Berners-Lee chose the high road, becoming director of the **World Wide Web Consortium (W3C),** a not-for-profit research organization geared toward promoting standards and innovations in Web-based communication. To this day, Berners-Lee remains at the W3C, promoting the standards for HTML design used worldwide. Recently hailed as one of the top 100 minds of all time, he has even authored a best-selling book based upon his invention. On the other hand, Andreessen teamed up with Jim Clark, a Silicon Valley venture capitalist who also founded industry giants Silicon Graphics and Healtheon. Together, Andreessen and Clark founded Netscape Communications (now owned by America Online), and helped reinvent the way the world communicates. Playing out the societal roles of rogue sage and capitalist, these two conceived a vast frontier where anyone who knew the code, the language, could stake their claim in cyberspace.

CHARACTERISTICS OF HTML

HTML is an easy formatting code to learn. In fact, after you read this chapter you should be able to identify and create the essential features of the Web. However, you should know up front that it is not our goal to make you a completely proficient HTML author. If you want to learn advanced HTML, we suggest several well-written books on our website. While learning the basics of HTML can be accomplished in one chapter, mastering the code is a much more time-consuming process. What follows is a list of the general characteristics involving HTML, and how these characteristics are authored via HTML source code.

RESOLVES SYSTEM INCOMPATIBILITY ISSUES

You are no doubt aware that computers come in many different flavors: Windows-based machines, Macintoshes, VAX, Unix, Linux–the list goes on and on. Remember that one of the main reasons Berners-Lee invented HTML was to create a coding system that would bridge the gap between these machines. This system incompatibility is resolved by HTML in four ways:

1. HTML is completely authored in text. Almost all computers use the **American Standard Code for Information Interchange (ASCII)** character set for text. Remember that computers deal with electrical currents that are converted into binary numbers— if the current is off, it's a 0; if it is on, it's a 1. ASCII uses a seven-bit long binary code for each letter. For example, *a* is 1100001 (which you know as 97). Using this standardized code to represent numbers and letters makes HTML readable by every platform (Burns 1998). If you create a file on your Windows machine and save it in ASCII text format, you can be sure it will be understood by a Macintosh or a Linux machine.

2. HTML uses that plain text to create universally browser-recognized "tags" or "arguments." Tags are the symbolic means of manipulating webpage content. Every browser, on every platform, recognizes a tag by its distinctive less-than, greater-than encapsulation. One of the codes you need to know, for example, is the first code that will appear on every webpage you author: <html>. This tag is recognized by the browser because it has been programmed to treat **<anything inside these mathematical symbols>** that matches the HTML vocabulary as a command. In this case, the <html> command informs the browser that it is about to read an HTML document and should therefore treat all forthcoming tags according to HTML code.

3. HTML works on a simplistic on/off formatting principle. Whenever the browser encounters a tag, it turns on that setting. Until another tag tells the browser to stop, it will continue to apply that tag's function. For example, when the browser comes across the tag that tells it to start italicizing text, <i> *everything after that will be displayed in italics until it is shut off by the ending tag* </i>. End tags are created by putting a slash in front of the command letter(s). In this case, if you didn't include the </i> tag, everything on the rest of the page would be in italics too.

4. New HTML tags are released in versions by the World Wide Web Consortium and are universally incorporated into all new browsers. The fact that the various manufacturers of Web browsers support the W3C as the *de facto* authority of HTML keeps the code consistent between browsers. Because the W3C works to ensure that HTML cannot be usurped by any corporation, the code remains an open source for anyone to use. However, several companies have begun to manufacture their own **proprietary codes** that only work in their browser and will not function within their competition's browser (Barksdale 1997). For example, Netscape has several different tags to create layers on the page that are not supported by Internet Explorer. These new proprietary codes

mean that quite often pages look very different from one browser to the next. They also make life more complicated for new webpage designers.

FORMATS TEXT

Another of the major issues confronting Berners-Lee was that his computer network flattened all word-processed formatting whenever documents were sent via text-based e-mail. This means that any document lost all formatting–be it boldfacing, underlining, colorization, etc.–once copied and pasted into older e-mail utilities. Of course, files could be attached to e-mail messages, but it was originally a complicated and unknown procedure for most. So HTML was designed with text-formatting commands. This way, more complicated documents could be created and viewed on different machines around the world. **Table 8.1** lists the primary text-formatting HTML codes.

CREATES INTERACTIVE DOCUMENTS

Another important characteristic of HTML is that it makes documents interactive through **hyperlinks.** A hyperlink is the selectable text or graphic on a webpage that tells your browser to retrieve other content located online; this content can be new webpages, specific places targeted within webpages, multimedia files, or even e-mail addresses. The ability to transfer a user from document A to document B, K, or Z is why we call it the Web. By hyperlinking reference points throughout the Internet with HTML, we create a web of data.

The power of the Web, of course, lies in its **referential immediacy:** a medium's ability to refer the user immediately to another media or resource. Say you put up a page, and on it you refer to another page. With the high referential immediacy of the Web, you can create a link to that other page, and your audience can jump to it with ease. On the other hand, if you were to publish that information in a book, magazine, or scholarly journal article (on paper), the lack of referential immediacy creates extra effort. Your audience would have to go and physically locate the other information to which you referred. The little time and effort required to go from one document to another, when compared to the traditional library, makes the Web a lucrative tool for libraries, universities, and major corporations who all require the expedient dissemination and retrieval of data. The referential nature of the Web helps us think of associations between information. Creating a link between pages is done in HTML with the anchor tag:

```
<a href = "http://www.wherever.com/">
      The words of the link</a>
```

Table 8.1

BASIC HTML TEXT FORMATTING COMMANDS

THE HTML TAGS	WHAT THE SOURCE CODE LOOKS LIKE	WHAT THE FINAL PRODUCT LOOKS LIKE
	TEXT FORMATTING	
<b></b>	<b>This is boldfacing</b>	**This is boldfacing**
<i></i> <cite></cite>	<i>This is italicization</i>	*This is italicization*
<u></u>	<u>This is underlining</u>	<u>This is underlining</u>
<tt></tt>	<tt>Appears as a typewriter</tt>	`Appears as a typewriter`
	HEADING LEVELS	
<h1></h1>	<h1>Heading 1</h1>	Heading 1
<h2></h2>	<h2>Heading 2</h2>	Heading 2
<h3></h3>	<h3>Heading 3</h3>	Heading 3
<h4></h4>	<h4>Heading 4</h4>	Heading 4
<h5></h5>	<h5>Heading 5</h5>	Heading 5
<h6></h6>	<h6>Heading 6</h6>	Heading 6
	FONT SIZE	
<font size = "+6"></font>	<font size = "+6">Font size 6</font>	Font size 6
<font size = "+5"></font>	<font size = "+5">Font size 5</font>	Font size 5
<font size = "+4"></font>	<font size = "+4">Font size 4</font>	Font size 4
<font size = "+3"></font>	<font size = "+3">Font size 3</font>	Font size 3
<font size = "+2"></font>	<font size = "+2">Font size 2</font>	Font size 2
<font size = "+1"></font>	<font size = "+1">Font size 1</font>	Font size 1
<font size = "-1"></font>	<font size = "-1">Font size -1</font>	Font size -1
<font size = "-2"></font>	<font size = "-2">Font size -2</font>	Font size -2
<font size = "-3"></font>	<font size = "-3">Font size -3</font>	Font size -3
<font size = "-4"></font>	<font size = "-4">Font size -4</font>	Font size -4
<font size = "-5"></font>	<font size = "-5">Font size -5</font>	Font size -5
<font size = "-6"></font>	<font size = "-6">Font size -6</font>	Font size -6
	JUSTIFICATION	
<center>Centered text</center>	<center>Centered text</center>	Centered text
<p align = "right"></p>	<p align = "right">Right justified text</p>	Right justified text

- **a** is shorthand for **a**nchor. The browser needs to know that you are about to "anchor" this line of code to another page.
- href stands for **h**ypertext **ref**erence. This command tells the browser to "get" the next file.
- The equal sign tells the browser that the next address inside quotation marks represents the file to be downloaded.
- http://www.wherever.com/ is the Web address where the document is located.
- The words of the link are underlined when viewed in the browser and are what the person clicks on to jump to the new content.
- The </a> code stops the hyperlink command and keeps the browser from turning everything else on the page into a link.

INSERTS MULTIMEDIA CONTENT

HTML gives us the means to tailor fit media within a webpage. Graphics, pictures, audio, video—all can be easily channeled through a Web browser. Before HTML and the Web, these files had to be downloaded and experienced independently. There was no "multi" in our computer-mediated communication. If you wanted to hear an audio clip, you downloaded that file by itself. If you wanted to see a video clip, you downloaded that file by itself too. With the Web, however, HTML authors can not only make their webpages retrieve multiple files simultaneously but they can also ensure that their audience experiences these files in synch. Atom-films.com **(Figure 8.4),** as well as many other popular sites, demonstrates this effect well. Without HTML acting as a layout guide, these multimedia properties could not be merged into one unified browser interface.

While we intend to show you much more concerning online multimedia in chapter 10, here we want to show you how HTML incorporates the most basic type of multimedia: images. Any image that you can scan, save from the Internet, or create in a simple graphic application can be placed within a webpage. The following code inserts a graphic file in a webpage:

```
<img src = "filename.gif">
```

- **img** stands for image, **src** stands for source.
- The equal sign tells the browser to retrieve the file listed next, which happens to be a graphical image, and display it within the webpage—in exactly the spot where the code is placed in the page.
- The name of the image to be retrieved, in this case "filename.gif", is always placed within quotations; sometimes a more complete

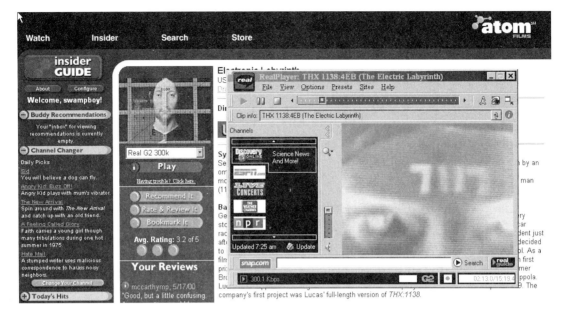

Fig. 8.4. Atomfilms.com uses the full range of available multimedia properties to make the Web browser come alive.

address for the file is given, such as, "http://www.wherever.com/directory/images/filename.gif".

• One key difference is that multimedia tags typically do not require closing tags.

Graphic images can be inserted anywhere on a page. When combined with an anchor code, they can even be turned into links. For example, if you wanted people to be able to click on the image home.jpg to get to the homepage of your site, the code might look like this: <a href = "home.htm"><img src = "home.jpg"></a>.

PLACES DATA INTO A GLOBAL COMMUNICATION CONTEXT

HTML advances human communication in so many ways that we cannot fathom the full impact yet. When our data is showcased via HTML in the global village that is the Web, the entire range of human experience becomes mediated into a public consciousness. If we choose to, we can confirm or disconfirm the consciousness of others around the world–and do so publicly, in small-group settings, or interpersonally. And if we choose not to accept the communicated thoughts of the other person, we can move on to the next webpage that strikes our fancy. HTML allows us to surf over one million pages, channels, or portals of data.

The true elegance of HTML, however, lies in its universality and portability. It can circulate through every computer, or operating system, across all geographies and time zones. It can empower individuals, agencies, and even the social body with a means of "being" with data. With HTML we can cut, paste, copy, send, save, interact with, and even alter data. It is an extremely pliable medium, by design, which creates both a context and a content for macromediated communication, *where any combination of data can be disseminated through any combination of media to any combination of audiences, whether intended or unintended.*

WYSIWYG HTML EDITOR BASICS

The purpose of this section is to provide you with a better appreciation of *What You See is What You Get* (WYSIWYG) HTML editors, their layout, and their various benefits and drawbacks. Our purpose here is not to train you in the uses of any particular WYSIWYG editor–that requires another text. We simply want you to be able to recognize the application and have an appreciation for general WYSIWYG technique. While there are a number of different WYSIWYG editors available, we are using Dreamweaver by Macromedia for demonstration purposes (a 30-day trial version has been provided on the CD with this textbook). Dreamweaver not only meets the needs of the basic or beginning Web designer but it is also equipped with advanced techniques that you will most certainly desire as you become more proficient in designing webpages.

WHAT IS A WYSIWYG HTML EDITOR?

WYSIWYG HTML editors function much like a word processor, but are geared uniquely around the communicative dynamics of the Web. Using a WYSIWYG editor, authors may craft HTML documents in a user-friendly click-button environment. Before these programs were created in 1996, webpage builders had to write out all of the codes by hand in a simple text editor. In recent years, WYSIWIG editors have evolved into very stable and simple to use applications. This stability, paired with a user-friendly interface, has allowed many Web novices to construct highly sophisticated documents in a fraction of the time it would have taken merely four years ago (Burns 1998). Now, anyone possessing the ability to use a word processor can make a webpage in a matter of minutes. This has also accelerated the time required for full-scale website construction from weeks or months to mere days.

GENERAL LAYOUT OF THE WYSIWYG EDITOR: DREAMWEAVER 3

Most WYSIWYG editors look like word processors, but possess the added capacity to hyperlink text, display graphics in specialized ways, and portray color as an integral component of page layout. Dreamweaver 3 has taken a somewhat unique approach to their interface design, although it is not too radically different from other products. While all of their system tools are still available in drop-down menus (as is normally the case with most WYSIWYGs), Dreamweaver 3 uses five different **design pallets (Figure 8.5),** or small floating islands of buttons that remain constantly accessible, to construct webpages. Each of these design pallets contains a set of design features.

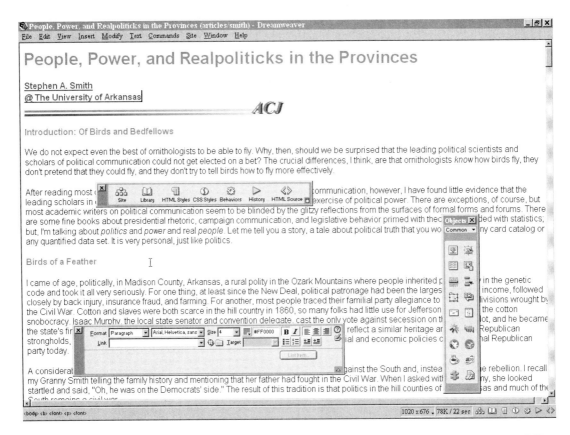

Fig. 8.5. The Macromedia Dreamweaver WYSIWYG interface. A click-button for every HTML tag supported by the W3 Consortium, and then some.

By and large, all WYSIWYG editors have many of the same design tools. They are distinct from one another in: (1) how they arrange their creative environments, (2) the number of advanced features each possesses, and (3) the degree of coapplications embedded within each WYSIWYG to streamline the editing process. For instance, some of the better WYSIWYG editors have FTP coapplications installed within the WYSIWYG environment to manage site construction. Some even have graphics packages embedded within the WYSIWYG to expedite the manipulation of images within the designing environment. Selecting a WYSIWYG is a matter of preference, comfort, and ultimately, an issue of how serious you intend to become about Web design.

Editors such as Dreamweaver allow a novice to quickly and easily create a webpage. We have included an exercise in this chapter to walk you through the creation of a simple webpage that shouldn't take much time at all. Once you understand that WYSIWYG editors are very similar to word processors, your comfort level should rapidly increase. And as you make use of the editor's help files, your skills will also grow rapidly.

BENEFITS

There are two major benefits to using a WYSIWYG editor. Clearly, the most important benefit comes in not having to write the code by hand. In the dark ages (or golden years, depending on your perspective) of five to six years ago, webpage authors spent hours coding pages at the source level. When WYSIWYG editors came along, they freed many coders from staring into a hypnotic field of raw HTML. While the WYSIWYGs were awkward at first, and lacked precision, in time they matured to become reliable means of formatting online content.

The second major benefit of a WYSIWYG editor is that you literally get to see the page as you develop it. Once again, those who code HTML by hand must do so in the dark, resting in the faith that their code is somehow flawless until they can view the page in a Web browser later on. With a WYSIWYG editor, authors can format text, design page properties, and manipulate graphics with a visual efficiency that would be impossible to accomplish at the source code level. In short, if you want to see what's going on with your document as you make your necessary formatting changes, WYSIWYGs are a must.

DRAWBACKS

When working with WYSIWYG editors, realize that there are three major drawbacks. In our opinion, the most important drawback is that you will lose contact with HTML at the source code level. While this may not seem like such a bad thing, over time your lack of contact with HTML will cause your coding skills to diminish. When this happens, you will become more and more dependent upon the WYSIWYG for webpage production. Perhaps it is the inevitable progression of new media technology that HTML be relegated as a transitional formatting code, and that WYSIWYG editors become the common means of production. Even so, we believe it critically important for you to keep your coding skills sharp for a great number of reasons. We will discuss these reasons in the final segment of this chapter.

The second major drawback is that WYSIWYG editors are not error free. As you continue to create online content, you will discover that WYSIWYGs can never substitute for a working knowledge of HTML. In many cases, you will be placed in situations that require you to manage source code by hand. In fact, most of the WYSIWYGs have built-in editing boxes that allow authors to directly manipulate HTML tags while working on a visible document. This is evidence that even the programmers of these tools recognize the limits of their WYSIWYG editors. So when, not if, the WYSIWYG editor fails, you will need to understand how to rework the source code by hand.

The final drawback to the WYSIWYG editor is that it is still considered something of a specialist's program and is therefore not presently available on a vast number of machines. As a result, you will frequently encounter computers without a WYSIWYG editor. Imagine being in a situation where you desperately need to hang some hypertext-based content online, but do not have a WYSIWYG editor. While some people will download one of the free-ware or trial-ware editors for large tasks in these emergency situations, those who can quickly author a webpage in any text editor (such as Notepad) will be at an advantage.

BOX 8.1

SETTING UP YOUR FIRST WEBPAGE

For your introduction to HTML editing, we're going to walk you through the creation of an online version of your resume. You can use any webpage editor, but in this example we will be referring to Dreamweaver by Macromedia. A 30-day trial version is included on the CD-ROM that came with your text, and installation instructions are also included. In this exercise we will be showing you how to use different features of Dreamweaver, and the end result will probably violate many of the design principles we'll talk about in the next chapter. That's okay, because for now we just want you to get comfortable with WYSIWYG editing.

1. The first thing you should do is save the file, even before you start working on it. If you're working through this exercise on a lab computer, you'll probably need to save the file on a floppy disk; if you're working on your own computer,

you can save it in any directory that you desire. Name the file resume.html, and save it.

2. Once the file is saved, you can begin setting up the page properties. Right-clicking anywhere on the page will pull up the page properties dialog box **(Figure 8.6).** Here you should give the page a title, which shows up at the top of the browser window when people visit your page. You can also designate the colors for text, links, and the background of the page. The background can also be an image that you select, which will be tiled across and down the page. Go ahead and try out different color schemes, and when you are satisfied move on to putting in the content.

3. Since this is supposed to be a resume, you probably want to put your name and any address information you feel comfortable revealing at the top (a P.O. box would be safest, if you are concerned about your privacy). Note that if you hit Enter at the end of a line, Dreamweaver puts in an extra line. This is because the new paragraph code, <P>, which is inserted when you hit Enter, tells the browser to jump down a line. If you want to start on the next line immediately below the line that you're on, hit Shift-Enter. This inserts a break code, <BR>, instead of a new paragraph one.

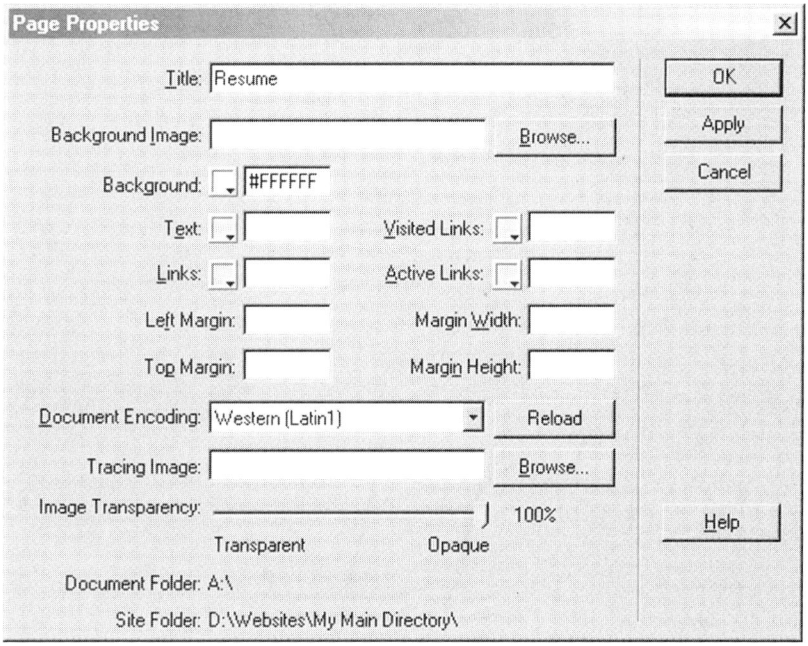

Fig. 8.6. Right-clicking anywhere on the page lets you set the page properties.

4. You can increase the size of your name by highlighting it and then selecting a new size in the properties dialog box **(Figure 8.7).** In this example, we've increased the font size by two. You can also change the font itself; just remember that if you use an unusual font, some people visiting your page might not have that font on their computer, and it won't show up as you intended. Your best bet is to stick with common fonts. Using the property box, you can even change the colors if you want, although be warned that multiple colors get annoying. Try changing the alignment of this address info; see if you like it best left, center, or right justified. Finally, you can bold or italicize the text as well.

5. Make a link to your e-mail address. Put the cursor where you want the address to appear, and then click on Insert > E-mail Link in the menu bar. In the box that pops up **(Figure 8.8),** enter in the text that you want to appear on the page (your best bet is your actual e-mail address) and then the e-mail address. Dreamweaver will then put an active link on your page that people can click on to e-mail you.

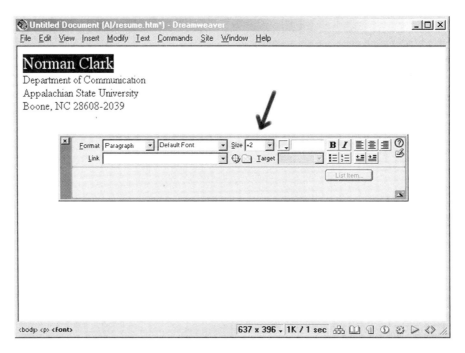

Fig. 8.7. You can change the size of the text by choosing from the options in this drop-down box.

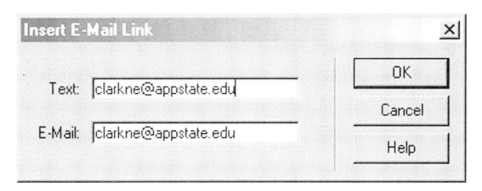

Fig. 8.8. Inserting an e-mail link.

6. Now you should have a list of the sections of your resume, so people can quickly jump to the part they want to read. First enter a heading ("Sections," maybe?), highlight it, and use the format section of the properties box to set it at whatever heading level you want (we would suggest Heading 2). Change the format back to None (do this any time the text is formatted and you don't want it to be) and click on the button in the properties box that has bullets next to lines **(Figure 8.9).** This will create an unordered list. Now enter in a few section names, including Goals, Education, Experience, and any others you think appropriate. When you're done with your list, hit Enter one more time and then click on the unordered list button again to shut it off.

7. Make up a goals statement. First, put in the heading ("Goals"), then hit enter and type in what you want out of life. Go back and highlight "Goals" and set the format to whatever heading level you want in the properties box.

8. Put in an Education section heading. Below it, put in a table that has two columns and two rows by clicking on Insert > Table. Notice that when you're working with the table, the property box adds options to allow you to change things such as the color of the table cell and the alignment of objects or text in the cells **(Figure 8.10).** Write in the first column the degrees you earned, and in the second column the schools you went to (make some up if necessary!).

9. Put in a line after this section (just for practice) by clicking on Insert > Horizontal Rule. Note that once again the properties box changes so you can set the options for the line.

10. Now put in some targets so people can move around your document easily. Put the cursor in front of the Goals section. Then click on Insert > Named Anchor (or hit Control-Alt-A). Give it an easy to remember name (like goals). Do this for the Education section also.

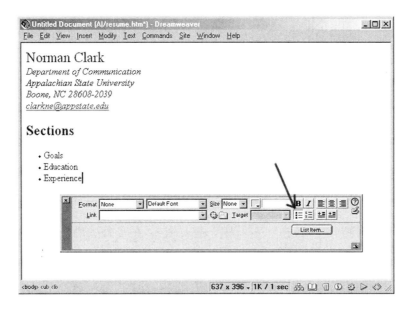

Fig. 8.9. Click this button to create an unordered list.

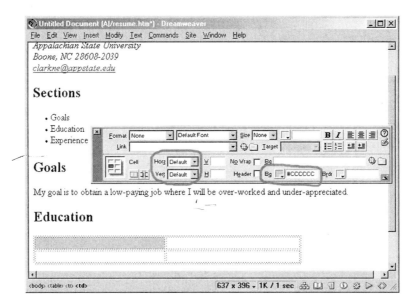

Fig. 8.10. The properties box makes it easy to change the properties of the table.

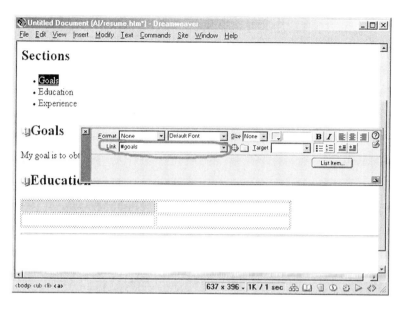

Fig. 8.11. Setting up a link to an anchor.

11. Now go back to your section list at the top of the page. Highlight the word "Goals." In the Link section of the property box, type in the correct target, preceded by a "#": in this case, you would type in "#goals" **(Figure 8.11).** Now when people click on Goals, it will move the page down to the goals section. Do this for "Education" too.

Go ahead and save your file again. You can preview how it will appear to people visiting your page by clicking on File > Preview in Browser (you may have to tell Dreamweaver the location of the browser if that wasn't set when Dreamweaver was installed). Just remember, the end product probably doesn't look anything like what designers would recommend. In the next chapter, we will give you plenty of advice on how to craft your pages well.

BOX 8.2

PUBLISHING YOUR PAGE

Once you've created a page, you still need to take one more step so that other people can see it: you need to publish it. It's important for you to remember that when you are working on pages, you normally save them on the computer in front of you, called the local computer. Even though that computer is (probably) set up to access other pages from the Web, it is (almost certainly) not set up to *deliver* pages to other computers on the Web. If you want to deliver your pages to other people, you have to store them on a Web server.

Chances are good that your school provides you with space on their server; if not, you'll need to get an account with an ISP. Normally you are provided with your own directory, which is often given the same name as your user name. Other people access your pages by entering in the address of your Web server, followed by your directory. For example, one of your authors teaches at Appalachian State University, and his Web directory address is http:// www1.appstate. edu/~clarkne/. You'll need to check with your school or ISP to learn what your Web directory address is.

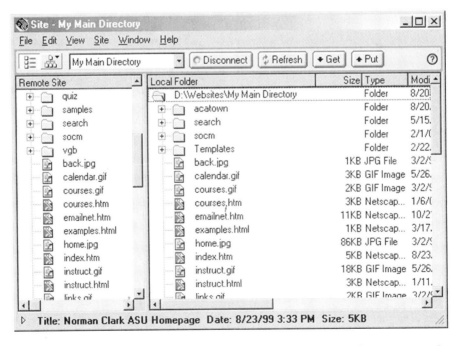

Fig. 8.12. The site manager shows you the files on your local computer and on your Web server and transfers them in either direction.

Your pages are put into your space on the Web server through FTP. To make the process of publishing a webpage easier, Dreamweaver includes FTP capabilities, along with many other features, in its site manager. Once you have the site manager set up, you'll be able to easily see the files in your directory on the remote server in the left-hand window frame, and the files on your local computer in the right-hand window frame **(Figure 8.12).** Then you can either **Get** pages from the server to work on them, or **Put** them into the server directory when you're ready for them to be visited.

But before you can begin publishing pages, you need to set up the site in Dreamweaver. Let's try publishing your resume. Go to the menu and click on Site > New Site to enter in the necessary information. The two main categories you'll need to define are the **Local Info (Figure 8.13)** and the **Web Server Info (Figure 8.14).** In the Local Info options, name the site Testing, call the local root folder a:\ (or wherever it was that you saved the resume file), and enter in your Web directory address (the address that other people use to visit your pages). Setting up the Web Server Info options requires some information that you will need to get from either your instructor, your school, or your ISP. The server access will be FTP. You'll need to learn the exact name of the server you're using, as well as the name of the host directory (usually public_html or www). Hopefully you know your user ID and password. If your Web server is using a firewall, you'll have to get specific set-up information from them. Otherwise, once you have set these options your site should be ready to go.

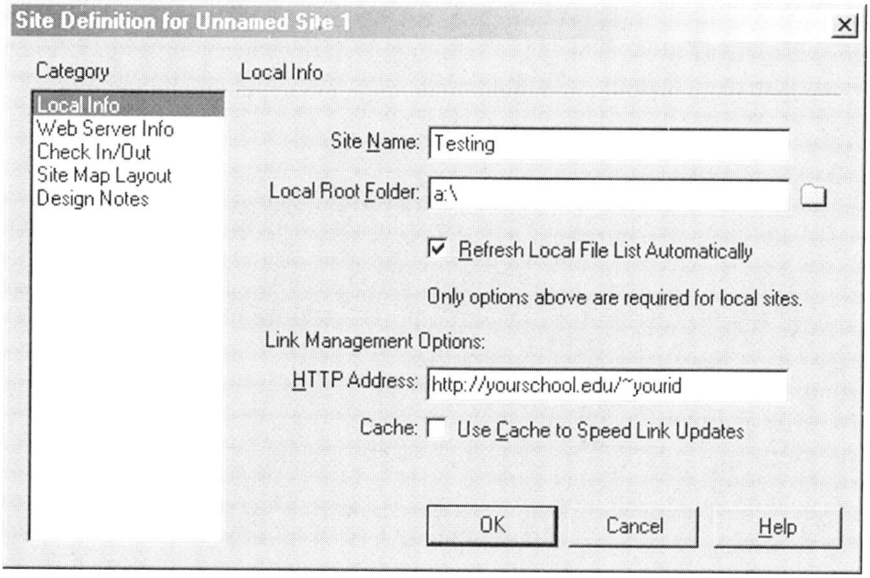

Fig. 8.13. Local Info options.

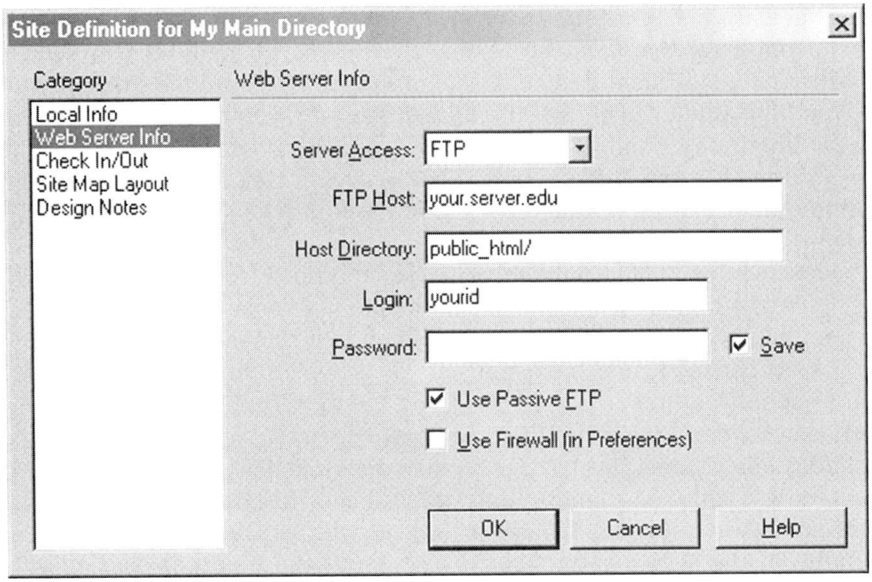

Fig. 8.14. Web Server Info options.

When you get the options correctly entered, you should be able to connect to that site by hitting the Connect button in the Site window. You should see something that looks like **Figure 8.15,** only you won't see the same files (if any) listed in the remote site (the left-hand window frame). All you have to do is click on the resume.html file and then hit the Put button. In a matter of seconds, your file will be placed on the

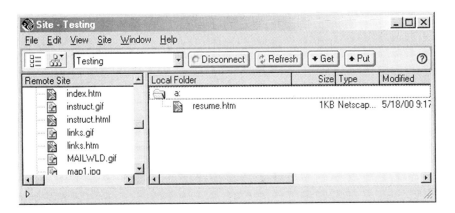

Fig. 8.15. All ready to "put" that resume onto the Web!

Web server where it will be available for anyone to see. When you're done, hit the Disconnect button to terminate your FTP connection.

Dreamweaver's site manager can do much more, including automatically updating links. We encourage you to take some time to read through the help file provided by Macromedia.

WHY BE PROFICIENT IN HTML?

You might be asking, now that WYSIWYG editors make your life so easy, why bother learning about HTML code? We'd like to offer three reasons why every online communicator should remain proficient in HTML. First, your familiarity with the behind-the-scenes code will increase your ability to teach others how to create webpages. While it is generally important for you, as an individual, to remain proficient in HTML, the Internet often creates among its users a strong sense of community. Members of this global network have a responsibility to share ideas, shortcuts, tricks-of-the-trade, and in sum, their knowledge about improving and bettering online communication.

Secondly, understanding HTML will better enable you to understand new developments at the source code level. We have only skimmed HTML in this chapter; if you continue to educate yourself about the source code you will learn that advanced HTML is much more complex than it first appears. For example, recently the W3C has endorsed a new coding language called XHTML, shortened to XML. **XML** is an altered form of HTML that has been designed around wireless Internet protocols. Most Web engineers believe that the Internet will eventually develop into a communal pool for all media, and are therefore preparing for a wave of smaller, more portable devices that can access the network: cell phones, palm-tops, and other specialized electronic devices designed for niche markets. As the Web continues to adapt to satisfy our human communication needs, so too will the source code. Knowing how HTML functions today is key to understanding how it (and other evolving codes) will function tomorrow.

The final reason as to why we should maintain a respectable understanding of HTML is that, from time to time, you will want to borrow design elements from other websites. While browsing the Web, you will inevitably discover other sites that you admire and wish to emulate. Site envy is probably a natural part of becoming a competent Web master. Imagine looking at an innovative new design and deciding that you want to replicate it. If all you know is how to work a WYSIWYG editor, certainly you could take a few guesses at how the site was constructed. On the other hand, if you know HTML, you will understand how the author achieved such an effect. With this knowledge you could return to your trusty WYSIWYG editor and mirror the feat.

BACK UP AND RELOAD

Who would have thought that our means of communicating with one another and with machines would have come so far, so fast? Within a decade, we have witnessed the popular diffusion of both the PC and the Web at a truly astounding rate. What's more, we have witnessed this diffusion in our homes, schools, and workplaces. Given the sweeping changes that have altered our communication landscape, it is hard to imagine what tomorrow will hold. However, one thing remains certain: the Web will likely play a central role in that very decentralized future.

Had Tim Berners-Lee not been revolutionary minded enough to invent a common means of uniting different computer platforms over online networks (and thus uniting human minds), we might still be arguing about the differences between PC clones and Macintoshes. Functionally speaking, however, the Web changed all of that. It brought us a means to create textually rich, interactive documents and add multimedia to our pages. What Berners-Lee had unknowingly done was to put the power of multimediated global communication in the hands of any user who knew the code. In recent years, the creation of WYSIWYG editors has made it even easier for novices to create content for the Web, since it allows them to see what they are creating. Even though these editors have drawbacks, they have opened up online publishing to people who would have been intimidated by the thought of learning the language of HTML. And even though WYSIWYG editors are simplifying the Web, an understanding of what is going on behind the scenes will help you communicate more effectively. Knowing the language in a foreign country is crucial to understanding what is going on; knowing the language of the Web is crucial to understanding our evolving world and the changing human condition.

BROWSE and BUILD

For sites to visit, exercises, quizzes to test your learning, and more, go to
www.harcourtcollege.com/ communication/inetcomm

References and Readings

Abbate, J. 1999. *Inventing the Internet.* Boston: MIT Press.

Barksdale, K., ed. 1997. *HTML activities: Webtop publishing on the superhighway.* Cincinnati: South-Western Publishing.

Berners-Lee, T., M. Fischetti, and M. Derotouzos. 1999. *Weaving the Web: The original design and ultimate destiny of the World Wide Web by its inventor.* San Francisco: Harper.

Burns, J. 1998. *HTML Goodies.* Indianapolis: MacMillan Publishing.

Cailliau, R. and J. Gillies. 2000. *How the Web was born: The story of the World Wide Web.* Oxford: Oxford University Press.

Moschovitis, C. J. P., H. Poole, T. Schuyler, and T. M. Senft. 1999. *History of the Internet: A chronology, 1843 to present.* Santa Barbara, Calif.: ABC Clio.

Reid, R. H. 1997. *Architects of the Web: 1,000 days that built the future of business.* New York: John Wiley & Sons.

Segaller, S. 1998. *Nerds 2.0.1: A brief history of the Internet.* New York: TV Books.

CHAPTER 9
Eyesore or Eye Candy?

Designing Webpages

By Peter Zale ©2000 Peter Zale, www.peterzale.com   Distributed by Tribune Media Services, www.comicspage.com

By the end of this chapter, you should:

I.   Know to begin the design process by identifying your purpose and audience.

II. Be able to apply the four basic design principles to webpages:
   A. contrast,
   B. repetition,
   C. alignment, and
   D. proximity.

III. Understand the importance of and keys to a good navigational system, focusing on:
   A. organization,
   B. links, and
   C. frames.

IV. Know the dos and don'ts for:
   A. colors,
   B. animation,
   C. page size,
   D. content, and
   E. bells and whistles.

Chances are, if you've done any amount of browsing on the WWW (which you ought to have done by now!), you have encountered some ghastly websites, so badly designed that your monitor probably blanked out in protest. With a mishmash of colors, fonts, animated graphics, blinking text, and dozens of other violations against your senses, these pages are digital eyesores. The homepage for the movie *GalaxyQuest* is a good example of the worst in Web design; of course, it was intentionally designed to look as if it had been made by a not-too-skilled fan. In print, we couldn't fully capture the horror of this site, since the blinking text doesn't show up on paper and much of the page is not visible. For the full effect, you'll have to visit the site by using the link on the textbook website.

Why are there so many poorly designed pages on the Web? First, since it is so easy to set up a webpage, many people have done so without first learning some principles of good design. Many so-called Web masters have very little training in visual principles, and yet they can sell their services to unsuspecting people who are even less familiar with HTML editors. Second, you are more likely to notice the bad examples, because a fundamental tenant of good design is that people shouldn't notice the design. A good design doesn't call attention to itself; instead, it focuses your attention on the content. A bad design grabs you, shakes you up, and leaves you feeling a bit nauseous. This chapter will cover how to make sure that the design of your page assists your communication, instead of hindering it. Since one of the best ways to learn design is by example, you should visit the textbook website, where we provide links to some of the best and worst the Web has to offer, as well as links to other sites offering design advice.

PURPOSE AND AUDIENCE

Before you even begin to create your website, you need to first consider two interconnected questions: What is my purpose, and who is my intended audience? The purpose of your site should come through clearly to any visitor. If you are primarily providing information, the design should call attention to the content. People should not have to hunt to find the information; it should be easy to get to as quickly as possible. Sites like Yahoo.com emphasize the content by featuring a categorical sorting system that begins on the homepage of the site. If you are attempting to use the Web for e-commerce, access to your product should be emphasized. Detailed and searchable information, pictures, online support, and simple purchasing options are just a few of the elements you will need to include in your design if you hope to make a sale. Of course, if you are putting up webpages to tell people about yourself, the design of your pages will need to reflect your personality.

Deeply related to your purpose is your intended audience. Who will be visiting your pages: friends, customers, students, or everyone in the world (might as well dream big)? Will they naturally be interested in your content–for example, your relatives–or will you need to attract them to your site? How likely is it that they will have the most current browser with all of the most popular plug-ins? How fast will their Internet connection be? If you think that your audience will be primarily using older computers, with an old version of the browser and connecting with a slow modem, you probably don't want to design a multimedia-intense site. Instead, you ought to create a fast-loading site, with an emphasis on text instead of glitz.

Don't ignore this important first step. Carefully identify your purpose and audience. Throughout the process of designing your website, you will be faced with numerous choices. If you don't have a clear sense of purpose and audience, you are likely to make choices at random, and your pages will suffer from a lack of purpose. But if you are guided in your choices by your identified purpose and audience, your site will win the only design "award" that really matters: repeat visitors.

BASIC DESIGN PRINCIPLES: CRAP

Becoming a skilled Web designer will take time. The aesthetic sense that good designers possess does not develop overnight. Of course, some people are blessed with a natural sense of balance and color, but even those people have to put that gift into practice. And while practice may help you reach perfection, it will be a much faster journey if you begin with an understanding of the basic principles of design. Robin Williams, a highly respected designer and author of several design textbooks, emphasizes four key principles: contrast, repetition, alignment, and proximity (Williams and Tollett 1998). These words create an acronym that should be fairly easy to remember and should help keep your pages from looking that way.

CONTRAST

Contrast, at the most basic level, is the difference between elements on a page. The primary purpose for contrast is to emphasize some elements, and de-emphasize others. In other words, it is used to create focal points that draw peoples' eyes. So the key thing to remember with contrast is that if you're going to make it different, make it *different.* If you are going to use a different font, color, or size to draw attention to an element, don't use one that is almost the same. Make the contrast noticeable. Subtlety

Fig. 9.1. Not much contrast here.

Fig. 9.2. Now your eyes know what's important.

has its place, but not when you are trying to show relative importance, focus attention, and guide people through your page.

Compare **Figures 9.1** and **9.2.** Notice how in the first example nothing really catches your eye. It is difficult to tell which elements are more important than others, since nothing has been given enough contrast to take priority. When you try to make everything look important, nothing does. The gray background makes it difficult for your eyes to focus on the text. In the second example, however, you can clearly spot the focal element of the page. All of the other elements are clearly subordinate to it, and yet they still maintain enough contrast among themselves to help you focus on what's important.

REPETITION

We know from communication research that repetition can greatly aid your audience in remembering information. But when it comes to design, repetition is used to pull your site together, so that individual pages are clearly connected to one another. This means that every page on your site ought to share elements with other pages: the same colors, graphic images, fonts, and so forth. Many times when new designers first begin creating pages, their first impulse is to use all sorts of fonts, colors, graphics, and type styles. But instead of being visually stimulating (which is the intention of novice designers), these pages end up being visually frustrating. Instead of using multiple elements, you should repeat just a few to keep your page from becoming cluttered and over-designed.

The repetition of these elements creates the theme of your site. A strong theme is what will separate your site from the rest of the Web. Since hyperlinks make it so easy to jump from one page to another, people can easily get lost when browsing, forgetting what site they came from and what site they are currently visiting. But if all of the pages on your site share the same theme, your visitors will always know when they are on your site and when they have left it.

Notice the repetition of elements in **Figures 9.3** and **9.4.** is the homepage of the site, and **9.4** shows a subpage. The fill pattern used for the letters of the primary links and site title, and for the horizontal lines, is actually a section cut out of the graphic image on the homepage. The same green shades are used for links. All of the subpages repeat the design elements that you see in **9.4.** They have identical image links that show up in the same place (on the left-hand edge of the page). The background for the links repeats the themes and colors of the two images on the homepage. The same fonts and colors are used throughout the site. In this way, even though the subpages are different from the homepage, enough repetition is present to show that these pages are part of the same site.

Fig. 9.3. Repetition of colors and fonts can help tie a page together.

Syllabus

- Goals
- Materials
- Performance
- Trouble-Shooting
- Philosophy
- Daily Schedule

Goals

This course has three main objectives: 1) to introduce students to communication theories and practices; 2) to help students determine whether or not they wish to pursue studies in communication; and 3) to begin the lifelong process of becoming literate, critical consumers and producers of messages. In case you couldn't guess, it's that last goal that will drive this entire course. The assignments are designed to increase your skills at listening to messages, analyzing them internally, and making the private knowledge you gained public through various means of communication.

Communication is importantly a liberal art. As such, studying communication liberates by providing the tools necessary for critically thinking through issues. We will engage a number of issues not to promote cynicism or conformity, but to increase our abilities, and to understand how language shapes our interactions with others.

Fig. 9.4. Repetition tells visitors thay are still on the same site.

ALIGNMENT

If you've ever used a word processor, you already know that **alignment** is how the text is lined up on the page. Text can be lined up on the left, the right, or down the center of the page. The best advice for alignment is to choose one and stick with it throughout the page. Most beginning Web designers center the title of their page, left align most other things, and sometimes right align special content. Though it might be fun to play with alignment, the fact is that many alignments on a page make it look messy. If everything is lined up the same way on the page, it creates an imaginary but very strong edge.

Centered alignment on a page is very balanced, calm and formal, and it is appropriate when your intent is to be calm and formal. It works well for opening splash screens and homepages. But left or right alignment, when it is done consistently on the whole page, unifies the content and makes it easier to read. Content in tables that is consistently aligned to the left margin makes it possible to remove the borders of the table, because the constant edge of the content creates its own invisible lines.

You also need to keep vertical alignment in mind. Tables allow you to align the content at either the top, middle, or bottom of the cell. Aligning it at the top will ensure that the **baselines** (the lines that text sits on) will be lined up. Using middle alignment will mean that text that spans two lines will not align with single lines of text.

Figures **9.5** and **9.6** show the start of the same resume. In **Figure 9.5,** the multiple alignments weaken the page and make the content difficult to follow. With the alignment problems fixed in the second version, the page gains balance and strength and is easier to read. The consistent left and top alignment in the table gives this resume more elegance. Your pages will communicate much more effectively if they consistently use the same type of alignment. This resume still has problems, however, which the next section addresses.

PROXIMITY

Proximity is the distance between two objects. Everyone who has been in a relationship knows that when people are more intimate, they get a little closer—sometimes a lot closer. The same thing should be true of

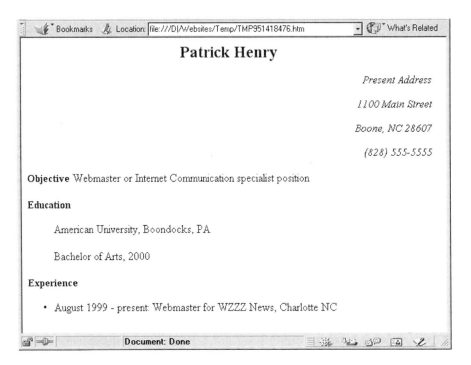

F i g . 9 . 5 . Multiple alignments weaken the design of this page.

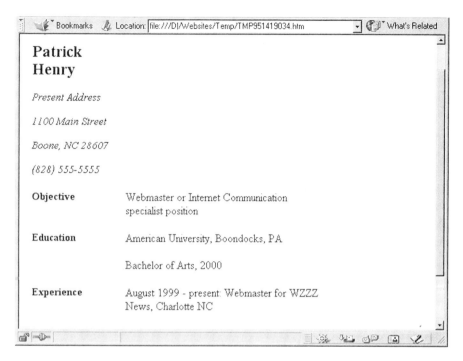

Fig. 9.6. Using one horizontal and one vertical alignment strengthens this resume.

your content. The more intimately related your content is, the closer together it should be. Placing content in close proximity on the page implies a connection, while putting space between items disconnects them from one another. When you glance at a webpage, the visual layout ought to group elements together.

One simple tip will help you a great deal when designing your pages: know the difference between the **paragraph** and **break codes.** A paragraph code in HTML, <P>, ends the current line and starts a new line, *placing a blank line in between.* A break code, <BR>, ends the line and starts a new one *without* putting an extra line between them. So if you want to end a line, but the content of the next line is related to it and needs to be in close proximity, use a break code instead of a paragraph code. A break code is created by hitting Shift-Enter, while a paragraph code is inserted every time you hit Enter.

Another problem that often baffles new designers is that they don't understand why they cannot keep a section of text close to a headline without having all of the text be as big as the headline. Say you type in a headline and hit Shift-Enter (which inserts a <BR>), so you can keep the following text nice and close to the headline. If you go back and highlight

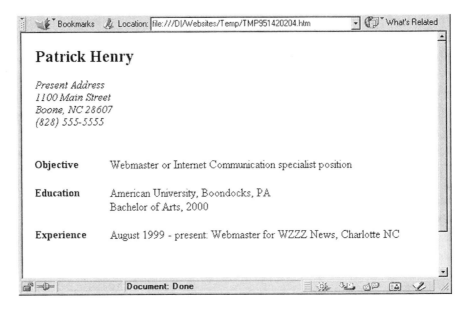

F i g . 9 . 7 . Get a little closer, don't be shy . . . and remember the principle of proximity.

the headline, and format it as Heading 1, both the headline *as well as the text below it* will be that size. This is because *heading codes apply to whole paragraphs.* Since you put a break code between the headline and the text, instead of a new paragraph code, you've only got one paragraph there. So the <h1> code around the headline actually causes everything until the next <p> (paragraph) code to be huge. To fix this, use a text formatting code that can be applied to individual words. For example, if you highlight the headline and use the *font size +2* code, it will increase the size of the headline without altering the rest of the text.

Figure 9.7 takes our sample resume and cleans it up. Notice how the changes in proximity make the connections between different content clear. The improved version should be easier to read (since your eye does not have to jump around as much) and also easier to grasp in a glance.

NAVIGATING THE LINKS

When you first begin designing webpages, you may start with only one page. But as soon as you begin to create multiple pages, you need to begin considering another important aspect of design: organization and navigation. How will the pages of your site be organized? How will visitors get from one page to another? Think of the organizational structure of your site as the skeleton, and the navigational system as the nervous system. If the skeleton isn't strong, and the nerve connections don't work well, it doesn't matter how colorful the clothing is. A visually stimulating site that visitors can't figure out how to navigate is a site that they won't revisit. In this section we will focus on how to organize a site so it is easy to navigate, and how to design links that are effective.

ORGANIZATION

More important than how cool your buttons look is the underlying structure of your site. To create a strong skeleton, keep the following advice in mind.

- Think of relationships: how are the pages of your site connected together? What are the relationships between the pages? One of the best ways to organize your site is to think of metaphors. An organizing metaphor can give you a novel and effective way to lay out your site, and in the case of the Web spatial metaphors are particularly effective. For example, if you are setting up an e-commerce site, you could organize the site around three key "places": a showroom, a checkout counter, and a customer service center. A personal site could be designed around different shoes: dress shoes for work-related information, tennis shoes for hobbies, slippers for personal or family information, and so forth.

- Think of categories: can you imagine how long it would take you to shop at the grocery store if all of the items were placed on the shelves at random, instead of organized by types of food? Some novice Web builders make the mistake of creating a homepage with links to every other page on their site, listed in apparently random order. If you only have three or four pages, this isn't a problem. But if you have many pages, you need to think of ways to group them into categories, and perhaps even subcategories. A goal for your homepage should be to present visitors with as few main categories as makes sense for the size of your site.

- Think levels: when deciding on your categories and subcategories, you also need to determine how many levels are appropriate for your site. Most people will not be willing to drill down through page after page to get to the content they desire, especially if they are using a modem connection. So you need to strike a balance between on the one hand overwhelming people with too many options at once, and on the other hand frustrating them with submenu after submenu. There is no hard-and-fast rule for this, but we would suggest that for a small website, three levels should be sufficient.

- Think express: if you have more than one level to your site, make sure that important content is located on the top levels. Critical content, such as the homepage, a search tool, and the main categories, should be reachable from any page in just one click. Well-designed sites have a navigation bar that allows people to get to these frequently visited pages.

- Think repetition: with navigational systems, this design principle is probably the most crucial. **Navigation bars,** which are horizontal or vertical tables with either textual or graphical links to critical pages on the site, should show up in the same place on every page and look the same. On particularly long pages, duplicate the primary links at the top and bottom of the page so people can get around your site without having to scroll back up to the top of the page.

- Think Web: remember that one of the strengths of the Web is that you can hyperlink pages to each other in infinite ways. Take advantage of this strength by giving people different ways to arrive at the same place. Try to avoid being a tyrant, forcing people to navigate through your site in only one way. Instead, let them follow the path that makes the most sense to them.

- Think big: if you have a particularly large site, you should consider providing your visitors with one of two tools—a site map or a search engine. You could create a simple site map by making an index: listing pages and nesting their subpages beneath them, and then making the titles of the pages into links. Dreamweaver can create a graphical representation of all the pages on your site, showing how pages are nested and linked together **(Figure 9.8).** However, it is just a graphic image and you cannot get to the various pages by clicking on them. If you're particularly ambitious, you could set up a search engine for your website. However, this would require knowledge of scripts, which you will have to learn either in another course or on your own.

- Think simple: the best organizational systems are clear and simple. Where people go wrong is focusing first on how they want things to look, instead of on how things will be organized. They end up creating visually appealing but complicated navigational systems that quite simply do not function well. Focus on creating a simple and clear structure for your site first, and let the look follow.

LINKS

As you know by now, the Web is all about connections. A basic purpose of HTML is to allow you to navigate from one page to the next. Creating a link in Dreamweaver is very simple. All you need to do, as is shown in

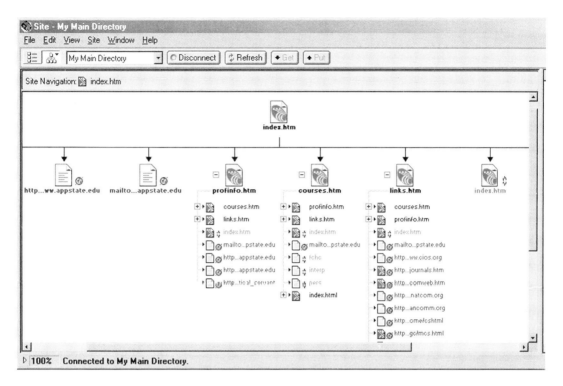

Fig. 9.8. Dreamweaver can generate graphical site maps.

Figure 9.9, is highlight the word that you want to turn into a link. Then type in the page that you want to connect to in the <u>L</u>ink option of the Properties palette. As a designer of webpages, your goal should be to provide people with efficient and effective links to your material. Keep in mind the following tips when turning words or graphics into links:

- Make sure your links serve the purpose of your website. Many new Web designers put links on their pages to major search engines such as Yahoo.com, browser download sites (those nasty little "Netscape Now" buttons, for example), and other pages that have no connection to the purpose of their site. Ask yourself if the link you are creating is specific to your goal, or if it is just a link that everyone else has. If the latter, don't bother.

- Limit the number of **external links** that you put on your page. An external link is one that takes people to a page on a different site. Again, this is related to your purpose. You have gone to a lot of effort to attract people to your page. Do you really want to give them lots of opportunities to leave your site quickly and easily? Sometimes the purpose of a page is to provide people with an

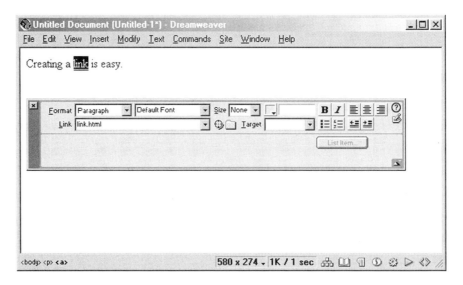

Fig. 9.9. Highlight the word, enter in the Link address, and you've got yourself a hyperlink!

index of links to other sites related to a particular topic. For example, you might be interested in solar energy and decide to share the links that you have found with other people who share that interest. In this case, the external links serve your purpose. However, we would caution you to check first and see if someone else has already put up a similar index. If so, there's not much point to putting up another index page.

- Make sure that your links work. Very few things are more annoying to people who visit your page than clicking on a link and seeing "404: Not Found." Dreamweaver can automatically check and fix your **internal links** (links to pages on your own site). Some other HTML editors will check the external links, and you can download shareware programs designed just for this purpose. Or you can do it the old-fashioned way: simply open up your page in a browser and click on your links to see if they work. If they don't, either fix them or remove them.

- Take advantage of the site manager. Dreamweaver and other high-end editors come with site managers. Taking the time to learn how to use the site manager will save you hours of time down the road. One major benefit of using this tool is that it can keep track of the links on your pages and keep them correct. For example, if you develop a website with different subdirectories and decide to move a page into a different directory, the site manager can automatically change all links to that page on the other webpages in your site so that they point to the correct location. This automatic managing and updating of your links will save you a great deal of effort and frustration.

- Choose the words that you turn into links carefully. A common mistake that many Web designers make is using the phrase "click here." For example: <u>Click here</u> to see Dr. Norman Clark's curriculum vita for more details. You should avoid using the phrase "click here" because it draws attention to the mechanisms of the Web. Most people browsing the Web know they can click on underlined words. It is also not a good idea to turn a whole sentence, or even a long phrase, into a link: <u>Click here to see Dr. Norman Clark's curriculum vita for more details.</u> Since a link is designated by underlining the word, it adds emphasis to that word. Because of this, you should work your links into the sentence structure and choose the word(s) that ought to be emphasized. In this case, the logical choice would be: See Dr. Norman Clark's <u>curriculum vita</u> for more details.

- Give people clear departure and arrival information. Make sure that the words of the link give people enough information about what will appear when they click on it. When possible, use the title of the coming page as a link. This way, when they get to that page, the title will confirm that they have arrived at the intended place. If you have space, a short description about the destination page is greatly appreciated, especially by people browsing with a slow connection. Nothing is more annoying than waiting five minutes for a page that ends up being completely irrelevant.

- If you use graphic images for links, be sure to provide duplicate text links somewhere on the page **(Figure 9.10).** Otherwise, if a visitor to your page has limited graphical capability or their graphics turned off they won't be able to see the links. These duplicate text links also make sure your page is accessible to all members of your audience, including blind people using text-to-Braille or text-to-voice converters.

- Use **anchors** in long documents. Anchors allow you to move to a specific section of a page. For example, say you create an HTML version of your resume with Dreamweaver. You might have three sections labeled Education, Work Experience, and References. To help viewers get to a specific section quickly, type up a list of those three sections at the top of the resume page. Then move the cursor down the page to the start of the Education section, and insert an anchor by pressing Ctrl+Alt+A. Dreamweaver will ask you to name the anchor; your best bet is to give it the same name as the section: education. Now, go up and highlight the word

Fig. 9.10. The buttons in the picture are duplicated in the text immediately below.

"Education" in the list of sections you put at the top of the page. In the Link option on the Properties palette, you would enter in the name of the anchor that you want connected to that word, preceded by a #: in this case, "#education." Now, when someone clicks on the word Education in the list at the top of your resume, the browser will jump to that section of the page. You would follow the same procedure for the other sections. Another useful tip is to put an anchor at the top of your page, named "top." Then, at the end of large sections on a long page, you could type in the words "Up to Top," and link them to the "#top" anchor.

All experienced communicators realize that a strong, logical organizational structure is one of the best ways to avoid overloading your audience with information. On the Web, where information overload has almost become a way of life, a functional and intuitive navigational system paired with effective and efficient links will set your page apart. The ability to quickly and easily reach the information that they want will bring visitors back to your site, not your fancy background image.

FRAMES

Frames allow you to divide a page up into sections. Many people make use of frames for navigational links. They divide a page up into two sections: one small section along either the top or side edge of the page, which holds links to different pages of the site, and one large section where those pages appear. When a visitor clicks on a link in the navigation frame, the corresponding page shows up in the main frame without changing the content of the navigation frame. You can scroll down a long page in the main frame without losing the navigational links in the other frame. In the example in **Figure 9.11,** clicking on Kehvon's Library in the left-hand frame would cause a story written by a daughter of one of the authors to appear in the right-hand frame, but all of the links would remain in the left-hand frame. If you were to scroll down through the story, the links would still be visible.

At first glance frames seem to be a great way to set up a consistent navigation system. However, frames are far from perfect. One major

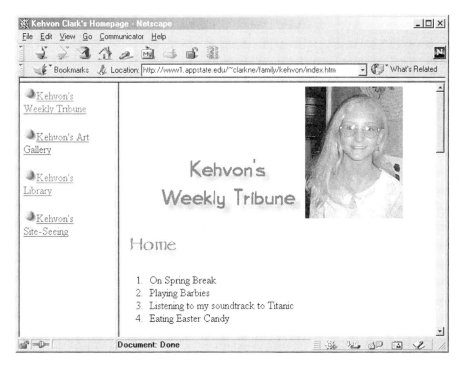

Fig. 9.11. An example of frames used not so well.

drawback is that frames do not bookmark well. Framed pages are created by a separate document that sets up the size of the frames and their initial content. **Figure 9.11** shows the content that is initially loaded by the frame-setting file. Let's say you click on <u>Kehvon's Library</u> and you like the story that you find there. So you create a bookmark to it in your browser. Later, you click on that bookmark to return to that page. However, what will appear on your screen is what you see in **Figure 9.11.** That is because the bookmark points to the frame-setting file (named index.htm), which is set to initially load up Kehvon's Weekly Tribune in the right-hand frame. In this case, this would not be major problem, since one click would take you to the page you wanted. But imagine your frustration if you had to click through several submenus to get to the page that you bookmarked, only to find that your bookmark forces you to go through the whole process of digging down to that page again. There are other drawbacks to frames as well. Older browsers won't back up to a previous frame. Instead, they will back up to the document you visited just before you got to the first framed page. Even older browsers won't be able to show a framed page at all. Quite often framed pages do not print out very well either.

For these and other reasons, *we would advise you to avoid using frames* most of the time. You can consider using them for navigation within one large document, where setting a bookmark would still pull up

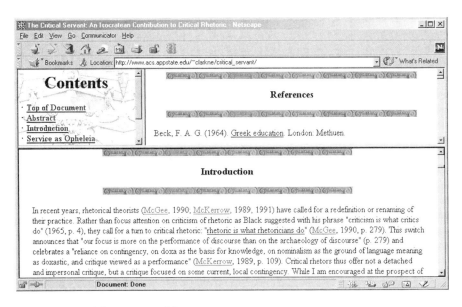

Fig. 9.12. A better use of frames.

the correct page. For example, **Figure 9.12** shows an online version of a research paper. Clicking on the names of cited authors in the main document moves the reference list in the upper right-hand frame to the correct citation. Clicking on headings in the table of contents window in the upper left moves the main document to the corresponding section. In this example the frames serve two functional purposes: they allow you to quickly jump to a specific section of the document and to check a reference citation without losing your place in the article. When used cautiously, frames can be useful. However, because of their drawbacks our final word of advice to you is to avoid using frames.

DESIGN DOS AND DON'TS

Every Web designer has their own list of pet peeves, of things they never do, and of things they always do. The textbook website has links to several sites that offer you design advice. Here we've collected what we think are some of the most important things to do, and to not do, when designing your webpages.

COLOR

- Down, boy! Keep your color use to a minimum. Five or fewer per page (except for pictures, of course) is a good rule of thumb.

- Use structural elements (such as heading levels, font sizes, font styles) to organize your content, not colors. A blind person using a text-to-Braille or text-to-voice converter visiting your site will not be able to tell that you are using dark blue for the text in the body of a paragraph and red for the headings. Even a sighted person visiting your site will be able to distinguish headings from paragraphs more easily if you use structural features instead of colors to set them apart. And you might have some visitors out there who are using a text-only browser, which cannot display different colors anyway.

- Remember the principle of contrast. Make sure there is enough contrast between the background and text colors so that your text is readable. Look at your page on a variety of monitors to double-check this.

- Black text on a white background may seem boring to new designers, but frankly it is what people have come to expect from reading books, and it is extremely readable (due to high contrast). Remember that black and white are colors, too.

ANIMATION

- Blinking text is evil. Don't use it. Just don't.

- All motion on your page competes with the rest of your message. It draws attention to itself and away from your content. So use it for a specific purpose and not just because it looks cool. Those e-mail images that start out with a letter that folds itself and then flies away don't really serve a purpose. Animated images that display how your product works do.

- Moving text may be visually interesting but it is also less readable than stationary text. If you are going to set up something like a scrolling news ticker, make the critical blocks of text stationary.

PAGE SIZE

- Opening splash screens and homepages (usually named index.html) ought to fit completely in a standard browser window. Your visitor should not have to scroll down to get to key links to the rest of your site—it should all be right there in front of them. Set the size of the index.html page to match the monitor resolution that you expect your visitors will be using. Dreamweaver makes this very easy. At the bottom of the editing window is a box with numbers in it that allows you to set the size of your page. Clicking on that box pulls up a list of standard sizes. Most visitors will probably be using a monitor resolution of 800 x 600. When the browser window is maximized, this leaves you with a page size of 760 x 420, because portions of the screen are used up by the browser's tool and scroll bars. If you want to be absolutely certain that your page will fit on everyone's screen, use the 600 x 300 setting, which will fit in a maximized window on a monitor set at 640 x 480.

- As much as you can, avoid making people scroll sideways on your page to see material. You can put all of the content on your page inside a table set to be only 760 pixels wide. This will ensure that people using an 800 x 600 resolution will never have to scroll sideways.

- Shorter pages are easier to maintain. They also take less time to download. Longer pages may start to annoy people, unless they expect it and you provide internal anchors to jump around the document quickly. As a general rule of thumb, try not to make your audience scroll down more than four screens. Breaking the page up into smaller subpages and providing an index page will make access to the pages faster and more satisfying for your audience.

CONTENT

- If you want people to return to your site, you have to provide them with something that they need. Expert power is based on having specialized information that other people desire. People will return to your site if they find valuable content on it. So analyze your audience, determine what content they need, determine what specialized knowledge you have in that area, and provide it.

- Besides having value, your content should also be of high quality. Check your grammar and spelling. Remember that when online, people will form their opinion of you based on the way that you communicate. So craft an expert persona on your webpage by carefully constructing your message, as you should do on e-mail.

- Start putting content at the upper levels of your site, as high up as your organizational structure allows. Don't force people to dig down four or five levels before they start getting valuable information. If you force them to wade through too many submenus, they may lose patience and leave your site. So design your organizational structure to feature important information at the upper levels of the site.

- Tell people if your content is **dynamic.** Dynamic content changes; static content stays constant. You are more likely to get return visitors if your content changes. The reason why sites like Weather.com get many hits is because they provide dynamic content–the weather is always changing. The easiest way to let people know that your information has changed, or will change, is to date it. Tell people when the information was last updated, and when it will be updated again.

- Of course, it follows from this that you need to keep your content current and updated. If you put up a website about yourself and then don't update any of the information on it for a year, you are probably better off shutting down that site.

- If you've gone through the trouble of publishing content to the Web, you should identify yourself as the author of that content. If it is your own site, provide a little information about yourself, perhaps on a separate page. If you are designing a site for someone else, you should simply identify yourself in a relatively inconspicuous place. For instance, you could write at the bottom of the page, "Webmaster: Norman Clark." In either case, you should provide an e-mail link so that people can send you feedback about your content (or design). In Dreamweaver, click on Insert > E-mail Link. You will then be asked to enter the text that will appear on the page, and the e-mail address. We suggest using the e-mail address as the text, too. By now, most people will recognize that clicking on an e-mail address on a webpage will pull up an e-mail composition window, allowing them to send a message to you.

BELLS AND WHISTLES

- Keep your pages simple. Avoid the impulse to add all of the latest cool tricks. Flying images, music clips, and other gratuitous additions to your pages take time to load and build. If they're not purposeful, they waste your time and your visitors' time. Fancy form cannot make up for a lack of valuable content.

- If you put the latest and greatest new tricks on your page, tricks that use the newest plug-ins, chances are good that your visitors might not have that plug-in. So if it is essential to your site that you keep this content on the page, make sure you designate the plug-in URL in the Properties (we'll cover how to do this in more detail in the next chapter). This way visitors will automatically be pointed to the site from which they can download that plug-in.

- Many people place a counter on their page that shows how many times it has been visited. Think twice before you do so. Most people (except for sheep) will return to your page because of the value of its content, not because of the number on its counter. Counters are also easy to falsify since they usually store the number of visits in a simple text file. If you need to keep track of visitors for some reason, you should use more sophisticated software than a simple counter. In any case, you don't need to bother your visitors with site statistics. Let the value of your content speak for itself. If you need to prove to your boss that the site is being visited, provide a separate page with site statistics instead of putting the counter front and center on the homepage.

As you design more of your own pages, you may decide to reject some of the advice we have given you here. Your instructor might give you differing advice as well. That's OK. Design, after all, is partly (perhaps even largely) a matter of taste. Rules of design, like all rules, are made to be broken. Just remember that when you break rules and principles, there are consequences. Think through what the consequences will be if you break or bend a rule. Sometimes you will decide that what you gain from breaking the rule is greater than what you lose. In any case, if you let your purpose and audience guide your design, you should be able to effectively communicate on the Web.

TEXT BOX 9.1

GETTING YOUR PAGE NOTICED

Now that you've gone through all of the effort to design an effective page, you would probably like some visitors. You can give out your Web address to friends and relatives, but to reach a broader audience you need to get your page properly indexed by some search engines. Search engines look at a number of different elements of a page, giving some different weight (according to the searching algorithm used by that engine). Here are some specific things you should do with your page to make sure that search engines index it correctly.

- Give it a good title: make sure that the title of your page, which you set in the page properties box, describes the content of the page. If the page is your resume, title it "Joe Schmoe's Resume" (well, using your own name would be best). Most search engines assign high importance to the title of a page.

- Set the **meta** tags: meta tags are HTML codes that are placed in the header of a webpage and are never actually seen by people visiting the page (unless they look at the source code). Two important meta tags are <description> and <keywords>. You can set these tags in Dreamweaver by clicking on Insert > Head > Keywords or Description. In the keywords tag, type in a few words that sum up the primary content of your page. Think about what words people might be searching for when looking for a page like yours. In the description tag, you can write a sentence or two about the page. Again, search engines pay close attention to these tags.

- Put important words at the top: one other thing that search engines often rank highly are the words in the first paragraph, or first few lines, at the top of your page. If you can work into the first few sentences some keywords that describe the content of your page, your page will be more likely to turn up when people search for those words.

If you want to make sure that search engines have your page in their databases, you can register your page. This allows you to designate specific keywords to be attached to your page and submits it directly to the search engine database. Many search engines have pages on their site where you can fill out a form to register your page with that engine. Or you can go to submission services such as http://register-it.com/ or http://submit-it.com that will register your site with several search engines at once. Register-it.com will submit your site to 12 engines for free; Submit- it.com charges a fee.

Finally, don't underestimate the power of word-of-mouth—or byte-of-computer—advertising. Announce the address of your website on appropriate listservs or newsgroups. If other people have similar pages, offer to do a **link exchange:** "I'll link to your page if you'll link to mine." If you're really going for the glory, submit your page to various award-givers.

BACK UP AND RELOAD

The Web, as you now know, is a visual medium. This means that if you wish to effectively communicate on it, you need to understand basic visual principles. But all communication has to begin with a consideration of your purpose and audience, and building webpages is no exception. The type of site you are creating, and the audience you intend to reach, must guide the decisions that you make when constructing your site.

Four basic principles of visual design are critical to constructing a pleasing and effective webpage. The principle of contrast means you must make the differences noticeable–don't be shy when setting something apart. Repetition is vital on a website, so that your visitors sense the connections between pages. A consistent alignment will give your page strength and balance. Finally, keep your content cozy by putting related items in close proximity to each other.

Moving from webpages to sites requires you to think about how your visitors will navigate though your content. An effective navigational system relies first on a strong organizational structure. Concentrate on simple and clear relationships and on dividing up your content into logical categories. Remember the design principle of repetition when you create navigational bars and use the same bar on every page. The second component of an effective navigational system is links. Make sure that all of your links serve the purpose of your page, and that they work. Choose the words of the links carefully to ensure that people know where the links will take them. Remember also that you can create links to specific sections of pages by using anchors, a particularly good idea with long pages. Finally, many designers are tempted to put their navigational links into frames. Because of the problems that frames create, we advise against using them.

Several other considerations come into play when designing for the Web. Use color judiciously and with restraint. If you decide to include some animation, remember that it will compete with the rest of your content for the audience's attention. Most visitors will be happier if you do not make them scroll down too much, and scrolling sideways will definitely make them cranky. Dynamic, high quality, and valuable content is what will bring visitors back to your page, so make sure that your design calls attention to what you have to offer. Avoid the temptation to put all of the latest tricks on your page, since many of your visitors will be connecting through slower connections and will consider them a waste of time. In all things, keep your purpose and audience foremost in your mind. Then your design shall be a thing of beauty, not a blight upon the earth.

BROWSE *and* BUILD

For sites to visit, exercises, quizzes to test your learning, and more, go to *www.harcourtcollege.com/ communication/inetcomm*

References and Readings

Davis, J., and S. Merritt. 1998. *The Web design wow! book: Showcasing the best of on-screen communication.* Berkeley, Calif.: Peachpit Press.

Head, A. 1999. *Design wise: A guide for evaluating the interface design of information resources.* Medford, N.J.: CyberAge Books.

Jacobson, R. 1999. *Information design.* Cambridge, Mass.: MIT Press.

Landow, G. 1992. *Hypertext: The convergence of contemporary critical theory and technology.* Baltimore: Johns Hopkins University Press.

Lynch, P., and S. Horton. 1999. *Web style guide: Basic design principles for creating web sites.* New Haven, Conn.: Yale University Press.

Rohan, R. 1998. *Building better Web pages.* San Diego, Calif.: AP Professional.

Siegel, D. 1997. *Creating killer Web sites: The art of third-generation site design.* Indianapolis: Hayden Books.

Walton, R. 1998. *Cool sites: Freeze-framed and down cold.* New York: Hearst Books.

Williams, R., and J. Tollett. 1998. *The non-designers Web book.* Berkeley, Calif.: Peachpit Press.

CHAPTER 10

Bring on the Multimedia!

Graphics and Beyond

By Peter Zale ©2000 Peter Zale, www.peterzale.com   Distributed by Tribune Media Services, www.comicspage.com

By the end of this chapter, you should:
I.   Appreciate the benefits of multimedia on the Web:
    A. sensory appeal and
    B. informative content.
II. Be aware of the limitations placed on Web multimedia by two factors:
    A. need for multiplatform support and
    B. need for speed.
III. Understand how browsers incorporate multimedia elements.
IV. Be familiar with the two primary types of Web graphics:
    A. GIF and
    B. JPEG.
V.   Be able to effectively:
    A. create graphics,
    B. optimize graphics, and
    C. use graphics.
VI. Know the basics of incorporating audio and video files into a webpage.
VII. Have a sense of the future of multimedia on the Web.

Long before you learn to read, you learn how to make sense of your perceptions, of the sights, sounds, smells, tastes, and textures around you. In school, you eventually were taught a lot more about interpreting words than images, and you may have gotten the sense that pictures were somehow "beneath" words. But in everyday life, we tend to prefer rich interactions. For example, which would you prefer: to read a newspaper account of a basketball game, or to go to the game, eat popcorn, see the players, read the scoreboard, hear the shouts, feel the electricity of the crowd, and smell the hot dogs? In the past, communicating this level of richness to someone far away was a great challenge. But the capabilities of computers, combined with the medium of the Internet, are making it easier to distribute sensory-intense information. In this chapter, we move beyond the world of text to help you learn to effectively use the multimedia capabilities of the Web.

MULTIMEDIA ON THE WEB

WHY MOVE BEYOND TEXT?

In chapter 2, we discussed the key characteristics of the Internet. One characteristic was that the Internet allows you to publish content in a wide range of formats. Through the Web, and increasingly through other interfaces such as e-mail, you can send text, graphics, sound, and video. In short, the Internet makes it possible to distribute multimedia. And as we noted in our discussion of visual rhetoric, images can be powerful persuasive tools. It is important for you to keep this in mind as you design webpages. You ought to make effective use of the multimedia capabilities of the Internet, not just because they are there but because they can help make your message more powerful. Three key benefits to using multimedia on webpages are that they can give your site sensory appeal, establish an identity, and add informative content.

Increase Sensory Appeal

For example, if you were going to tell someone about a trip you had, you could write about it in an essay (as you probably had to do for an assignment in grade school). But your message could have much greater impact if you added multimedia: told people about what you did, showed them pictures that you took, let them see a video, played them a recording of some local music, and so on. Great writers understand that a powerful story allows people to *experience* the events; great speakers know that to be effective, a persuasive speech must allow the audience to *visualize* the positive results of the proposed plan. Photographers know that a powerful picture isn't just a snapshot: it *tells a story.* And effective Web designers realize that a website needs to make use of as many of the audience's senses as possible. This is important for two reasons. First, presenting information in different formats allows you to reach people with different learning styles: for example, people who learn visually versus those who learn auditorially. Second, when your audience interacts with information in more than one way, each new type of interaction with the same data reinforces the overall message. Reading about it, seeing it, hearing it–on a multimedia webpage, your audience gets exposed to repeated versions of your message. By encoding your message in several slightly different ways, you increase the chance that your audience will be reached and will remember what you communicated. Of course, this means that your multimedia elements need to reinforce the overall message and not distract from it.

Establish an Identity

Well-planned graphics can give a webpage or site a distinct feel, or visual appeal. If webpages could only use text, you would see relatively little variation from one site to the next, especially since HTML does not give you the complex text-formatting tools of a word processor or publishing program. But with the addition of graphics, colors, and other multimedia elements, sites can take on entirely different characteristics. One of the goals of adding multimedia to your webpage is to distinguish it from the rest of the Web by giving it a unique identity.

A well-designed graphical theme–one that follows the principle of repetition–sets the tone of your site. Graphics can be used to create a fun-and-friendly feeling or a professional aura. When combined with your words, graphics can give your visitors a wide range of impressions: serious, casual, impersonal, intimate, etc. It is critical that you think about the tone that your graphics set for the site, because this tone has a great impact on your credibility. In public speaking, we know that speakers who have charisma are perceived as more trustworthy and believable. On webpages, charisma is created through your use of words and images. Your graphics should enhance, rather than detract from, your credibility.

Obviously, you want the identity of your site to match up with your audience's sense of identity. If your goal is to establish your site as the premier destination for college students, you'll need to craft with your images an identity that they would share. According to the critical theorist Kenneth Burke, identification happens through the sharing of basic substances: physical, experiential, and philosophical possessions. So to attract students, you would use images (and words) that make reference to things that they might own, do, or believe. By doing this, you give your site an identity that appeals to your visitors, because they say to themselves, This site is speaking to people like me, or to the person I would like to be.

Add Informative Content

In our example of telling a story about your trip, adding multimedia allowed you to appeal to many senses. But it also allowed you to tell much more about your trip. With graphics, audio, and video, you can present information and ideas that are difficult, if not impossible, to put into words. When combined with the interactive capabilities of the Web, online multimedia can be an extremely powerful and effective way to present large amounts of information. For example, if you were to set up a website about a trip you took, you could include all of the previously mentioned content plus links to other information. You could set up links to maps of the region, historical sites that give background about the place you visited, current news items, and much more. No doubt most if not all of those sites will also make use of multimedia. The net effect (no pun intended) is a exponential increase in information, accessible when users want it, and otherwise out of sight (or hearing).

REALIZING YOUR LIMITS

With the rich and exciting possibilities of multimedia, it is not surprising that less experienced communicators can get carried away. A healthy appreciation of the limits on multimedia use, as well as the possibilities, is one thing that separates an experienced webpage builder from a novice. Here we will discuss two crucial limits on multimedia delivered over the Web: the needs for speed and multiplatform support.

Need for Speed

It's true that the speed of the Internet has been increasing (as we discussed in chapter 2). However, multimedia elements always require more bandwidth than text, since graphic, audio, and video files are so much larger than text files. Thus, if you overload your website with pictures, audio files, and more, it will take an eternity for your webpages to reach your audience. Every image increases the time it takes for your page to load, so make sure that they serve a purpose. You can also make use of compression techniques that we will discuss in this chapter to make your multimedia elements as small as possible. One thing we have learned from research is that people will not wait long for webpages. If a page takes too long to load, they will simply click on the Stop button and move to a different page. Don't let your page become a bandwidth hog, because outside of state fairs, not many people are willing to spend time waiting to see a pig.

Need for Multiplatform Support

The Web was designed from the beginning to be accessible from any type of computer. HTML-encoded pages are readable on computers running nearly any operating system (OS), whether it is Windows, Mac OS, Unix, etc. While this is a great advantage for Web users, it creates a definite challenge for Web designers. And even though we call some HTML editors WYSIWYG, they are really more like **WISIWIG,** or **"What I See Is What I Get."** The layout of your page and the colors of your graphics may not appear the same from one computer to the next. Some monitors display millions of colors, while others may only show 256. Some may be set at very high resolutions, showing 1024 x 768 **pixels** (extremely tiny squares) on the screen, while others may be set to show only 640 x 480. **Figures 10.1** and **10.2** show how the exact same page can look when viewed on two computers set up differently. When adding multimedia to your webpages, it is important to keep in mind the wide variety of computers, operating systems, browsers, monitor setups, etc. that are out there. If you are designing a page to reach a diverse audience, you will probably need to restrict your use of multimedia to the most widely supported elements, or design two different pages: one multimedia-intense page for people with a lightning-fast Internet connection, a high-end graphics card and monitor, and the most up-to-date browser; and another more basic page for the rest of the people in the world.

BROWSERS AND MULTIMEDIA

How your page will appear on some else's screen depends in part on how browsers handle multimedia content. When the browser encounters a tag

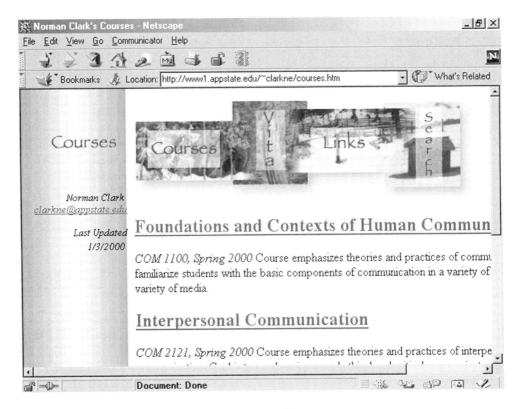

Fig. 10.1. Web page viewed at 640 x 480 resolution.

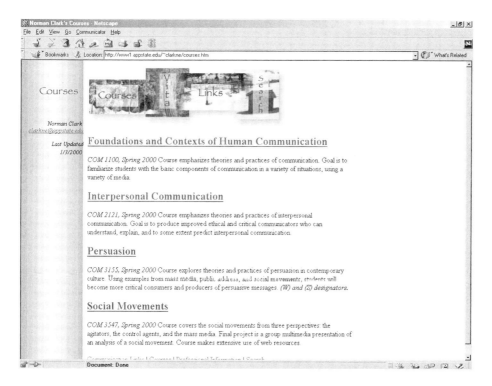

Fig. 10.2. page viewed at 1,024 x 768 resolution.

that designates something other than text, the program will use one of three methods to deal with it: **inline,** with a **plug-in,** or with a **helper application** (or **helper app**). Web browsers can display most graphics inline, or right next to the text on the webpage. Pictures, buttons, and the like are displayed without any extra effort on the part of the user. However, some forms of multimedia, including audio files, require an additional program to reach your senses. Two different types of programs can play back these more complex multimedia files. A plug-in, as you learned in chapter 2, works from within the browser and shows up inside the browser window. A helper app, on the other hand, opens up a separate program window. Some formats can be displayed in both ways. For example, RealAudio's video files can show up either inside the browser window **(Figure 10.3),** or in a completely different program **(Figure 10.4).**

A crucial difference between helper apps and plug-ins is that a helper app can run even if your browser is not running, while a plug-in cannot. However, plug-ins are usually more appealing to a Web audience because they make experiencing the multimedia content a seamless part of browsing. In either case, both the producer of such multimedia

Fig. 10.3. Here the video is displayed in the browser window.

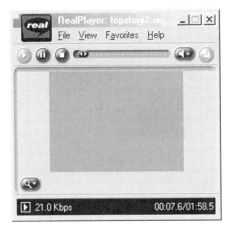

Fig. 10.4. Here the video pops up in a separate window.

content and the audience have to install additional programs. The producer has to have a program that encodes the multimedia content, and the audience has to have a program that in turn decodes it. Most plug-ins have an automatic download feature. For example, if visitors to your site click on the link to an audio file that you have put on your site, and do not have the appropriate plug-in installed on their computer to play it, the browser will ask if they wish to download and install the plug-in. If they say yes, their browser will automatically take them to the site where the plug-in is available so they can proceed to download and install it.

In this chapter, we will spend the majority of our time dealing with graphics, primarily because they are viewed inline and are thus the simplest multimedia for novices to add to their webpages. We will devote some attention to adding other multimedia elements. However, teaching you how to produce multimedia-intensive websites is not the goal of this text, or of most introductory courses on the Internet. Regardless of the complexity of your site, keeping in mind the benefits, limitations, and methods of incorporating multimedia will help you communicate more effectively.

GRAPHICS

Almost every webpage that you visit today has at least one graphic on it. It is not surprising that of all the possible multimedia content, graphics are the most widely used on the Web. This is because computers moved from textual to graphical interfaces long ago, and the Web quickly followed suit. If we had switched to voice-activated computer interfaces, the Web would no doubt make much greater use of sound. As it is, graphics have been on the Web for quite some time, and thus the tools to create them have matured, and the tools to incorporate them into webpages have become easier to use as well. For examples of working with graphics, we will be using screen shots from Macromedia's Fireworks. A 30-day evaluation version of this program is included on the CD-ROM that comes with this book. In this section we will discuss how to choose between the two primary graphic formats used on the Web, how to create and optimize graphics, and how to effectively insert them into a webpage.

GRAPHIC FORMATS

GIF

One of the two most widely used formats for graphics on the Web is the Graphics Interchange Format, or GIF (pronounced with either a hard or soft "g," depending on whom you ask). GIFs use **lossless compression,** which means that the file size is reduced without reducing the quality of the picture. Essentially, when a GIF file is created, it scans the picture line by line, and turns a long block of one color into two numbers: one that tells what color the block is, and another that tells how long the block is. GIFs are made up of many pixels that combine together like a mosaic to form the picture. GIFs use a maximum of eight bits per pixel to store the color information. Since computers use a binary number system, the number of colors possible in a given pixel, and thus in the entire image, is equal to 2^{bits}: in the case of GIFs, $2^8 = 256$. Because they are limited to 256 colors, and because of the method of compression, GIFs are best used for drawings, bullets, icons, lines, and other images made up primarily of large blocks of color.

Two additions to the GIF format have made them even more popular on webpages: animation and transparency. **Animated GIFs** are made by creating a series of frames that the computer cycles through. By making minor variations to each consecutive frame, you can make the graphic seem to rotate, wave, change color, or do any number of transformations. Unfortunately GIFs are always square, but you can simulate any imaginable shape by designating the **transparency.** Say you draw your image on a white background. When you save it as a GIF file, most graphic programs will allow you to designate one color as transparent. If you choose white to be transparent, then when the GIF file is shown on your webpage the background color of the page will show through all of the formerly white areas of the image **(Figure 10.5).**

JPEG (or JPG)

The second most widely used graphic format was established by the Joint Photographic Experts Group, hence the name JPEG (pronounced "jaypeg"). Like GIFs, JPEGs use pixels, but JPEGs use 24 bits per pixel. Because of this, JPEGs can include over 16 million colors ($2^{24} = 16,777,216$). To reduce the size of the graphic files, JPEGs use a **lossy** compression scheme. In lossy compression, some of the information in the image is discarded, which reduces the quality of the image slightly. However, given the amount of data in a picture, the files can be greatly reduced in size without a noticeable loss in quality. Since JPEGs can have over 16 million colors, this format is usually used for photographs, textures, smooth gradients, and other complex images.

CREATING GRAPHICS

Some people are blessed with great artistic skills. Luckily for the rest of us who stuck to stick figures in art class, the graphics programs that are now available make it relatively easy for anyone to create appealing graphics. Of course, if your stick figures look like chicken scratchings, or you are pressed for time, you might decide to download your graphic images from one of the many collections available online. The textbook

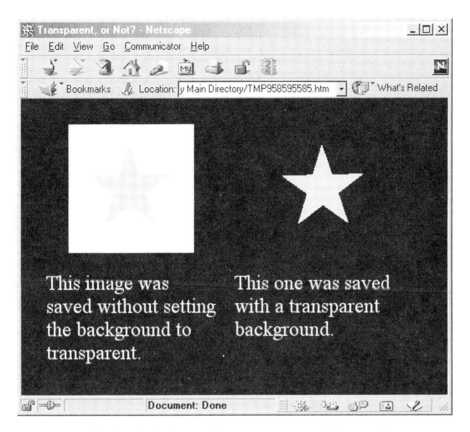

Fig. 10.5. Setting the background as transparent can help your images blend into the page.

website has a page of links to graphic collections. Quite often, this is the best place to start. After all, why spend time creating a graphic image when someone has already made one that will serve your purpose? However, just be sure that either (1) the graphic you download is in the public domain (not copyrighted), or (2) you ask permission from the creator to use it. Obtaining graphics that others have created is a relatively simple process. If you right-click on any image in the browser window, one of the options that will pop up is to save that image on your local computer.

However, sometimes you won't find an image you like, or you may need images with a special theme. In this case, you will have to create your own. We don't really have time or space here to discuss in great detail all of the graphics you can create, so we will focus on some basic instructions for the types you are likely to create: backgrounds, buttons, and scanned photographs. We will not cover **clip art** (graphic images

---

BOX 10.1

PNG, THE GRAPHIC FORMAT OF THE FUTURE?

While GIFs and JPEGs are the most popular formats for Internet graphics at present, a new format is slowly gaining popularity: the Portable Network Graphic, or PNG (pronounced "ping"). If you use Fireworks to create graphics, you'll be working with and saving PNG graphics. PNG is a format that tries to combine the best of GIFs and JPEGs, and adds some new features as well. PNGs use an even better form of lossless compression than GIFs and can be saved in 32-bit format ($2^{32} = 4,294,967,296$ colors!). Thus with the PNG format you can save and resave a very high-quality, full-color image, without losing any of the information (which happens with JPEG images). This makes the PNG format especially useful for working on graphics in an editor, where you tend to resave the file quite often.

PNGs have two other advantages over GIFs: **alpha channels** and **gamma correction.** An alpha channel allows you to set variable transparencies for an image. With GIFs, you can select a color of the image to be transparent–but it has to be completely transparent. With PNGs, you can make some portions of the image partly transparent, others completely transparent, and still others completely opaque. So instead of only two levels of transparency (transparent or not), you can have 254 levels. Gamma correction allows you to control the brightness level of an image across different platforms. People who work with graphics a lot know that if you create an image on a Macintosh and view it on a PC it will tend to look too dark, and PC-created images will look too bright on a Macintosh. The PNG image carries with it a gamma value that ensures that it will have the correct brightness level on any system.

PNGs have several other technical advances over GIFs and are expected to replace GIFs eventually. For now, however, when it is time to put your graphic on a webpage, your best bet is to export it as a JPEG or GIF. Not all browsers support the PNG format, and JPEGs end up being much smaller.

---

that illustrate a topic), because most people make use of premade art, and because designing clip art is the subject of a whole other course.

Backgrounds

HTML allows you to designate an image as the background of a page, instead of just a color. In Dreamweaver, clicking on Modify > Page Properties pulls up a dialog box that has an option line where you can enter in the name of an image file to use as the background **(Figure 10.6).** The image is tiled across the page, repeated from left to right and continuing down the entire page. Because of this, most background images are either textures or repeating patterns. Fireworks, like most graphics programs, comes with a number of textures that you can use to create a new background. Alternatively, you can create a tile that when repeated produces an interesting effect. For example, you have probably seen webpages with a column running down the left edge of the page and a white background on the rest of the page. To create this effect, you actually create a very wide but very short image (perhaps 1,024 pixels wide by 3 high) with a white background. Then you would fill in the first 100 pixels with either a solid color or a **gradient**–a gradual transition from one color to another. An example is in the top portion of **Figure 10.7.** When this image is used as the background, the webpage will look similar to the one in the lower portion of **Figure 10.7.**

Buttons

As we noted in the last chapter, graphics can be made into links to other webpages, just as words can. Many people take advantage of this capability and liven up their pages with buttons. Typically, buttons are used

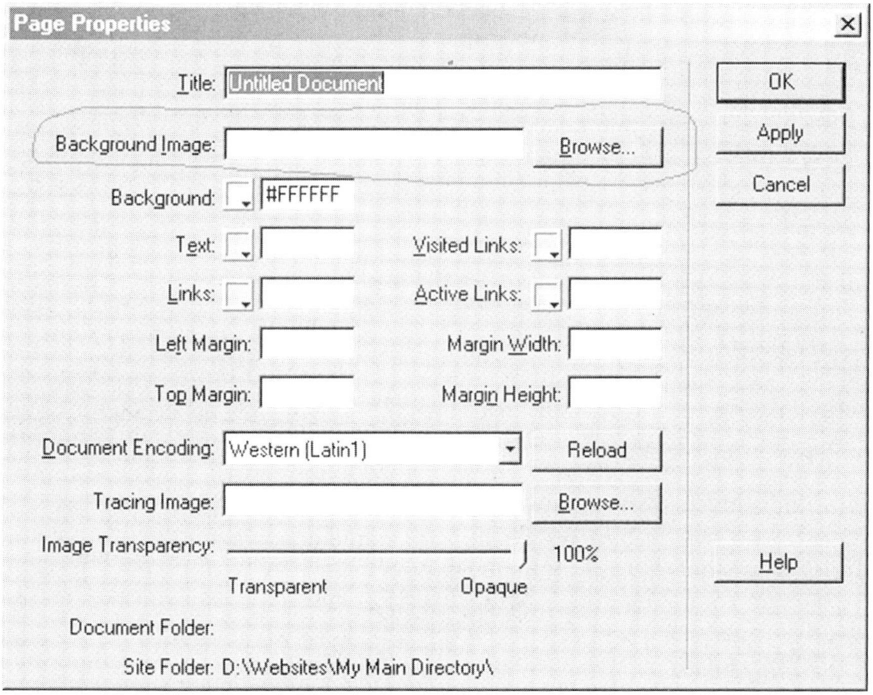

Fig. 10.6. The Page Properties allows you to designate a background image, as well as set the title and colors of the page.

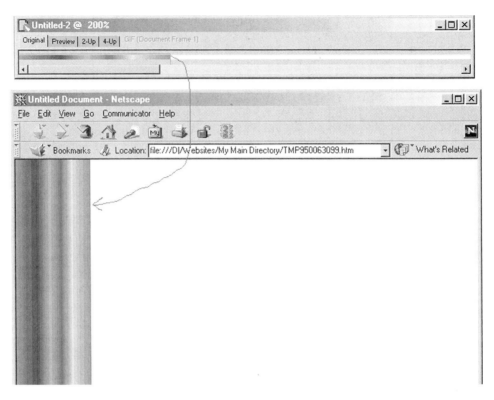

Fig. 10.7. When the graphic file at the top (shown magnified to 200%) is used as a background, it creates a column on the page.

for the navigational system within the site, providing visitors with a colorful and visually stimulating way to see which page they are on and which pages they can go to. Buttons range widely in complexity, as you can see in **Figure 10.8,** which shows some prebuilt buttons available in Fireworks. Web graphics programs make it very easy to create buttons. The Effect design pallet of Fireworks allows you to easily and automatically apply several different button effects, including embossing, beveling, adding shadows and glows, and more **(Figure 10.9).** Once you are happy with the format of the button, it is a simple matter to add the appropriate text to it.

Graphical navigational systems can get much more elaborate. By taking the time to get familiar with Web graphics programs, you can very quickly and with relative ease create buttons that change when you move the mouse over them. You can go one step further by creating an **image map.** An image map is a graphic file with **hotspots,** which are areas of the image that are actually links. When the mouse pointer is over the

Fig. 10.8. Some of the many prebuilt buttons available in Fireworks.

hotspot, it turns into a hand, letting the user know that clicking here will open up a new page. These more advanced systems are getting easier to implement, as graphic programs like Fireworks assist you with creating the graphics and then generate the HTML code that makes the image maps work.

Scanned Photographs

The first webpages that most people build are personal ones: pages about themselves or their families. Quite often, these pages are put up so that friends and relatives (and perhaps future employers) can see what that person is currently doing. What better way to show what is happening than with photographs? If you have access to a computer with a scanner,

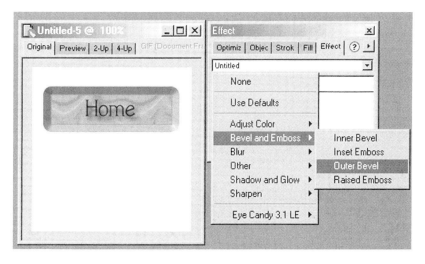

Fig. 10.9. Creating your own buttons is simple in Fireworks, thanks to built-in effects.

it is a relatively simple matter to digitize a photograph, which can then be placed on a webpage. If the scanner has been installed on that computer correctly, then a graphics program on that same computer will have the Acquire option enabled (usually found on the File menu). Clicking on Acquire will pull up a dialog box that allows you to adjust the settings on the scanner and then scan the photograph into the graphics program. Of course, once the photo has been digitized, you can perform any number of manipulations on it with your graphics program, including touching it up, applying various special effects filters, or turning it into an image map.

OPTIMIZING GRAPHICS

As we noted earlier, people browsing the Web have little patience for slow-loading pages. What typically slows down the loading of a page is an overabundance of large graphic files. Thankfully, both GIF and JPEG formats allow you to compress the size of the graphic file, and Web graphics programs allow you to easily alter the way that you want the file saved. Fireworks's Optimize palette **(Figures 10.10 and 10.11)** provides you with a variety of options for saving the file. Fireworks will let you preview what the image will look like once it has been saved with those settings (simply click on the Preview tab of your image) and even tell you how long it will take to download. A general rule of thumb is to try to keep your graphic files smaller than 30K (the K stands for kilobytes, or 1024 bytes).You can reduce the file size in several ways:

Fig. 10.10. WebSnap mode reduces the number of colors saved with a GIF file.

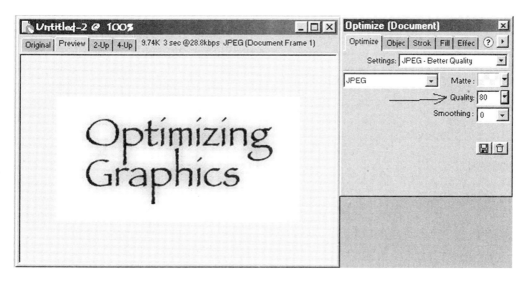

Fig. 10.11. Reducing the quality of a JPEG reduces the file size.

- Reduce the color depth: if you are saving a GIF file (such as a button), one quick way to shrink its size is to reduce the maximum number of colors that can be assigned to any given pixel. If you save it in 256-color mode, that means that each pixel has to have 8 bits assigned to it (since $2^8 = 256$). However, if your bullet only has 4 colors in it, you could save it in 4-color mode where each pixel would only need 2 bits ($2^2 = 4$). This would cut the file size by three-fourths. Fireworks makes this task even easier by automatically reducing the color depth if you use the WebSnap setting **(Figure 10.10).** If you want to ensure that your image looks the same regardless of what monitor it is displayed on, tell your graphics program to save it using only Web-safe colors. This will limit your picture to 216 specific colors, but you can rest easy knowing that these colors will look nearly the same on any visitor's computer.

- Reduce the resolution: the resolution of a file is the number of pixels per square inch. The lower the resolution, the smaller the file size. While printers can print out images at a resolution level as high as 1200 **dpi** (dots per inch), monitor screens can only display 72 pixels/inch. So if you are scanning in a picture, or creating a new one, and you plan to only put it on a webpage, it makes sense to set the resolution level at 72 pixels/inch, reducing the file size considerably. Often when Web designers think people might want to print out an image, they will provide a separate link to a high resolution version of the file. This way the page still downloads quickly, but if people are willing to wait they can obtain a high-quality file suitable for printing.

- Reduce the quality: JPEGs, as you no doubt remember, use a lossy compression strategy. They reduce the size of the file by losing data. You can reduce the file size by increasing the amount of lost data, which means decreasing the image quality. This is where Web graphics programs such as Fireworks can help you greatly. Using the Optimize palette **(Figure 10.11),** you can lower the quality of the image. You can see how it will affect the image by clicking on the Preview tab. Obviously, if you decrease the quality too much the image will look horrible. But Fireworks's preview feature makes it easy to create a file that looks great and is less filling, too—or at least uses less bandwidth.

- Reduce the size: it should be obvious that a graphic that is 1,000 x 1,000 pixels will be saved as a much larger file than one that is 100 x 100. Say you scan in a 4" × 6" photograph. If you leave this image at full size, it will take up a considerable portion of the screen, as well as a considerable chunk of memory. You can make the image smaller in two ways. First, you could digitally **crop** the image, using the cropping tool to draw a box around the part of the picture you want to keep and discarding the rest. Or you could resize the image **(Figure 10.12).** Fireworks allows you to set a specific size in pixels for the image or to reduce the size by a certain percentage. If you keep the <u>C</u>onstrain Proportions box checked, changing the width will proportionally change the height, and vice versa.

USING GRAPHICS ON A WEBPAGE

Placing a graphic on a webpage is very simple with a WYSIWYG editor like Dreamweaver: simply insert it by clicking on the small tree icon on the Objects palette, or by selecting <u>I</u>nsert > <u>I</u>mage on the menu. This will pull up a window that allows you to browse for the image on your computer. To make sure that things go smoothly, we suggest that you store your image files and your webpage file in the same location, and save the webpage before you start adding images. If you are using a lab computer, this most likely means on a floppy disk. By doing this, you ensure that when you upload all of your files to a directory on the server, it will be able to find all of the images. If you set up a more complicated site, with subdirectories, we suggest you read through the site management help files in Dreamweaver to ensure that the URLs for your images are correct.

But using graphics *effectively* involves more than just inserting them onto the page. To use them well, follow these tips:

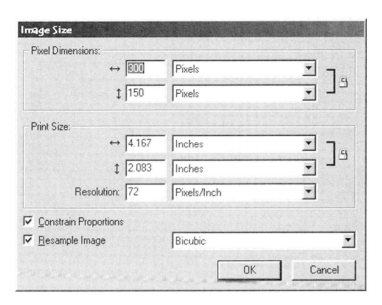

Fig. 10.12. Obviously, making the graphic physically smaller makes the file smaller too.

- Use the Alt parameter: if you click on the image in Dreamweaver, the Properties palette changes to show the image properties. In the Alt section, you should enter in a description of the image. This description is what will be displayed if the person visiting your page has their images turned off or if they have a text-only browser. The description will also appear in a pop-up box next to the pointer if they hold it over the image (and will also be converted to Braille or sound for blind people visiting your site). Use a succinct phrase or even one word that summarizes the content and/or purpose of the image.

- Consider using **thumbnail** images: if you have several large, complicated graphic files that will take a long time to load, create small versions of the files by resizing them. Then link these thumbnails to the larger version of the file. For example, NASA does this with images from the Hubble Space Telescope **(Figure 10.13).** A page with a listing of the various images in thumbnail form downloads very quickly, allowing visitors to get a preview of what the larger image will look like. This way they can decide which ones they want to look at badly enough to wait for them to download.

- Reuse graphics: if you create your own lines, bullets, buttons, and so forth, reuse the same image as often as possible. Doing this saves time for people visiting your page. Their browser will

Nebulae

Light and Shadow in the Carina Nebula

An Expanding Bubble in Space

Star Birth in the Trifid Nebula

Fig. 10.13. NASA makes very effective use of thumbnails.

download one copy of the file and store it in the cache on their computer. Then, when that image is used on another page, it is retrieved instantly from the computer's memory or hard drive, instead of having to be downloaded over the Internet.

- Use the height and width parameters: make sure that the height and width values are present in the parameters for the image (which show up in the Properties palette in Dreamweaver if the image is selected). When you place a graphic on a page, Dream-weaver automatically enters in these values, but some HTML editors do not. If your editor does not, use your graphics program to learn the dimensions of your image and enter them into the image properties. This will allow the page to load faster, since the browser will immediately know how big the image is and can format and display the rest of the page without having to wait for the whole picture to download.

- Use tables to position graphics and text: HTML does not allow you to do elaborate layout and formatting. However, you can use a table to make sure that your images and text appear where you want. This is especially useful if you want your text to show up right beside an image. If you create a table with one row and two columns and set it to have no border, you can place the image in either the right or left cell and then type the text into the other cell. You can also use a table to position several graphic images right next to each other in a row or column.

- Use graphics sparingly: new Web builders have a tendency to overfill their pages with graphics. They put horizontal lines in at every new paragraph, clip art for every topic, and soon the page becomes a jumbled mess. Try to avoid this temptation. Ask yourself, Does this image serve a purpose? If not, remove it. Remember that unless you are selling images, most people are coming to your page for the textual content. Thus the multimedia elements should compliment and accent the content, not overwhelm it.

- Use backgrounds cautiously: keep your background image files as small as possible. Keep the colors pale and muted, so they do not interfere with the readability of the text. Be sure to check what your background image will look like at different color depths. If you create a beautiful texture image with millions of colors, it might end up looking horribly blotched when viewed on a monitor displaying only 256 colors. Worse yet, it might make the text completely unreadable.

You can do much more with graphics than what we have covered. One way to learn more advanced techniques is to look at other people's webpages and see what they have done. Another is to learn to use the advanced features of a Web graphics program. In either case, adding multimedia ought to be done carefully, with an eye toward how it will affect the overall design of the page.

AUDIO AND VIDEO

If you are a newcomer to webpage creation and are taking an introductory level course on the Internet, chances are that you won't be ready yet to delve into the world of audio and video files. Nor will your instructor have time to cover them in any great detail. But we would be remiss if we didn't at least point out the other types of multimedia content that you can add and the basics of how to insert them into a webpage. We would also like to remind you to check out the textbook website, where you will find links to the homepages of various multimedia formats. On these sites, you can find more information about how to incorporate these files into your webpages.

Audio and video content can be created by a number of different programs and saved in a number of different formats. **Table 10.1** lists the different types of formats and the extension with which they are saved. For example, if you create a QuickTime movie about your vacation and save it, its full name will be *vacation.qt.* Two of the most advanced and yet also easy-to-use multimedia formats are Shockwave Flash and Shockwave Director. With these files, you can combine animated graphics and

Table 10.1
COMMON ADVANCED MULTIMEDIA FORMATS

NAME	EXTENSION	DETAILS
AUDIO		
Wave Audio	.wav	Used for sound effects or small recordings; can be created with Microsoft's Recorder, which comes with Windows 95 and higher, and a microphone
MIDI	.mid, .midi	Used for music files, can reproduce the sounds of a wide range of musical instruments; can be created with a MIDI instrument such as a keyboard attached to a computer equipped with an audio editor
RealAudio	.ra, .rmp	Used for live broadcasts and other streaming audio; requires RealCreator to make the files and RealServer to deliver them over the Internet
AIFF, AU	.aiff, .au	Macintosh formats similar to wave files
VIDEO		
Video for Windows	.avi	Originally created for Windows machines
Quicktime	.qt, .mov, .qtvr	Originally created for Macintosh machines; can be used to create virtual reality files that allow the user to manipulate an image
RealVideo	.ram, .rmp	Used for live broadcasts and other streaming video; requires RealCreator to make the files and RealServer to deliver them over the Internet
INTERACTIVE MULTIMEDIA		
Shockwave Flash	.swf, .spl	Interactive vector graphics and animations; created with Macromedia Flash
Shockwave for Director	.dir, .dxr, .dcr	Interactive Shockwave movies; created with Macromedia Director

video with synchronized music, creating a powerful multimedia experience. They are also interactive, allowing you to create multimedia games, product displays, and much more. However, since these files can do so much, they also can get large, and thus they require a fast Internet connection. To see some examples of what people are doing with Shockwave, check out the links provided on the textbook website.

What all of these formats have in common is that they require a separate program to reach your senses. HTML uses the <embed> tag to designate content that is played by a plug-in or helper application. When a Web browser encounters the <embed> tag, it looks at the extension of the file. Then it checks its list of installed plug-ins to see if one has been designated to handle that type of file. If the browser has the required plug-in, it is used to display or play back the content. In Dreamweaver, inserting multimedia content is very simple: place the cursor where you want the content to appear (or where you want the plug-in controls to appear), then click on the appropriate button in the Object palette. If, for example, you wanted to insert an audio file called hello.wav, you would click on the icon that looks like a puzzle piece (the default icon used by browsers for embedded content). You would then browse to find the file and then select it. The code that would be generated would look like this:

```
<embed src="hello.wav" width="32" height="32"></embed>
```

Using the Properties palette, you can set a wide variety of options (depending on the type of content that you are embedding), including one very important one: the Plg URL. If a visitor to your page does not have that plug-in installed, this setting will automatically direct them to the location from which they can download the plug-in.

BRING ON THE FUTURE

As the overall bandwidth of the Internet increases and more people have faster access to it, more complex multimedia will be possible. For example, **virtual reality** (VR) is a digital environment in which you can interact with objects and even people who show up as digital characters called **avatars (Figure 10.14).** VR is used on the Web for a wide range of 3-D simulations, including virtual museums, tours of cities, views of stadiums (so you can see the view from your seat before you purchase the ticket), product demonstrations, games, and much more. At present, VR is still not used very widely on the Internet since it requires a lot of data and hence a very fast connection. But the possibilities for its use are great. You've probably seen commercials in which doctors operate on a patient from a location on the other side of the country. Such operations are already taking place on a limited scale.

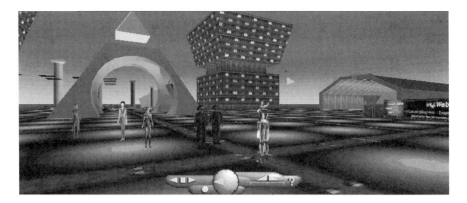

Fig. 10.14. Cybertown, a virtual community. The controls for moving and interacting are at the bottom center.

One of the defining characteristics of the Internet that we discussed in chapter 2 is that it is digital. And once information can be encoded digitally, it can be almost infinitely manipulated and transmitted. Theoretically, any information can be converted into digital data. Thus the possible multimedia content that could be delivered over the Internet is only limited by our imaginations (and available bandwidth, of course). So imagine this: you get a virtual greeting card from your significant other, and when you "open" it you are greeted with the smell of roses. Impossible? Actually, it is already possible. Researchers have found a way to digitally encode smells, and these digital signals can be sent over the Internet. On the receiving end, a small device filled with basic scent oils and a fan is connected to your computer. When the odor file is received, the device reads the file, doles out the appropriate mixture of oils, and then uses the fan to blow the odor out into the air (Platt 1999). It gives a whole new meaning to spam: imagine receiving an e-mail that actually smells like canned ham!

BACK UP AND RELOAD

Ever since the first graphical browser was written, the Web has continually moved beyond text to include more multimedia content. The addition of multimedia to the Web has had three great benefits: greater sensory appeal, stronger identity creation, and more informational content. At the same time, however, the structure of the Internet has limited multimedia content because of its need for speed and multiplatform support. Nevertheless, current browsers support a wide range of multimedia content, playing it through helper applications that either appear inside the browser or in an external window.

Graphics are the most widely used multimedia content on webpages. The two most popular formats are GIFs, used for simple graphics, and JPEGs, used for photographs. For the most part, new webpage builders make use of prebuilt graphics. However, Web graphic programs make it very easy for novices to construct their own images or scan in their own photographs. The same programs can help you optimize your graphic images. Since graphic files can greatly increase the time it takes a page to load, it is important that you make use of a variety of techniques to make them as small as possible. Once you have obtained or created the file, WYSIWYG editors allow you to simply insert them into a webpage. However, as is always the case, effectively using graphics means paying attention to the details.

More advanced multimedia content, such as audio and video files, require a bit more effort. They have to be created, embedded on the page, and then played back with a separate program. But they can greatly enhance the sensory impact, identity creation, and informational content of a page. As the speed that data flows over the Internet increases, you can expect to see more and more types of multimedia content–even, incredibly enough and sooner than you might think, smells.

Browse *and* Build	For sites to visit, exercises, quizzes to test your learning, and more, go to *www.harcourtcollege.com/ communication/inetcomm*

References and Readings

Botto, F. 1999. *Dictionary of multimedia and internet applications: A guide for developers and users.* Chichester, N.Y.: Wiley.

Faber, L. 1998. *The Internet design project: The best in graphic art on the Web.* New York: Universe Publishing.

Gehris, D. 1998. *Using multimedia tools and applications on the Internet.* Belmont, Calif.: Integrated Media Group.

Goralski, W., M. Poli, and P. Vogel. 1997. *VRML: Exploring virtual worlds on the Internet.* Upper Saddle River, N.J.: Prentice Hall.

Hughes, B. 2000. *Dust or magic: Secrets of successful multimedia design.* New York: Addison-Wesley.

Lopuck, L. 1996. *Designing multimedia: A visual guide to multimedia and online graphic design.* Berkeley, Calif.: Peachpit Press.

Platt, C. 1999. You've got smell! *Wired* 7(11):256–63.

Exiting Cyberspace: Implications of the Internet

[Cyberspace is] the ultimate extension of the exclusion of daily life. With cyberspace as I describe it you can literally wrap yourself in media and not have to see what's really going on around you.

WILLIAM GIBSON

Prediction is extremely difficult. Especially about the future.

NEILS BOHR

We've spent a lot of time exploring this new medium. But it's time now to step back and look at how it is affecting the world around us. Unthinking and uncritical use of anything can be dangerous, and the Internet is no exception. We began this book by taking an historical and theoretical look at what the Internet *is*. We then applied various theories to the practical *use* of this medium as a communication tool. The final step we need to take is to ask one of the most important questions you can ask when learning: *Now what?* What happens when we start communicating with this new medium? Where are we headed? And even though the future is uncertain, there's little doubt that looking ahead is better than blindly rushing forward.

Chapter 11

What about My MTV?

Impacts on Traditional Media

By Peter Zale ©2000 Peter Zale, www.peterzale.com   Distributed by Tribune Media Services, www.comicspage.com

By the end of this chapter, you should:
I.   Recognize the trends that follow the introduction of a new medium, especially in the U.S.:
   A. depiction as satan or savior,
   B. commercialization, and
   C. concentration.
II. Be aware of the current (and potential) ways that the Internet interacts with:
   A. books,
   B. newspapers/magazines,
   C. radio/recordings,
   D. film, and
   E. television.

Throughout this textbook, we've been treating the Internet as a new communication medium. It's important to realize the dual significance of the word "new" here: first, this isn't the only communication medium, and so its development and characteristics are influenced by the older, previously existing media. Second, as the latest medium, it is forcing older media to adapt and change. Naturally then, as is the case with most advances, there is a cyclical relationship between the Internet and older media: they both influence and are influenced by each other. We'll be examining this complex interaction in this chapter, first by looking at the trends that new media typically follow when they are introduced and then at how the Internet and older media affect each other.

TRENDS IN NEW MEDIA INTRODUCTIONS

Once upon a time, the inventor of a new communication medium demonstrated it to a chief executive officer. The inventor was very excited by his creation, as can be expected. But the CEO was less enthusiastic. He argued that this new medium would weaken peoples' minds and their ability to remember. Creativity could be destroyed, because people would rely on external images instead of the workings of their own minds. He was also afraid that it would give people all sorts of information and make them think they were knowledgeable. But in fact, they would only have the illusion of wisdom: information without understanding.

Try to guess what the invention was. If you said television, you would be off by a few years—actually, a few millennia. The invention was *writing*, the inventor was the Egyptian god Theuth, and the CEO was the pharaoh Ammon (you can find this story in Plato's *Phaedrus*). The point of this brief trip into the classics is to help you understand that every time a new medium is introduced, it evokes very old reactions and goes through stages quite similar to those that all of our older media have traversed. This is because humans typically make sense and use of new things in the same way that they made sense and use of the old. Three very typical trends follow the introduction of a new medium, particularly in Western countries, and most particularly in America: depiction as satan or savior, commercialization, and concentration.

DEPICTION AS SATAN OR SAVIOR

As was the case with writing, the introduction of any new medium often creates polarized reactions. On the one hand, critics of the medium see it as the destroyer of civilization. As we noted in chapter 2, communication media make it possible for us to communicate with people far away. For some critics, this ability causes more problems than it is worth. All mass media make it possible to participate without getting involved or committed (Scannell 1996). What this means is that when you talk with someone in a far-off place, it is easy to step away and keep your distance from the other person's problems. For some people, the chance of developing a new superficial relationship with someone far away is more appealing than putting in the work necessary to develop existing connections. With 500 channels, a new world that you can watch from a distance without getting involved is just a click of the remote away. The only things critics see people really committing to when new media arrive are the new forms of entertainment possible.

On the other hand, supporters believe the new medium will save society from impending doom. A long-standing tradition in America is to continually proclaim every new medium to be the new savior of participatory democracy. Assuming that new communication must mean better communication, many in America have celebrated each new advance, from photography to communications satellites (Zynda 1984). Local media such as radio and community newspapers have always been hailed by some as the best means to revitalize the public sphere, making it possible for everyone to have their opinions heard by everyone else. Or perhaps a new medium can save society by revolutionizing education. Radio, television, and now the Internet have all been pitched as promising educational tools. Perhaps you had *Cable in the Classroom* at your elementary school; certainly you have heard of *Sesame Street*!

We will be covering some of the implications of these issues in more detail in the upcoming chapters. For now, you need to realize that the shining promises and gloomy predictions about the Internet are not new ones. In fact, the claims made about this new medium are little different from those made about previous media. The end result of the Internet will probably not be the resurrection of New England town-hall meetings and a revived commitment to political action. Nor will it mean the collapse of society as in the days of Rome, with everyone glued to the virtual equivalent of a gladiator contest: destroying roaming demons and aliens in network-wide video games while ignoring the decay in the world around them. No, the future of the medium lies somewhere in between, down a path shaped by two other trends.

COMMERCIALIZATION

The earliest samples of writing that we have are not great sagas or moving poems but records of grain harvests. The earliest radio stations were owned by local furniture stores and other merchants. When communication media are introduced, enterprising people quickly find ways to use the increased connectivity to increase their profits. And even though the Internet began as a joint project between the military and the academy, it has quickly become primarily a commercial enterprise. Sites ending in .com vastly outnumber those ending in .edu, and .mil is almost nonexistent these days.

We can see the increase in commercialization in two areas: **e-commerce** and advertising. E-commerce, or the use of the Internet for commercial sales, is growing at a phenomenal rate. In 1999, an estimated $25 billion was spent online, $10 to $13 billion during the holiday season alone according to Ernst and Young. Retail sites were the fastest growing type of website during 1999, increasing by 52% from June to November according to Nielsen/NetRating. Estimates for online spending by the year 2003 range from $133 billion to $162 billion according to eMarketer. More and more time online is being spent on shopping, and more and more money is flowing to our emerging online retailers.

With so much money being spent online, it's not surprising that advertisers are flocking to the Web as well. But the growth in online advertising is more than just a knee-jerk response; it represents a significant aspect of the trend toward commercialization in Western media. You probably noticed at some point that you don't have to pay to receive radio or television broadcasts (other than buying the set, but we will deal with that issue later)—at least, not in America. But it is somewhat misleading to say you don't pay for broadcast radio or TV, because you do end up paying for it eventually. This is because in America, and some other countries, these broadcasts are supported by advertising revenues.

This is not the case in all of the world, as you hopefully know. In many countries, broadcast media are supported by government funding. While many Americans get upset at the thought of government control over the media, they don't think twice about paying extra for a product that has to cost more to pay for the advertisements. The cycle goes like this: companies pay broadcasters to air an ad, you watch the "free" programming, and then you pay a higher price for the product. Two things are going on here: first, you are paying companies to persuade you to buy their product. Second, the purpose of broadcast media becomes rounding up an audience to sell to advertisers. The key point is this: the recent trend of "free" Internet services that are actually paid for by advertising (e.g., free long distance through companies such as Dialpad.com) is not really a recent phenomenon at all. It is the model Western media have been following for quite some time.

Nor is the critique of the West's advertising-driven media a new phenomenon either. Certainly you can think of advantages to this model: free (at least on the surface) services and content. But many critics argue that this commercialization of our existence has a net negative effect. It is becoming increasingly impossible to make any choices that aren't somehow related to products (Luria 1996). On the World Wide Web, even searching for information requires a corporate sponsor. The advertisements are everywhere, and they constantly pressure us to buy a product to make up for personal inadequacies. In a consumer culture, shopping can quickly turn from the second most popular form of entertainment (behind television) into a compulsive illness (Sedgwick 1994). As an informed Internet communicator, you need to ask yourself, How closely do I want what I have to say tied to what I buy?

TEXT BOX 11.1

DIALPAD.COM AND INTERNET TELEPHONY

As you learned in chapter 5, the Internet can also be used for voice-based communication. This form of communication is executed between two computers. An online communicator can enter the Internet address of another online user, establishing a live voice connection, with the appropriate software. These conversations occur through a simple PC microphone. The main problem with this model, of course, is that both parties must be connected to the Internet at the same time. For this reason, only frequent long-distance partners (or internationals) make much use of this technology. However, it is definitely cheaper than the traditional route of using a telephone (especially for international phone calls). Two local calls to an ISP, allowing the Internet to disperse and reassemble the audio signal, effectively kills long-distance charges.

But what if your other party is not online savvy? Or worse, what if they do not even have a computer? Several companies have emerged with a communication solution similar to the PC-to-PC telephony model. One of these companies, Dialpad.com, lets you make totally free long-distance phone calls from your PC to any traditional telephone, anywhere in the domestic United States. While you rush to your computer to view this site, you may be asking yourself, How they can do this for *free*–as in, where's the catch? The service is completely advertiser-driven. You will have to view several ad banners on your monitor while placing your telephone call. Still, if you are willing to submit to a little naked capitalism for the duration of your call, you can save yourself a pretty penny.

- To place a call, log in to the Internet. Remember, you have to be connected to the Internet for this to work.

- Next, turn your microphone on and test the audio levels by listening to yourself through your speakers (we strongly suggest purchasing a microphone headset for this, once you are more comfortable with the interface).

- Then, go to Dialpad.com. You'll have to download a small Java applet (or program) that will automatically set itself up. Once this is done, you will see a phonebook that you can use to store numbers and a number pad that you can use to punch in the desired number just as you would with a normal telephone **(Figure 11.1).** So make that call!

- Your party will answer. Begin talking.

- Adjust your microphone and speaker levels using the sliders on the Dialpad window as needed. Check with your conversation partner to make sure they can hear you clearly.

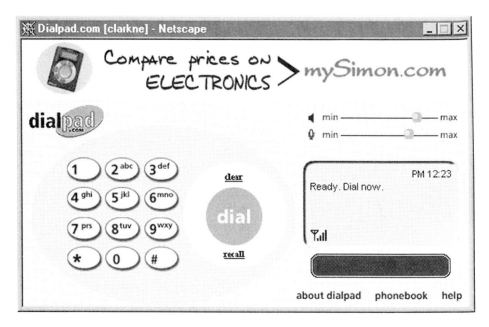

F i g. 11.1. Dialpad's point-and-click interface makes it easy to reach out and digitize someone.

So, how does all of this stuff actually work? Well, what happens is that the website transmits your desired telephone number to a company-owned server. This server then contacts another company server located geographically in the area code from your desired telephone number. The distant server, recognizing the area code and local telephone number, places a local call to your long-distance party. The distant server then digitizes the distant voice signal, "Hello? Johnson residence . . ." sending it back to you through the Internet. As you say, "Wwhhaazzuupp?" to your friend, your voice is digitally encoded by your computer and sent to the distant server. This server, in turn, relays the signal through the local phone lines. And there you have it. You just bypassed AT&T, Sprint, and 1-800-COLLECT all in one fell swoop.

One drawback is that the process of converting the voice signals takes time. So there will be some delay between the time you speak and the time the other person hears you. And obviously, Dialpad.com's servers can get a little busy. So if you get disconnected, simply retry the connection again later. It is also good etiquette to inform your distant party that you are on Dialpad.com at the beginning of the conversation, just to let them know you aren't being rude if your ISP suddenly gets net congestion.

In the very near future, Internet telephony may advance to the point where we no longer have long-distance telephone charges. Instead, we will subscribe to national ISPs that will provide services much like Dialpad.com. Or, on the other hand, long-distance telephone rates will continue to drop lower and lower until Internet telephony is abandoned for being too clumsy. Where exactly Internet telephony is going in the continually emerging world of new communication technologies is still a mystery. But because the Internet has made it so easy to control long-distance voice communications, we are likely to see increased competition in this market sector, which should translate into better services and lower costs.

CONCENTRATION

You no doubt learned at some point in your education that capitalism thrives on, and even depends upon, open competition in a free market. You might even have heard some stirring speeches about how America is great because it encourages and even forces companies to compete with one another, producing better and better products at lower and lower prices. All of this presumably benefits the consumer. But how many of you remember Betamax? Or, to pick something more recent, the streaming audio format called Crescendo? On the other hand, unless you've been glued to a MUD for the past couple of years, you probably do remember the antitrust lawsuit against that little company called Microsoft. What ties these three things together? One word: concentration. And it occurs in two ways: standardization and mergers.

Imagine what your life would be like without standards. Say you wanted to listen to a CD. If every CD manufacturer out there used their own **proprietary** (or unique, special) format, then you would either have to have a different adapter to play each type of CD, or worse yet, a whole different player. As far-fetched as this may sound, it actually is a scenario that gets played out over and over when new technologies are introduced. When something like digital videotape is invented, it is often worked on by several different companies simultaneously, and each company might have come up with a slightly different format. These companies realize that unless they can come to an agreement about the format, no one will buy their products. After all, would you buy six different CD players? So the major players get together and propose a set of standards that all will follow. We saw this in the past with digital videotape, as VHS tapes eventually took over the market, pushing Sony's (in many ways superior) Betamax format into oblivion. More recently, new television broadcasting standards have solidified, so that before long most of you will be watching **HDTV (high-definition television).**

While the benefits of standardization should be obvious, the drawbacks might not be. For the consumer, it means that they do not have to worry (as much) that the video or audio format that they start buying into is going to disappear next week. Anyone reading this have any digital audiotapes (DATs)? Standards are also what makes competition possible. Imagine what sports would be like if the rules were not standardized, and each football team had their own rules. But the drawback is that standardization also stops innovation to a certain extent, and sometimes it stops it in the wrong place. Many times the agreed-upon format is not the best, but simply the format with the most powerful backers, or backers with the most political clout. This was the case with the battle between VHS and Betamax. Sony's Betamax had many advantages over VHS, including sharper colors, higher resolution, and a larger head drum that resulted in a better signal-to-noise ratio, less problems with tracking, and less tape wear (since fewer heads were needed than with VHS to achieve the same effects). But in the end, Betamax lost to the more powerfully backed VHS. As a result, consumers lost as well, as they were left with the inferior format.

Standards are not the only pressure toward concentration. In recent years, we have seen a rapid increase in media mergers. ABC and Disney, Time and Warner, and Viacom and CBS have paired up over the past decade to become massive media conglomerates, buying up other media companies of every imaginable type and size. By the end of 1999, the three largest media companies had a combined total revenue of $69 billion, owning companies in every medium including television and radio stations, film and record companies, and newspaper and book publishers (not to mention theme parks!). Online, we have seen companies such as Microsoft, Amazon.com, and AOL/Netscape do the same thing, buying up smaller content providers and technology companies as quickly as their over-valued stocks would allow. Competition declines as the concentration forces of standardization and mergers enable strong companies to grow stronger, buy out smaller companies, and grow stronger yet again.

As the Internet matures, you can expect to see these three trends that follow the introduction of a new medium shape its development. Opponents and proponents will continue to overestimate its impact, either negatively or positively. The Web's growth will be tied to the growth of e-commerce and advertising as sources of revenue. And finally, standards and mergers will increase the concentration of media ownership, as more and more smaller online companies will be swallowed up by the giants of the Internet. A prime example of these trends: on January 10, 2000, Time/Warner and AOL announced a planned merger that would form a company with a net worth of $350 billion. Whether you believe the Internet is satan or savior, you can't deny its commercial nature and resulting societal impact.

MEDIA INTERACTION

People in Western cultures often have a tendency to see cause and effect relationships where none exist. A black cat crosses your path, and later in that day you stub your toe. Why, it must have been be*cause* of the black cat, right? While you probably don't have much trouble dismissing this example as mere superstition, the fact remains that you often take two phenomena that occur together and label the first one the cause and the second the effect. While you might be tempted to conclude that the introduction of the Internet is *causing* many changes in older media, you would be better off concluding that the Internet and older media are undergoing mutual change. In this section, we'll examine the interactions of the Internet with books, newspapers and magazines, the radio and recording industries, film, and television.

INTERNET/BOOKS

Online Sales

Probably the most obvious connection between the Internet and books is the rapid growth of online booksellers. Amazon.com, which now sells a wide variety of products, began as a book retailer. In fact, according to Ernst and Young, more people who shopped online in 1999 bought books than any other type of product. Even so, online book sales were projected to only account for 10.8% of the total U.S. sales in 1999, and 14.6% by 2002 (eMarketer 1999). Thus it appears that most people still prefer to browse through physical books, picking them up and flipping through the pages before they purchase them. Another explanation is that many people still do not trust the security of the Internet enough to use their credit cards for online purchases. Or perhaps some people are unwilling to wait for the book to be shipped to them. Even though traditional brick-and-mortar bookstores still sell the majority of books, many of them are setting up websites, turning themselves into "click and mortar" businesses. In 1999, BarnesandNoble.com was the next largest online book retailer after Amazon.com.

One reason why Amazon.com and other online book retailers have been so successful is that they have taken advantage of the interactivity possible on the Web. As we noted earlier, websites can keep track of your earlier purchases and make recommendations about what other books you might like to buy, either by recommending books in the same category or books purchased by other people who bought that same book. What they provide in effect is a digital version of a knowledgeable and attentive sales clerk, who knows your personal tastes and lets you know when new books that you might find interesting arrive. Of course, most sites don't only let you interact with a program. They also allow you to rate the book, write a review about the book, or read reviews that others have written. Finally, you can also interact with other information, following links provided by the website to learn more about the author or content of the book.

E-Books

If Amazon.com is the most obvious connection between the Internet and books, electronic books are, for many, the most exciting connection. E-books, like NuvoMedia's Rocket eBook **(Figure 11.2),** allow you to download books off of the Internet and store them on a portable reader about the size of a paperback book. These readers can store thousands of pages of text and have many additional features, including the ability to search for specific text, add digital bookmarks, underline text, add notes, look up words in a dictionary, and change the font size for easier reading. When innovations come out, they are usually hampered by high costs. E-books are no exception. At the end of 1999, low-end readers sold for $199, and downloadable versions of books were priced the same as paper copies. As these costs come down, and as the readers are made lighter and brighter, e-books will probably become more popular.

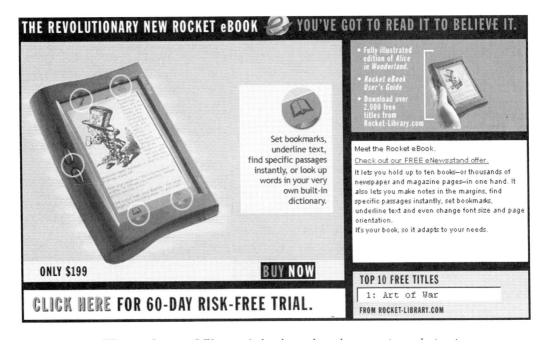

Fig. 11.2. Who needs paper? Electronic books and readers save trees, but not money.

Death of the Book?

Does this mean that traditional paper books are doomed to extinction? Perhaps, but doubtfully. E-books will be adopted by people who are enthusiastic about new technology. However, avid book readers and buyers enjoy *experiencing* books: leafing through them in the bookstore, getting hardcover versions autographed by the author, and building up a library that they can see on their shelves. Additionally, e-books will be viewed by many as an inappropriate use of technology. Traditional paper books have been around for centuries and are a good example of "just enough" technology. Unlike an e-book, they do not require batteries and can be read in almost any light. If you drop a paperback book into your bathtub, you've only lost $5 (if it can't be dried) instead of $200 (or perhaps your life!).

A better question is, does the Internet mean the death of book culture? Remember, the definition of *culture* that we are using here is a set of attitudes, values, and practices. It is definitely the case that the culture surrounding the Internet is very different from the culture surrounding books. Books are relatively closed and fixed: they have a specific beginning and end. This means that books emphasize a linear approach: you start at the beginning and follow the story or argument to its end. On the Web, discourses are woven together. Texts have links to other texts, advertisements, comments, etc., and do not have to be followed in any particular order. The culture that rose up around books emphasized grammar and rigid rules of composition. In contrast, the culture that rose up around e-mail and chat-rooms emphasized interactivity, fast and open forums, and a very casual attitude toward proper forms. Finally, in the culture of the book, knowledge is geologic: book after book is written, and the knowledge of the new book depends on and is added to the knowledge of prior books. But on the Web, knowledge is oceanic: a vast, simultaneously growing collection of cross-referenced material. Critics and scholars are still debating what the end result will be of this cultural clash. One thing you can be sure of is that these cultures will change each other, and your life as well.

INTERNET/NEWSPAPERS AND MAGAZINES

Supplementing or Circumventing

Online newspapers and magazines fall into one of two categories. Many are set up by already existing, traditional paper publications. Newspapers from the *Wall Street Journal* **(Figure 11.3)** to the *Grand Forks Herald* **(Figure 11.4)** have created digital versions of themselves, as have many magazines. Sometimes available free of charge and sometimes by subscription, these sites typically duplicate the print version while including some additional features. The supplemental features include late-breaking

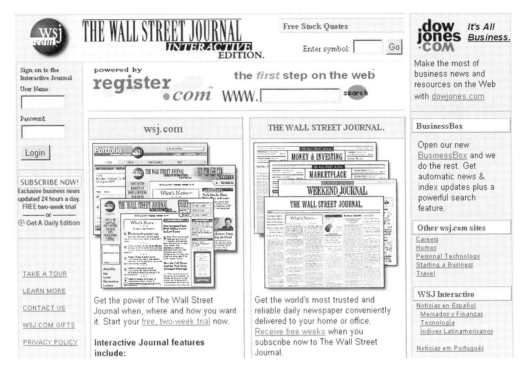

F i g . 1 1 . 3 . The *Wall Street Journal* has an online version, but it'll cost you.

news stories, links to other online content, the ability to personalize the content of the webpage, and searchable archives of previous editions.

However, some publishers are bypassing print completely and producing online "magazines" that are never published on paper. Salon.com is one example of a completely online publication **(Figure 11.5).** Of course, calling it a publication is incorrect since it is never published. Part of the challenge is figuring out what exactly to call the online versions of newspapers and magazines. Salon.com calls itself a "daily destination"; calling these sites **feature destinations** seems appropriate. Instead of sections, feature destinations have subsites for such topic areas as arts and entertainment, books, and technology. And unlike traditional newspapers and magazines, destinations are not limited by time deadlines. A quick glance at any of Salon.com's current pages reveals that the articles were written anytime during the previous week. Instead of being locked into final form and printed by a specific date, the content at feature destinations can be continually refreshed. New articles can be written and posted up to the appropriate site at any time, while older articles can be removed from the site and stored in an archive (from which they can still be retrieved). The articles can also be organized in many different

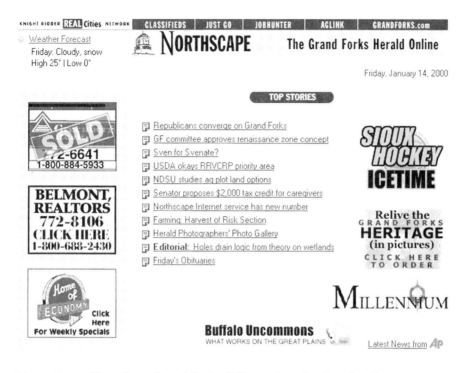

Fig. 11.4. News from Grand Forks, N.D., on the other hand, is free.

ways. Salon.com gives readers links organized by topic area, columnist, or date and allows readers to search by keyword.

Extending the Local

Traditionally, newspapers have been highly local media. Most of the content in the paper and most of the readers of the paper have come from a specific region: a town, a metropolitan area, a rural county, and so forth. The *Grand Forks Herald*, for example, is primarily read by residents living in the northern Red River Valley around the city of Grand Forks. In the past, if you moved from a city and wanted to keep up with the news from that region, you would probably have to purchase a subscription to the paper and have it mailed to your home. With more and more papers going online, it is becoming much easier (and cheaper) to keep up with local news from your old hometown. By extending the reach of local newspapers, the Internet is helping people stay in touch with communities in which they used to live. In a society that is increasingly mobile, the Internet might help some people feel a greater sense of connectedness by increasing the reach of local newspapers.

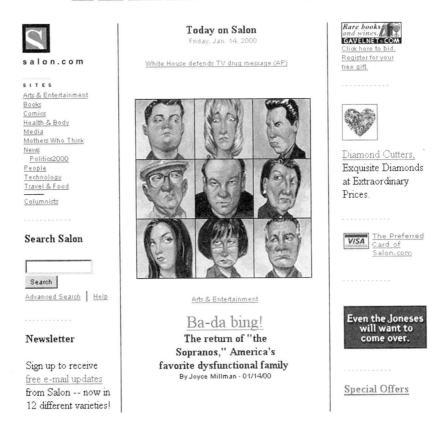

Fig. 11.5. Feature destinations combine the depth and focus of magazines with the speed of radio.

Targeting Interests

If newspapers are in part defined by their targeting of a specific region, magazines are in part defined by their targeting of specific interests. *Car and Driver, Fitness,* and *Field and Stream* have obvious target markets. If enough people are interested in the subject, someone (and perhaps many someones) will print a magazine devoted to it. The way the Internet is changing this is by redefining what we mean by the word *enough.* It does not cost any more to produce an online magazine for an audience of 5 than it does to produce it for an audience of 5,000. Since there are no printing or distribution costs, highly specialized special-interest destinations can be set up on the Web. Of course, whether or not these sites can be economically viable is a whole other issue that we will discuss shortly.

INTERNET/RADIO AND RECORDINGS

Making the Airwaves Surfer-Friendly

As the speed of the Internet has increased, it has made it possible for richer media to be transmitted over the Web. No longer limited to text, we can now send audio and video as well. But one of the more significant advances has been the development of **streaming audio.** With streaming audio, audio files can begin playing while they are being downloaded into your computer. Prior to this, you had to wait for the entire file to be sent to your computer before you could begin playing it. For a long audio file, this downloading process could take several minutes. But with streaming audio, the audio file can start playing as soon as it has stored a few seconds into your computer's memory (a process called **buffering,** shown in progress in **Figure 11.6**). This has made it possible for people to virtually broadcast over the Internet. With a streaming audio server such as RealAudio's RealServer, anyone can send out a continual stream of music, talk shows, and any other audio content over the Web. And anyone else can listen to this content by simply installing on their computer a streaming audio player such as RealAudio's RealPlayer **(Figure 11.6)** and then clicking on a link to an audio stream.

Fig. 11.6. Incoming audio stream being buffered on RealPlayer.

Just as the Internet is making it possible for newspapers to reach people far beyond the range of their delivery trucks, so too is the Internet making it possible for radio stations to reach audiences far beyond the range of their broadcasting towers. You can now listen to radio stations from every state in the United States and from 76 other countries broadcasting every imaginable format live over the Internet. And these "stations" are not necessarily tied to a specific physical location. Some of them are tied to a time period, some tied to a theme, some tied to a music movement. In fact, even online magazines like Salon.com have their own radio program that they send out through streaming audio. In a sense, we're returning to the early days of radio, when stations were owned by furniture stores and car dealerships and were used to announce sales.

What hasn't been figured out yet is the economics of Internet radio. Local radio stations rely on local advertising to pay for their broadcasts. If a local radio station makes their broadcast available over the Internet, it can be heard by an audience around the world. Say an Internet user in California is listening to a RealAudio stream from a radio station located in New York. Chances are slim that he or she will patronize any of the local (as in New York) businesses that advertise on the radio station. In fact, many local radio stations are concerned that Internet broadcasts will cut down on the number of local listeners, thus decreasing the rates they can charge for advertising. Arbitron, the company that compiles data on radio listening that radio stations use to set their advertising rates, now also tracks Web audio listening. Local stations are concerned that their shares and rating points will be cut by online audio outlets, unless the time spent listening to Web audio is tracked and recorded in a different category.

Custom CDs and MP3s

Like books, CDs and tapes can now be purchased over the Internet, at many of the same websites. Music clubs, such as Columbia House and BMG, now offer their services online as well. But one of the revolutionary changes that the Internet brings to the marketing of music is customization. At websites like CDNow.com, you can pick and choose what songs you want, and have them "burned" onto a custom CD **(Figure 11.7).** So instead of having to buy a CD with one song that you like and eight others you have never heard, you can build your own "greatest hits" CD with songs from multiple artists, or a personalized Valentine's CD for that special someone.

But the greatest change that the Internet brings to the recording industry is the completely digital distribution of CD-quality sound via MP3 files. As we mentioned back in chapter 2, MP3 is a format for digitally encoding sound. CD audio files can be easily converted into MP3 files, uploaded to the Internet, then downloaded and listened to on a

F i g . 1 1 . 7 . Custom CDs are only a mouse-click away.

computer or converted back into CD audio files that can be recorded onto a CD. Sites such as MP3.com allow aspiring artists to upload their songs, which can then be downloaded either for free or for a small fee by Web users. Obviously, the possibility for computer users to take songs off of CDs and send the files over the Internet to other users, who can then rerecord those songs onto their own CDs, has recording companies concerned. We will discuss the ways that copyright law is being adapted to the changes brought about by the Internet in chapter 12.

Proponents of MP3 files argue that it opens up the music industry. Instead of large companies controlling what music is heard by controlling which artists get produced, now individual artists can produce and sell their own music with a computer and an Internet connection. MP3.com, for example, offers a service for high school bands to digitally encode their own music, which can then be sold online as either MP3 files or as complete CDs for fund-raising efforts. But so far, the explosion of artists on the national scene predicted by MP3 visionaries has not occurred. According to industry figures, during the month of August 1999, the top three online independent music sites (IUMA, MP3.com, and Riffage.com) sold an average of a half a CD per artist. However, this figure could increase rapidly as more portable MP3 players are sold, and as more mergers between radio labels and Internet companies are made (such as the merger in January 2000 of EMI and AOL/Time Warner).

INTERNET/FILM

Microcinema

If the recording industry is being revolutionized by MP3 files on the Internet, so too is the film industry being shaken up by the combination of digital video cameras, editing suites that run on personal computers, and the Internet. For around $10,000, independent filmmakers can purchase a digital camera, computer, and editing software that will allow them to produce an infinite number of films. When you add in the possibility of distributing these films through streaming video over the Internet, you have a unique situation: the average person can shoot, edit, and distribute their own film without having to go through a studio. The **microcinema movement,** a term coined in 1991, is a community of independent filmmakers who produce everything from animated shorts to feature-length movies at a fraction of the cost of the major studios. With digital equipment, these films are now rivaling the quality of multi-million dollar productions. And now, with the Web as a distribution medium, the microcinema community is rapidly growing. Sites such as AtomFilms.com **(Figure 11.8)** feature new shows each week, providing a direct connection between independent filmmakers and audiences. If you are wondering if there is any profit in the microcinema world, answer this question: have you ever heard of *The Blair Witch Project?* This film, shot on Hi8 video and 16mm film cameras by the actors and produced for $40,000, grossed over $150 million.

Higher Hype

Part of the success of *The Blair Witch Project* was due to another connection between the Internet and film: online marketing campaigns. Thanks to a clever and suspenseful website and private individuals spreading word about the film through e-mail, this film managed to create a high level of hype despite a minuscule budget. Nearly every film produced today has a website. Quite often, as was the case with *Star Wars: Episode I* **(Figure 11.9),** the website is online long before the film is actually shown in theaters. Film websites help promote movies by providing access to downloadable trailers; "behind the scenes" information about production, stars, and plotlines; and (of course) movie-related merchandise. But beyond increasing the hype level, the Internet is not affecting the Hollywood film industry very much yet. In part, this is because the two media are very different: films are designed to be viewed on massive screens in dark theaters; the Internet is accessed from a personal computer.

Fig. 11.8. They aren't *Terminator 3*, but the creativity and quality of the films at Atom Films will surprise you.

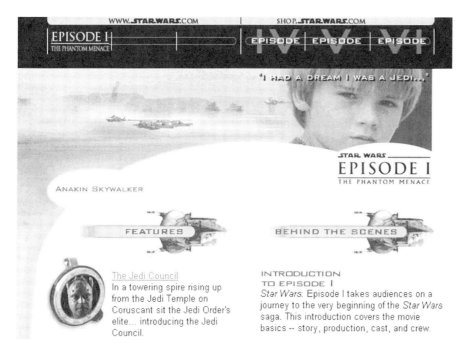

Fig. 11.9. Big-budget films, big-budget Web sites.

But as films make increasing use of digital technologies, such as computer-generated graphics, you should expect to see more connections between these two media.

Online Films

On May 5, 2000, Metafilmics (a production company) and Sightsound.com began distributing a full-length feature film called *Quantum Project* over the Web. This $3 million film could only be seen by visiting the website at http://www.quantumproject.com and downloading the movie. The movie wasn't free: a standard resolution version cost $3.95 and a high-res version $5.95. Once you downloaded the movie, you could watch it anytime, and as many times as you wished, on your computer–no waiting in line, and no need to pay $4 for popcorn. At the time this book went into print, it was too soon to report the success or failure of this venture. But Metafilmics and other production companies are already planning to release more films over the Internet. Keep an eye on this cutting-edge method of film distribution!

INTERNET/TELEVISION

Blurring the Lines

Just as many newspapers now have websites that serve to supplement their print publication, so too do the major television networks. ABC, CBS, NBC, and even Home and Garden Television all have websites that offer programming schedules, late-breaking news, more in-depth stories, and even games. And just as we are also seeing completely online magazines, so too will we soon see more and more completely online television stations. For example, ImOn.com TV sells complete packages ranging in price from $31,000 to $84,000 that allow anyone with the money to start their own online interactive television station. Anyone with a standard browser on a computer with an Internet connection can watch these Web casts while surfing sites that are linked to a show.

This is only a hint of things to come; most industry insiders, and most of the major players, are predicting that soon you won't be able to distinguish between your PC, your television, and the Internet. They are investing large sums of money in an attempt to converge these technologies into one easy-to-use interface that will make interactive television a viable, popular medium. Bill Gates frequently refers to this forthcoming device as an "information appliance." Microsoft's purchase of WebTV, a product that allows you to surf the Web from a television set, shows just how serious the move to unite television and the Web really is.

The convergence of television and the Web is moving forward slowly, in part because different companies have different visions of what the final merging should look like. This causes consumers to hesitate before purchasing a product because they are not sure that it won't be obsolete in a few months. For example, in January 2000 WebTV had only one million subscribers. Additionally, the technologies of the Web and television are still fairly far apart. It is possible, with the addition of a TV tuner card, to watch television on your computer. And it is possible with a set-top unit such as WebTV to browse the Internet on your television. What is slow in coming is a seamless connection between the two, so that as you watch a television show on one half of the screen a page of links to related sites shows up in the Web browser portion of the screen. One current solution to this problem is to produce simultaneous Web casts and broadcasts. For example, ABC's Enhanced TV **(Figure 11.10)** allows people to pull up statistics about football players, predict the next play, and get other detailed information using their Web browser while they simultaneously watch the football game on their television set.

Fig. 11.10. Interactive television is still in its infancy, but sites such as ABC's Enhanced TV are breaking new ground.

Lazy Interactivity

Most experts foresee that people will not be using their interactive televisions to access information but to purchase products. Because after all, American media are particularly driven by the advertising and consumption of consumer goods. They imagine the following scenario: you sit down to watch your favorite television show. As the theme song plays, a link appears on the side of your screen that urges you to "buy the soundtrack CD now!" You use the button on your remote to move the mouse over to that link, click on it, and your PC/TV instantly transmits over the Internet your credit card information and mailing address to the company selling the soundtrack. Two days later, the CD arrives at your door. This simple, easy-to-use, basic level of interactivity is what marketers dream of, but many critics fear. The combination of these technologies could launch impulse purchasing to new heights, which, in turn, could increase consumer debt to unheard-of levels.

Faster News, or Bigger Rumors?

Traditionally, television and radio broadcasters have had one major advantage over newspaper and magazine publishers when it comes to the news: speed. While newspapers and magazines come out periodically, television and radio stations broadcast around the clock. Thus when there is breaking news, television and radio stations can announce it between programs at the top of the hour or even interrupt programs when the news is particularly important, while newspapers and magazines have to wait until the next day, or week, or month. But the coming of the Internet has leveled the playing field, since now they all can publish news as quickly as their Web masters can code a new page. However, many critics are concerned that the push for ever-faster news may cause media outlets to publish unverified information in their attempt to be the first with the story. This happened in 1999 during the Clinton/Lewinsky scandal, when several news websites published a rumor about a Secret Service agent who supposedly had witnessed the two together. When this turned out to be untrue, the pages were taken off of the websites, but the damage had already been done. In this age, when mass media are pushing the envelope of speed, it becomes even more important to verify information.

BACK UP AND RELOAD

As is the case with any new medium, the Internet is following patterns and trends established by the media that preceded it. Its introduction has led to polarized predictions, with critics seeing the Internet as the destroyer of civilization and proponents seeing it as the savior of participatory democracy and education. As the Internet matures, it is being shaped by two powerful forces: commercialization, which is increasing in the selling and advertising of goods online; and concentration, which is reducing the number of players (and strengthening the ones that remain) through standards and mergers.

As is also the case with any new medium, the Internet is being put to many of the same uses that prior media were. Thus it cannot avoid being shaped by older media. At the same time, the unique characteristics of this new medium are also forcing its ancestors to adapt. Online booksellers such as Amazon.com are slowly growing in size, while electronic books combined with the digital distribution of the Internet hint at revolutionary changes in the publishing industry just over the horizon. Newspapers and magazine publishers are making use of the Web to either supplement or supplant their traditional paper format. By doing so, it is possible for newspapers to reach people far outside of their region, and for special-interest magazines to target groups far smaller than was possible with printed publications. Streaming audio makes it possible for stations to broadcast over the Internet, while the MP3 format allows private individuals to easily record, upload, and download CD-quality audio files. Using the Web, independent film producers can get easily distribute inexpensively made, all-digital films to the world. At the same time, major studios use websites to increase the hype for big-budget blockbusters. Finally, we are seeing a rapid convergence of the PC, the television set, and the Internet. If the major corporations investing in the Internet have their way, it won't be long before you won't be able to notice a difference between these once very different technologies.

BROWSE
and
BUILD

For sites to visit, exercises, quizzes to test your learning, and more, go to
*www.harcourtcollege.com/
communication/inetcomm*

References and Readings

Adair, S. 1999. *Information sources for the press and broadcast media.* London: Bowker-Saur.

eMarketer. 1999. *eRetail report.* Accessed 11 January 2000 <http://www.emarketer.com/estats/s_cons_prev.html>.

———. 2000. *Is online retail growth slowing?* Accessed 6 January 2000 <http://www.emarketer.com/estats/010400_wharton.html>.

Harper, C. 1998. *And that's the way it will be: News and information in a digital world.* New York: New York University Press.

Luria, C. 1996. *Consumer Culture.* New Brunswick, N.J.: Rutgers University Press.

Marvin, C. 1988. *When old technologies were new: Thinking about electric communication in the late nineteenth century.* New York: Oxford University Press.

Owen, B. 1999. *The Internet challenge to television.* Cambridge, Mass.: Harvard University Press.

Sedgwick, E. 1994. *Tendencies.* London: Routledge.

Scannell, P. 1996. *Radio, television and modern life: A phenomenological approach.* New York: Blackwell Publishers.

Wolf, M., P. Ensor, and M. A. Thomas. 1998. *Information imagineering: Meeting at the interface.* Chicago: American Library Association.

Zynda, T. 1984. Fantasy America: Television and the ideal community. In *Interpreting television: Current research perspectives,* edited by W. Rowland Jr. and B. Watkins, 250–66. Beverly Hills: Sage Publications.

Chapter 12

What about My Rights?

The Internet and U.S. Law

By Peter Zale ©2000 Peter Zale, www.peterzale.com   Distributed by Tribune Media Services, www.comicspage.com

By the end of this chapter, you should:

I. Understand how intellectual property law is affected by the Internet:
- A. copyright law,
- B. trademark law, and
- C. patent law.

II. Be aware of the First Amendment issues raised by the Internet:
- A. what free speech law is,
- B. unpopular, controversial, and offensive communications,
- C. indecent and obscene communications, and
- D. controversies over filtering devices.

III. Understand how to avoid liability when online:
- A. what tort law is,
- B. privacy law, and
- C. defamation–libel and slander.

For many attorneys, communications law has become one of the most complex areas in which to practice. This is not because the theories behind communications law are any more complex than those governing, say, criminal or corporate law. Rather, it is because in many cases we do not yet have fully developed precedents (Lawson 1999). Throughout the course of history, every mass medium has temporarily befuddled the governments of the world and their judicial systems. Of course, this is to be expected. Governments and legal institutions always incur something of a "system shock" whenever encountering unorthodox issues (Reidenberg 1998). This is especially the case considering how quickly Internet technologies have spread throughout society during the 1990s. How could our judges, attorneys, and jurors have been expected to know how these technologies worked? How could they render fair decisions when some might not have used e-mail, or maybe even a personal computer?

We are faced with this dilemma in part because innovations are, by their very namesake, innovative. They bring new ideas and challenges to the legal context. Even though facing these challenges can be confusing, we must confront them because our powerful new communication media continue to become more popularl. No longer are people merely the consumers of rich media. Each and every individual can now become a multimedia producer and distributor right in the comfort of his or her own home, thanks to the Internet. In this environment of increasingly powerful new communication technologies, the government and our courts are struggling to keep communications law current. In this chapter, we will look at the three major areas of communications law affected by the Internet: intellectual property law, First Amendment issues, and tort liability.

INTELLECTUAL PROPERTY LAW

Ideas are not like physical material. They cannot be easily contained. They are thoughts, free to move between minds given the conduit of communication. The only thing that gives ideas any legal gravity is recording them, at which point intellectual property law provides penalties for abusing another party's famous marks, copy, or inventions. Because ideas are so important to us—especially in our emerging information society—it is critical that you recognize the ground rules for dealing with information when communicating online.

There are three main areas to intellectual property law: copyright law, trademark law, and patent law. In the United States each of these areas is guided by its own set of federal statutes. The sum of these federal statutes is the *U.S. Code* (or federal code). Every year, Congress passes acts or amendments to update the *U.S. Code*. It is the duty of Congress to make these new laws where socially necessary, while it is the duty of the courts to rule upon the constitutionality of these laws. Congress has updated the *U.S. Code* with several amendments lately, reflecting many of the difficult legal issues being produced by the Internet. Let's first consider the case of copyright law to see how Congress is attempting to deal with our new communications context.

COPYRIGHT LAW

What Copyright Law Is

Copyright law, recorded in Title 17 of the *U.S. Code*, is principally consti-tuted by the sweeping changes made in the Copyright Act of 1976. Most important to our analysis here, however, will be the Digital Millennium Copyright Act of 1998 (DMCA). Before we review the DMCA, let's first try to get a better understanding of how copyright law functions. Then we'll consider how the Internet complicates copyright law and how the DMCA attempts to solve these problems.

Copyright law is designed to protect the *expression* of ideas. Once an idea is fixed in a tangible form, it is eligible for protection by copyright law. According to Title 17, section 102, "works of authorship include the following categories: (1) literary works; (2) musical works, including any accompanying words; (3) dramatic works, including any accompanying music; (4) pantomimes and choreographic works; (5) pictorial, graphic, and sculptural works; (6) motion pictures and other audiovisual works; (7) sound recordings; and (8) architectural works." This means that when you are browsing the Web, the graphic images, sound files, text on webpages, e-mail messages, and Java programs that you encounter can all be protected by copyright. Some computer programs, though, are more likely to be granted a patent than a copyright, depending upon the amount of original content being used.

The crucial terms to copyright law are *expressed* and *fixed.* This means that intangible things, such as an "idea, procedure, process, sys-tem, method of operation, concept, principle, or discovery" (*U.S. Code,* Title 17, section 102) cannot be protected, only the tangible expression of an intangible thing. So if you have an idea for a really great logo, but you never actually create it, you can't claim to own that idea. Some other things that cannot be protected are facts (such as $2 + 2 = 4$, or the earth is round), titles, names, or short phrases.

So what do you have to do to protect your website? Nothing, really. The second you express your ideas in a fixed form, the work is protected by statutory copyright. To demonstrate that you wish to have your copy-right respected, you may use the © symbol to declare your copyright. Usually this symbol is used in conjunction with the name of the owner of the work and the first year of copy publication. Of course, to register your copyright, a $30 application can be filed with the U.S. Copyright Office. Whether you go through the U.S. Copyright Office formally or declare a statutory copyright, the copyright is good for the life of the author plus 70 years (to protect inheritance rights). If the copy is made as work for hire then the copyright extends to the holder for 95 years from publication or 120 years from creation.

But what exactly does it mean to say that something is protected by copyright law? If you break apart the word, you will see that it means that only the author of the work (or owner of the copyright) has the *right* to *copy* it (or in some cases, perform, display, or even synchronize the property with other media). The assumption behind copyright law is that copying should *not* occur, unless the copyright owner grants permission. Sometimes that permission comes at a price: for example, the cartoons used throughout this textbook are copyrighted, and we had to pay the author to use them in this book.

As with any rule, there are exceptions to copyright law. Generally speaking, you can use copyrighted materials without seeking permission as long as your use constitutes **fair use.** Fair use is a slippery concept, determined by four factors listed in section 107 of Title 17:

- Purpose and character of use: fair use purposes include criticism, comment, news reporting, teaching, scholarship, or research. This test also considers whether or not the use is for a nonprofit educational purpose or for profit. Obviously if you're going to profit from using something, it is less likely to be considered fair use.

- Nature of the work: this test essentially asks, is the original work worthy of copyright protection?

- Relevant amount: the most slippery test of all, this factor asks if a reasonable amount of the work was copied. Copying an entire book would never be judged fair use, while copying a paragraph probably would be. However, the courts have not set an exact ratio or percentage of how much you can copy. They look at both the quantity as well as the importance of what you've copied.

- Effect on the market: finally, the courts look at the potential harm that your copying of the work may have on the sales of the original work.

However, every fair use issue must be weighed on the merits of its own case. Some educational uses are designed more for profit and some for the classroom. Some fair uses are more warranted, and some less warranted, than others.

Take this textbook, for example. It is considered a for profit fair use venture. When we quote a sentence or two from an article or book, we do not have to ask permission from the author because it is considered fair use (although we must cite the author). Yet we did have to ask permission to use screen shots of websites (notice the copyright permission appearing underneath them). After all, if a website has only four or five pages, printing one of those pages in this textbook means that we are using a considerable portion of that work (Phan 1998). You are probably starting to get a sense of how complicated the application of the fair use exclusion is. Different tests are weighted more heavily at different times and applied in different ways.

Complications of the Internet

Copyright law establishes that once the expression of an idea is fixed, it becomes intellectual property. If you make a copy of this book, you are basically stealing our property. As we noted above, the underlying premise is that copying should *not* take place. But the Internet violates this premise everyday. When you visit a webpage, the server sends that page to your computer. At this point, a copy of that page now resides in the memory of your computer, and usually on the hard drive in your browser's cache. Is this a copyright violation? Most reasonable people would say no. This is not the point, however. The point is that on the Internet, copying does, should, and even *must* take place on a regular basis (Reindl 1998). It is the operational nature of the medium.

Say you decide that you like the layout of a webpage, so you save the HTML source code on your hard drive. Later you copy large portions of that code into your own page. Have you violated copyright law? The answer is now yes, depending on whether or not your use falls under the fair use exception. Or let's say you are a big *Star Trek* fan. You decide to set up your own fan site and go to Paramount's *Star Trek* site (http://www.startrek.com/) to download some graphics for your own site. You have now definitely violated copyright law. Paramount is well known for searching the Web for pages using their licensed images without permission, and you'll probably receive a notice from their lawyers. Even though the practice of borrowing HTML code and graphics is fairly common, this does not mean it is necessarily legal.

This is only the beginning of the convoluted mess that this new medium has created for copyright law (Carlson 1997). Because of the Web's ability to hyperlink material, it is quite easy for you to build a **composite webpage** that pulls different elements of other pages together from different Web servers. So you could potentially have background images, pictures, and sound files on your page that you never actually copied to your server, but instead simply call up from the original server using the appropriate HTTP address. Is this copyright infringement? Any individual link, like a title, cannot be copyrighted, but what about a list of links? The courts have ruled that telephone books cannot be protected because alphabetizing is not an original expression. But what if someone spent hours compiling the list, organizing it into categories, evaluating the sites?

What if you have discovered that someone is using a great deal of your website in a frameset? When people first go to the frameset site, they might get the impression that your pages are the property of the frameset site owner. Federal courts have ruled that it is legal to link to someone else's website or webpage. But it is a copyright infringement to knowingly use another party's work to create the impression that it is, in fact, your work. If you use frames, make sure that you note explicitly when a link is–or is not–your original content. It might also be good manners to e-mail the owner and ask for permission, just to be safe.

The Digital Millennium Copyright Act of 1998

Copyright law was written for a different age, when works were recorded on paper, magnetic tape, and other stationary media. The basic premise of copyright has made it unwieldy, inadequate, and even useless when applied to the Internet. Congress addressed this, in part, on October 12, 1998, when it passed the Digital Millennium Copyright Act (DMCA). Unfortunately, the DMCA did not address many of the fundamental issues inherent to how the Internet operates. It did limit copyright infringement liability for ISPs and higher education institutions, however. For example, if you create a page that includes copyrighted images and store it on your university's server, the university (under most circumstances) would not be held liable for your copyright infringement. The DMCA also required the Register of Copyrights to make recommendations to Congress on how to balance the rights of copyright owners and the needs of users in our new digital age. We have yet to see what those recommendations might be.

However, the DMCA does not completely free ISPs from responsibility in all matters of copyright. If, for instance, someone were to file a copyright infringement complaint with an ISP about one of the sites it hosts and the ISP did not shut the site down, then the ISP could also be held liable for copyright infringement damages. In such a case, the owner of the site in question has little recourse. The site in question, according to the DMCA, should be shut down by the ISP (unless the ISP decides to risk incurring liability). While the owner of the site in question can defend their actions as either mistake or coincidence, the site must remain inoperable until the dispute is settled.

This makes ISPs the enforcing arm of Internet law until the courts can render a verdict. And it nicely insulates the ISP from both violations against copyright and free speech. Again, one must look at the genesis of the DMCA to fully understand its implications. The DMCA was written primarily by ISP attorneys as an attempt to shield ISPs from liability. In this manner, the act is highly effective. But this legislation has been widely criticized by free speech advocates due to its top-heavy nature.

Copyright verses Copy-Respect

The DMCA specifically included language to protect the fair use defense. Most average uses of the Internet would probably fall under this protection. If you are making webpages, your best bet is to create the page entirely on your own, scan in your own photographs, and create your own graphics. By using original material, you would be totally immune from any copyright prosecution. If you are not creative enough to draw your own graphics, then your next best bet would be to go to one of the many public domain collections of copyright-free graphics. If something is identified as residing in the public domain, this means that it is free to be copied. Of course, if you use a public domain picture on your site that has a person in it, that person could potentially file a right of publicity lawsuit. But this is unlikely to happen unless you use a recognizable person's likeness for commercial gain (e.g., using a picture of Michael Jordan for your logo on your sporting goods e-commerce site).

But what if you come across a graphic image on someone's page that you really want to use? In this case, we would encourage you to think about **copy-respect** instead of copyright. The culture of the Internet evolved from some pretty freewheeling roots. It was designed to make it easy to share information, to connect ideas, and to make as many things as possible freely available: research, computer programs, and so on. This culture was based on the simple principle of respect: if you wanted to use something that someone else had created, you just had to ask. This free spirit has been eroded somewhat by the commercialization of the Internet. Still, if you ask someone if you can link to a graphic image they created, or even copy it and save it on your own Web server, they will likely say yes. The assumption here is that if someone else asks you to use something you have created, you will also say yes. Among honest, collegial, and respectful users of the Internet, most copyright issues can be easily resolved without having to resort to Title 17 of the *U.S. Code*. The rest of the issues will have to wait until Congress and the courts revise copyright law to meet the unique demands of this dynamic new medium.

TRADEMARK LAW

What Trademark Law Is

Title 15, chapter 22 of the *U.S. Code* encompasses trademark law. The key legislation guiding Title 15 today is the Trademark Act of 1946, popularly known as the Lanham Act. As has been the case with copyright law, trademark law has undergone several changes during its two-century-old evolution. Still, the engine of the 1946 Lanham Act remains intact–a testimony to its effectiveness as intellectual property law. However, leave it to the Internet to challenge the basic assumptions of a working federal law. In 1995, Congress passed the Federal Trademark Dilution Act (FTDA), which holds several legal implications where online communication is concerned. Also, the Intellectual Property and Communications Reform Act of 1999 contained a piece of rider legislation known as the Anticybersquatting Consumer Protection Act (ACPA). The ACPA rectified several trademarking issues not even imagined in the Lanham Act. We'll update you on both the FTDA and the ACPA after we've covered the basics of trademark law.

A **trademark** can be a logo, acronym, word, color scheme, combination of sounds, or any other symbolic device used to distinguish a product or service as unique. For instance, Domino's Pizza has developed the slogan "Delivering a Million Smiles a Day!" through much expense and effort. Domino's is quite serious about its financial investment in that phrase, as is the case with Coca-Cola, Dodge, Nike, or any other major company that uses advertising heavily. It should go without saying, then, that companies will protect this consumer recognition whenever it is threatened.

As you know, copyright does not extend to the names that a company calls itself or its products. This is where trademark law has evolved as a means to solve issues of identity conflict. Trademarks protect company logos and names, product brand names, slogans, jingles, and the like. This legal protection can be exercised when one company believes that another company has encroached upon the distinguishing elements of a certain trademark. Unlike copyrights or patents that have a preset expiration date, trademarks can endure forever. Some trademarks in the United States are more than 100 years old. As long as the company keeps using the famous marks, trademark law can provide indefinite legal protection through trademark renewal.

For a trademark to have standing in the eyes of the court, three criteria must be met: (1) the trademark must be in active use by the company for a specified product or service, (2) the trademark cannot be ambiguous or ordinary, such as calling a new broom you have developed "The Broom," and (3) the trademark cannot be misleadingly comparable to preexisting trademarks in the marketplace. This last point needs some explanation. Often products will be called the same thing but not be made by the same company or even be in the same product line. For example, "Mean Green" the all-purpose cleaner is not the same thing as "Mean Green" the weed eater. Here the courts assume that the reasonable consumer will recognize the limits of language and not confuse such divergent consumer categories. Yet, if any of these three above criteria are not met, then the trademark can be rendered null and void by the court.

Complications of the Internet

The Internet complicates trademark law in a variety of ways. At this point, you should realize that online communication is about the immediateness of communication, if nothing else. When communication is so immediate for so many around the world, the law must expand to enforce certain ground rules for discourse. We will examine the issues of preexisting trademark claims, global trademark disputes, trademark dilution, domain name disputes, and the resulting introduction of the Anticybersquatting Consumer Protection Act of 1999.

Preexisting trademark claims can cause problems when people declare statutory trademarks on intellectual properties without having searched for potentially conflicting claims. Inexperienced executives will sometimes declare a trademark without having explored whether or not the property is truly unique in the marketplace. They may, in haste, assume that the name is distinctive enough to avoid the protocols of registering the trademark. This could turn into a hard lesson in the making, however, since rarely does someone come up with a completely unique idea. Corning Fiberglass once won a lawsuit against a competitor because they held the trademark to pink fiberglass. Tricky law, no?

Many trademark infringement cases are emerging in state and federal courts due to this casual oversight. The Internet makes it easy for entities to immediately and publicly declare statutory trademarks, making subsequent similar requests a violation of trademark law. Since the Internet is one of the most effective tools for conducting exact searches, the ability to easily find potential infringements has caused a sharp increase in legal disputes. The moral to this story, of course, is that you should invest in research assistance before committing to a slogan, logo, or other distinct trademark attribute. This should become even more apparent when you recognize that different states have different state statutes in operation, some of which do not report to the *Federal Register*. Even if the research is not wholly accurate, doing some homework will reduce your liability if, indeed, a similar trademark does exist in the universe.

Global trademark disputes are becoming more and more common in this global communication context. Before the Internet, the parameters of trademark law were somewhat negotiable. The World Intellectual Property Organization (WIPO) has, historically, served as the principal arbitration agency between disputing parties for some time now. In fact, they have been fairly successful in resolving these disputes. Yet the overwhelming surge in global participation on the Internet that we are witnessing, particularly among international corporations, has made international trademark disputes an important issue (Dueker 1996). Could companies in Canada with similar trademarks as those operating in Louisiana file complaints because of an infringement, for example? Or vice versa? Legally speaking, U.S. law generally stops at its borders, as does Canadian law.

Trademark dilution is another important issue in trademark law, dealing with the diminishment of a trademark's value. For instance, McDonald's cannot take the widely recognized Burger King logo and negatively position it in their advertisements without consent. Of course, obtaining such consent is unlikely. But imagine that a clandestine corporate executive took one of the two hamburger chain logos and prominently pasted in a picture of a dead rat. Worse, imagine that this image were anonymously posted to thousands of recipients on a fast-food listserv, who then sent the image on to their friends and family. The Internet provides a simple and effective way to diminish the value of a trademark to the corporation. The Federal Trademark Dilution Act of 1995 protects companies by making such attacks on their trademarks illegal.

Disputes over domain names often crop up because during the early years of domain name registration those who could see the coming of the Web as a device for commerce began securing both humorous and profitable URL addresses. This practice, called cybersquatting, mirrors the settlement of the Wild West during the 1800s–except in this case, the squatters used computers instead of pistols. Once e-commerce became popular, many brick-and-mortar companies tried to use the name of their business as part of their URL, only to discover that another pseudo-organization or individual had purchased that domain name already (Landau 1997). Most of these issues settled themselves naturally, of course. The company would offer a purchase price to the cybersquatter, and negotiations would ensue until a settlement could be reached. However, sometimes a mutual price could not be reached between the two parties. That's when the expense of legal action became necessary, and the government was prompted to intervene.

The 1999 Anticybersquatting Consumer Protection Act updated Title 15, chapter 22. President Clinton signed the act into law on November 29, 1999; it allows companies to legally act against those who would, in bad faith, profiteer on their famous marks. It is a violation of trademark law if: (1) a party uses a mark that is "identical or confusingly similar to a mark that was distinctive when the domain name was registered," (2) a party uses a mark that is "dilutive of a mark that was famous when the domain name was registered," or (3) a party infringes upon "marks and names protected by statute such as the Olympic symbol or Red Cross" (Deutsch 2000). The ACPA legislation is retroactive, meaning that the act applies to domain names registered on or before the passage of the legislation on November 29, 1999. And while most of the usual .com domain names have already been selected, remember that the .cc suffix has also emerged as a secondary means of providing digital territory for commerce-based websites. Within this new domain, companies will be able to start fresh, aware of the e-commerce context (this time) and armed with the provisions provided by the ACPA.

PATENT LAW

What Patent Law Is

Title 35 of the *U.S. Code* details how U.S. patent law is to be applied. Many people confuse patent law with trademark and copyright law. Patent law is specific to "any new and useful process, machine, manufacture, or composition of matter, or any new and useful improvement thereof." For

---

TEXT BOX 12.1

CLASSIC DOMAIN NAME DISPUTES

- Adam Curry, once a video jockey for Music Television, was an early adopter of Internet technologies. He secured the domain name MTV.com to promote the network via the Internet in 1993. When he was released as a VJ, Curry continued to promote the domain name and website until MTV filed suit against Curry. The issue was eventually settled out of court.

- The People for Eating Tasty Animals (PETA) purchased domain name rights to peta.org in 1995, lampooning the People for the Ethical Treatment of Animals (PETA). That domain name has been disabled until the matter can be resolved by the courts.

- Hasbro Industries, makers of the classic children's game Candyland, in 1996 won their case against the Internet Entertainment Group, Inc., who purchased Candyland.com for an adult entertainment site. In part, the Hasbro ruling was based on the premise that Hasbro held trademark rights to such a distinctive entertainment moniker. But, in larger measure, the spirit of the ruling also held that the domain name could be confusing for children venturing into cyberspace (as you can no doubt vividly imagine . . .).

---

instance, Kentucky Fried Chicken has a patent on their batter recipe. What is most important for you to understand is that the Patent and Trademark Office is bound to two important patent-granting criteria: (1) the product must serve some useful purpose to individuals or society, and (2) the product must be explicitly detailed. Abstract ideas cannot be patented. Inventions must be explicit, certain, and clearly demonstrate their impact. A patent provides the inventor with the right to prevent foreigners or domestics from "making, using, offering for sale, or selling" (*U.S. Code*, Title 35, part 3, chapter 8) the invention in the United States for 20 years after the patent was initially filed (assuming it is granted). Patent law protects the discovery from being capitalized upon by another.

Complications of the Internet

The Internet doesn't exactly effect patent law directly, but its ability to communicate new ideas so easily causes some concern (Reindl 1998). Because e-mail, the Web, and attached data files are used so much in business communication today, patent development secrets face increasing risks (Hodkowski 1997). This is a serious concern for major corporations and start-up firms alike looking to secure a patent. At any stage along the development of a particular idea, from the abstract to the concrete, a party on the inside can communicate critically important information to a party on the outside. This communication could seem innocent enough–a moment of glee sent to a close friend from college in an e-mail: "We found it! We found the missing R2811X gene! Man, we're gonna be rich!" Or it could be more subversive, using anonymous e-mail accounts to reveal the full specifications of company secrets. Remember, the Patent and Trademark Office will not accept requests for a patent grant unless the idea is fully developed. An unsuspecting premature e-mail could, most definitely, jeopardize years of research efforts and the resulting proceeds from securing a profitable patent.

FIRST AMENDMENT ISSUES

As we noted in the introduction to the intellectual property law section, ideas are difficult to contain. Intellectual property laws try to protect the profitability of creativity, but another genre of law tries to protect general human expression. Perhaps more than at any other time in the history of humankind, free speech philosophy is being widely and popularly advocated. It is our opinion that the love for free speech would not be as great as it is, currently, unless the Internet made the act of communicating so commonplace in our lives. Practically speaking, we can now send and receive all types of information with the click of a mouse button, to or from Istanbul, Mexico City, Moscow, Berlin, Tokyo–a matter of individual will and the right e-address. But exactly how far do these individual freedoms run before they violate law? Just how free are you, really, to communicate with the world as you might choose?

WHAT FREE SPEECH LAW IS

The First Amendment to the U.S. Constitution reads: "Congress shall make no law respecting an establishment of religion, or prohibiting the free exercise thereof; or abridging the freedom of speech, or of the press; or the right of the people peaceably to assemble, and to petition the government for a redress of grievances." Of all the amendments, this is the one most commonly cited by U.S. citizens during everyday conversation. We cite our right to free speech whenever feeling oppressed or declaring an authority out-of-bounds. Clearly, though, you should not get into the habit of trusting the conversational legal analysis of those who offhandedly cite the First Amendment. Our popular understandings of how free speech works are not always consistent with how Congress or the courts have interpreted law. In other words, before you freely express yourself, it is best to have a working understanding of the law.

You see, while Congress "shall make no law" abridging these freedoms, on occasion it has (Tedford 1997). And in some cases, the Supreme Court has even upheld these laws due to "compelling state interests." Why is this? Basically, this is because the U.S. Supreme Court has subscribed to a centrist interpretation of the First Amendment. This means that some of the justices, during the history of U.S. rulings, decided that the words of the First Amendment needed to be softened to ensure the functioning of society. Since none of the authors of the Constitution remain with us, what they intended becomes a matter of interpretation. And, when interpretation is involved, these are matters upon which reasonable justices will disagree. The first thing that you must recognize about free speech law is that certain types of speech are treated differently by the courts. For example, the Supreme Court would be more inclined to uphold a citizen's right to publicly debate the merits of socialism than another citizen's decision to loudly proclaim their sexual delights in a park. Thomas Jefferson and Karl Marx get the utmost levels of constitutional protection, whereas Larry Flynt and Hugh Hefner are more vulnerable. You can say what you will, but you must recognize that your individual rights, under certain circumstances, can be forfeited if you go against the prevailing wishes of society (Salbu 1998). Most people do not recognize this and, to their own detriment, interpret the First Amendment literally. While many free speech scholars and attorneys might applaud your idealism, idealism and the law are treated differently before the bench.

Where the Internet and free speech are concerned, almost all of the contemporary cases revolve around one of three dynamics. The first concerns whether or not the First Amendment should be extended to protect unpopular, controversial, and even offensive communications. The second deals with issues of online indecency and obscenity. The final dynamic deals with the use of screening or filtering devices, both in the home and at public institutions.

UNPOPULAR, CONTROVERSIAL, AND OFFENSIVE COMMUNICATIONS

We have all encountered unpopular, controversial, or offensive communications. In fact, you may have even done some of this communication yourself. After all, everyone has their own set of standards for what constitutes unpopular, controversial, and offensive meaning. One person's brilliance is another person's annoyance. The main issue here concerns whether or not content conveyed over the Internet that is unpopular, controversial, or offensive should enjoy First Amendment protection. In the following section, we look at cyberstalking, spam, and hate speech to help us understand how free speech law functions online.

Cyberstalking

Suppose someone sends you 20-30 uninvited e-mails a day. Imagine what your life might be like if these e-mails became threatening or harassing in nature. Would you want to even open your e-mail account? The Interstate Stalking Act of 1996 already provides federal protection against those who physically cross state lines to stalk another party. Title 18, section 875(c) of the federal code makes it a federal crime "to transmit any communication in interstate or foreign commerce containing a threat to injure the person of another." Even so, many lawyers argue that the statute is not specific enough. In an attempt to make such legislation tailored to the communicative dynamics of the Internet, the Department of Justice released a report in 1999 titled *Cyberstalking: A New Challenge for Law Enforcement and Industry.* The report argues that federal law must be changed to "prohibit the transmission of any communication in interstate or foreign commerce with intent to threaten or harass another person, where such communication places another person in fear of death or bodily injury to themselves or another person."

So, then, how is this a free speech issue? Philosophically, many free speech advocates argue that people should be left alone to communicate to one another however they wish. In other words, words are mere words. Legally, where do you draw the line between actual threats of violence or duress and jokes, humor, and the like? Beyond the fact that the Internet does not convey the nuances of humor very well absent the trusty emoticon ;-), it is not good practice to tell someone (even if a close friend) that you intend to do them harm (even in play). One person's joke is another person's sleep-consuming nightmare. So, for your own sake as well as everyone else's, please try to refrain from using such precarious language.

Spam

As you'll recall from chapter 3, spam is a form of electronic junk mail that includes such messages as get-rich-quick scams, advertisements for pornography sites, diet programs, and other content that you (and maybe hundreds of others) didn't ask to receive. The basic question here is, Does spam enjoy First Amendment protection? As of June 2000, the answer was still yes. There are no federal laws preventing marketers from doing bulk e-mail distributions over the Internet (several state laws do exist). This could be changing, however. The Unsolicited Electronic Mail Act of 2000 (H.R.3113) is being considered before the 106th Congress. Roughly speaking, H.R.3113 treats spam in the same manner that communications law treats junk phone calls. Spam marketers could be liable for a $500 fine if they send an e-mail message to a recipient who has explicitly requested to be taken off their contact list. These restrictions could be considered First Amendment infringements upon commercial expression, of course (Marcus 1998). But here is an example where the legislature may determine that an entire class of unpopular communications needs to be restricted in favor of protecting the larger community interests involved.

Hate Speech and Hate Literature

Some of the most violent communication is very difficult to regulate because extremist political speech enjoys sweeping First Amendment protection. Even if the statements and opinions offered by those on the fringes of discourse violate the sensibilities of the reasonable person, the courts have protected the open expression of political content above and beyond all other forms of speech. The Internet has brought new challenges to those who wish to stop such expressions. Even if our courts began deciding that certain forms of speech did not enjoy First Amendment protection, how could the Department of Justice enforce such rulings upon the rest of the world? For example, if someone ran a site proclaiming that the Jewish Holocaust is a mere hoax–and then stored these viewpoints on a server in the Netherlands–how could U.S. law affect them? The enforcing arm of U.S. law could only control the downloading of such information within its borders (O'Rourke 1998).

Private entities enjoy private rules over their own equipment. If the agency is a private corporation or university, the proprietor of the equipment governs what can or cannot be communicated on their machines (Hash and Ibrahim 1996; Gantt 1995). This is not a violation of First Amendment law, since the government has not made any provision against the free exercise of speech. Ordinarily, extremist expressions will not be tolerated by these monitored services because of liability concerns. ISPs also enjoy the right to terminate a user's service contract whenever provisions of that contract are broken. Almost all ISP contracts incorporate statements that make harassing, threatening, and extremist speech grounds for termination.

Public universities, long known for their protection of free and open discourse, are an emerging legal issue. On most campuses today, a quiet debate rages over whether or not the public institution (representing the state) should be allowed to intervene when computer-mediated communications become unpopular, controversial, or offensive. Several institutions have resolved this issue by arguing that any information communicated via public university equipment must–in some tangible fashion–be directly related to the mission of the institution. The interpretation of what is, and what is not, tangibly related to the university mission rests in the hands of the campus information technology administrator.

Extremist speech loses its First Amendment protection, however, when it becomes directly threatening or harassing toward any specific person or group. Communications of this genre fall under tort liability, which will be covered in greater detail later in this chapter. If threats, harassment, or acts of violence forewarned in communications can be linked to ethnic, racial, cultural, religious, or even gender-based hate, the courts can issue an enhanced sentence depending upon the infraction. The Anti-Defamation League reports that some 40 states currently have hate-enhancement laws on the books, with more considering them during the new legislative season.

INDECENT AND OBSCENE COMMUNICATIONS

Every new communication medium has had to balance the issues of human sexuality and free speech. Some of the first materials ever produced on the printing press were not only Gutenberg Bibles but also off-color limericks written by wayward monks. When photography emerged as a popular medium, the art of nude portrait (of both the male and female forms) became quite the underground phenomena. Likewise, as film, television, cable, and portable video debuted, each medium had to survive its own round of public criticism and scrutiny in order to define its appropriate place within the community. Certainly by now you have heard of "cyberporn" or "Internet pornography."

On July 3, 1995, *Time* magazine ran a cover story by Philip Elmer-Dewitt with the title: "On a Screen Near You: Cyberporn." Citing the preliminary research of U.S. Senator Jim Exon (D-NE), the article concluded that this new form of interactive pornography might best be left at the corner video store. The resulting public awareness (which bordered on hysteria) about this newfangled place called cyberspace, and its ability to provide endless categories of point-and-click risqué material, created a significant amount of discussion—in our legislatures, universities, barber shops, and personal bedrooms. It was only a matter of time before the issue finally presented itself to Congress in the form of legislation. When it did, it pitted conservative society against liberal society in a contest that would eventually appear before the highest court in the land.

The CDA

The Communications Decency Act of 1996 (CDA) was a subsection (Title V) of the larger Telecommunications Reform Act of 1996. Introduced by Senators Jim Exon (D-NE) and Dan Coats (R-IN), the CDA sought to amend Title 47 of the *U.S. Code*. The CDA tried to achieve several content-specific restrictions: (1) to ensure that the existing federal communications laws barring obscene material also applied to the Internet, (2) to

TEXT BOX 12.2

SO WHAT IS OBSCENE, REALLY?

To grasp the significance of laws about online pornography, you need to understand what is meant legally by the word "obscene." The *Miller v. California, 413 U.S. 15 (1973)* case produced the "Miller obscenity test," which is used to determine what materials are obscene. In Miller and subsequent decisions, the courts determined that a work is legally obscene if to the average adult person or its intended or probable recipient group:

1. the work, taken as a whole, appeals to the prurient interest or is advertised as if it appeals to the prurient interest; and,

2. the work depicts or describes, in a patently offensive way, sexual conduct specifically defined by applicable state law, or which the judge or member of the jury believes was intended to be included in the definition even though no exhaustive list is supplied; and

3. if to the "reasonable person" the work, taken as a whole, lacks serious literary, artistic, or political value. (Tedford 1997, 146).

criminalize the display or transmission of indecent (i.e., nonobscene) material on the Internet where children might encounter the material, and (3) to prohibit the availability of information referring to abortion services. The bulk of the change propose by the CDA would have been applied to section 223:

Whoever in interstate or foreign communications knowingly uses an interactive computer service to send to a specific person or persons under 18 years of age, or uses any interactive computer service to display in a manner available to a person under 18 years of age, any comment, request, suggestion, proposal, image, or other communication that, in context, depicts or describes, in terms patently offensive as measured by contemporary community standards, sexual or excretory activities or organs, regardless of whether the user of such service placed the call or initiated the communication; or knowingly permits any telecommunications facility under such person's control to be used for an activity prohibited by paragraph with the intent that it be used for such activity, shall be fined under Title 18, United States Code, or imprisoned not more than two years, or both.

In the election year of 1996, Congress quickly approved the act, passing it on to President Clinton, who signed it into law. Clinton noted that the CDA would help parents by keeping their children from "being exposed to objectionable material transmitted though computer networks."

Reno v. ACLU

The American Civil Liberties Union (ACLU) and American Library Association (ALA) wasted no time in filing a joint lawsuit against the Department of Justice. Strategically, the ACLU decided not to oppose the legislation bearing upon obscenity, since obscene content (e.g., bestiality, child pornography, snuff films, etc.) was already illegal. The ACLU focused its efforts instead upon reversing the indecency and abortion aspects of the CDA. Estimating that the abortion legislation was likely unconstitutional, the Department of Justice focused its efforts upon defending the CDA's indecency statutes. What was truly at issue here was whether legally indecent matter would enjoy constitutional immunity under the First Amendment. In other words, should legally indecent content be allowed to freely reside online? The government claimed that all other communications mediums had socially mandated age-verification procedures. On the other hand, the ACLU claimed that the Internet was unlike any of these other mediums, citing the fact that the network would circumvent any unconstitutional regulations upon online speech in any case.

In June of 1996, the U.S. District Court for the Eastern District of Pennsylvania overturned the indecency sections of the CDA, noting their unmistakable breach upon the First Amendment. It also upheld the federal obscenity legislation aspects, extending these laws to include the Internet. Predictably, the court deemed the restrictions upon communications involving abortion procedures unlawful. In the end, the three-panel Federal District Court in Philadelphia found the contested indecency legislation unconstitutional because: (1) the laws were geared toward ordinary citizens and not merely pornographers, (2) the means of securing an age-verification system on the network was both unavailable and likely a financial burden upon the average citizen, (3) the law would be an unnecessary burden upon the adult citizen's right to discuss or exchange adult content, (4) any age-verification system proposed could not possibly be foolproof, (5) the terms "indecent" and "patently offensive" were unfair absent an existing legal measurable standard, (6) such a law would only allow for scant enforcement causing an imbalance in due process, and (7) the law would create an unnecessary "chilling effect" upon kindred forms of speech, thus diminishing expressive diversity. In short, the court ruled that free speech would be needlessly burdened by the CDA.

The Department of Justice pursued the matter further by appealing the lower court's decision (*Reno v. ACLU*, 521 U.S. 844, 117 S. Ct. 2329). In June of 1997, the Supreme Court unanimously upheld the district court's decision, overturning major sections of the CDA as violations of the First Amendment. Writing for the majority, Justice John Paul Stevens said, "As a matter of constitutional tradition, in the absence of evidence to the contrary, we presume that governmental regulation of the content of speech is more likely to interfere with the free exchange of ideas than to encourage it." In the end, while history may record that the Congress and president of the United States consciously authorized constitutionally doomed legislation during an election year to garner the support of voting constituencies, what will be recorded by law is that it is not illegal to display or transmit indecent material online.

The COPA

In October of 1998, Congress drafted and President Clinton signed into law a revised version of the CDA named the Child Online Protection Act of 1998 (COPA). This act sought to remedy the apparent constitutional flaws of the CDA by using the Supreme Court's opinions as a gauge for what might be considered constitutional limitations to the Internet. This time, the legislation targeted Title 47, section 231 of the *U.S. Code,* seeking penalties for the "commercial" circulation of any material that could be considered "harmful to minors."

Nicknamed the Son of CDA, CDA II, and now Reno v. ACLU II for its similarity to the CDA, COPA was challenged by the ACLU as unconstitutional. Backed by the Electronic Frontier Foundation (http://www.eff.org) and the Electronic Privacy Information Center (http://www.epic.org) as coplaintiffs, their first line of attack was to amass a list of plaintiffs who, alongside their counsel, would testify that the law injured their right to free speech. Of course, securing these commercial plaintiffs was not a difficult task.

The ACLU then filed for a restraining and injunction order against the law in light of its predecessor's unconstitutionality. On November 19, 1998, Federal Justice Lowell A. Reed granted the restraining order but not the injunction order, making the law temporarily unenforceable until he could rule upon the necessity for an injunction. On February 1, 1999, Justice Reed ruled for a temporary injunction against the COPA. Justice Reed also acknowledged that the ACLU's arguments were likely to succeed if the matter were left in his court. On April 2, the Department of Justice appealed Justice Reed's injunction, requiring yet another hearing in the matter. As of June 2000, the randomly selected three-panel Third Circuit Court of Appeals based in Philadelphia had yet to rule on the injunction.

The ACLU remains confident in its battle against the COPA, however, claiming that the net effects of the legislation are strikingly similar to the CDA. The ACLU notes that the law is hampered by: (1) its lack of substantive definitions for what constitutes commercial speech, (2) its attempt to create a PIN system for adults in such a manner that might compromise their online privacy, thus creating a de facto system of prior restraint upon free speech, and (3) the legislation's allowance of a regionalized community-standards approach to be applied for what constitutes indecent content without regard to the global nature of the Internet.

Students of both free speech and the Internet must carefully watch this decision as it unfolds. It will likely be another landmark case similar to *Reno v. ACLU*, defining the parameters of law explicitly for commercial vendors of adult content.

CONTROVERSIES OVER FILTERING DEVICES

One of the popular solutions to protecting children from objectionable online material is the use of Internet filtering devices. These controversial tools, supported by many parental advocacy groups, place restraints upon what a browser may or may not retrieve from the Internet. Cybersitter, NetNanny, and CyberPatrol—just to name a few that are available for purchase—screen the Internet for category-specific content. With this software, if you didn't want your PC to be able to retrieve pages containing full nudity, all you'd have to do is select the No Full Nudity box (Wagner 1999). If you didn't want your browser to be able to retrieve pages containing offensive language, then you'd select the No Offensive Language box. The local software (called "censorware" by its opponents) then works in two distinct ways when a remote Internet connection is made: (1) it retrieves the software company's **blocked list** from a downloadable online directory, ensuring that the remote browser remains current, and (2) it previews all incoming pages by scanning them against an objectionable "buzzword" list. When an objectionable website is detected by the filter, the browser defaults to an HTML page telling the user that the site has been blocked **(Figure 12.1).**

Filtering Device Problems

So how exactly do these filtering devices work? NetNanny, for instance, maintains a staff of reviewers who scan the Internet for objectionable material. After training, these reviewers label their determinations by

Fig. 12.1. Warning: The content you are about to experience may be unsuitable for young viewers . . .

offensive category in NetNanny's central database. This database is then culled by a manager who places the strike-list file into one of several downloadable directories for everyone using their service. If you have selected not to view sites related to alcohol or drugs or cults, upon connecting to the Internet, NetNanny will automatically load that strike-list file from the directory. Once the strike-list file is loaded, your browser will not be able to view sites based upon the topic you've selected.

Of course, nothing is foolproof. When you stop to consider that the Internet is growing faster than the size of these reviewer staffs, it is only logical that the selection process would become more reliant upon automation. It would take hundreds of reviewers, amassed in a coordinated effort, countless years to humanly determine what is and is not objectionable given each category. What's more troubling, of course, is that the Web is constantly in motion, ever expanding. It is *always* changing. Today's nice website may be tomorrow's naughty website, or vice versa. As a result, many of the human determinations of late are already outdated. When *time* is added into the determination process, the necessity for automation becomes apparent.

And sometimes, perfectly acceptable sites get wrongly refereed as being unacceptable. This will result in a lot of frustration and anger–especially if you are the owner of the allegedly objectionable website. Whether the mistake were made by a human or by a program that misread something on a page will not matter. Your site is now being blacklisted by a site-blocking service. You are now being censored by every filtered browser in the world using that service. It is for this very reason that many people are not supportive of a software architecture that, admittedly, has design flaws. Still, if you do not mind your children not being able to see some of the sites that have been unfairly blocked in order to keep them from seeing most of the "objectionable" sites (CyberPatrol boasts a 97% success rate), these filtering devices might be your means to a more respectable version of the Internet.

Yet, what if these devices were installed not simply at your home (where it is your choice to regulate the flow of information as you wish), but at your public school or library? Or maybe even your workplace? Does a public agency possess the right, if not the duty, to protect children from viewing indecent material? Can this right be animated in the form of a governing software architecture over the Internet? Well, that depends upon several pieces of legislation making their way through Congress and how the ACLU plans to respond.

The Children's Internet Protection Act of 1999 (H.R.896 and S.97)

Introduced by Congressman Bob Franks (R-NJ) as part of the Juvenile Justice Bill of 1999, the Children's Internet Protection Act proposes that all public schools (K-12) must install an FCC-approved filtering device on their Internet applications. Focusing on Title 47 of the *U.S. Code*, this legislation seeks to amend section 254 of the Communications Act of 1934. Before being adopted by the House on June 15, 1999, the bill went through three rounds of subcommittee editing to finally read:

> To be eligible to receive universal service assistance . . . an elementary or secondary school shall certify to the Commission that it has (A) selected a technology for computers with Internet access to filter or block (i) child pornographic materials . . . (ii) obscene materials . . . and (iii) during use by minors, materials deemed to be harmful to minors . . . and (B) installed, or will install, and uses or will use, as soon as it obtains computers with Internet access, a technology to filter or block such material.

Noncompliance with the law would make the public school and/or library no longer eligible for U.S. "e-rate" subsidies (known by many as the "Gore Tax"). These monies are commonly used by schools to purchase new computers, software, and networking equipment. Focusing exclusively on the public school and library's responsibility to install Internet filter software, the resolution is being backed by John McCain (R-AZ) and Ernest Hollings (R-SC) in the Senate, who have proposed a companion bill in the Senate (S.97). In this version the phrase "materials deemed to be harmful to minors" has been removed, suggesting that such wording would give too much censoring power to the community authority. Both the House and Senate bills were referred to subcommittees for further discussion. As of June 2000, the amendment had been approved by the Senate Commerce Committee and awaited consideration by the Senate.

The Neighborhood Children's Internet Protection Act of 1999 (S.1545)

This bill is an alternative to the two bills listed above. Rather than *requiring* public schools and libraries to use Internet filtering software, this legislation merely *allows* them to install it by providing congressional sanctioning. In order to determine the constitutionality of any given law, one must first exist. So this Senate bill simply requires public schools and libraries using federal monies to either install filtering software or implement a formal minor usage policy. As of June 2000, the legislation was in the Senate Commerce Committee pending review.

Of course, the ACLU and other noteworthy civil rights activist groups are not likely to take the passage of any such legislation easily. Already armed with one district court precedent *(Mainstream Loudoun, et. al. v. Board of Trustees of the Loudoun County Public Libraries, et. al. in Alexandria, Virginia)* where a federal judge ruled in favor of removing blocking software from a public library based upon First Amendment grounds, the Department of Justice and the ACLU seem to be headed for the

Supreme Court once again. If any of these bills do emerge from Congress and are signed into law by the president, you can rest assured the conservative society and libertarian society will square off once again in a battle for the minds of U.S. children.

Free speech and the First Amendment are not something that the student of online communication should regard lightly. If it were not for free speech, the U.S. Constitution would not be the powerful living document that it is today. It is our willingness to exercise our right to readily and openly communicate that ensures that our ideas, in earnest, are known by others. And it is this right that allows others to communicate honestly and openly with us, so that we may understand them better. Absent this right, and absent our exercising this right, democracy dies. Furthermore, the bonds of society forged by communication become strained. Because our free speech laws are being challenged on a daily basis, it is critical that you remain ever vigilant about your constitutional rights—on a personal and local level. To know these rights, you must remain a student of the courts of our land. This is especially the case concerning the Internet, since it is quite clear that the legal context for online communication is still forming.

TORT LIABILITY

WHAT TORT LAW IS

Tort law is an extremely broad area of law dealing with civil wrongs. Civil wrongs are matters in which the state does not get involved. The state will only get involved if *criminal* infractions have occurred. Torts are wrongs caused to a party for which another party is liable. Tort law is about civil court cases involving monetary damages if you hurt someone wrongfully. For the most part, torts are physical world issues: someone rear-ends your car, runs your cat over, or punches you—just to name a few of the common examples. But in communications law, rarely if ever is tort liability a physical issue. Unless parties are dealing with property rights—for example, signal frequencies, cable-line ownership, tax surcharge rights—communications law generally focuses upon three areas of nonphysical tort: (1) the invasion of privacy, (2) the intentional infliction of mental distress, and (3) defamation, which includes libel and slander. These three areas focus on the harm caused to someone's personal privacy, psychological state, or personal or professional reputation. Before we explicitly cover these three areas, however, it is imperative that you understand how malice and a lighter burden of proof are important in tort liability.

The Importance of Malice

So, you might be asking, why is it that establishing malice is not a requirement in tort cases? Remember that we are dealing with *civil* matters here. All the civil court is charged to do by the state is to determine who possesses liability and how much, and then attempt to make the damaged party whole again. Even if the tort were caused by accident, the wrongdoer is still liable for compensatory damages to some extent. Thus malice is clearly not necessary for securing **actual damages.** When malice can be proven, however, this does increase the possibility of securing **punitive damages.** Punitive damages are the court's special way of sending a stronger message to the wrongdoing party. It is an attempt to punish the wrongdoer into compliance with societal expectations, while overcompensating the injured party for suffering a clear injustice.

A Lighter Burden of Proof for Civil Action

It is crucial for you to understand that civil and criminal violations are mutually exclusive, according to the law. Civil and criminal law are practiced with different rules, using different burdens of proof. For example, in civil matters, the burden of proof for the plaintiff is "a preponderance of the evidence," whereas in criminal issues, the burden of proof for the state is "beyond a reasonable doubt." It should be somewhat obvious that "a preponderance of the evidence" is much easier to prove than "beyond a reasonable doubt." For this reason, our civil courts have seen a sharp rise in civil liability suits during the late 1900s.

PRIVACY LAW

When we say that someone's privacy has been wronged, we're assuming that we have a right to privacy. A theorized right to privacy was first proposed by two Boston attorneys, Louis Brandeis and Samuel Warren, in what has become an historic *Harvard Law Review* article (1890). In that article, they assert that people should have the right to be left alone to perform their daily life duties. This article comes from the fact that the two attorneys were being hounded by the media in both their private and public places. As it was, however, it was just an article. It possessed no legal clout. In 1903, New York adopted a formal right to privacy using many of the ideas generated by Brandeis and Warren. Eventually every state in the United States adopted a policy, creating a haphazard smattering of privacy rights throughout the country. Congress has not yet seen it fit to generate any legislation specific to a federal right to privacy. What does exist is the right to privacy ensured by state statutes and a battery of diverse federal regulations covering specialized areas of the law—educational records, medical records, and the like.

The Four Privacy Torts

Today, the right to privacy has been interpreted to mean that we have a right to be left alone, we have a right to be portrayed correctly in the news, and we have a right not to be commercially exploited. Of course, any variations on these laws will depend largely upon your state of residence. Let's now examine the mechanics of the four privacy torts and their applications where the Internet is specifically concerned.

1. Public disclosure of embarrassing private facts–Defined as the publication and dissemination of nonnewsworthy private facts about a person's life that would be considered highly offensive to the reasonable person. Some examples include, but are not limited to, information about someone's sexual activity, health, or economic position. Remember that private facts are *true*, therefore plaintiffs cannot really sue for defamation. However, any online communications–e-mail, websites, or attached e-mail documents–that publicly disclose embarrassing private facts could incur liability. Online communicators are strongly advised not to electronically transmit any material of a private or sensitive matter for that very reason.

2. Intrusion–Defined as an intentional intrusion into an individual's private space, seclusion, or solitude, caused by an electronic, mechanical, or physical means. This tort involves trespassing, but is usually hinged to some technological means of invasion. No published materials need exist for this tort to occur since it bears more upon the civil improprieties wrought by intrusive information-gathering techniques. Third-party wiretapping, paparazzi photography, and hidden videotaping of sexual acts are excellent examples of privacy intrusion. Many of the new Internet broadcasting technologies being released directly apply here. The use of hidden video cameras is not recommended unless they are for home security purposes. Any techniques that unlawfully intrude into an individual's privacy present certain liability issues.

3. False light–Occurs when someone knowingly disseminates highly offensive erroneous publicity with reckless disregard for its lack of merit or truth. Thus the phrase "false light." For example, if you were to publish stories that contain bogus "facts" about a person's life on a listserv or on a website, you have likely opened yourself up to civil prosecution. Even if the names of the persons involved are fictionalized in a false light narrative, the story can be considered a thin disguise depending upon how the tort is interpreted in the given state. It is for this reason that we encourage you to be true to life in all of your online

communications. Honesty is not only a virtue, it is also an excellent way to insulate yourself from the tort of false light.

4.   Commercial appropriation–Occurs when a profiting agency uses a person's name, likeness, or symbolic identity for commercial purposes without obtaining prior consent. The theory working behind the law here is that people get to control the symbolism related to their personhood, thus safeguarding themselves from exploitation. News agencies are free of this concern, by and large, since they are sanctioned to report newsworthy information to the public. Even websites not carrying the clout of a full news agency enjoy the right to newsworthiness. Pictures taken in the public sphere are considered safe for publication, excepting those which have a clear commercial interest at stake. Of course, you should also remember copyright law, which declares the commercial appropriation of an image to be a violation of copyright. So in order to protect yourself from liability, make certain that whenever you use someone's name or likeness online you obtain explicit, signed prior consent. The same should be respected for other people's intellectual property.

As abstracted above, these four torts represent the body of law available to you if you believe that your privacy has been invaded. They also represent the expectations that the law has for all of us concerning matters of civility and privacy. However, in 1986, the federal government did pass some very important legislation specific to the emerging area of online communications.

The Electronic Communications Privacy Act of 1986

The Electronic Communication Privacy Act (ECPA) makes it illegal for the government or a third party to intercept an e-mail. The ECPA provides certain exclusions to this act, many of which are geared toward assisting system operators in their duties. The ECPA provides a legal basis for these sysops to intercept e-mails given any combination of the following scenarios: (1) if the message appears to pertain to the commission of a crime, then the message can be disclosed to legal officials, (2) if either the sender or one of the recipients deems it permissible, and (3) if the message incurs transmission difficulties and must be opened to route it to one of its addressed recipients. Of course, these exclusions are provided mainly to private e-mail accounts only. If you use a company-owned e-mail account, recognize that the account is company property. As company property, it can be monitored without much opportunity for recourse. Interestingly, many people obtain private ISP accounts to free themselves of potential censorship and invasion of privacy issues. What many of these users do not recognize is that many of their service contracts provide the ISP with sweeping powers to intercept messages when necessary. By clicking Accept to the contractual agreement window, the user waives a great deal of his or her rights to privacy. And, if those rights are waived contractually, they are waived actually. ISPs also have the right to back up all messages sent and received as a means of insulating the company from incurring any liability for a user's activity (Lawson 1999). So, whether your e-mail is communicated via an ISP, a company, or even a public university, recognize that privacy functions more in theory than reality.

You should also know that ISPs and universities often maintain network logs to monitor the browsing behavior that occurs on any given PC. Additionally, marketing firms like Doubleclick have become experts in the use of cookies, which are small programs that track user activity and report it back to a central database. As a result of the efficiency of our technology, privacy seems to be more of a legal promise than a real-world possibility. Given this ambiguous context, what are the things you should do to protect your privacy online? For some excellent advice, check out the text box below detailing the Electronic Frontier Foundation's Top 12 ways to protect your privacy when online.

DEFAMATION

Defamation, which includes libel and slander, occurs when someone communicates untrue information that lowers a person's status or subjects a person to public disdain, embarrassment, or humiliation. Specifically, defamation must demonstrate the following legal elements: (1) a false statement of fact about an entity, not an opinion, (2) an unprivileged publication of that false statement to a third party, (3) fault or wrongdoing with malice, and (4) a documented level of harm or damage. The Supreme Court has done away with constitutional restraints on defamation, meaning that you can openly defame another without having criminal charges brought against you by the state. But, if for some reason you do commit defamation, remember that you are still open to civil suit.

Libel and Slander

Libel deals with *written untruths* about an entity published to third parties, and slander deals with *spoken untruths* about an entity to third parties. While libel and slander are both defined easily enough, determining what constitutes actual libelous or slanderous communications can sometimes be difficult. The statement cannot simply be perceived as false by the person (or entity) being discussed. The statement must also be found false by the court. To determine this, the court requires a thorough-going investigation into all of the legal elements constituting defamation. This research can be costly, tedious, and potentially embarrassing. Many attorneys attempt to dissuade their clients from defamation suits for this very reason.

THE EFF'S TOP 12 WAYS TO PROTECT YOUR ONLINE PRIVACY. VERS. 1.2, DEC. 6, 1999

1. Do not reveal personal information inadvertently.

You may be "shedding" personal details, including e-mail addresses and other contact information, without even knowing it unless you properly configure your Web browser. In your browser's "Setup," "Options," or "Preferences" menus, you may wish to use a pseudonym instead of your real name, and not enter an e-mail address nor provide other personally identifiable information that you don't wish to share. When visiting a site you trust, you can choose to give them your info in forms on their site; there is no need for your browser to potentially make this information available to all comers. Also be on the lookout for system-wide "Internet defaults" programs on your computer (some examples include Window's Internet Control Panel, and MacOS's Configuration Manager, and the third-party Mac utility named Internet Config). While they are useful for various things, like keeping multiple Web browsers and other Internet tools consistent in how they treat downloaded files and such, they should probably also be anonymized just like your browser itself if they contain any fields for personal information. Households with children may have an additional "security problem"–have you set clear rules for your kids, so that they know not to reveal personal information unless you OK it on a site-by-site basis?

2. Turn on cookie notices in your Web browser, and/or use cookie management software.

"Cookies" are tidbits of information that websites store on your computer, temporarily or more-or-less permanently. In many cases cookies are useful and innocuous. They may be passwords and user ID's, so that you do not have to keep retyping them every time you load a new page at the site that issued the cookie. Other cookies, however, can be used for "data mining" purposes, to track your motions through a website, the time you spend there, what links you click on and other details that the company wants to record, usually for marketing purposes. Most cookies can only be read by the party that created them. However, some companies that manage online banner advertising are, in essence, cookie sharing rings. They can track which pages you load, which ads you click on, etc., and share this information with all of their client websites (who may number in the hundreds, even thousands). It is unknown whether all of these cookie rings (some examples of which are Double-Click and Link Exchange) do in fact share user data, but they certainly can do so potentially.

Browsers are starting to allow user control over cookies. Netscape, for example, allows you to see a notice when a site tries to write a cookie file to your hard drive, and gives you some information about it, allowing you to decide whether or not to accept it. (Be on the lookout for cookies the function of which is not apparent, which go to other sites than the one you are trying to load, or which are not temporary.) It also allows you to automatically block all cookies that are being sent to third parties (or to block all cookies, entirely, but this will make some sites inoperable). Internet Explorer has a cookie management interface in addition to Netscape-like features, allowing you to selectively enable or disable cookies on a site-by-site basis, even to allow cookies for a site generally, but delete a specific cookie you are suspicious about. With Internet Explorer you can also turn on cookies for a site temporarily then disable them when you no longer need them (e.g., at an online bookstore that requires cookies to process an order, but whom you don't want to track what books you are looking at, what links you are following, etc., the rest of the time). Turning on cookie warnings will cause alert boxes to pop up, but after some practice you may learn to hit "Decline" so fast that you hardly notice them any more. The idea is to only enable cookies on sites that require them AND whom you trust.

You can also use cookie management software and services. One example is the Internet Junkbuster Proxy (http://www.junkbusters. com/ht/en/ijb.html). It runs on Win95/98/NT and Unix (no Mac version), and can selectively block cookies for you (and banner ads, to boot). interMute (http://www.intermute.com/) does likewise (and more—blocks popup windows, etc.; only runs under Windows). A Java-based solution called Muffin (http://muffin.doit.org/) is also available. While it will run on Mac, Win and Unix systems, it is definitely for "power users," as it is complicated to set up and operate effectively. There are also numerous "cookie eater" applications, some which run on a schedule or in the background, that delete cookie files for you. As with turning off cookies entirely, you may have trouble accessing sites that require certain cookies (though in most cases the worst that will happen is that you'll have to re-enter a login ID and password you thought were saved). "Eating" the cookies periodically still permits sites to track what you're doing for a short time (i.e., the time between successive deletion of your cookie file), but thwarts attempts to discern and record your actions over time.

The best solution doesn't exist yet: Full cookie management abilities built into the browsers themselves. Only increased user pressure on Microsoft, Netscape and other browser makers can make this happen. Users should ultimately be able to reject cookies on a whole-domain basis, reject all cookies that are not essential for the transaction at hand, receive notice of exactly what a cookie is intended for, and be able to set default behaviors and permissions rather than have to interact with cookies on a page-by-page basis. This just isn't possible yet.

3. Keep a "clean" e-mail address.

When mailing to unknown parties; posting to newsgroups, mailing lists, chat rooms and other public spaces on the Net; or publishing a webpage that mentions your e-mail address, it is best to do this from a "side" account, some pseudonymous or simply alternate address, and to use your main or preferred address only on small, members-only lists and with known, trusted individuals. Addresses that are posted (even as part of message headers) in public spaces can be easily discovered by spammers (online junk mailers) and added to their list of targets. If your public "throw away" address gets spammed enough to become annoying, you can simply kill it off, and start a new one. Your friends, boss, etc., will still know your "real" address. You can use a free (advertising-supported) e-mail service provider like Yahoo Mail or Hotmail for such "side" accounts. It is best to use a "real" Internet service provider for your main account, and to examine their privacy policies and terms of service, as some "freemail" services may have poor privacy track records. You may find it works best to use an e-mail package that allows multiple user ID's and addresses (a.k.a. "personalities," "aliases") so that you do not have to switch between multiple programs to manage and use more than one e-mail address.

4. Don't reveal personal details to strangers or just-met "friends."

The speed of the Internet is often reflected in rapid online acquaintanceships and friendships. But it is important to realize that you don't really know who these people are or what they are like in real life. A thousand miles away, you don't have friends-of-friends or other references about this person. Be also wary of face-to-face meetings. If you and your new e-friend wish to meet in person, do it in a public place. Bringing a friend along can also be a good idea. One needn't be paranoid, but one should not be an easy mark, either. Some personal information you might wish to withhold until you know someone much better would include your full name, place of employment, phone number, and street address (among more obvious things like credit card numbers, etc.). Needless to say, such information should not be put on personal homepages. (If you have a work homepage, it may well have work contact information on it, but you needn't reveal this page to everyone you meet in a chat room.) For this and other reasons, many people maintain two personal home pages, a work-related one, and an "off-duty" version.

5. Realize you may be monitored at work, avoid sending highly personal e-mail to mailing lists, and keep sensitive files on your home computer.

In most states, employees have little if any privacy protection from monitoring by employers. When discussing sensitive matters in e-mail or other online media, be certain who you are talking to. If you replied to a mailing list post, check the headers—is your reply going to the person you think it is, or to the whole list? Also be aware that an increasing number of employers are monitoring and recording employee Web usage, as well as email. This could compromise home banking passwords and other sensitive information. Keep private data and private Net usage private, at home.

6. Beware sites that offer some sort of reward or prize in exchange for your contact or other information.

There's a high probability that they are gathering this information for direct marketing purposes. In many cases your name and address are worth much more to them (because they can sell it to other marketers, who can do the same again—a snowball effect) than what you are (supposedly) getting from them. Be especially wary of sweepstakes and contests. You probably won't win, but the marketer sure will if you give them your information.

7. Do not reply to spammers, for any reason.

"Spam," or unsolicited bulk e-mail, is something you are probably already familiar with (and tired of). If you get a spammed advertisement, certainly don't take the sender up on whatever offer they are making, but also don't bother replying with "REMOVE" in the subject line, or whatever (probably bogus) unsubscribe instructions you've been given. This simply confirms that your address is being read by a real person, and you'll find yourself on dozens more spammers' lists in no time. If you open the message, watch your outgoing mail queue to make sure that a "return receipt" message was not generated to be sent back to the spammer automatically. (It is best to queue your mail and send manually, rather than send immediately, so that you can see what's about to go out before it's actually sent.) If you have a good Internet service provider, you may be able to forward copies of spam e-mail to the system administrators, who can route a complaint to the ISP of the spammer (or if you know a lot about mail headers and DNS [domain name server] tools, you can probably contact these ISPs yourself to complain about the spammer.)

8. Be conscious of Web security.

Never submit a credit card number or other highly sensitive personal information without first making sure your connection is secure (encrypted). In Netscape, look for a closed lock (Windows) or unbroken key (Mac) icon at the bottom of the browser window. In Internet Explorer, look for a closed lock icon at the bottom (Windows) or near the top (Mac) of the browser window. In any browser, look at the URL (Web address) line—a secure connection will begin "https://" instead of "http://." If you are at a page that asks for such information but shows "http://" try adding the "s" yourself and hitting enter to reload the page (for Netscape or IE; use whatever method is required by your browser to reload the page at the new URL). If you get an error message that the page or site does not exist, this probably means that the company is so clueless—and careless with your information and your money—that they don't even have Web security. Take your business elsewhere.

9. Be conscious of home computer security.

On the other side of the coin, your own computer may be a trouble spot for Internet security. If you have a DSL [digital subscriber line] or other connection to the Internet that is up and running 24 hours, unlike a modem-and-phone-line connection, be sure to turn your computer off when you are not using it. Most home PCs have pitifully poor security compared to the Unix workstations that power most commercial websites. System crackers search for vulnerable, unattended DSL-connected home computers, and can invade them with surprising ease, rifling through files looking for credit card numbers or other sensitive data, or even "taking over" the computer and quietly using it for their own purposes, such as launching attacks on other computers elsewhere—attacks you could initially be blamed for.

10. Examine privacy policies and seals.

When you are considering whether or not to do business with a website, there are other factors than a secure connection you have to consider that are equally important to Web security. Does the site provide offline contact information, including a postal address? Does the site have a prominently posted privacy policy? If so, what does it say? (Just because they call it a "privacy policy" doesn't mean it will protect you—read it for yourself. Many are little more than disclaimers saying that you have no privacy! So read them carefully.) If the policy sounds OK to you, do you have a reason to believe it? Have you ever heard of this company? What is their reputation? And are they backing up their privacy statement with a seal program such as TRUSTe (http://www.truste.org) or BBBonline (http://www.bbbonline.org)? (Such programs hold websites to some baseline standards, and may revoke seal licenses, with much fanfare, of bad-acting companies that do not keep their word.) If you see a seal, is it real? Check with the seal-issuing site to make sure the seal isn't a fake. And examine terms carefully, especially if you are subscribing to a service rather than buying a product. Look out for auto-rebilling scams and hidden fees.

11. Remember that YOU decide what information about yourself to reveal, when, why, and to whom.

Don't give out personally-identifiable information too easily. Just as you might think twice about giving some clerk at the mall your home address and phone number, keep in mind that simply because a site asks for or demands personal information from you does not mean you have to give it. You do have to give accurate billing information if you are buying something, of course, but if you are registering with a free site that is a little too nosy for you, there is no law against providing them with pseudonymous information. (However, it would probably be polite to use obviously fake addresses, such as "123 No Such Street, Nowhere, DC 01010." If they are generating mailings based on this information—presumably in accordance with the terms of their privacy policy—they can probably weed such addresses out and not waste the postage on them.)

12. Use encryption!

Last but certainly not least, there are other privacy threats besides abusive marketers, nosy bosses, spammers and scammers. Some of the threats include industrial espionage, government surveillance, identity theft, disgruntled former associates, and system crackers. Relatively easy-to-use e-mail and file encryption software is available for free, such as Pretty Good Privacy (PGP, available at: http://www. pgpi.org), which runs on almost all computers and even integrates seamlessly with most major e-mail software. Good encryption uses very robust secret codes, that are difficult if not impossible to crack, to protect your data. You can also use specialized services (some free, some pay), such as the Anonymizer (http://www.anonymizer. com), which can completely disguise to websites where you are coming from and who you are (and block all cookies). Some ISPs are beginning to offer secure, encrypted dial-up accounts and other security features. Hopefully some day soon, good encryption and computer security will simply be included in all such services, but for now you have to actively seek out good service providers.

While no actual federal defamation laws exist in the *U.S. Code*, every state in the United States maintains its own set of statutes. Interestingly, in the cases of libel and slander, the U.S. Supreme Court has exercised its federal decision-making authority to rule upon cases that cannot be adequately settled at the state level. As you might have guessed, free speech law and defamation law often intersect on a number of levels. In fact, some scholars believe that they are completely opposed to one another. To sum up those interactions in a phrase: defamation law is a state statutory means of keeping people from defaming others, while free speech law seeks to allow for the free and unfettered expression of ideas—be they factual, political, or critical.

There are a number of defenses that one can use against defamation suits. If the statement is true, it does not meet the definition of defamation. Opinions are also protected under the law because they do not constitute facts. Here, the court gets to determine whether or not statements were made on the basis of fact or opinion. There are, of course, a number of other qualified privileges that can be used in a defamation defense. Qualified privileges include the accurate reporting of material that is in the public record, including court records, statements made at government proceedings, and so forth.

New York Times v. Sullivan

In the landmark case of *New York Times v. Sullivan* (1964), the Supreme Court ruled that before a public official could receive damages for defamatory statements, he or she must first prove that the statement was made with "actual malice." This determination federally trumped all lower state statutes providing for the recovery of accidental (negligent) defamation. In a later decision, the court expanded the ruling to include public figures, meaning people who involve themselves in public controversies. What this essentially did was to require that all parties involved in the *public sphere* interested in bringing defamation suits to trial have proof of actual malice to receive any compensation for injury.

So what does this mean for your online communications? Obviously the Internet makes the dissemination of information much easier today than ever before. One simple e-mail posted to a listserv of 15 individuals could be delivered to 2 or 3 associates who, in turn, send it to 30 or 40 more recipients—and on and on and on. When making potentially critical comments about people on the Internet, remember that the diffused model of online communications can cause serious, perhaps even irreparable, personal or professional harm. Of course, defamation law is quite ill-equipped to handle the almost random nature of online communications delivery. In order to insulate yourself from incurring defamation liability online, follow mom's loving advice: "If you can't say something nice, don't say anything at all."

BACK UP AND RELOAD

If your head is spinning a bit at this point, it's understandable. Communications law was complicated enough before the new medium of the Internet came along and rendered most of the laws out of date and in some cases nearly useless. Each of the three primary areas of communications law—intellectual properties, free speech, and tort liability—are in need of adjustment now that we have access to a global digital medium.

In this chapter we first learned about intellectual property law and why it is important for you to respect the words, images, and inventions of others. Intellectual property law helps us control the flow of information, while attributing credits and rights to the deserving party. Next, we learned about free speech law, and all of the problems and issues that are incurred when we apply the First Amendment online. And finally, we delved into tort liability, involving matters of civil dispute and injury resolution. These three areas of communications law, generally speaking, are the areas where the Internet is having the greatest impact.

It is appropriate, and probably more than a little ironic, that we end this legal chapter with a disclaimer. The Internet, communications law, and the courts are not standing still. By the time you read this chapter, new decisions will have been made about what is or isn't legal when you are communicating online. We encourage you to check the textbook website for more up-to-date information. You should not use this chapter for legal advice if you are charged with a violation of one of these laws. Instead, seek competent counsel. Because even the best communications law attorneys are challenged by the complications we are now facing, thanks to the Internet.

BROWSE *and* **BUILD**   For sites to visit, exercises, quizzes to test your learning, and more, go to *www.harcourtcollege.com/ communication/inetcomm*

References and Readings

Attorney General. 1999. *Cyberstalking: A new challenge for law enforcement and industry.* Accessed 21 May 2000 <I>http://www.usdoj.gov/criminal/cybercrime/cyberstalking.htm>.

Baughman, M. 1999. Recent legislation: Regulating the Internet. *Harvard Journal on Legislation* 36:230.

Bauman, L. 1997. Personal jurisdiction and Internet advertising. *The Computer Lawyer* 1:14.

Benkler, Y. 1999. Free as the air to common use: First Amendment constraints on enclosure of the public domain. *New York University Law Review* 74:354.

Carlson, B. 1997. Balancing the digital scales of copyright law. *Southern Methodist University Law Review* 50:825.

Carmichael, J. 1996. In support of the white paper: Why on-line service providers should not receive immunity from traditional notions of vicarious and contributory liability for copyright infringement. *Loyola Los Angeles Entertainment Law Journal* 16:759.

Carter, P. I. 1999. Health information privacy: Can Congress protect confidential medical information in the information age? *William Mitchell Law Review* 25:223.

Deutsch, S. 2000. Anticybersquatting Consumer Protection Act. *International Trademarking Association Website.* New York: International Trademarking Association. Accessed 21 May 2000 <http://www.inta.org/cyberpiracy.htm>.

Dueker, K. S. 1996. Trademark law lost in Cyberspace: Trademark protection for Internet addresses. *Harvard Journal of Law & Technology* 9:483.

Fraser, S. 1998. The conflict between the First Amendment and copyright law and its impact on the Internet. *Cardozo Arts & Entertainment Law Journal* 16:1.

Gantt, L. O. 1995. An affront to human dignity: Electronic mail monitoring in the private sector. *Harvard Journal of Law and Technology* 8:345.

Good, A. B. 1998. Trade secrets and the new realities of the Internet age. *Marquette Intellectual Properties Law Review* 2:51.

Hash, P. E., and Ibrahim, C. M. 1996. E-mail, electronic monitoring, and employee privacy. *Texas Law Review* 37:893.

Hodkowski, W. A. 1997. The future of Internet security: How new technologies will shape the Internet and affect the law. *Santa Clara Computer and High Technology Law Journal* 217:13.

Landau, M. B. 1997. Problems arising out of the use of "www. trademark.com": The application of principles of trademark law to Internet domain disputes. *Georgia State University Law Review* 13:455.

Lawson, J. 1999. *The complete Internet handbook for lawyers.* Chicago: American Bar Association.

Lee, L. W. 1999. Child pornography prevention act of 1996: Confronting the challenges of virtual reality. *Southern California Interdisciplinary Law Journal* 8:639.

Lemley, M., and E. Volokh. 1998. Freedom of speech and injunctions in intellectual property cases. *Duke Law Journal* 48:147.

Lessig, L. 1996. Reading the Constitution in Cyberspace. *Emory Law Journal* 869:45.

Lyman, P. 1998. The Article 2B debate and the sociology of the information age. *Berkeley Technology Law Journal* 13:1063.

Marcus, J. 1998. Commercial speech on the Internet: Spam and the First Amendment. *Cardozo Arts & Entertainment Law Journal* 16:245.

Ohm, P. K. 1999. Comment: On regulating the Internet: Usenet, a case study. *UCLA Law Review* 46:1941.

O'Rourke, M. 1998. Fencing Cyberspace: Drawing borders in a virtual world. *Minnesota Law Review* 82:609.

Phan, D. T. 1998. Will fair use function on the Internet? *Columbia Law Review* 98:169.

Reidenberg, J. R. 1998. Lex informatica: The formulation of information policy rules through technology. *Texas Law Review* 553:76.

Reindl, A. P. 1998. Choosing law in Cyberspace: Copyright conflicts on global networks. *Michigan Journal of International Law* 19:729.

Rose, L., S. Rogers, and J. Cuthbertson. 1995. *Netlaw: Your rights in an online world.* New York: Osborne Publishing.

Salbu, S. R. 1998. Who should govern the Internet? Monitoring and supporting a new frontier. *Harvard Journal of Law & Technology* 429:11.

Stepka, D. T. 1997. Obscenity on-line: A transactional approach to computer transfers of potentially obscene material. *Cornell Law Review* 905:82.

Tedford, T. 1997. *Freedom of speech in the United States.* State College, Pa.: Strata.

Wagner, R. P. 1999. Filters and the First Amendment. *Minnesota Law Review* 83:755.

CHAPTER 13

What about My Life?

Society, Individuals, and the Internet

By Peter Zale ©2000 Peter Zale, www.peterzale.com   Distributed by Tribune Media Services, www.comicspage.com

By the end of this chapter, you should:

I. Understand how technologies like the Internet become accepted by societies, organizations, and cultures via:

    A. the Elites-Popularization-Specialization (EPS) cycle and

    B. change agents.

II. Know how the Internet is de-centering:

    A. the government,

    B. education,

    C. the economy,

    D. the concept of community, and

    E. the individual.

III. Comprehend where the Internet may be headed:

    A. wireless Internet protocols and portable connectivity and

    B. virtual and augmented reality.

When Gutenberg invented the printing press in 1450, the church was unprepared for a machine that could automate the work of a hundred monks in a fraction of the time. When Marconi debuted his wireless telegraph in 1890, the state was equally unprepared for a medium more difficult to govern than mass-produced print. History offers countless examples like these, where media innovations are made, employed, and societies must then adapt to the new practice of communication (Jonash

1999). Similarly, the Internet has caught almost everyone unprepared–changing how radio, film, television, telephony, print publication, and even interpersonal correspondence is being practiced (Owen 1999).

Even more intriguing about the Internet, though, is the rate at which the new medium has spread. When you consider that a publicly accessible Internet has been available for less than a decade, its pervasiveness as a communication medium among governments, companies, organizations, cultures, and individuals is nothing short of astounding (Canton 1999). How has the Internet been accepted by society so rapidly? How have our concepts of community and self been altered? What in the world could possibly be coming next?

ADOPTING A MEDIUM

Mass communication theory helps us explain how mass media have matured over time. It stands to reason that these theories would also provide us with some insights concerning the recent social adoption of the Internet over the past decade. One of the leading theories of mass media adoption is the **Elites-Popularization-Specialization (EPS) cycle,** formulated in 1971 by Merrill and Lowenstein. The EPS cycle suggests that all mass communication media are first introduced to (or by) elites, then get dispersed among the population, and finally expand in availability so that content can become specialized **(Figure 13.1).**

PHASE ONE: ELITES

In general, a new medium is expensive when it is first introduced. It will likely offer communicative (and thus strategic) advantages over

Fig. 13.1. The Elites-Popularization-Specialization cycle.

preexisting media, but the new medium inevitably requires different, and initially expensive, equipment. Consequently, our traditional power structures–government, military, higher education, and research and development organizations–usually gain access to such equipment first. Due to the fact that these power structures have access to large amounts of money, time, intellect, and knowledge, they will often be the very ones inventing the new media in the first place.

Once an innovation has been experimented with by the primary elites and has been deemed socially acceptable, it is then introduced to the public. If it is deemed unacceptable, policies and enforcement attempt to harness the diffusion of the innovation. A clear example of this existed when the U.S. Bureau of Export Administration issued a usage and export ban in 1996 against certain encryption programs that scrambled data to protect both the sender and recipient from a third-party interception: a.k.a. espionage. These encryption tools, federal authorities argued, could be easily employed by terrorists to evade monitoring. As this example shows, governments desire to remain in control of potentially equalizing media. In the United States, this control is typically maintained by the **Federal Communications Commission** (http://www.fcc.org/). The FCC, established by the Communications Act of 1934, is responsible to Congress and charged with regulating both national and international communication.

If you will recall how the Internet was initially developed (chapter 1), it began as a government project. As time progressed, the government slowly began pulling itself away from the project, dedicating large segments of the physical network to public use. Eventually, in the early 1990s, the popularity of the Internet exploded, whereupon we have witnessed an infusion of millions of new users (Shenk 1998). When this happened, the EPS cycle moved into the next phase.

PHASE TWO: POPULARIZATION

As more individuals discover the benefits of a given innovation, they will translate these benefits into meaningful social and individual applications. This new appreciation is then passed on from person to person in something of a grassroots campaign. Ask yourself, for example, how many times one of your friends has mentioned the Internet to you. This appreciation is also promoted by companies using commercialized advertising and strategic public relations efforts. Consider for a moment how many dot-com commercials you have seen recently on television. However they heard about it, suddenly everyone is discussing the new medium. It has happened this way with print, radio, television, citizens' band (CB), cable television, VCRs, radar detectors, CDs, and now the Internet. The new medium becomes a part of the culture in coffee shop discussions, radio and television programming, and formalized class-room instruction.

Once the public becomes aware of the emerging medium, an informal self-literacy movement usually commences. This is where members of society begin to educate themselves, alerting the state (usually through universities and colleges) to the need for popular instruction. For example, following the popular emergence of radio, the state eventually believed it important enough to offer curriculum in radio broadcasting (and later television broadcasting), where citizens could be properly trained in the theories and applications of the medium. The same EPS cycle pattern is occurring with the Internet.

Social adoption depends upon a great number of economic forces, too. For instance, if we were all appropriately educated, many of us might find a great number of uses for our own low-power television station. Yet with a whopping price tag of around $600,000, the chances of a popular, widespread adoption of this medium are rather low. On the other hand, as the *power* of PC technology continues to increase, while the *costs* of PC technology continue to decrease, we are seeing an increase in home computer ownership (Gleick 1999). And, since several ISPs will supply users with a free personal computer (via rebates) if they sign a long-term subscription contract, adoption of this new medium becomes possible for a mere $19.95 per month.

The trend emerging from the 1990s suggests that the 2000s will likely be a decade marked by continued PC and Internet penetration world-wide. In 2000, the Stanford Institute for the Quantitative Study of Society (SIQSS) suggested that 55% of the U.S. populace is now engaged in online communication, with 43% of U.S. households connected to the Internet. In short, if the medium warrants it, popularization happens. It happens when you begin spending hours instead of minutes online every week. It happens when our news magazines and newspapers begin covering the Internet as front-page stories. And it happens when your little sister or brother knows more about website development than you do. The rapidity and reach of the Internet revolution in the United States is irrefutable proof that we are popularizing the medium (Tapscott 1997). To what extent, degree, and end is still undetermined.

PHASE THREE: SPECIALIZATION

Once the popularization phase of the EPS cycle is underway, mass media have the tendency to demassify. **Demassification** occurs when mass media saturate the market and are then reconfigured (or reinvented) to capture niche audiences. To explain how demassification works, let's consider the examples of cable television and direct satellite broadcast feeds. During the late 1970s when cable television lines were being installed in our neighborhoods and communities, most television owners could not understand why. After all, their television sets already received ABC, CBS, and NBC (depending upon the weather). What could cable possibly do that television antennas could not? As we all now know, cable television purified and boosted the existing signals of the three major networks. More importantly, cable television also introduced us to new programming stations such as CNN, ESPN, MTV, the Weather Channel, and TBS. Cable made it possible for stations to target a more specialized audience because that audience would still be large enough since it was drawn from a nationwide pool of viewers. A local station that tried to target do-it-yourselfers within its broadcasting range would have too small of an audience to be commercially viable. But by delivering specialized programming to a nationwide audience, cable makes stations such as Home and Garden Television profitable for advertisers and broadcasters alike.

This is how demassification works. Better technology allows for more demassification, and therefore more media and audience specialization. As cable service providers began to reach the maximum number of stations that they could carry over cable lines, direct satellite broadcast systems evolved to allow for further medium specialization. CNN added CNNfn (financial news) and CNNsi *(Sports Illustrated),* and music lovers were targeted more narrowly as MTV was joined by Video Hits 1 (VH1), Black Entertainment Television (BET), and Country Music Television (CMT).

Of course, no one is really certain what our preoccupation with a fragmented media landscape might be doing to us, either as a community or as individuals (Johnson 1997). New technologies like the Internet are making it possible to target audiences with increasing precision. The downside to this, critics argue, is that we focus our attention on fragments of our mediated human existence rather than the whole. Highly specialized sites could begin to assume more importance in our lives than the local news or the presidential State of the Union address. Over time, the critics fear, we may lose touch with those things, those thoughts, those symbols that were once at the center of our community-negotiated social realities. As technology makes further fragmentation of the audience possible, we might find ourselves one day with thousands of micro-societies that cannot communicate with each other.

Because the Internet allows for both the consumption as well as the production of content, specialization has occurred even more quickly than usual. Once popularization of the Internet began, the average user could become a producer, not just a consumer. Anyone, anywhere, can display anything for whatever reason he or she may desire. Websites are about as diverse as humanity and imagination allow. Christianity, pornography, recipes for explosive devices, recipes for chocolate chip cookies, even pictures of your cousin at the Grand Canyon National Park—the public and the personal—everything conveniently hyperlinked for our browsing pleasure (Negroponte 1996). Fascinating times are ahead, whether you are an advocate or critic of this popularized medium.

THE ROLE OF CHANGE AGENTS IN THE DIFFUSION OF INNOVATIONS

While the EPS cycle explains the larger social processes involved in adopting new technologies, diffusion of innovations theory offers more subtle insights about the interpersonal nature of change. Proposed by Rogers in the late 1950s, the theory suggests that interpersonal networks (and the power brokers governing these networks) sometimes have more to do with the adoption of new ideas than the ideas themselves. To explain how social systems work, Rogers (1995) identified five adoption profiles that he argues exist in all organizations and cultures: (1) innovators, (2) early adopters, (3) members of the early majority, (4) members of the late majority, and (5) laggards. Of course, some of us are extremely open to change by nature. Likewise, some of us are highly resistant to change. As would normally be expected, most people fall somewhere in one of the two majorities:

- Innovators (2.5% of the average sample): adventuresome, cosmopolite, networked with fellow innovators and early adopters, have access to financial resources, have high exposure to mass-mediated content, understand complex technical knowledge, are able to cope with high degrees of uncertainty.

- Early adopters (13.5%): respected, innovative, networked with other early adopters and innovators, prefer a local geography more than the innovator, have access to financial resources, have high exposure to mass-mediated content, provide strong opinion leadership with the organization or culture, can deal with uncertainty but prefers certainty.

- Early majority (34%): members prefer a local geography, interact frequently with their peers for data, have access to relatively modest financial resources, have medium exposure to mass-mediated content, seldom hold positions of opinion leadership, are rarely innovative, prefer certainty.

- Late majority (34%): members are skeptical, cautious, prefer a local geography, interact infrequently with peers for data, have access to relatively modest financial resources, have medium exposure to mass-mediated content, rarely hold positions of opinion leadership, are seldom innovative, prefer certainty, innovation adoption might result from economic/social necessity due to the diffusion effect.

- Laggards (16%): suspicious, doubtful, most localite, point of reference is the past, wary of change agents and innovations, generally have meager resources, may never adopt the innovation.

If you placed yourself within one of the first two adoption categories listed above, there is a distinct possibility that you could be a change agent in waiting. Rogers defines a **change agent** as "an individual who influences clients' innovation-decisions in a direction deemed desirable by a change agency" (Rogers 1995, 355). In most organizations and cultures, it is the change agents who encourage others to adopt the technology of the Internet. These people are the first to set up their own webpage, use Dialpad.com for their long-distance communication, and videoconference with people on the other side of the globe. But most importantly, they tell others in their organization about how wonderful it all is. By doing so, they speed up the EPS cycle as they help popularize the new medium. Of course, since innovation and change are often political issues in organizations and cultures—which are ordinarily more concerned with holding on to power than innovating—change agents sometimes encounter resistance to their ideas, even if their ideas are valid. But without these innovators and early adopters of technology, and their interpersonally persuasive contacts with those who are slower to change, the Internet would never have moved out of research circles and into your home.

DE-CENTERING OUR WORLD

Before the Internet, you had to go to the post office to get things like postage stamps and tax forms. Before the Internet, you had to word process a letter, print it out on paper, and physically mail it to the recipient(s) in an envelope. Before the Internet, you had to go to a department store, possibly even using actual money to purchase your goods. Today, we have online services like stamps.com and electronic tax filing. We use e-mail to communicate with our friends and colleagues throughout the world. And we use e-commerce to buy almost anything we could ever possibly want without leaving our homes.

This is because the Internet works by way of a distributed data model. Data is data, whether it is mediated by a person or a computer. So the points of data contact and exchange can be de-centered and spread out to thousands of computers, rather than being centralized within a brick-and-mortar location (open between 9:00 A.M. and 4:30 P.M.). All you need is (1) access to an Internet-ready PC and (2) some of the basic Internet literacy skills that we have covered in this book. **Figure 13.2** is a simple diagram of how a traditional centralized communication structure differs

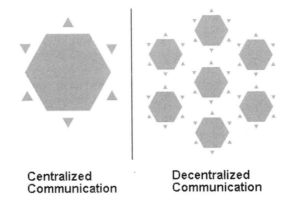

Centralized
Communication

Decentralized
Communication

F i g . 1 3 . 2 . Centralized versus decentralized communication structures.

from an online decentralized communication environment. Instead of one central source producing messages that are then dispersed to audiences, in a decentralized system the production and consumption of information is spread throughout society. As a result, we are faced with two important questions: how does decentralized communication alter the way we interact with and perceive our traditional societal institutions (including government, education, the economy, and community), and how does it change our selves?

DE-CENTERING GOVERNMENT

On an international, federal, state, and local level, the decentralized networks provided by the Internet have allowed governments to disseminate an enormous amount of data online (Garson 1999). And, while almost every nation in the world maintains a Web presence, not every nation boasts the architecture necessary (e.g., computers, phone lines, networking systems, and strength of satellite connectivity) to reach its citizenry. So, until such a time exists when lesser-developed countries become equipped with a stable online infrastructure, most of these governmental websites basically target an international audience.

Finding Government Information Online

Targeting international audiences is not the case in the United States or in other more technologically developed nations. The White House (http://www.whitehouse.gov/), U.S. Senate (http://www.senate.gov/), and U.S. House of Representatives (http://www.house.gov/) each have a website dedicated to public data. And all you need to do to find your respective state government online is to go to http://www.state.ny.us/, substituting the abbreviation of your state for the "ny" in the address. Certainly city and county government directories are a bit more complicated to find when online. But a good place to start is always with the official state government site. Most of these sites list links to major cities and communities. If this still does not provide you with the sites you need, sometimes the actual city name followed by a .com suffix (e.g., http://www.boston.com/) will put you within two clicks of the government site.

Gatekeeping

What is more intriguing to us than the data-delivery aspects of government websites is their data-receiving potential. Before the Internet became something of a public medium, elected officials normally heard from their constituents in one of three manners: (1) a direct letter or telegram, (2) a phone call, or (3) an office visit. In either of these three scenarios, the public official's staff functioned as a gatekeeping mechanism. And for good reason, too. Imagine having to field upwards of 500 communiqués on any given workday. That is why political figures *have* staffs. Obviously, the same dynamic occurs to some extent with e-mail. No one should believe for a moment that an e-mail they send to thepresident@whitehouse.gov is actually being read by the public official himself, without it first having progressed through the proper gatekeeping channels.

On the other hand, within our federal, state, and local bureaucracies, midlevel officials can be directly located and contacted without much, if any, gatekeeping. That is the beauty of decentralized communication systems. Here, the citizen could shop the bureaucracy and pinpoint exactly whom they should consult about their issue with very little running around. This has the potential to increase participation in state, county, and city government, if public servants engage in an active online dialogue with their constituents. This dialogue, in theory, should provide for a wider spectrum of ideas, beliefs, and values upon which to draw when making important community decisions. This, as we all know from our third-grade civics course, is how democracies theoretically function (Kamarck 1999).

Bypassing the Traditional Media

As usual, politicians also recognize that they will likely be candidates again and must therefore stand for reelection. Most candidates today recognize the important outreach function that online technology offers and, therefore, directly incorporate it into their campaign. This is usually done via listservs and websites. Campaign websites have come to function as a base for fund-raising efforts, strategic public relations, and direct constituency contact. For many politicians, though, the most exciting part of their website is its ability to bypass the media entirely. Since free presses were first conceived, politicians have been leery of a broadcast media prone to sound-bite journalism and editorialization. Creating their own webpages allows politicians to put out "unadulterated" public relations messages.

Politicking among the Digital Provinces

When we look more closely at how the Internet works, perhaps a greater "beast" than the national press corps awaits the candidate who enters into the Web (Morris 1999). For instance, when George W. Bush began his 2000 presidential bid, his staff discovered that several cybersquatters had purchased rather uncomplimentary domain names and were using them to lampoon the Bush 2000 campaign. To counteract this problem, the campaign staff purchased the rights to as many of the derogatory URLs that they could possibly find, such as http://www.bushsucks.com/, and then rerouted them to the legitimate campaign site at http://www.georgewbush.com/.

What could be more damaging than the satirical domain name itself is what might appear on a site employing such a domain name, and what uncritical audiences might be led to believe. Imagine, for example, that you have just received a digitally reconfigured picture of a political figure engaged in some form of disreputable activity. It appears quite real and maybe even plausible. What will you do with this unverified image? Might you forward such an image on to your friends with a cheeky comment? Or would you delete it out of high virtue, understanding that the Internet can circulate bogus as well as valid data? The fact that some of us might forward the image on to our friends, and so on and so on, proves that online data has an immediacy well beyond our traditional media expectations. More problematic, this form of disinformation can accelerate through our interpersonal network streams, with no means of verification. Then again, the recurrence of such events might cause Internet users to become increasingly skeptical with every piece of information they encounter (Davis 1999).

What will become of online government is still unclear. As with ourselves, our government institutions are inherently a part of this grand experiment. Will we someday hold our political elections online? Will we even have a need for these political elections? Is it possible that we could move democracy to a new form of government by direct public referendum? The answers to these questions are obviously more about the distribution of power than the ready capabilities of our new media technologies. How a medium as slippery and elusive as the Internet will, once firmly rooted in an educated global public, restructure these notions of centralized authority is yet to be seen. Moreover, how centralized institutions like government will have to rethink the very ways in which they have traditionally *represented* the masses, who can now arguably represent themselves, is probably a much more unknown dynamic.

DE-CENTERING EDUCATION

Self-Instruction

The most important contribution that the Internet has provided to education comes in its ability to allow the user to teach the self (Palloff and Pratt 1999). Let's say, for example, that you happen to reside in the deep recesses of the Amazon jungle, where no formal education exists. Here, the Internet might evolve as a de facto community library. Think about all of the social programs and agricultural bounties that could be gained through a simple laptop and cellular connection in that isolated region of the world. Likewise, even in more developed nations like the United States, when a student goes online to discover how oil and gas teams pinpoint hydrocarbons deep within the Earth, this also constitutes a form of education. In this way, the Internet works to empower the individual and the community. For this very reason, academic institutions find the Internet both empowering and frightening. By its very anarchic nature, the Internet challenges the centrality of the university with a decentralized educational paradigm. With the Internet, some might argue, who needs a teacher?

Decentralizing the Institution and the Classroom

The most obvious change occurring in our academic institutions is the amount of computer equipment being used. It seems that everywhere we turn, another computer lab is either being installed or upgraded. This is probably for good reason, too, since no matter whether you are studying communication, mathematics, or music, computers have evolved as the chief means by which we now do our study. It should also go without saying that a major reason why institutions are installing this equipment is to get their students online. Both educators and administrators recognize the value of promoting decentralized communication portals via the Internet. Doing so can alleviate the tedium of question-and-answer stress on faculty and staff, while also reducing the informational complexity that students often face in bureaucratic institutions. And given that students can easily afford their own Internet-ready computer and obtain connectivity through either their university dial-up lines or a private ISP, the traditional centralized educational model has, in effect, decentralized away from campus. Where students used to meet only in class, they can now also meet in listservs and chat-rooms.

The Rise of the Virtual University

Distance learning, where students learn without physically being on campus, began long before the Internet became a popular medium. Throughout the 1970s and 1980s, in fact, most distance learning courses were offered via the postal service. During the late 1980s and early 1990s, cable television helped institutions further promote the concept of "tele-education" within their local communities. When the Internet roared into our schools and homes during the 1990s, most distance learning programs shifted to the new online, or virtual, delivery systems.

The emergence of online courses offered by traditional brick-and-mortar institutions, and by virtual universities that exist entirely online, has made it possible to obtain almost any form of education via the Internet. Undoubtedly, many private and public institutions are concerned that someday all education will be delivered via the virtual model. Critics argue that the campus will always hold a certain face-to-face aesthetic that the online environment will never be able to simulate. Either way, the concept of virtual education has emerged as a realistic model. Now, the institution and the student begin the social negotiation process to determine the feasibility of such a model.

De-centering the Children

One of the major initiatives undertaken by the Clinton-Gore administration during the 1990s is the promise to provide "Internet access in every school and in every classroom, throughout the nation." In a 2000 report, the National Center for Education Statistics (NCES) indicates that this goal is near completion with 95% of all schools and 63% of all classrooms now connected. But no good deed ever goes unpunished. What information could K-12 students, mere children, possibly find online? Detailed instructions to build a gas grill bomb? Pornography? Some began to question if this was such a good idea after all. As discussed in chapter 12, the First Amendment and the Internet have had, and will continue to have, repeated encounters.

Regardless of the software available that makes the Web "safer" to browse for children (which can be found at Cybersitter.com, Netnanny. com, and Cyberpatrol.com), a much more subtle education is at work here. Rather than receiving traditional linear instruction, which enforces the concepts of centralization, order, and if-then causal reasoning— Generation E is growing up with the logic of decentralization, distribution, and associational reasoning. Regardless of whether or not they think this is a positive thing, scholars of the Internet are agreed that we are training our children to think very differently than our grandparents did.

DE-CENTERING THE ECONOMY

Even if you don't follow the stock market closely, chances are good that you have still heard about the enormous wealth being generated in the information technology sector. Up until 1995, the U.S. economy had been traditionally led by conventional industrial, energy, agricultural, and service-related markets. Since early 1995, however, the U.S. economy has been driven by a raging-bull market in the information technology sector. Between the years of 1995 and 2000, the Dow Jones Industrial

Average rose nearly 188%, while the technology-rich NASDAQ went up an astounding 466%. **Figures 13.3 and 13.4** document this explosive growth in both the DJIA and the NASDAQ.

Led by industry giants Intel, Motorola, Microsoft, Cisco Systems, and AOL, our need to connect to the Internet has ushered in a new economy, and with it a new paradigm of practicing business (Canton 1999). The decentralized communication systems of the Internet have provided modern capitalism with a distributed method of engaging nearly every aspect of commerce. From the raw materials broker, to the manufacturer, to the distributor, to retail—our entire means of assimilating, delivering, marketing, and selling products is being forever revolutionized. Little by little, the intermediaries who once weighted down Adam Smith's vision of a "friction-free capitalism" (where the buyer and seller could identify one another's best price without brokers) are now being replaced by highly reliable automated information systems (Schiller 1099)

The Virtual Office

One of the first applications that emerged from the Internet was the virtual office. The virtual office was not a product made by any manufacturer, per se, although a few have used that title to sell their wares. It was

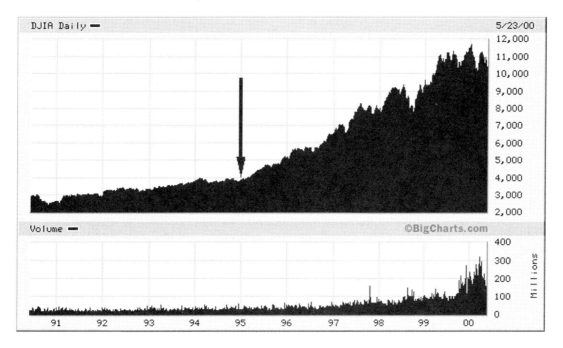

Fig. 13.3. The Dow Jones Industrial Average entered a bull market on January 1, 1995, and has not looked back.

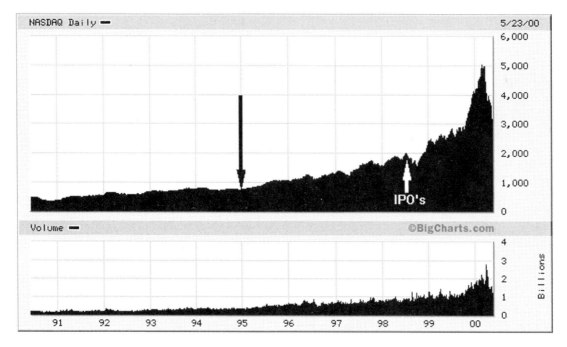

Fig. 13.4. The NASDAQ entered into a light bull market on January 1, 1995. However, recent vertical gains are directly attributed to the dot-com and technology-heavy initial public offerings (IPOs) being made on the NASDAQ since October of 1998. Many people believe that the technology-heavy NASDAQ will soon overtake the DJIA, signaling the dominance of the U.S. information technology over industrials.

a concept. You see, once the Internet was understood by early innovators in business and industry, they began to apply its functionality into their office and plant operations. E-mail became commonplace, expected, a way of using flextime to communicate across vast geography. Naturally, the Web emerged as a means of publicly distributing data, even practicing corporate public relations. Consequently, in 1995 offices everywhere began installing new computers and network lines. As the virtualization of the office continued throughout the late 1990s, the demand for computer equipment also soared, creating a pattern of self-perpetuation of technology. Companies purchased faster computers, other companies created new uses for those computers, which in turn required faster computers, which computer manufactures were more than happy to sell. Now, with a laptop and a cellular modem, business users can access their e-mail, company databases, their organization's **intranet** (secure internal computer networks that use the same protocols as the Internet), and critical information from anywhere in the world. Highly sophisticated collaborative applications that go far beyond the basic videoconferencing programs we talked about in chapter 5 make it possible for people distributed around the planet to work together as a team.

E-commerce

Since its inception, people have been using the Internet to conduct business. **E-commerce** (also known as **e-tail**) is a form of consumer-direct sales conducted through the Web. It is usually as simple as going to the company's site, selecting a category, and then locating your desired item. If you want to purchase the item, you simply select the Buy button nearby and take your "shopping cart" to the online "checkout counter." Golf equipment, plane tickets, new cars, air purifiers, Rolex watches–all online, 24 hours a day, 7 days a week (De Kare-Silver 1999).

Many prefer e-tail shopping because: (1) you do not have to travel to the store in order to examine an item, (2) there are no crowds or lines at the virtual checkout counter, (3) the selection is often better, (4) it is easier to compare prices, and (5) the selected product is delivered directly to your home. On the other hand, many dislike e-tail shopping because: (1) you never get to see and touch what it is that you are going to buy, (2) it takes the fun out of shopping as an activity, and (3) you must often wait three to five business days for the product to be delivered to your residence. Regardless of your preference, e-tailers are certain that as the Internet's reach continues to expand and people become more comfortable with online shopping, their businesses will flourish. Since more than 20 million people to date have purchased something online already, it seems that the early majority is leading society into a new distributed model of commerce.

If you happen to be one of the 20 million who have already purchased something online, then you also know just how many e-tail merchants exist. What you may or may not find surprising, however, is that e-tail can be quite slippery from a marketing perspective. Because websites are less expensive to create than new stores, some e-tail outlets will simply replicate their e-commerce engine in four to five different themes, brand names, and locations. In appearance it may seem like you are shopping at another e-store. But, in all actuality, the products and prices are the same from one site to the next. All that has changed is the marketing and appearance for each e-commerce site. These multiple storefronts provide the e-merchant with more opportunity to encounter a potential customer, and thus, profits.

However, e-commerce has to overcome one major hurdle: lack of consumer trust. Many buyers are cautious about entering in their credit card number on a webpage, even though they do not hesitate to give that number out over the phone or even hand their card to someone else (such as a waiter). In the scheme of things, your credit card number is actually safer online, especially when a **secure-sockets layer** is used to

TEXTBOX 13.1

AUCTIONS

Looking for a rare Japanese Pokemon card? Or perhaps you want to go on a cruise, but you can't afford to pay full price? Then you might want to check out an auction site, where almost anything imaginable is sold (and even some unimaginable things), and where you can often get a good deal. Just as in real-life auctions, goods in online auctions are sold to the highest bidder. Most online auctions use a Dutch auction format, where the earliest and highest bidder wins. Typically, you enter in the maximum amount you're willing to pay, and the auction site starts your bid off at the current highest bid. Then as other people bid higher, your bid is automatically increased until it reaches the limit you set. These auctions are time limited, and if no one bids higher than you before the deadline, that tournament foosball table is yours.

Two different types of auction sites exist, and they are differentiated by one important criteria: who can sell. Some sites, such as Egghead.com **(Figure 13.5),** auction products from businesses only. The advantage of this is that Egghead serves as a

Fig. 13.5. Going, going, gone: Online auctions can be effective and fun ways to get a good deal.

programs we talked about in chapter 5 make it possible for people distributed around the planet to work together as a team.

E-commerce

Since its inception, people have been using the Internet to conduct business. **E-commerce** (also known as **e-tail**) is a form of consumer-direct sales conducted through the Web. It is usually as simple as going to the company's site, selecting a category, and then locating your desired item. If you want to purchase the item, you simply select the Buy button nearby and take your "shopping cart" to the online "checkout counter." Golf equipment, plane tickets, new cars, air purifiers, Rolex watches–all online, 24 hours a day, 7 days a week (De Kare-Silver 1999).

Many prefer e-tail shopping because: (1) you do not have to travel to the store in order to examine an item, (2) there are no crowds or lines at the virtual checkout counter, (3) the selection is often better, (4) it is easier to compare prices, and (5) the selected product is delivered directly to your home. On the other hand, many dislike e-tail shopping because: (1) you never get to see and touch what it is that you are going to buy, (2) it takes the fun out of shopping as an activity, and (3) you must often wait three to five business days for the product to be delivered to your residence. Regardless of your preference, e-tailers are certain that as the Internet's reach continues to expand and people become more comfortable with online shopping, their businesses will flourish. Since more than 20 million people to date have purchased something online already, it seems that the early majority is leading society into a new distributed model of commerce.

If you happen to be one of the 20 million who have already purchased something online, then you also know just how many e-tail merchants exist. What you may or may not find surprising, however, is that e-tail can be quite slippery from a marketing perspective. Because websites are less expensive to create than new stores, some e-tail outlets will simply replicate their e-commerce engine in four to five different themes, brand names, and locations. In appearance it may seem like you are shopping at another e-store. But, in all actuality, the products and prices are the same from one site to the next. All that has changed is the marketing and appearance for each e-commerce site. These multiple storefronts provide the e-merchant with more opportunity to encounter a potential customer, and thus, profits.

However, e-commerce has to overcome one major hurdle: lack of consumer trust. Many buyers are cautious about entering in their credit card number on a webpage, even though they do not hesitate to give that number out over the phone or even hand their card to someone else (such as a waiter). In the scheme of things, your credit card number is actually safer online, especially when a **secure-sockets layer** is used to

TEXTBOX 13.1

AUCTIONS

Looking for a rare Japanese Pokemon card? Or perhaps you want to go on a cruise, but you can't afford to pay full price? Then you might want to check out an auction site, where almost anything imaginable is sold (and even some unimaginable things), and where you can often get a good deal. Just as in real-life auctions, goods in online auctions are sold to the highest bidder. Most online auctions use a Dutch auction format, where the earliest and highest bidder wins. Typically, you enter in the maximum amount you're willing to pay, and the auction site starts your bid off at the current highest bid. Then as other people bid higher, your bid is automatically increased until it reaches the limit you set. These auctions are time limited, and if no one bids higher than you before the deadline, that tournament foosball table is yours.

Two different types of auction sites exist, and they are differentiated by one important criteria: who can sell. Some sites, such as Egghead.com **(Figure 13.5),** auction products from businesses only. The advantage of this is that Egghead serves as a

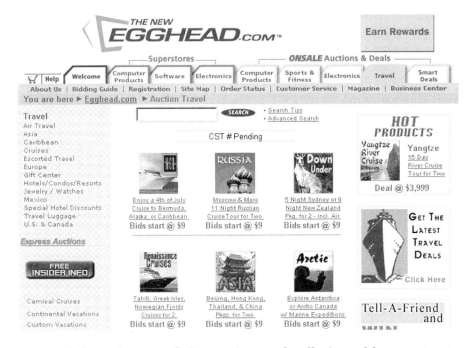

Fig. 13.5. Going, going, gone: Online auctions can be effective and fun ways to get a good deal.

mediator between the person selling and the person buying, which allows the buyer to pay Egghead with a credit card and then Egghead passes the money along to the seller. This additional security and convenience makes auction sites like Egghead popular.

Other sites, such as eBay.com, allow anyone to sell (almost) anything they want. So if you have a rare Beanie Baby, you could list it for sale on eBay, set the number of days you want the auction to run, and sit back and wait. Since eBay allows private individuals as well as businesses to sell items, you can find almost anything for sale. In fact, eBay has had to deal with pranksters who have listed items such as a human liver for sale. eBay does not get involved with the exchange of money for auctioned items; however, other companies such as PayPal.com have sprung up to make it easier and safer for auction winners to pay sellers.

What eBay has done to make auctioning more attractive to people is the addition of feedback. Buyers can rate sellers' performances in categories such as speed of delivery, quality of goods, and service, while sellers can rate buyers performances in terms of payment follow-through and promptness. This feedback system allows both buyers and sellers to get a sense of the trustworthiness of the person with whom they are dealing. And if there is anything we know about commerce on the Internet, it is that trust is critical. By providing feedback forums (see **Figure 1.3**), eBay allows buyers and sellers to reduce their apprehension through the exchange of information–an important aspect of interpersonal communication.

Auctions can be an exciting way to get a great deal on almost anything–from cruises to cruise missiles (well, maybe not . . .). But if you decide to dive into a bidding war, keep a close watch on yourself. If you aren't careful, you could get into a bidding frenzy and end up paying more for the item than it is worth. It's a good idea to check around at other e-commerce sites to see what the item retails for normally.

encrypt the data, than it is when you count off the digits over an insecure phone line. People also hesitate to shop at an online vendor that they do not recognize, just as they might hesitate to shop at an unfamiliar supermarket. But as e-commerce gets diffused throughout society, these fears will gradually be replaced by trust for many people. And since a great deal of our knowledge about the Internet comes through our interpersonal networks (O'Donnell 1998), most people will likely be convinced by the positive experiences that their friends share with them.

Business-to-Business (b2b) Models

Gaining a commanding lead within the e-tail industry was so important to the early venture capitalists who moved into the online investment arena that the much larger profit margins in the wholesale industry went completely ignored for a full year. But now, **business-to-business** (b2b) e-commerce portals attempt to match industry-specific needs by using a more ambitious e-commerce model. Rather than selling general commerce like a retail outlet might, these portals function as communities where manufacturers, wholesalers, distributors, and retailers can virtually meet and lower their costs by eliminating intermediaries. Most b2b sites also provide news information (usually about product research) developing within each specific industry.

For example, let's say that you are a large milk producer in Wisconsin. You are interested in purchasing some milk chillers so that your product will not spoil before being delivered to market. But you know that you cannot exactly go to any of the general e-tail sites and find one of these products online. Instead, you could go to a site like Verticalnet.com to find a community specifically constructed to meet the needs of the milk and milk products industry. Suddenly, not only have you found your milk chiller but you have found a new information "home" geared around your livelihood. B2b commerce online has a lot of potential for growth, and b2b sites such as Comercis.com and Verticalnet.com are popping up all over the Web.

DE-CENTERING THE COMMUNITY

Once upon a time, in a land not so far away, people met in town halls and schools to discuss issues as communities. They would enter into a public building of some sort where other stranger-citizens were gathered, get a bad cup of coffee, take a seat, and an official would smack a gavel down to begin the meeting. While these assemblies still occur, a great deal of our communal discourse has shifted to the electronic. Beginning in the mid-1970s, some people saw computer networks as a way to serve local community needs. Since that time, the use of computer networks as a community communication medium has taken many forms and been called by many names: community networks, local bulletin boards, civic networking, telecottages, community information systems, community computing, community telecomputing, Free-Nets, and more. Whatever form or name community networks take, they share four goals: connecting all members of their community to the Internet for no cost or a minimal fee; advancing local issues; providing an electronic space for local news, announcements, and information; and preaching the gospel of political empowerment to local residents (Schuler 1996).

These community networks see one of their primary missions to be the rebinding of people in a particular place. But by moving to the Internet, the community network now makes it even easier for residents to leave their local community. Because the Internet is a global medium, it obviously adheres to no geography. From the beginning, it was driven by the goal to eradicate the boundary of space and to remove any problems that arose in spatially distant communication. This is very important to remember when discussing the concept of community, because traditionally our notion of *community* was rooted in geography. If you were holding a town meeting, it was usually about something in town. If you were at a school board meeting, the topic was likely to be about issues within the district–again, a geographic concept. In the online environment, we define communities by topic. Perhaps this topic might be Miami, Florida, or Seattle, Washington–but it could just as easily be fly-fishing, or model trains, or the Beatles. The function of the online community is to bring a centralized sense of order to the decentralized engineering of the Internet. When you get right down to it, how else could we possibly search the Internet if not by topic, or at least some sense of shared meaning?

These topic communities can be highly developed and specialized because they build upon themselves over time. As they grow in membership and in data, they evolve a certain community personality, if not communality. This is why many virtual communities have a FAQ file listed prominently in their directory; this ensures that new users will engage the community on a more evolved level of interaction than asking repeated ". . . does anyone know how?" questions. There is a topic community dedicated to just about any possible interest that you can imagine, provided it is broad enough for general interest. As evidence of this, Egroups.com sponsors more than 300,000 topic communities. Inside these online civic centers, members can discuss issues, post multimedia content, and ruminate about their postings to absorb prior knowledge.

This is not to say that our actual communities have been substituted for virtual communities. But it is to say that we are spending a great deal more of our time in communities that are not tied to any specific *place*. Instead, people search for and interact with people around the world who share a common *interest* (Rheingold 1993). For instance, if we are interested in tennis or bowling or canoeing, we can become part of a worldwide virtual community before we encounter the actual local community involved in the activity. This occurred before the Internet, of course, but the Internet has brought interest communities to a whole new level. Instead of having three major networks, or 280 satellite broadcast channels, we now have approximately 8,000,000 websites at our point-and-click disposal (Owen 1999). Unlike television, these websites invite our feedback. They draw us into the dialogue. With this many minds going in this many directions, it is no wonder that community has been de-centered from our traditional notions. People can access information from around the globe, engage in correspondence with people on different continents, or get involved in issues that matter to them personally but are of little or no relevance to their neighbors. Critics of virtual communities fear that as people become increasingly de-centered from their physical communities, they may become increasingly oblivious to the problems in their town, as they spend more time seeking out the fulfillment of their own interests.

DE-CENTERING THE INDIVIDUAL

We've seen some ways that the Internet is de-centering our social institutions. But what about the individual? Most of our current academic research focuses upon how the Internet affects us as a society, leaving us to deduce how these answers bear upon the individual. We do know some things about how people are using the Internet. For instance, the Stanford SIQSS 2000 Internet Survey reports that we primarily use the Internet to compose and read e-mail (90% of respondents answered in the affirmative). Likewise, it seems that we also use the Web to locate general data (77%) via surfing (69%) or reading (67%). The most prominent online categories of interest relate to either our personal hobbies (63%), product data (62%), or travel data (54%). Indicating that the Internet has either not yet penetrated our workplaces fully or that many professions do not require its use, less than half of all respondents said they use the medium for their work (46%).

Logical Diversity and Desensitization

But what happens to individuals as they use the Internet? With over 8,000,000 websites, boasting over 8,000,000 different avenues of content, we end up with a society composed of individuals experiencing an infinite number of differently arranged messages. This is where it becomes difficult to know exactly how the Internet is affecting the individual. The logical diversity available on the Internet is astounding. As you already know, you will encounter a great deal of data online—the good, the bad, and the ugly. Critical audiences will carefully evaluate information, but is that enough? Some critics contend that our interaction with potentially unsound data subtly desensitizes us. In other words, as we continually encounter bad data, our proverbial moral and ethical bells no longer go off. So, from this perspective, we intellectually consume everything with a lack of consideration for the self (Shenk 1999; Shenk 1998). The equally valid counterpoint to this argument is that desensitization is really just another form of sensitization. By experiencing the new and unique, we are actually learning about each other—the good, the bad, and the ugly. In other words, the more we encounter data, the better off our knowledge (Shapiro 1999; Davidson 1997).

A third perspective is that it need not be one or the other, and that both of these processes are continually at work. Everyday, a user on the Internet can learn something new. This new information can either confirm or deny his or her previously held assumptions. Either way, each new argument encountered forces the individual to reconsider previously held assumptions; this will happen even if the new argument is not accepted. By contemplating the new thought, symbol, or referent, the preexisting framework of what we feel is reasonable, logical, just, or sound gets stretched, pulled, shifted, and moved. So, in a sense, we are logically de-centering ourselves: not dogmatically rejecting bad data, or uncritically accepting everything, but adjusting the boundaries of our understanding.

Social Isolation

If you are a curious person, the Internet can be both a blessing and a curse. It can be a blessing because you enjoy the process of learning a great deal, flirting with logical de-centering at every possible turn. Yet, if you find yourself becoming a "mouse potato" lately, staying up until 3:00 A.M. to browse the Web, you also realize how the Internet can be a curse (Rawlins 1998). The Stanford statistics further indicate that the longer we have had Internet access, the more time we spend with the medium. This would ordinarily make sense, of course, since the more you use the Internet, the more you discover all of the neat things you can do with it. The potentially disturbing issue lying dormant in these statistics, however, is that the more time we spend with our computers generally means the less time we have to engage in other life activities. Researchers are concerned that Internet aficionados are engaging the data on the Internet as a means to synthetically substitute for face-to-face real-life interactions.

Lifestyle Impacts

The Stanford study also demonstrates that we are increasingly spending: (1) less time talking with our friends and family over the phone, (2) less time with our friends and family, and (3) less time at actual events away from the home. Because heavy Internet users seem to communicate less in face-to-face dynamics than nonusers, this does not mean that they are necessarily communicating less. In fact, they could be using technology to communicate *more* than nonusers. That said, Internet users are clearly engaging the world in a much different way than nonusers ordinarily engage it (Negroponte 1996). Of course, it is important to realize that there aren't just users and nonusers, but different levels of use. The key thing to examine in your own life, as you spend more time using this new medium, is where that time is coming from. Any activity requires sacrificing some other activity. The Internet, while technologically advanced, is not a time machine and thus is no exception to this rule.

WHERE IS THE INTERNET SOCIETY HEADED?

The airplane, the submarine, the missions to the moon—each of these visions had their opponents who declared the impossibility of such lofty goals ever becoming realities. "If man were meant to fly, he would have been born with wings," critics would chuckle at the Wright Brothers during their trial flights. It has always been easy to be a critic. Critics critique, they offer their opinion. They do not construct. But it was the innovator who endured the labors of invention, bringing forth thoughts, models, and products from sheer nothingness. They had a vision and dared to bring it to the marketplace of reality. They dared to dream. This is why our best innovators are some of the most celebrated minds among history.

Let's take a moment to look ahead to where some of the cutting-edge visionaries believe that the Internet is headed. Like the Wright Brothers and Jules Verne, remember that these visions of the future may seem far-fetched to you at the moment. But to negate the possibility that these visions might evolve into realities negates humankind's journey toward exploration itself. It vexes what it means to be human. So before you read these final few pages, we would like you to keep your mind open. Consider the possibilities of what could be before you interject the state of that which is. If you have some difficulty doing this, recall what things were like without all of these technologies at our disposal merely a decade ago. A pretty dramatic change, to say the least.

A WIRELESS INTERNET: THE NEXT CONTEXT

You have probably seen someone using a PalmPilot handheld personal digital assistant (PDA) by now. If not, you should become more familiar with these devices. Today's futurists generally agree that our computing devices will evolve from the "wired Internet" much as our phones have due to cellular telephony (Harte and Kellogg 1998; Williams 1995). It is not that much of a leap since several wireless handheld devices and telephones utilize the Internet already. But these devices are still in their infancy. Because laptops are heavy, engineers have designed lighter breakaway devices that target specific data needs. For instance, if you trade on the stock market, you can purchase a Flextrader.com portable to keep you connected to your brokerage. Or you can even browse the Web for information via your cell phone. As of yet, no truly pocket-portable device can give you full PC compatibility and Internet connectivity in a slim-cased all-in-one design. When, not if, this day comes, the Internet will de-center the human being from the wired Internet. You will be able to connect to the Internet from anywhere, at any time.

Imagine someday opening a soft-covered portfolio-like folder where on the right side of your "InterPad" there is a touchscreen LCD. Because voice-recognition software will have evolved into a stable human-computer interface, you will speak into your InterPad device asking it to connect you to the Internet. A small motorized rubber antenna will protrude from the top of the unit, and the your mini-modem will instantly connect you to the Internet. You say the following commands into the device, "Teleconference with my son." The InterPad places a teleconfer-ence call through the Internet and locates your son. His InterPad beeps as he opens an incoming-call permission window. You see that he is once again "studying" at the library with his new girlfriend. To the left of your InterPad resides the camera and microphone through which you carry on an embarrassing live teleconference about his recent report card and the importance of studying more–alone. As you realize you are fighting a losing battle, you tell him that you will see him at home for dinner around 7:00 to discuss the issue later. You disconnect from your session by saying, "Complete teleconference."

Then you remember that you promised your spouse that you would cook dinner tonight because s/he would be in a long face-to-face meet-ing. You access your home PC control system by saying, "Home interface, kitchen." Immediately you see a control panel interface for your kitchen on your InterPad screen. You instruct the microwave to begin cooking the frozen dish that you placed there earlier that morning. As you arrive home, the odor of rotten fish fills the air, which prompts you to quickly order pizza. All done through your InterPad, all done through the Inter-net, and all done by our emerging communication technologies. This future, and the appliances that will work off such a communication land-scape, is probably less than a decade away. Imagine a decentralized, dis-tributed, wireless Internet not binding you to a line in your office or home. This will be the next revolutionary context of the Internet. Sending and receiving all forms of data will occur on-cell, as well as online–a term that might soon disappear.

VIRTUAL AND AUGMENTED REALITY

To some extent, virtual reality has already been explained in the fiction of our feature films (and in chapter 9). Yet only a few of these techno-thrillers have discussed the possibility of online VR. These simulated realities are becoming increasingly interactive in the sense that users can experience even the perception of bodily movement, provided they have the requisite full-body suit and other gear (Hayles 1999). When the de-corporealizing technologies of VR are paired with the wireless con-duits to the Internet, we are presented with wireless VR. Imagine the possibility of someday shaking hands with your colleagues at a VR con-vention via your InterPad while sitting in a restaurant near the interstate off-ramp.

And while wireless VR would be the exact same experience for the human mind whether it were being conducted in an office building or through an InterPad-like device, another emerging technology called augmented reality (AR) is challenging our notions of single-screen VR (Mizel, Behringer, and Klinker 1998). **Augmented reality** is a means of pairing multiple reality feeds into an orchestrated human experience, whether these feeds are real, synthetic, or a mixture of both. This may be difficult to imagine at first, but try to envision a television set displaying two overlapping signals at the same time. This double image would likely be a little confusing to the normal mind. But, if we could better manage the two feeds, we could essentially merge both into a fused environment. How exactly could we do this, you might wonder?

The U.S. government is now experimenting with AR technologies that will provide better management over reality via a developmental form of VR. Users of this augmented reality equipment wear a special set of VR goggles with a camera attached to the rim of their headset. The headset camera feeds a vision of what the user would be looking at in actual reality directly into the VR glasses (Field 1). So, here, you would essentially be looking at a picture of what you would ordinarily see minus the glasses. The second image would be, say, a program that recognizes the shapes, sizes, and surface effects of the items being represented in Field 1. This program (Field 2) is an augmented reality overlay system (AROS). The AROS determines, using a visual-object database, where a scanned Field 1 part is located in an engineering schematic by comparing it to Field 2. Engineers at Boeing are also experimenting with such equipment, since this technology would free their developers from thousands of needless hours of manual consultation when designing aircraft. They could look at a part on an airplane and see in their goggles specifications, settings, part numbers, and more. Like the Terminator, we humans could scan reality and match it against a visual-object database, stored online and thus accessible from anywhere in the world, for more pertinent data.

BACK UP AND RELOAD

If there's one thing you can count on in this world (besides death and taxes), it is change. The past few decades have brought enormous changes to our world and to the way we communicate. But to quote another cliché, the more things change, the more they stay the same. Even though new technologies are entering our lives at a faster and faster pace, they all still follow the same cycle. Moving through three phases, new technologies typically start with elites, spread to the general population, and finally expand so much that they begin to be specialized. Of course, technologies do not move through the EPS cycle on their own. Change agents persuade other people to begin using the technology, and through this process of interpersonal networking help diffuse the innovation throughout the society.

Take a look again at the opening cartoons for this chapter and chapter 1. As you should remember, the Internet was originally designed to help the military communicate in the event of a nuclear war. It did so by decentralizing the communication system—spreading it out so it could not be taken out by a single strike. When the Internet became a popular medium, it maintained this decentralized structure. But as we know from our studies of other communication media, the structure of our media impacts the structure of our society and even our own identities. In this case, we can point to some decentralized trends in government, education, the economy, communities, and individuals that are connected to the global spread of the World Wide Web.

If change is really constant, and if the pace of change is increasing, we can expect to see even more innovations in the future. Wireless Internet connections will make this global data network even more a part of our daily lives. And virtual and augmented reality will make Internet communication even more lifelike—or perhaps even more surreal. How can you keep up with these changes? Well, you've taken an important first step: you've begun to learn. Nathan Pusey, the president of Harvard, said the following back in 1963: "We live in a time of such rapid change and growth of knowledge that only [one] who is in a fundamental sense a scholar—that is, a person who continues to learn and inquire—can hope to keep pace, let alone play the role of guide." Keep your eyes, ears, and most importantly your mind open for the rest of your life, and keep learning, and you will remain an effective communicator on the Internet.

BROWSE *and* **BUILD**

For sites to visit, exercises, quizzes to test your learning, and more, go to *www.harcourtcollege.com/ communication/inetcomm*

References and Readings

Canton, J. 1999. *Technofutures: How leading-edge technology will transform business in the 21st century.* Carlsbad, Calif.: Hay House Press.

Carter, R., and C. Frith. 1999. *Mapping the mind.* Berkeley: University of California Press.

Cochrane, P. 1999. *Tips for time travelers: Visionary insights into a new technology, life and the future on the edge of technology.* New York: McGraw-Hill.

Davidson, J. D. 1997. *The sovereign individual: How to survive and thrive during the collapse of the welfare state.* New York: Simon & Schuster.

Davis, R. 1999. *The web of politics: The Internet's impact on the American political system.* Oxford: Oxford University Press.

De Kare-Silver, M. 1999. *E-shock: The electronic shopping revolution: Strategies for retailers and manufacturers.* New York: American Manufacturing Association.

Fukuyama, F. 1999. *The great disruption: Human nature and the reconstitution of social order.* New York: Free Press.

Garson, G. D. 1999. *Information technology and computer applications in public administration: Issues and trends.* Harrisburg, Pa.: Idea Group Publishing.

Gershenfeld, N. A. 1999. *When things start to think.* New York: Henry Holt and Company.

Gleick, J. 1999. *Faster: The acceleration of just about everything.* New York: Pantheon Books.

Harte, L., and S. Kellogg. 1998. *The comprehensive guide to wireless technologies.* New York: APDG Technologies.

Hayles, N. K. 1999. *How we become post-human: Virtual bodies in cybernetics, literature, and informatics.* Chicago: University of Chicago Press.

Heim, M. 1997. *Virtual realism.* Oxford: Oxford University Press.

Johnson, S. 1997. *Interface culture: How new technology transforms the way we create and communicate.* San Francisco: Harper San Francisco.

Jonash, R. S. 1999. *The innovation premium.* New York: Perseus Books.

Kamarck, E. C. 1999. *Democracy.com: Governance in a networked world.* Hollis, N.H.: Hollis Publishing Company.

Mizel, D., R. Behringer, R., and G. Klinker. 1998. *Augmented reality: Proceedings of IWAR 1998.* Wellesley, Mass.: A. K. Peters Ltd.

Morris, D. 1999. *Vote.com: How big-money lobbyists and the media are losing their influence, and the Internet is giving power back to the people.* Los Angeles: Renaissance Books.

Negroponte, N. 1996. *Being digital.* New York: Vintage Books.

O'Donnell, J. J. 1998. *Avatars of the word: From papyrus to Cyberspace.* Cambridge: Harvard University Press.

Owen, B. M. 1999. *The Internet challenge to television.* Cambridge: Harvard University Press.

Palloff, R. M., and K. Pratt. 1999. *Building learning communities in Cyberspace: Effective strategies for the online classroom.* San Francisco: Jossey-Bass Publishers.

Pusey, N. 1963. *The age of the scholar.* Harvard: Belknap Press.

Rawlins, G. J. E. 1998. *Slaves of the machine: The quickening of computer technology.* Cambridge: MIT Press.

Rheingold, H. 1993. *The virtual community: Homesteading on the electronic frontier. Reading,* Mass.: Addison-Wesley.

Rogers, E. M. 1995. *Diffusion of innovations.* New York: Free Press.

Schiller, D. 1999. *Digital capitalism: Networking the global market system.* Cambridge: MIT Press.

Schuler, D. 1996. *New community networks: Wired for change.* New York: ACM Press.

Schwartau, W. 1996. *Information warfare: Chaos on the electronic superhighway.* New York: Thunder's Mouth Press.

Shapiro, A. L. 1999. *The control revolution: How the Internet is putting individuals in charge and changing the world we know.* New York: The Century Foundation.

Shenk, D. 1998. *Data smog: Surviving the information glut.* San Francisco: Harper San Francisco.

–––. 1999. *The end of patience: Cautionary notes on the information revolution.* Bloomington: Indiana University Press.

Stefik, M. 1999. *The Internet edge: Social, legal, and technological challenges for a networked world.* Cambridge: MIT Press.

Tapscott, D. 1997. *Growing up digital: The rise of the net generation.* New York: McGraw-Hill.

Williams, V. 1995. *Wireless computing primer.* Chicago: IDG Books.

GLOSSARY

actual damages Money paid for injuries incurred, without any need to prove malice.

Adobe Acrobat Reader A program and plug-in that can read .pdf files.

algorithms Formulae used for manipulating data.

alignment How the text is lined up on the page, either on the left or right edge, or down the center.

alpha channels A feature of PNG graphic files that allows you to set variable transparencies for an image.

alphanumeric Either letters or numbers.

anchors Allow you to move to a specific section of an HTML page.

AND A Boolean operator that forces a search engine to pull up only pages that contain all of the words that you enter.

animated GIFs Moving images made by creating a series of frames that the computer cycles through.

APA (American Psychological Association) **Style** One of the most commonly used style guides for academic writing.

arousal How interested another person is in us, communicated through cues such as an animated voice, face, or body posture.

ARPA (Advanced Research Projects Agency) The agency formed in 1958 by the U.S. government to consider the tactical issues of new technological developments; the organization that provided the host computers for ARPANET.

ARPANET The first full-scale effort to build a national computer-mediated communication infrastructure by the United States, developed by ARPA in 1968.

ASCII (American Standard Code for Information Interchange) Character set for text.

asterisk A wild card character (*) used in searches to stand for "anything else." A search for "health*" will find health, healthy, healthiness, etc.

asynchronous Not at the same time.

@join A MOO command that allows you to teleport to the designated person's side.

attachments Files sent with an e-mail message.

@who A MOO command that lists not only "who" is in the MOO but also "where" they are located.

augmented reality A means of pairing multiple reality feeds into an orchestrated human experience, whether these feeds are real, synthetic, or a mixture of both.

avatars Digital characters.

baselines The lines that text characters "sit" on.

BBS (bulletin board service) Early online communities using telephone lines and modems. Allowed participants to post text messages to a virtual bulletin board for public reading.

bibliographic databases Focused collections of reference and research materials such as journals, books, etc. These databases are put together by professionals, indexed according to keywords, and often have abstracts of the article or book or may even have the complete text.

blocked list   A list of sites that will not be retrieved, downloaded from an online directory by filtering software.

bookmarks   Just like real bookmarks, virtual ones allow you to go straight to the desired webpage.

Boolean operators   Terms used to manage the logical operations of a search engine.

break code   Ends the line and starts a new one without putting an extra line between them.

burn   Record a CD.

b2b (business-to-business)   E-commerce portals that attempt to connect industry-specific businesses, allowing them to sell directly to each other.

buttons   Used for the navigational system within the site, providing visitors with a colorful and visually stimulating way to see which page they are on and which pages they can go to.

cache   Temporary storage on your local computer, either in memory or on the hard drive.

CCD (charged coupled device)   Inexpensive chips that are used in digital video cameras to capture images.

CDA (Communications Decency Act of 1996)   A subsection of the larger United States Telecommunications Reform Act of 1996, the CDA tried to achieve several content-specific restrictions over the Internet but was ruled unconstitutional by the Supreme Court in the *Reno v. ACLU* decision.

CGI (Common Gateway Interface)   A standard that allows programs to interface with Web servers.

change agent   An individual who influences innovation-decisions.

characterological coherence   The expectation we have that people will act reliably.

chat-room   A synchronous portal where communicators can engage in an abrupt text-based conversation.

clip art   Graphic images that illustrate a topic.

collabication   Contraction of "collaboration" and "communication," used to denote the dual nature of conferencing tools.

commercial appropriation   Occurs when a profiting agency uses a person's name, likeness, or symbolic identity for commercial purposes without obtaining prior consent.

composite webpage   Pulls different elements of other pages together from different Web servers.

compression   Using sophisticated **algorithms** to reduce the size, and thus downloading time, of large graphic files or video clips.

conference   Task-oriented meeting between two or more people.

content level of meaning   Refers to the pure data that you are communicating.

contrast   The difference between elements on a page.

convergence   The integration of the once separate technologies and industries of print, broadcasting, and telecommunications.

COPA (Child Online Protection Act of 1998)   This act sought to remedy the apparent constitutional flaws of the CDA. Often referred to as the "Son of CDA," it is currently being challenged.

copy-respect   The general attitude to maintain toward online materials, invoking common courtesy as a guide.

crop   Using a tool to draw a box around the part of the picture you want to keep, and discarding the rest.

culture   The shared activities, values, ways of life, and problem-solutions of a group of people.

data chaos   Occurs when authors lose track or control of their webpages, resulting in time-based stagnation, multiple counterfeit versions, or false authorship.

de-centering   The loss of a single organizing principle.

demassification   Occurs when mass media saturate the market and are then reconfigured (or reinvented) to capture niche audiences.

design pallets Small floating islands of click-buttons that remain constantly accessible while using a program.

destination protocols The "where from" and "where to" information attached to packets during transmission.

digest A listserv command that tells the mailing program to send you only one message that contains a set number of messages or the messages received in a certain time period.

directory outline An extensive series of general to specific lists of subtopics and websites that can either be browsed through or searched.

dock Lock a floating tool in place.

dominance Greater power in an interpersonal setting.

dpi (dots per inch) The measurement of resolution for a printer. A higher dpi yields a clearer print-out.

drop A MOO command that subtracts an object from your inventory, placing it in the room.

DSPs (digital signal processors) A chip that performs computations on video and audio signals.

dynamic Changing; in this case, applied to a webpage with changing content.

dystopic Darkly pessimistic.

early adopters People who are respected, innovative, networked with other early adopters and innovators, prefer a local geography more than the innovator, have access to financial resources, have high exposure to mass-mediated content, provide strong opinion leadership with the organization or culture, and can deal with uncertainty but prefer certainty.

early majority People who prefer a local geography, interact frequently with their peers for data, have access to relatively modest financial resources, have medium exposure to mass mediated content, seldom hold positions of opinion leadership, are rarely innovative, and prefer certainty.

e-commerce Use of the Internet for commercial sales.

ECPA (The Electronic Communication Privacy Act of 1986) Bill that made it illegal for the government or a third party to intercept an e-mail.

editorial checks The system set up in traditional publishing where a team of editors and reviewers verifies the accuracy of information before publication.

e-mail A shortened version of the phrase "electronic mail" that refers to messages exchanged through networked computers.

emote A MOO command that allows you to announce whatever follows the command to those in the same room.

emoticons Typographical emotional symbols.

EPS (Elites-Popularization-Specialization cycle) A theory that suggests that all mass media are first introduced to (or by) elites, then get dispersed among the population, and finally expand in availability so that content can become specialized.

etiquette Proper social behavior as prescribed by some authority.

examine (object) A MOO command that can be used to look specifically at the object in question.

expert inquiries Direct requests for data from a recognized authority.

external links A link that takes people to a page on a different site.

fair use An exception to copyright law that allows works to be copied under certain situations for the purpose of criticism, comment, news reporting, teaching, scholarship, or research.

false light Occurs when someone knowingly disseminates highly offensive erroneous publicity with reckless disregard for its lack of merit or truth.

FAQ (Frequently Asked Question) **library** Websites dedicated to storing and updating FAQ pages.

FAQ (Frequently Asked Question) **Pages** Compilations of the most frequently asked questions pertaining to a given topic, usually assembled on a single webpage that is updated by the proprietor.

FCC (Federal Communications Commission) The government agency established by the Communications Act of 1934, responsible to Congress, and charged with regulating both national and international communication.

feature destinations Online "magazines" that have subsites for such topic areas as arts and entertainment, books, and technology, and are not restricted by deadlines.

flames Strong opinions expressed bluntly over the Internet.

flamewar The degeneration of a listserv into an unending series of personal attacks.

FPS (frames per second) The number of times that an image is captured in a given time period to create a video. Higher FPS rates yield smoother video images.

frames Virtual dividers that allow you to divide a webpage into sections.

FTF (face-to-face) Direct physical contact with another person.

full duplex An audio transmission format that allows both people to speak at the same time.

gagging A MOO command that allows you to mute communication from a specified player.

gamma correction A feature of PNG graphic files that allows you to control the brightness level of an image across different platforms.

get A MOO command that adds an object to your inventory.

GIF (Graphic Interchange Format) One of the most popular types of online graphic files, typically used for buttons, icons, and other items with few colors, because it is limited to 256 colors.

give A MOO command that gives an object to another participant.

go (direction) A MOO command that, when combined with a direction, moves your character.

gradient Gradual transition from one color to another.

half duplex An audio transmission format that only allows one person to speak at a time.

hand A MOO command that gives an object to another participant.

header The part of a packet or e-mail message that identifies: (1) who and where the packet is from, (2) when it was issued according to the sending server clock, (3) to whom and where the packet is headed, (4) the subject of the data, or datatype, and (5) transmission error information.

helper application (or helper app) A program that opens up a separate window, called up by a Web browser to show other types of content (such as video, audio, etc).

hosts Computers open to access over a network.

hotspots Areas of an image that are hyperlinks.

HTML (hypertext markup language) A simple programming language designed to designate the form and content of a webpage.

HTTP (hypertext transfer protocol) A special set of protocols used for retrieving webpages.

hypermedia Electronically interconnected information in a variety of forms.

hypertextuality The ability to link any type of content to any other type of content.

icons In semiotics, signs that are similar or analogous to the object that they represent.

immediacy Cues that communicate liking, such as leaning forward, reaching toward people, smiling, etc.

IMAP (Internet Message Access Protocol) An e-mail system that allows you to view your messages as if they were stored on your computer, while they stay stored on a remote mail server.

inbox The initial e-mail folder into which all new mail is put.

indexes In semiotics, signs that point to an object's existence.

inline Displaying multimedia content right next to the text on the webpage.

innovators People who are adventuresome, cosmopolite, networked with fellow innovators and early adopters, have access to financial resources, have high exposure to mass-mediated content, understand complex technical knowledge, and are able to cope with high degrees of uncertainty.

instant messenger chat-box   A program run on your local computer that alerts you whenever people on your "friend" or "buddy" list open their chat-box, providing the opportunity for interpersonal exchange.

insulated   The quality of online power that results in online messages being not as persuasive as face-to-face encounters.

internal links   Links to pages on your own site.

Internet   The worldwide network of computer networks and all of the supporting structure.

Internet telephony   Audio-only network-mediated communication; using your computer as a telephone.

intertextuality   Term used to denote the connections between texts.

intranet   Secure internal computer networks that use the same protocols as the Internet.

intrusion   An intentional invasion of an individual's private space, seclusion, or solitude, caused by an electronic, mechanical, or physical means.

inventory   A MOO command that lists the items in your inventory available for use.

IP address   The address assigned to a computer by an Internet service provider.

IRC-d (Internet Relay Chat daemon)   An early program used for multi-user real-time communication.

Java   A simple programming language, designed to run on any computer platform.

Java scripts   Simple programs, embedded in webpages.

JPEG (or JPG; Joint Photographic Experts Group)   A popular graphic file format, typically used for photographs and other complex images because it can include up to 16 million colors.

Kbps   Thousands of bytes per second.

keywords metatag   A line in the HTML code of a page that programmers can use to identify what the page is about.

knowbots   Programs designed to retrieve all of the publicly available data posted on the Internet and store it in a compact version on the main search engine server.

laggards   People who are suspicious and doubtful, strongly tied to the local region, look to the past, are wary of change agents and innovations, generally have meager resources, and may never adopt an innovation.

late majority   People who are skeptical, cautious, prefer a local geography, interact infrequently with peers for data, have access to relatively modest financial resources, have medium exposure to mass-mediated content, rarely hold positions of opinion leadership, are seldom innovative, prefer certainty, and might adopt innovations out of economic/social necessity due to the diffusion effect.

libel   Written untruths about an entity published to third parties.

linked ethos   The tendency to transfer your trust of the source of the original page to the source of a nonrelated linked page.

link exchange   A conventional courtesy of the Internet, where people create links to each other's pages.

linking loops   Two or more websites linked to the same information.

link rot   The deletion or relocating of a particular website without its location being erased or corrected in search engine databases.

listserv   A server-maintained database of subscribers' addresses, allowing messages to easily be sent to a group.

look   A MOO command that tells you everything that can be "seen" in the room.

lossless compression   A method of reducing the file size of an image without reducing the quality of the picture.

lossy compression   A method of reducing the file size of an image in which some of the information in the image is discarded, which reduces the quality of the image slightly.

macromedium Used to refer to the Internet because it is immense in size and can be used to reach audiences on a global scale, and at the same time to access or publish the smallest bits of personal trivia, or webpages tailored to an audience of one.

mailto An HTML command that calls up a message composition window so you can send an e-mail to the designated address.

maintenance roles Group behaviors that keep people happy with the group.

Mbps Millions of bytes of data per second.

metamedium Used to refer to the Internet as a medium of media since it serves as a platform for older media, including telephony, print, and broadcasting.

metasearch engines (metaengines) Search engines that submit a key term to several independent search engines, comparing and contrasting the results.

metatags HTML codes that are placed in the header of a webpage, and are never actually seen by people visiting the page (unless they look at the source code).

microcinema movement A community of independent filmmakers who produce everything from animated shorts to feature-length movies at a fraction of the cost of the major studios.

micro-expressions Facial expressions that last as little as 200 milliseconds.

MLA (Modern Language Association) **Style** One of the most commonly used style guides for academic writing.

moderated A listserv set up with one person or a group of people who serve as gatekeepers, who read through messages and sort out ones that aren't on topic or are too inflammatory, and then pass on to the subscribers only those messages that fit the topic and environment of the list.

MOO (multiuser, object-oriented interface) A professional version of MUDs that allows people to virtually get together and interact for educational or business purposes.

MUCK (multiuser character/chat kingdom) A type of MUD that simulates the environment of a motion picture (typically a Disney film).

MUD (multiuser dungeons) Text-based, real-time fantasy role-playing game where communicators have the ability to navigate their way through an imaginary environment.

multivocality Many voices.

MUSH (multiuser simulated hallucination) A type of MUD that simulates a free-falling adventure paralleling hallucination, similar to "Alice in Wonderland."

navigation bars Horizontal or vertical tables with either textual or graphical links to important pages on the site.

NEAR A Boolean operator that pulls up pages with specific words located close to each other.

net conference An umbrella term that refers to any conference mediated by networked computers.

netiquette Rules of proper online behavior.

newbies Newcomers to the Internet.

newsgroup A topical online bulletin board where interested parties may post and view one another's messages.

nodes Computers that serve as major connecting points on the Internet.

NOT A Boolean operator that excludes pages that have a particular term in them.

NSCA (National Supercomputing Agency's) **Mosaic** The first multimedia-capable browser.

NSFNET Developed in 1986 by the National Science Foundation as a massive new information superstructure; successor to ARPANET; precursor to current Internet.

on the fly In real time, as a webpage is being displayed.

OR A Boolean operator that expands the search to include pages that contain any of the words that you enter.

packets Small bundles of data that make traffic more manageable across the Internet.

packet switching The network's process of redirecting data and literally "switching" flow to the path of least resistance.

page   A MOO command that allows you to communicate with people throughout the complex.

paragraph code   Ends the current line and starts a new line, placing a blank line in between.

para-proxemics   The illusion of physical distance that is created by how close the camera is to the person being recorded.

PDF (Print Document Format)   A file format widely used on the Internet, PDFs allow organizations to seamlessly convert their paper documentation into an online version that will retain the document's original formatting, style, and layout.

persona   Constructed identity.

pixels   Extremely tiny squares, the basic building blocks of an image on a screen.

plagiarism   Presenting someone else's ideas as your own.

plug-in   A program that works with a browser, and shows special content inside the browser window.

PNG (Portable Network Graphic)   A new graphic format gaining in popularity online because it has several advantages over both GIFs and JPEGs.

POP3 (Post Office Protocol)   E-mail reading system that acts as a bridge between your PC and the server where your e-mail is collected, transferring messages to the local PC.

portals   Customizable entry-points to the Internet.

POTS (plain old telephone service)   Normal copper lines used for telephone connections.

proprietary   Unique, special format.

proprietary codes   HTML commands that only work in a specific browser and will not function in a competition's browser.

protocols   The generally accepted rules governing the transmission, delivery, and reception of data on the Internet, normally programmed into a universally installed software suite so that no one computer has a different set of standards than any other machine.

proximity   The amount of distance between two things.

punitive damages   The court's special way of sending a stronger message to the wrong-doing party by requiring them to pay a much higher sum to the injured party; requires proof of malice.

put   A MOO command that takes an object from your inventory and places it someplace.

QuickTime   A file format, produced by Apple, for video, sound, animation, graphics, text, music, and 360-degree scenes.

RealPlayer   A program that plays back digital media content transferred over the Internet, including live-time television, streaming video clips, live-audio events, Internet radio broadcasts, and prerecorded audio files.

referential immediacy   A medium's ability to instantly point a user to another media or resource.

relational level of meaning   Information about the relationship between you and the other person that is embedded in any message.

routers   The machines dictating where packets will travel on the network.

search engine   Device that allows the user to submit key-term requests to an online database that stores most of the data on the Web in a compressed format.

secure-sockets layer   Used to encrypt data transmitted online.

signal-to-noise ratio   The amount of useful messages or information compared to the useless ones.

site maps   Dedicated outlines of a site's layout, which can be used as a navigational guide.

site-specific search engines   Search engines that only search the data on a given website.

slander   Spoken untruths about an entity to third parties.

source code   The text file that a Web browser reads from left to right, top to bottom, assembles, and then displays onscreen.

spam   Unwanted mass e-mail.

streaming audio   Audio files that can begin playing while they are being downloaded into your computer.

symbol   In semiotics, an arbitrarily chosen sign.

synchronously   At the same time.

take   A MOO command that adds an object to your inventory.

Talk   A simple program that allowed users on networked computers to type messages to one another in real time.

task roles   Group behaviors related to getting the job completed.

TCP/IP (Transmission Control Protocol/Internet Protocol)   Standards that govern the process of packet switching, making data transmission possible over the Internet.

Telnet   A program that connects your computer directly to a server, turning your system into a dumb terminal.

thread   An online dialogue of messages and replies.

throw   A MOO command that subtracts an object from your inventory, placing it in the room.

thumbnail   Small versions of graphic files.

TMSIs (text-based multi-user synchronous interfaces)   An alphanumeric context in which people type messages to others in close-to-real time, similar to a group conversation.

to   A MOO command that allows you to speak directly to a particular person within a room, while allowing everyone else to hear you.

topic rings (or webrings)   A method of interconnecting related material on the Web into an easily navigated collection.

trademark   A logo, acronym, word, color scheme, combination of sounds, or any other symbolic device used to distinguish a product or service as unique.

transparency   A color in a GIF file that will not be displayed, allowing the background of a webpage to show through.

urban legends   Stories that circulate throughout society, that might at one time have been based in fact but now have a life (and reality) of their own.

URL (uniform resource locator)   The host address that is entered into a Web browser to retrieve online documents.

USB (universal serial bus)   A fast port used to connect a wide range of devices, including video cameras, speakers, keyboards, mice, etc., to a computer.

Usenet   An extensive collection of electronic bulletin boards.

U.S. Explorer I   The first NASA satellite launched on January 31, 1958.

U.S.S.R. Sputnik I   Earth's first artificial satellite launched by the Soviet Union in October 4, 1957.

utopic   Idealistically optimistic.

videoconferencing   Refers to audio and video network-mediated communication.

visual rhetoric   The study of how images persuade.

VR (virtual reality)   A digital environment in which you can interact with objects and even people who show up as avatars.

VRML (virtual reality markup language)   A set of codes used to create artificial environments online.

whisper   A MOO command that allows you to speak quietly to people within the same room.

whiteboarding   Sharing a virtual drawing board while engaged in a net conference.

WWW (World Wide Web)   A hypertextual, multimedia interface to the Internet.

W3C (World Wide Web Consortium)   A not-for-profit research organization geared toward promoting standards and innovations in Web-based communication.

WYSIWYG (What You See Is What You Get)   An acronym used to describe advanced text and Web editors that show the creator what the product will look like as it is being created.

XML (or XHTML)   An altered form of HTML that has been designed around wireless Internet protocols.

INDEX